GREEK CLASSICS

EDITORIAL DIRECTOR Laurie Barnett
DIRECTOR OF TECHNOLOGY Tammy Hepps

SERIES EDITORS John Crowther, Justin Kestler
MANAGING EDITOR Vincent Janoski

WRITERS Roman Altshuler, Brian Ballentine, James Carmichael,
    Cloe Frances Cockburn, Ross Douthat, David Egan, Yael Goldstein,
    Lindsey Lusher, John Maier, Brian Phillips, Ignacio Prado, Henry Rich,
    Adam Rzepka, Bulbul Tiwari, Jonathan Weil, Caroline Whitbeck,
    Elizabeth Hartley Winthrop
EDITOR Matt Blanchard

Introduction: Stopping to Buy SparkNotes on a Snowy Evening

Whose words these are you *think* you know.
Your paper's due tomorrow, though;
We're glad to see you stopping here
To get some help before you go.

Lost your course? You'll find it here.
Face tests and essays without fear.
Between the words, good grades at stake:
Get great results throughout the year.

Once school bells caused your heart to quake
As teachers circled each mistake.
Use SparkNotes and no longer weep,
Ace every single test you take.

Yes, books are lovely, dark, and deep,
But only what you grasp you keep,
With hours to go before you sleep,
With hours to go before you sleep.

CONTENTS

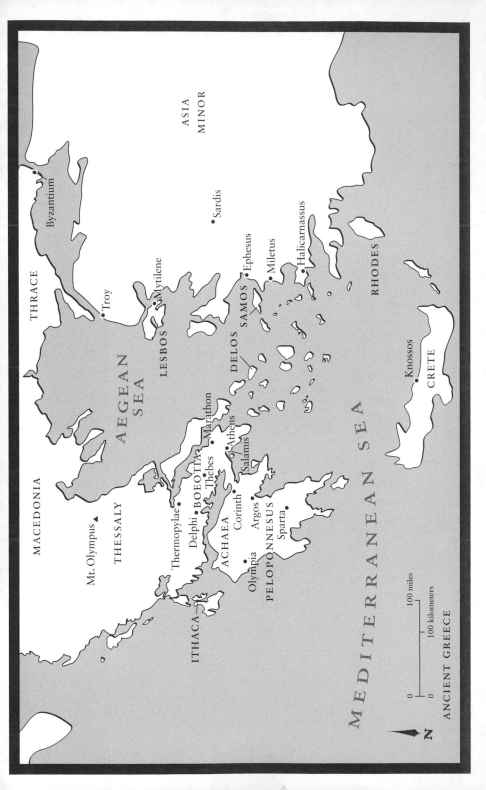

THRACE

Byzantium

MACEDONIA

Mt. Olympus ▲

THESSALY

Troy

AEGEAN
SEA

LESBOS

Mytilene

ASIA
MINOR

Sardis

Thermopylae

Delphi
BOEOTIA
Thebes
Marathon
Athens
Salamis
Corinth
Argos

ACHAEA

Olympia

Sparta

PELOPONNESUS

DELOS

SAMOS

Ephesus

Miletus

Halicarnassus

RHODES

ITHACA

Knossos

CRETE

MEDITERRANEAN SEA

N

0   100 miles
0   100 kilometers

ANCIENT GREECE

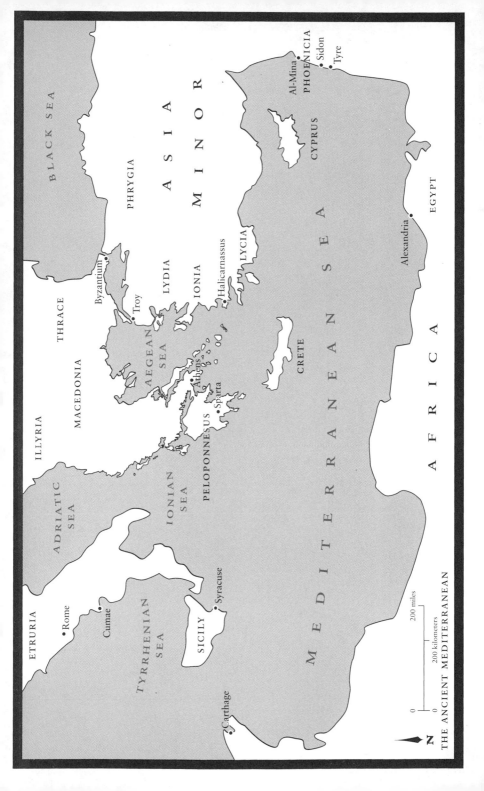

THE ANCIENT MEDITERRANEAN

N

0   200 miles
0   200 kilometers

BLACK SEA

ETRURIA
Rome
Cumae
TYRRHENIAN SEA
SICILY
Syracuse
Carthage

ADRIATIC SEA

ILLYRIA

MACEDONIA

THRACE

Byzantium

IONIAN SEA

PELOPONNESUS

Athens
Sparta

AEGEAN SEA

Troy

LYDIA

IONIA

Halicarnassus

LYCIA

PHRYGIA

ASIA MINOR

Al-Mina
PHOENICIA
Sidon
Tyre

CYPRUS

CRETE

MEDITERRANEAN SEA

Alexandria

EGYPT

AFRICA

EPIC POETRY

HOMER

CONTEXT AND BACKGROUND

Nearly 3,000 years after they were composed, the *Iliad* and the *Odyssey* remain two of the most celebrated and widely read stories ever told, yet next to nothing is known about their composer. He was certainly an accomplished Greek bard, and he probably lived in the late eighth and early seventh centuries B.C. Scholars traditionally ascribe authorship of the *Iliad* and the *Odyssey* to a blind poet named Homer, and it is under this name that the works are still published. Greeks of the third and second centuries B.C., however, already questioned whether Homer existed and even whether the two epics were written by a single individual.

Most modern scholars believe that even if only one person wrote the epics, his work owed a great debt to a long tradition of oral poetry. Stories of a glorious expedition to the East and of its leaders' fateful journeys home had been circulating in Greece for hundreds of years before the *Iliad* and the *Odyssey* were composed. Casual storytellers and semiprofessional minstrels passed these stories down through generations, and each artist developed and polished the story as he told it. According to this theory, one poet, multiple poets working in collaboration, or perhaps a series of poets handing down their work in succession finally turned these stories into written works, again with each adding his own touch and expanding or contracting certain episodes in the overall narrative to fit his taste.

Although historical, archaeological, and linguistic evidence suggests that the epics were composed between 750 and 650 B.C., they are set in Greece in about the twelfth century B.C., during the Bronze Age. This earlier period, the Greeks believed, was a more glorious and sublime age, when gods still frequented the earth and heroic, godlike mortals with superhuman attributes populated Greece. Because the *Iliad* and the *Odyssey* strive to evoke this pristine age, they are written in a high style and generally depict life in a manner consistent with the Greeks' popular notions about life in the great kingdoms of the Bronze Age. The writer of the epics often refers to the Greeks as Achaeans, the name of a large tribe occupying Greece during the Bronze Age.

At the same time, Homer's portrayal of the Bronze Age often yields to the realities of eighth- and seventh-century B.C. Greece. The feudal social structure apparent in the background of the *Odyssey* seems more akin to Homer's Greece than to Odysseus's, and Homer substitutes the pantheon of deities of his own day for the related but different gods whom Mycenaean Greeks worshipped. Many other minor but obvious anachronisms—such as references to iron tools and to tribes that had not yet migrated to Greece by the Bronze Age—betray the poem's later, Iron Age origins.

For centuries, many scholars believed that the Trojan War and its participants were entirely the creation of the Greek imagination. In the late nineteenth century, however, an archaeologist named Heinrich Schliemann declared that he had discovered the remnants of Troy. The ruins that he uncovered sit a few dozen miles off of the Aegean coast in northwestern Turkey, a site that indeed fits the geographical descriptions of Homer's Troy. One layer of the site, which corresponds roughly to the point in history when the fall of Troy would have taken place, shows evidence of fire and destruction consistent with a sack. Although most scholars accept Schliemann's discovered city as the site of the ancient city of Troy, many remain skeptical as to whether Homer's Trojan War ever really took place. Evidence from Near Eastern literature suggests that episodes similar to those described in the *Iliad* may have circulated even before Schliemann's Troy was destroyed. Nonetheless, many scholars now admit the possibility that some truth may lie at the center of the *Iliad*, hidden beneath many layers of poetic embellishment.

Like the *Odyssey*, the *Iliad* was composed primarily in the Ionic dialect of Ancient Greek, which was spoken on the Aegean islands and in the coastal settlements of Asia Minor, now modern Turkey. Therefore, some scholars conclude that the poet hailed from somewhere in the eastern Greek world. More likely, however, the poet chose the Ionic dialect because he felt it more appropriate for the high style and grand scope of his work. Slightly later Greek literature suggests that poets varied the dialects of their poems according to the themes that they treated. Therefore, some poets may have written in dialects that they did not actually speak themselves. Homer's epics are Panhellenic (encompassing all of Greece) in spirit and use forms from several other dialects. This characteristic suggests that Homer suited his poems to the dialect that would best complement his ideas.

THE ILIAD

CHARACTERS

Achilles   The son of the military man Peleus and the sea-nymph Thetis. The most powerful warrior in the *Iliad*, Achilles commands the Myrmidons, soldiers from his homeland of Pythia in Greece. Proud and headstrong, he takes offense easily and reacts with blistering indignation when he perceives that his honor has been slighted. Achilles' wrath at Agamemnon for taking his war prize, the maiden Briseis, is central to the plot of the *Iliad*.

Agamemnon (also called Atrides)   King of Mycenae and leader of the Achaean army; brother of King Menelaus of Sparta. Arrogant and often selfish, Agamemnon provides the Achaeans with strong but sometimes reckless and self-serving leadership. Like Achilles, he lacks consideration and forethought. Perhaps most important, Agamemnon's tactless appropriation of Achilles' war prize, the maiden Briseis, creates a crisis for the Achaeans when it prompts the insulted Achilles to withdraw from the war.

Patroclus   Achilles' beloved friend, companion, and advisor. Patroclus grew up alongside the great warrior in Phthia, under the guardianship of Peleus. Devoted to both Achilles and the Achaean cause, Patroclus stands by the enraged Achilles but also dons Achilles' terrifying armor in an attempt to hold back the Trojans.

Odysseus   A fine warrior and the cleverest of the Achaean commanders. Along with Nestor, Odysseus is one of the Achaeans' two best public speakers. He helps mediate between Agamemnon and Achilles during their quarrel and often prevents them from making rash decisions.

Diomedes (also called Tydides) The youngest of the Achaean commanders. Diomedes is bold and sometimes impetuous. After Achilles withdraws from combat, Athena imbues Diomedes with such courage that he actually wounds two gods, Aphrodite and Ares.

Great Ajax An Achaean commander, Great Ajax (sometimes called Telamonian Ajax or simply Ajax) is the second mightiest Achaean warrior after Achilles. His extraordinary size and strength help him to wound Hector twice with boulders. He often fights alongside Little Ajax, and Homer frequently refers to the pair as the Aeantes.

Little Ajax An Achaean commander, Little Ajax is Oileus's son (to be distinguished from Great Ajax, Telamon's son). Little Ajax often fights alongside Great Ajax, whose considerable size and strength complement Little Ajax's nimbleness and speed. Homer sometimes calls the pair the Aeantes.

Nestor King of Pylos and the oldest Achaean commander. Although age has taken much of Nestor's physical strength, it has left him with great wisdom. He often acts as an advisor to the military commanders, especially Agamemnon. Nestor and Odysseus are the Achaeans' most deft and persuasive orators, although Nestor's speeches are sometimes long-winded.

Menelaus King of Sparta and the younger brother of Agamemnon. Although the Trojan War is sparked by an offense against Menelaus—the abduction of his wife, Helen, by Paris—Menelaus consistently proves quieter, less imposing, and less arrogant than Agamemnon. Menelaus has a stout heart, but he is not among the mightiest Achaean warriors.

Calchas   An important soothsayer. Calchas's identification of the cause of the plague ravaging the Achaean army in Book 1 leads inadvertently to the rift between Agamemnon and Achilles that occupies the first nineteen books of the *Iliad*.

Phoenix   A kindly old warrior. Phoenix helped raise Achilles while he himself was still a young man. Achilles deeply loves and trusts Phoenix, and Phoenix mediates between him and Agamemnon during their quarrel.

Hector   One of King Priam and Queen Hecuba's sons. Hector is the mightiest warrior in the Trojan army. He mirrors Achilles in some of his flaws, but his bloodlust is not so great as Achilles'. He is devoted to his wife, Andromache, and son, Astyanax, but resents his brother Paris for bringing war upon their family and city.

Priam   King of Troy and husband of Hecuba. Priam is the father of fifty Trojan warriors, including Hector and Paris. Although Priam is too old to fight, he has earned the respect of both the Trojans and the Achaeans by virtue of his levelheaded, wise, and benevolent rule. He treats Helen kindly, although he laments the war that her beauty has sparked.

Hecuba   Queen of Troy, wife of Priam, and mother of Hector and Paris.

Paris (also called Alexander)   One of Priam and Hecuba's sons and Hector's brother. Paris's abduction of the beautiful Helen, wife of Menelaus, sparked the Trojan War. Paris is self-centered and vain. He fights effectively with a bow and arrow (never with the sword or spear, which the Greeks considered more manly) but often lacks the spirit for battle and prefers to sit in his room making love to Helen while others fight for him, thus earning both Hector's and Helen's scorn.

Helen   The wife of Menelaus and the woman commonly regarded as the most beautiful woman in the ancient world. Before the start of the *Iliad,* Helen becomes embroiled with Paris and eventually leaves her husband, Menelaus. Although Helen does not bear full responsibility for this turn of events, she loathes herself for the misery that she believes she has caused so many Trojan and Achaean men. Helen's contempt extends to Paris as well, but she stays with him nonetheless.

Aeneas   A Trojan nobleman, the son of Aphrodite, and a mighty warrior. The Romans believed that Aeneas later founded the city of Rome. Aeneas is the protagonist of Virgil's masterpiece, the *Aeneid.*

Andromache Hector's loving wife. Andromache begs Hector to withdraw from the war and save himself before the Achaeans kill him.

Glaucus   A powerful Trojan warrior. Glaucus nearly fights a duel with Diomedes. The men's exchange of armor after they realize that their families are friends illustrates the value that ancients placed on kinship and camaraderie.

Sarpedon   One of Zeus's sons. Sarpedon's fate seems intertwined with the gods' quibbles, calling attention to the unclear nature of the gods' relationship to fate.

Briseis   A maiden who is Achilles' war prize. When Agamemnon is forced to return Chryseis to her father, he appropriates Briseis as compensation, sparking Achilles' great rage.

Zeus   King of the gods and Hera's husband. Zeus claims neutrality in the mortals' conflict and often tries to keep the other gods from participating in it. However, he throws his weight behind the Trojan side for much of the battle after the sulking Achilles has his mother, Thetis, ask the god to do so.

Hera   Queen of the gods and Zeus's wife. The conniving and
              headstrong Hera often goes behind Zeus's back in
              matters on which they disagree, working with Athena
              to crush the Trojans, whom she hates passionately.

Athena   The goddess of wisdom, purposeful battle, and the
              womanly arts; Zeus's daughter. Like Hera, Athena
              passionately hates the Trojans and often gives the
              Achaeans valuable aid.

Thetis   A sea-nymph and Achilles' devoted mother. Thetis
              convinces Zeus to help the Trojans and punish the
              Achaeans at the request of her angry son. When
              Achilles finally rejoins the battle, Thetis commissions
              the god Hephaestus to design him a new suit of armor.

Apollo   A son of Zeus and twin brother of the goddess Artemis.
              Apollo is god of the arts and archery. He supports the
              Trojans and often intervenes in the war on their behalf.

Aphrodite   Goddess of love and daughter of Zeus. Aphrodite is
              married to Hephaestus but maintains a romantic
              relationship with Ares. She supports Paris and the
              Trojans throughout the war, although she proves
              somewhat ineffectual in battle.

Poseidon   Zeus's brother and god of the sea. Poseidon holds a
              long-standing grudge against the Trojans because they
              never paid him for helping them to build their city. He
              therefore supports the Achaeans in the war.

Hephaestus God of fire and husband of Aphrodite. Hephaestus is
              the gods' metalsmith and is known as the lame or
              crippled god. Although the text of the *Iliad* does not
              make clear Hephaestus's sympathies in the mortals'
              struggle, he helps the Achaeans by forging a new set of
              armor for Achilles and by rescuing Achilles during his
              fight with a river god.

ANALYSIS OF MAJOR CHARACTERS

ACHILLES

Although Achilles possesses superhuman strength and has a close relationship with the gods, he may strike modern readers as less than heroic. He has all the marks of a great warrior, and indeed proves the mightiest man in the Achaean army, but his deep-seated character flaws consistently impede his ability to act with nobility and integrity. Achilles cannot control his pride or the rage that surges up when that pride is injured. This attribute so poisons him that he abandons his comrades and even prays that the Trojans will slaughter them, all because he has been slighted at the hands of his commander, Agamemnon. Achilles is driven primarily by a thirst for glory. Part of him yearns to live a long, easy life, but he knows that his fate forces him to choose between the two. Ultimately, he is willing to sacrifice everything else so that his name will be remembered.

Like most Homeric characters, Achilles does not develop significantly over the course of the epic. Although the death of Patroclus prompts Achilles to seek reconciliation with Agamemnon, it does not alleviate his rage but merely redirects it toward Hector. The event does not make Achilles a more deliberative or reflective character. Bloodlust, wrath, and pride continue to consume him. He mauls his opponents without mercy, brazenly takes on the river Xanthus, desecrates the body of Hector, and performs a savage sacrifice of twelve Trojan men at Patroclus's funeral. Achilles does not relent in this brutality until the final book of the *Iliad*, when King Priam, begging for the return of Hector's desecrated corpse, appeals to Achilles' memory of his father, Peleus. Yet it remains unclear whether a father's heartbroken pleas really have transformed Achilles or whether this scene merely testifies to Achilles' capacity for grief and acquaintance with anguish, which were already proven in his intense mourning of Patroclus.

HECTOR

The mightiest warrior in the Trojan army. Although he meets his match in Achilles, he wreaks havoc on the Achaean army while Achilles is absent. Hector leads the assault that finally penetrates the Achaean ramparts; he is the first and only Trojan to set fire to an Achaean ship; and he kills Patroclus. Yet Hector's leadership contains discernible flaws, especially toward the end of the *Iliad*, when the participation of first Patroclus and then Achilles reinvigorates the Achaean army. Hector demonstrates a certain cowardice when, twice in Book 17, he flees

Great Ajax. Indeed, Hector recovers his courage only after receiving his comrades' insults—first Glaucus's and then Aeneas's. Hectors own emotions often overwhelm him, as we see when he treats Patroclus and his other victims with rash cruelty. Later, swept up by a burst of confidence, Hector foolishly orders the Trojans to camp outside Troy's walls the night before Achilles returns to battle. This rash action leads to the routing of the Trojan forces and hastens Hector's fatal confrontation with Achilles.

Although Hector may prove overly impulsive and insufficiently prudent, he does not come across as arrogant or overbearing, as Agamemnon does. Moreover, the fact that Hector fights in his homeland, unlike any of the Achaean commanders, allows Homer to develop him as a tender, family-oriented man. Hector shows deep, sincere love for his wife and children. Indeed, he even treats his brother Paris with forgiveness and indulgence, despite Paris's lack of spirit and preference for lovemaking over military duty. Hector never turns violent with Paris but instead merely aims frustrated words at his cowardly brother. Moreover, although Hector loves his family, he never loses sight of his responsibility to Troy. Admittedly, he runs from Achilles at first and briefly entertains the delusional hope of negotiating his way out of a duel. However, in the end, Hector stands up to the mighty warrior, even when he realizes that the gods have abandoned him. His refusal to flee even in the face of vastly superior forces makes him the most tragic figure in the *Iliad*.

SUMMARY: BOOKS 1–3

The poet invokes the Muse to aid him in telling the story of the rage of Achilles, the greatest Greek hero to fight in the Trojan War. The narrative begins nine years after the start of the war, as the Achaeans sack a Trojan-allied town and capture two beautiful maidens, Chryseis and Briseis. Agamemnon, commander-in-chief of the Achaean army, takes Chryseis as his prize. Achilles, one of the Achaeans' most valuable warriors, claims Briseis. Chryseis's father, a man named Chryses who serves as a priest of the god Apollo, begs Agamemnon to return his daughter and offers to pay an enormous ransom. When Agamemnon refuses, Chryses prays to Apollo for help.

Apollo sends a plague upon the Greek camp, and many soldiers die. After ten days of suffering, Achilles calls an assembly of the Achaean army and asks for a soothsayer to reveal the cause of the plague. Calchas, a powerful seer, stands up and offers his services.

Although he fears retribution from Agamemnon, Calchas reveals the plague as a vengeful and strategic move by Chryses and Apollo. Agamemnon flies into a rage and says that he will return Chryseis only if Achilles gives him Briseis as compensation.

Agamemnon's demand humiliates and infuriates the proud Achilles. The men argue, and Achilles threatens to withdraw from battle and take his people, the Myrmidons, back home to Phthia. Agamemnon threatens to go to Achilles' tent in the army's camp and take Briseis himself. Achilles stands poised to draw his sword and kill the Achaean commander when the goddess Athena, sent by Hera, the queen of the gods, appears to Achilles and checks his anger. Athena's guidance, along with a speech by the wise advisor Nestor, finally succeeds in preventing the duel. That night, Odysseus returns the girl to her father.

Achilles, however, remains enraged. He calls on his mother, the goddess Thetis, to help him strike back against Agamemnon. Thetis promises to speak with Zeus. To help the Trojans, as promised, Zeus sends a dream to Agamemnon in which a figure in the form of Nestor persuades Agamemnon that he can take Troy if he launches a full-scale assault on the city's walls. The next day, Agamemnon gathers his troops for attack but, to test their courage, lies and tells them that he has decided to give up the war and return to Greece. To his dismay, they eagerly run to their ships.

When Hera sees the Achaeans fleeing, she alerts Athena, who inspires Odysseus, the most eloquent of the Achaeans, to call the men back. Odysseus shouts words of both encouragement and insult to goad them and restore their confidence. He reminds them of a prophecy that the soothsayer Calchas gave when the Achaeans were first preparing their soldiers back in Greece: a water snake had slithered to shore and devoured a nest of nine sparrows, and Calchas interpreted the sign to mean that nine years would pass before the Achaeans would finally take Troy. As Odysseus reminds the men, they vowed at that time not to abandon their struggle until the city fell.

The Trojan army marches from the city gates and advances to meet the Achaeans. Paris, the Trojan prince who precipitated the war by stealing the beautiful Helen from her husband, Menelaus, challenges the Achaeans to one-on-one combat with any of their warriors. When Menelaus steps forward, however, Paris loses heart and shrinks back into the Trojan ranks. Hector, Paris's brother and the leader of the Trojan forces, chastises Paris for his cowardice.

Stung by Hector's insult, Paris finally agrees to a duel with Mene-laus, declaring that the contest will establish peace between Trojans and Achaeans by deciding once and for all which man shall have Helen as his wife. Hector presents the terms to Menelaus, who accepts. Both armies look forward to ending the war at last.

Paris and Menelaus arm themselves and begin their duel. Neither is able to fell the other with his spear. Menelaus breaks his sword over Paris's helmet. He then grabs Paris by the helmet and drags him through the dirt, but the goddess Aphrodite, an ally of the Trojans, snaps the strap of the helmet so that it breaks off in Menelaus's hands. Frustrated, Menelaus retrieves his spear and is about to drive it into Paris when Aphrodite whisks Paris away to his room in Priam's palace. She summons Helen there too. Helen, after upbraid-ing Paris for his cowardice, lies down in bed with him. Back on the battlefield, both the Trojans and the Greeks search for Paris, who seems to have magically disappeared. Agamemnon, who insists that Menelaus has won the duel, demands Helen's return.

ANALYSIS: THE RAGE OF ACHILLES

Like other ancient epic poems, the *Iliad* presents its subject clearly from the outset. Indeed, the poem names its focus in its opening word: menin, or "rage." Specifically, the *Iliad* concerns itself with Achilles' rage—how it begins, how it cripples the Achaean army, and how he ultimately redirects it toward the Trojans. Although the Trojan War itself figures prominently in the work, this larger con-flict ultimately acts as background rather than subject matter. By the time Achilles and Agamemnon enter their quarrel, the Trojan War has been going on for nearly ten years. Achilles' absence from battle, on the other hand, lasts only a matter of days, and the epic ends soon after his return. The poem describes neither the origins nor the end of the war that frames Achilles' wrath. Instead, it scrutinizes the ori-gins and the end of this wrath, thus narrowing the scope of the poem from a larger conflict between warring peoples to a smaller one between warring individuals.

Although the *Iliad*'s central focus is the rage of a mortal, it also explores the gods' motivations and actions. Even before Homer describes the quarrel between Achilles and Agamemnon, he explains that Apollo was responsible for the conflict. In general, the gods in the poem participate in mortal affairs in two ways. First, they act as external forces upon the course of events, as when Apollo sends the plague upon the Achaean army. Second, they represent internal forces acting on individuals, as when Athena, the goddess of wisdom, prevents Achilles from abandoning all reason and persuades him to cut Agamemnon with words and insults rather than his sword. But while the gods determine grave matters of peace and violence, life and death, they also provide comic relief. Their intrigues, double-dealings, and inane squabbles often appear humorously petty in comparison with the wholesale slaughter that pervades the mortal realm. The bickering between Zeus and Hera, for example, provides a much lighter parallel to the heated exchange between Agamemnon and Achilles.

SUMMARY: BOOKS 4–6

While the Trojans and Achaeans swear a temporary truce, the gods engage in their own duels. Zeus argues that Menelaus has lost the duel and that the war should end as the mortals had agreed. But Hera, who has invested much in the Achaean cause, wants nothing less than the complete destruction of Troy. In the end, Zeus gives way and sends Athena to the battlefield to rekindle the fighting. Disguised as a Trojan soldier, Athena convinces the archer Pandarus to take aim at Menelaus. Pandarus fires, but Athena, who wants merely to give the Achaeans a pretext for fighting, deflects the arrow so that it only wounds Menelaus.

Agamemnon now rallies the Achaean ranks. He meets Nestor, Odysseus, and Diomedes, among others, and spurs them on by challenging their pride or recounting the great deeds of their fathers. Battle breaks out, and the blood flows freely. None of the major characters is killed or wounded, but Odysseus and Great Ajax kill a number of minor Trojan figures. The gods also get involved, with Athena helping the Achaeans and Apollo helping the Trojans. The efforts toward a truce have failed utterly.

As the battle rages, Pandarus wounds the Achaean hero Diomedes. Diomedes prays to Athena for revenge, and the goddess endows him with superhuman strength and the power to discern gods on the field of battle. She warns him, however, not to challenge any of them except Aphrodite. Diomedes fights like a man possessed, slaughtering all Trojans he meets. He destroys the overconfident Pandarus and wounds Aeneas, the noble Trojan hero immortalized in Virgil's *Aeneid*. When Aeneas's mother, Aphrodite, comes to his aid, Diomedes wounds her too, cutting her wrist and sending her back to Mount Olympus. When Apollo goes to tend to Aeneas in Aphrodite's stead, Diomedes attacks him as well. This act of aggression breaches Diomedes' agreement with Athena, who had limited him to challenging Aphrodite alone among the gods. Apollo issues a stern warning to Diomedes, effortlessly pushes him aside, and whisks Aeneas off the field. Aiming to enflame the passions of Aeneas's comrades, Apollo leaves a replica of Aeneas's body on the ground. He also rouses Ares, god of war, to fight on the Trojan side.

After Ares, the god of war, joins the ranks of the Trojans, Hera and Athena appeal to Zeus, who gives them permission to intervene on the Achaeans' behalf. Hera rallies the rest of the Achaean troops, while Athena encourages Diomedes. She withdraws her earlier injunction not to attack any of the gods except Aphrodite and even joins Diomedes to challenge Ares. The divinely driven chariot charges Ares, and in the seismic collision that follows, Diomedes wounds Ares. Ares immediately flies to Mount Olympus and complains to Zeus, but Zeus counters that Ares deserved his injury. Athena and Hera also depart the scene of the battle.

With the departure of the gods, the Achaeans rout the Trojans from the field of battle, and Hector retreats to the city to warn his mother of the pressing dangers. As he prepares to reenter the fray, he visits his wife, Andromache, whom he finds nursing their son Astyanax by the walls of the city. As Andromache cradles the child, she anxiously watches the struggle in the plain below. In a moving scene, she begs Hector not to go back, but he insists that he cannot escape his fate, whatever it may be. He kisses Astyanax, who, although initially frightened by the crest on Hector's helmet, greets his father happily. Hector then departs. Andromache, convinced that he will soon die, begins to mourn his death. Hector meets Paris on his way out of the city, and the brothers prepare to rejoin the battle.

Summary: Books 7–9

When Hector offers to end the battle by fighting any Achaean, no one has the courage to come forward. Finally, at the encouragement of Nestor, Great Ajax volunteers. Hector and Ajax begin their duel by tossing spears, but neither is successful. They then use their lances, and Ajax draws Hector's blood. The two are about to clash with swords when heralds, spurred by Zeus, call off the fight on account of nightfall. The two heroes exchange gifts and end their duel with a pact of friendship.

That night, Nestor gives a speech urging the Achaeans to ask for a day to bury their dead. He also advises them to build fortifications around their camp. Meanwhile, in the Trojan camp, King Priam makes a similar proposal regarding the Trojan dead. In addition, his son Antenor asks Paris to give up Helen and thereby end the war. Paris refuses but offers to return all of the loot that he took with Helen from Sparta. When the Trojans present this offer to the Achaeans the next day, however, the Achaeans sense the Trojans' desperation and reject the compromise. Nonetheless, both sides agree to observe a day of respite to bury their respective dead.

After prohibiting the other gods from interfering in the course of the war, Zeus travels to Mount Ida, which overlooks the Trojan plain. There, he weighs the fates of Troy and Achaea in his scale, and the Achaean side sinks down. With a shower of lightning upon the Achaean army, Zeus turns the tide of battle in the Trojans' favor, and the Greeks retreat in terror. Hera, seeing the Achaean army collapsing, inspires Agamemnon to rouse his troops. He stirs up their pride, begs them to have heart, and prays for relief from Zeus, who finally sends a sign—an eagle carrying a fawn in its talons. The divine symbol inspires the Achaeans to fight back.

As the Achaeans struggle to regain their power, the archer Teucer fells many Trojans. But Hector finally wounds Teucer, reversing the tide of battle yet again. Hector drives the Greeks behind their fortifications, all the way to their ships. Athena and Hera, unable to bear any further suffering on the part of their favored Greeks, prepare to enter the fray, but Zeus sends the goddess Iris to warn them of the consequences of interfering. Knowing that they cannot compete with Zeus, Athena and Hera relent and go back to Mount Olympus. When Zeus returns, he tells them that the next morning will provide their last chance to save the Achaeans. He notes that only Achilles can prevent the Greeks' destruction.

With the Trojans poised to drive the Achaeans back to their ships, the Achaean troops sit brokenhearted in their camp. Standing before them, Agamemnon weeps and declares the war a failure. He proposes returning to Greece in disgrace. Diomedes, however, rises and insists that he will stay and fight even if everyone else leaves. He buoys the soldiers by reminding them that Troy is fated to fall. Nestor also urges perseverance and suggests reconciliation with Achilles. Seeing the wisdom of this idea, Agamemnon decides to offer Achilles a great stockpile of gifts on the condition that he return to the Achaean lines. The king selects some of the Achaeans' best men, including Odysseus, Great Ajax, and Phoenix, to communicate the proposal to Achilles.

The embassy finds Achilles playing the lyre in his tent with his dear friend Patroclus. Odysseus presents Agamemnon's offer, but Achilles rejects it immediately. He announces that he intends to return to his homeland of Phthia, where he can live a long, humble life instead of the short, glorious one that is his fate should he stay. Achilles offers to take Phoenix, who helped rear him in Phthia, with him, but Phoenix launches into his own lengthy, emotional plea for Achilles to stay. Phoenix uses the ancient story of Meleager— another warrior who, in an episode of rage, refused to fight—to illustrate the importance of responding to the pleas of helpless friends. But Achilles stands firm, still feeling the sting of Agamemnon's insult. The embassy returns unsuccessful, and the army again sinks into despair.

SUMMARY: BOOKS 10–12

The next morning, Nestor suggests sending a spy to infiltrate the Trojan ranks, and Diomedes and Odysseus are quick to volunteer. As the two men set off, the Trojans devise their own reconnaissance. Hector wants to know whether the Achaeans are planning an escape. He selects Dolon, an unattractive but lightning-quick man, to serve as his scout, and promises to reward him with Achilles' chariot and horses once the Achaeans fall. Dolon sets out and soon encounters Diomedes and Odysseus. The two men interrogate Dolon, who, hoping to save his life, tells them the positions of the Trojans and all of their allies. He reveals to them that the Thracians, newly arrived, are especially vulnerable to attack. Diomedes then kills Dolon and strips him of his armor.

Diomedes and Odysseus proceed to the Thracian camp, where they kill twelve soldiers and the Thracian king, Rhesus. The two Achaean spies also steal Rhesus's chariot and horses. Athena warns them that some angry god may wake the other soldiers, so Diomedes and Odysseus ride Rhesus's chariot back to the Achaean camp. Nestor and the other Greeks, worried that their comrades had been killed, greet them warmly.

When the fighting starts again the next morning, Agamemnon pushes the Trojans back to their gates, only to be wounded by a Trojan named Coön. When Agamemnon is forced to retreat, Hector enters the battle. The Achaeans panic and stand poised to retreat, but the words of Odysseus and Diomedes imbue them with fresh courage. Diomedes hurls a spear that hits Hector's helmet—a brush with death that stuns Hector and forces him to retreat. Paris then wounds Diomedes with an arrow, thus sidelining the great warrior for the rest of the *Iliad*. Trojans now encircle Odysseus, who is left to fight alone. He beats all of them back, but not before the Trojan warrior Socus inflicts a wound through Odysseus's ribs. Great Ajax carries Odysseus back to camp before the Trojans can harm him further.

Hector resumes his assault on another part of the Achaean line. The Greeks initially hold him off, but they panic when Paris wounds the healer Machaon. Hector and his men force Ajax to retreat as Nestor conveys Machaon back to his tent. When Achilles learns of Machaon's injuries, he sends his companion Patroclus to inquire into Machaon's status. Nestor tells Patroclus about all of the wounds that the Trojans have inflicted upon the Achaean commanders. He begs Patroclus to persuade Achilles to rejoin the battle—or at least enter the battle himself disguised in Achilles' armor. This ruse would provide the benefit of Achilles' terrifying aura. Patroclus agrees to appeal to Achilles.

Undaunted by the trenches around the Greek fort, Hector, acting on the advice of the young commander Polydamas, orders his men to disembark from their chariots and storm the ramparts. Just as the Trojans prepare to cross the trenches, an eagle flies to the left-hand side of the Trojan line and drops a serpent in the soldiers' midst. Polydamas interprets this event as a sign that their charge will fail, but Hector refuses to retreat.

The Trojans Glaucus and Sarpedon now charge the ramparts, and Menestheus, aided by Great Ajax and Teucer, struggles to hold them back. Sarpedon makes the first breach, and Hector follows by shattering one of the gates with a boulder. The Trojans pour through the fortifications as the Achaeans, terrified, shrink back against the ships.

SUMMARY: BOOKS 13–15

Zeus, happy with the war's progress, leaves the battlefield. Poseidon, eager to help the Achaeans and realizing that Zeus has gone, visits Little Ajax and Great Ajax in the form of Calchas and gives them confidence to resist the Trojan assault. Poseidon also rouses the rest of the Achaeans, who have withdrawn in tears to the sides of the ships. The Aeantes (Little Ajax and Great Ajax) prove successful in driving Hector back. When Hector throws his lance at Teucer, Teucer dodges out of the way, and the weapon pierces and kills Poseidon's grandson Amphimachus. In vengeance, Poseidon imbues Idomeneus, one of the Achaean commanders, with raging power. Idomeneus cuts down a number of Trojan soldiers but hopes most of all to kill the warrior Deiphobus. Finding Deiphobus on the battlefield, Idomeneus taunts the Trojan, who summons Aeneas and other comrades to his assistance.

Nestor leaves the wounded Machaon in his tent and goes to meet the other wounded Achaean commanders by their ships. The men scan the battlefield and realize the terrible extent of their losses. Agamemnon proposes that they give up and set sail for home, but Odysseus declares this notion cowardly and disgraceful. Diomedes urges them all to the line to rally their troops. As they set out, Poseidon encourages Agamemnon and gives added strength to the Achaean army.

Hera spots Zeus on Mount Ida, overlooking Troy, and devises a plan to distract him so that she may help the Achaeans behind his back. She visits Aphrodite and tricks her into giving her an enchanted breast-band into which the powers of Love and Longing are woven, forceful enough to make even the sanest man go mad. Hera then visits the embodiment of Sleep, and by promising him one of her daughters in marriage, persuades him to lull Zeus to sleep. Sleep follows Hera to the peak of Mount Ida, where, disguised as a bird, he hides in a tree. Zeus sees Hera, and the enchanted breast-band seizes him with passion. He makes love to Hera and, as planned, soon falls asleep. Hera then calls to Poseidon and tells him that he now has free reign to steer the Achaeans to victory. Poseidon reassembles the Achaeans, who charge the Trojans. In the ensuing scuffle, Great Ajax knocks Hector to the ground with a boulder, and the Trojans are forced to carry the hero back to Troy. With Hector gone, the Achaeans trounce their enemies, and Trojans die in great numbers as the army flees back to the city.

Zeus wakes and sees the havoc that Hera and Poseidon have wreaked while he dozed in his enchanted sleep. Hera tries to blame Poseidon, but Zeus comforts her by making clear that he has no personal interest in a Trojan victory over the Achaeans. He tells her that he will again come to their aid but also says that Troy is still fated to fall and that Hector will die after he kills Patroclus. Zeus then orders Poseidon to leave the battlefield, while Apollo seeks out Hector and fills him and his comrades with fresh strength. Hector leads a charge against the Achaeans, and while their leaders initially hold their ground, they retreat in terror when Apollo himself enters the battle.

Apollo covers the trench in front of the Greek fortifications, allowing the Trojans to beat down the ramparts once again.

The armies fight all the way to the ships and very nearly into the Greek camp. At the base of the ships, furious hand-to-hand fighting breaks out. Great Ajax and Hector again tangle. The archer Teucer fells several Trojans, but Zeus snaps his bowstring when he takes aim at Hector. Ajax encourages his troops from the decks of the ships, but Hector rallies the Trojans, and inch by inch the Trojans advance until Hector is close enough to touch a ship.

SUMMARY: BOOKS 16–18

Meanwhile, Patroclus goes to Achilles' tent and begs to be allowed to wear Achilles' armor if Achilles still refuses to rejoin the battle himself. Achilles declines to fight but agrees to the exchange of armor, with the understanding that Patroclus will fight only long enough to save the ships. As Patroclus arms himself, the first ship goes up in flames. Achilles sends his Myrmidon soldiers, who have not been fighting during their commander's absence, out to accompany Patroclus. Achilles then prays to Zeus that Patroclus may return with both himself and the ships unharmed. Homer reveals, however, that Zeus will grant only one of these prayers.

When Patroclus appears in Achilles' armor, the battle quickly turns, and the Trojans retreat from the Achaean ships. At first, the Trojan line holds together, but when Hector retreats, the rest of the Trojans become trapped in the trenches. Patroclus slaughters every Trojan he encounters. Zeus considers saving his son Sarpedon, but Hera persuades Zeus that the other gods would either look down upon him for it or try to save their own mortal offspring in turn. Zeus resigns himself to Sarpedon's mortality. Not long after, Patroclus spears Sarpedon, and both sides fight over his armor. Hector returns briefly to the front in an attempt to retrieve the armor.

Zeus decides to kill Patroclus for slaying Sarpedon but first lets Patroclus rout the Trojans. Zeus then imbues Hector with a temporary cowardice, and Hector leads the retreat. Patroclus, disobeying Achilles, pursues the Trojans all the way to the gates of Troy. Homer explains that the city might have fallen at this moment had Apollo not intervened and driven Patroclus back from the gates. Apollo persuades Hector to charge Patroclus, but Patroclus kills Cebriones, the driver of Hector's chariot. Trojans and Achaeans fight for Cebriones' armor. Amid the chaos, Apollo sneaks up behind Patroclus and wounds him, and Hector easily finishes him off. Hector taunts the fallen man, but with his dying words Patroclus foretells Hector's own death.

At Patroclus's death, a great fight begins over the armor of Achilles and the body of Patroclus. Hector finally dons Achilles' armor himself. Aware of Hector's impending doom and perhaps pitying him, Zeus temporarily grants Hector great power. Ajax and Menelaus summon more Achaeans to help them, and they soon force the Trojans, including mighty Hector, to run for the city's walls. Aeneas, invigorated by Apollo, rallies the fleeing men to return to the fight, but even after much effort, they remain unable to take the corpse. Achilles' charioteer, Automedon, becomes involved in the fighting as Zeus imbues his team with fresh strength. Hector tries to kill Automedon so that he can steal the chariot, but Automedon dodges Hector's spear and brings down a Trojan in the process. Menelaus finally manages to steal away with the body of his comrade.

When Antilochus brings Achilles word of Patroclus's death, Achilles loses control of himself. He weeps, beats the ground with his fists, covers his face with dirt, and utters a "terrible, wrenching cry" so profound that Thetis hears him and comes with her water-nymph sisters from the ocean to learn what troubles her son. Achilles tells his mother of the tragedy and insists that he will avenge himself on Hector, despite his knowledge that, should he choose to live the life of a warrior, he is fated to die young. Thetis responds that since Hector now wears Achilles' armor, she will have the divine metalsmith Hephaestus make him a new set, if Achilles will delay exacting his revenge for one day.

Thetis departs, and Iris, sent by Hera, comes to tell Achilles that he must go outside and make an appearance on the battlefield. This appearance alone will scare the Trojans into abandoning the fight for Patroclus's body. Achilles leaves his tent, accompanied by Athena, and lets loose an enormous cry that does indeed send the Trojans fleeing.

That night, each army holds an assembly to plan its next move. In the Trojan camp, Polydamas urges his comrades to retreat to the city now that Achilles has decided to return to battle. Hector dismisses the idea as cowardly and insists on repeating the previous day's assault. His foolhardy plan wins the support of the Trojans, whom Athena has robbed of their wits. Meanwhile, in the Achaean camp, the men begin to mourn Patroclus.

SUMMARY: BOOKS 19–21

Achilles announces his intention to go to war at once. Odysseus persuades him to let the army eat first, but Achilles himself refuses to eat until he has slain Hector. All through breakfast, Achilles sits mourning his dear friend Patroclus and reminiscing. Even Briseis mourns, for Patroclus treated her kindly when she was first led away from her homeland. Zeus finds the scene moving and sends Athena down to fill Achilles' stomach with nectar and ambrosia in order to keep his hunger at bay. Achilles then dons his armor and mounts his chariot. As he does so, he chastises his horses, Roan Beauty and Charger, for leaving Patroclus on the battlefield to die. Roan Beauty replies that it was not he but a god who let Patroclus die and that the same is fated for Achilles. But Achilles needs no reminders of his fate, for he knows that by entering battle for his friend, he seals his destiny.

While the Achaeans and Trojans prepare for battle, Zeus summons the gods to Mount Olympus. He is aware that Achilles, if allowed to enter the battlefield unchecked, will decimate the Trojans and maybe even bring the city down before its fated time. Accordingly, Zeus removes his previous injunction against divine interference in the battle, and the gods stream down to earth. However, they soon decide merely to watch the fighting rather than involve themselves in it. They take their seats on opposite hills overlooking the battlefield, interested to see how their mortal teams will fare on their own.

Before Apollo resigns himself to a passive role, he encourages Aeneas to challenge Achilles. The two heroes meet on the battlefield and exchange insults. Achilles is about to stab Aeneas fatally when Poseidon, in a burst of sympathy for the Trojan—and much to the chagrin of the other, pro-Greek gods—whisks Aeneas away. Hector then approaches, but Apollo persuades him not to strike up a duel in front of the ranks but rather to wait with the other soldiers until Achilles comes to him. But when he sees Achilles slaughtering the Trojans, among them one of Hector's brothers, he again challenges Achilles. The fight goes poorly for Hector, and Apollo must save him a second time.

Achilles routs the Trojans and splits their ranks, pursuing half of them into the river known to the gods as Xanthus and to the mortals as Scamander. On the riverbank, Achilles mercilessly slaughters Lycaon, a son of Priam. The Trojan Asteropaeus, given fresh strength by the god of the river, makes a valiant stand, but Achilles kills him as well. The vengeful Achilles has no intention of sparing any Trojans now that they have killed Patroclus. He throws so many corpses into the river that its channels become clogged. The river god rises up and protests, and Achilles agrees to stop throwing people into the water but not to stop killing them. The river, sympathetic to the Trojans, calls for help from Apollo, but when Achilles hears the river's plea, he attacks the river. The river gets the upper hand and drags Achilles all the way downstream to a floodplain. He very nearly kills Achilles, but the gods intervene. Hephaestus, sent by Hera, sets the plain on fire and boils the river until he relents.

ANALYSIS: ACHILLES' RECONCILIATION

Although Achilles reconciles with Agamemnon, his other actions in Books 19 and 20 indicate that his character remains static. Achilles still demonstrates a tendency for the thoughtless rage that has brought so many Achaeans to their deaths. He remains so intent on vengeance, for example, that he initially intends for the men to go into battle without food, which could prove fatal in warfare that demands so much physical energy. Similarly, on the battlefield, Achilles demonstrates an obsessive concern with victory—to the exclusion of all other considerations. He cuts down the Trojan warrior Tros even though Tros supplicates him and begs to be saved; it is apparent that Achilles has done little soul-searching. Although he reconciles himself with the Achaean forces, this gesture does not alleviate his rage but rather refocuses it. Achilles now lashes out at the Trojans, expressing his anger through action rather than through pointed refusals to act. Burning with passion, he rejects all appeals to cool-headed reflection; the text compares him to an "inhuman fire" and, when he dons his shining armor, likens him to the sun. This imagery recalls his portrayal in Book 1 as "blazing Achilles."

Indeed, Achilles' internal dilemma as a character remains largely the same as in the beginning of the epic. Achilles has known throughout that his fate is either to live a short, glorious life at Troy or a long, obscure life back in Phthia. Now, as before, he must choose. Although he still feels torn between the two options, the shock of Patroclus's death has shifted the balance in favor of remaining at Troy. There is little reason to believe that Achilles would have made up his mind without such a powerful catalyst for his decision.

Summary: Books 22–24

Hector now stands as the only Trojan left outside Troy. Priam, over-looking the battlefield from the Trojan ramparts, begs him to come inside, but Hector, having given the overconfident order for the Tro-jans to camp outside their gates the night before, now feels too ashamed to join them in their retreat. When Achilles finally returns from chasing Apollo (disguised as Agenor), Hector confronts him. At first, Hector considers trying to negotiate with Achilles, but he soon realizes the hopelessness of his cause and flees. He runs around the city three times, with Achilles at his heels. Zeus considers saving Hector, but Athena persuades him that the mortal's time has come. Zeus places Hector's and Achilles' respective fates on a golden scale, and, indeed, Hector's sinks to the ground.

During Hector's fourth lap around the city walls, Athena appears before him, disguised as his ally Deiphobus, and convinces him that together they can take Achilles. Hector stops running and turns to face his opponent. He and Achilles exchange spear throws, but nei-ther scores a hit. Hector turns to Deiphobus to ask him for a lance; when he finds his friend gone, he realizes that the gods have betrayed him. With a perfectly timed thrust, Achilles puts his spear through Hector's throat. Near death, Hector pleads with Achilles to return his body to the Trojans for burial, but Achilles resolves to let the dogs and scavenger birds maul the Trojan hero.

The day after, following the burial of Patroclus's bones, Achilles holds a series of competitions in Patroclus's honor. Marvelous prizes are offered, and both the commanders and the soldiers compete. The events include boxing, wrestling, archery, and a chariot race, which Diomedes wins with some help from Athena.

Achilles continues to mourn Patroclus and abuses Hector's body, dragging it around his dead companion's tomb. Apollo, meanwhile, protects Hector's corpse from damage and rot and staves off dogs and scavengers. Finally, on the twelfth day after Hector's death, Apollo persuades Zeus that Achilles must let Hector's body be ran-somed. Zeus sends Thetis to bring the news to Achilles, while Iris goes to Priam to instruct him to initiate the ransom. Hecuba fears that Achilles will kill her husband, but Zeus reassures her by sending an eagle as a good omen.

Priam sets out with his driver, Idaeus, and a chariot full of trea-sure. Zeus sends Hermes, disguised as a benevolent Myrmidon sol-dier, to guide Priam through the Achaean camp. When the chariot arrives at Achilles' tent, Hermes reveals himself and then leaves

Priam alone with Achilles. Priam tearfully begs Achilles for Hector's body. He asks Achilles to think of his own father, Peleus, and the love between them. Achilles weeps for his father and for Patroclus. He accepts the ransom and agrees to relinquish the corpse.

That night, Priam sleeps in Achilles' tent, but Hermes comes to him in the middle of the night, rouses him, and warns him that he must not sleep among the enemy. Priam and Idaeus wake, place Hector in their chariot, and slip out of the camp unnoticed. All the women in Troy, from Andromache to Helen, cry out in grief when they first see Hector's body. For nine days, the Trojans prepare Hector's funeral pyre—Achilles has given them a reprieve from battle. The Trojans light Hector's pyre on the tenth day.

ANALYSIS: PRIAM MEETS ACHILLES

Despite the temporary bond formed between Priam and Achilles, Troy's remains fated to fall at the hands of the Achaeans, as Andromache reminds us when she sees soldiers carrying Hector's body into the city. Nonetheless, while Achilles and Priam remain enemies, their animosity has become a nobler, more respectful one.

This change ostensibly stems from Achilles' removal from the battlefield and his awareness of the imminence of his own death. Achilles begins the epic as a temperamental, prideful, selfish, and impulsive man, but in Book 24, he displays a sense of sympathy for others. Throughout the poem, Homer charts Achilles' inability to think beyond himself: his wounded pride interferes with his duty to lead the Achaeans, ensuring their defeat. Likewise, his rage at Patroclus's death prompts him to disrespect the noble Hector's corpse. At this point, however, Achilles not only respects Priam's plea by returning Hector's body but also allows the Trojan people a reprieve from battle in order to honor and grieve their hero properly.

The fact that Achilles' change of heart comes at the conclusion of the *Iliad* emphasizes the centrality of Achilles' rage to the poem. Homer chooses to conclude the *Iliad* not with the death of Achilles or the fall of Troy but rather with the softening of Achilles' mighty wrath. The thorough exploration of human emotion and the accompanying lack of dramatic climax typify the poem's basic anticlimactic nature. Homer's audience would have been familiar with the plot's outcome, and even a modern audience probably knows how things turn out. With the element of suspense gone, it makes perfect sense for Homer to wrap up his poem once the original conflict—Achilles' rage at Agamemnon—is resolved.

The Odyssey

Characters

Odysseus   The protagonist of the *Odyssey*. Odysseus fought among the other Greek heroes at Troy and now struggles to return to his kingdom in Ithaca. He is Queen Penelope's husband and Prince Telemachus's father. Though a strong and courageous warrior, Odysseus is most renowned for his cunning. He is a favorite of the goddess Athena, who often sends him divine aid, but a bitter enemy of Poseidon, who frustrates his journey at every turn.

Telemachus   Odysseus's son. An infant when Odysseus left for Troy, Telemachus is about twenty at the beginning of the story. He is a natural obstacle to the suitors doggedly courting his mother, but despite his courage and good heart, he initially lacks the poise and confidence to oppose them. His maturation, especially during his trip to Pylos and Sparta in Books 3 and 4, provides a subplot to the epic. Athena often assists Telemachus.

Penelope   Odysseus's wife and Telemachus's mother. Penelope spends her days in the palace pining for her husband, who left for Troy twenty years earlier and has yet to return. Homer portrays her as sometimes flighty and excitable but also clever and steadfastly true to her husband.

Athena   Zeus's daughter and the goddess of wisdom, purposeful battle, and the womanly arts. Athena assists Odysseus and Telemachus with divine powers throughout the *Odyssey* and speaks up for them in the councils of the gods on Mount Olympus. She often appears in disguise as Mentor, an old friend of Odysseus.

Poseidon God of the sea. As Penelope's suitors are Odysseus's mortal antagonists, Poseidon is his divine antagonist. Already predisposed against Odysseus and the greeks in the Trojan War, Poseidon despises Odysseus for blinding his son, the Cyclops Polyphemus, and constantly hampers his journey home. Ironically, Poseidon is the patron of the sea-faring Phaeacians, who ultimately help to return Odysseus to Ithaca.

Zeus King of the gods who mediates the disputes of the gods on Mount Olympus. Homer occasionally depicts Zeus as weighing men's fates on his scales. Zeus sometimes helps Odysseus or permits Athena to do so.

Antinous The most arrogant of Penelope's suitors. Antinous leads the campaign to have Telemachus killed. Although Homer portrays some of the other suitors with redeeming qualities, his portrayal of Antinous is unsympathetic. Antinous is the first to die when Odysseus returns.

Amphinomus Among the dozens of suitors, the only decent man seeking Penelope's hand in marriage. Amphinomus sometimes speaks up for Odysseus and Telemachus but dies with the rest of the suitors in the final fight.

Eumaeus A loyal shepherd who, along with the cowherd Philoetius, helps Odysseus reclaim his throne after his return to Ithaca. Even though Eumaeus does not know that the vagabond who appears at his hut is Odysseus, he gives the man food and shelter.

Eurycleia The elderly, loyal servant who nursed Odysseus and Telemachus when they were babies. Eurycleia is well-informed about palace intrigues and serves as confidant to her masters. She keeps Telemachus's journey secret from Penelope and later keeps Odysseus's identity a secret after she recognizes a scar on his leg.

Melanthius Melantho's brother. Melanthius is a treacherous and opportunistic goatherd who supports the suitors, especially Eurymachus, and abuses the beggar who appears in Odysseus's palace, not realizing that the man is Odysseus himself.

Calypso The beautiful nymph who falls in love with Odysseus when he lands on her island home of Ogygia. Calypso holds him prisoner there for seven years until Hermes, the messenger god, persuades her to let him go.

Polyphemus One of the Cyclopes (uncivilized one-eyed giants) whose island Odysseus reaches soon after leaving Troy. Polyphemus imprisons Odysseus and his crew and tries to eat them, but Odysseus blinds him through a clever ruse and manages to escape. In doing so, however, Odysseus angers Polyphemus's father, Poseidon.

Circe The beautiful witch-goddess who transforms Odysseus's crew into swine when they land on her island. With Hermes' help, Odysseus resists Circe's powers and then becomes her lover, living in luxury at her side for a year.

Laertes Odysseus's aging father, who resides on a farm in Ithaca. In despair and physical decline, Laertes regains his spirit when Odysseus returns and eventually kills Antinous's father.

Tiresias A Theban prophet who inhabits the underworld as a shade. Tiresias meets Odysseus when Odysseus journeys to the underworld in Book 11. He shows Odysseus how to get back to Ithaca and allows Odysseus to communicate with the other souls in Hades.

Nestor King of Pylos and a former warrior in the Trojan War. Like Odysseus, Nestor is known for being a clever speaker. Telemachus visits him in Book 3 to ask about his father, but Nestor has little information on Odysseus's whereabouts.

Menelaus   King of Sparta and brother of Agamemnon. Menelaus, the husband of Helen, helped lead the Greek forces in the Trojan War. He offers Telemachus assistance in his quest to find Odysseus when Telemachus visits him in Book 4.

Helen   Wife of Menelaus and queen of Sparta. Helen's abduction at the hands of the Trojans sparked the Trojan War. Her beauty is without parallel, but Homer sometimes paints her in a critical light for giving in to her Trojan captors and thereby costing many Greek men their lives. Helen offers Telemachus assistance in his quest to find his father.

Agamemnon   Former king of Mycenae, brother of Menelaus, and commander of the Achaean forces at Troy. Odysseus encounters Agamemnon's spirit in Hades. Agamemnon died at the hands of his wife, Clytemnestra, and her lover, Aegisthus, upon returning from the war. His son Orestes later avenged him. The story of Agamemnon's and Orestes' fates appears repeatedly in the *Odyssey* and offers an inverted image of the fortunes of Odysseus and Telemachus.

Nausicaa   The beautiful daughter of King Alcinous and Queen Arete of the Phaeacians. Nausicaa discovers Odysseus on the beach at Scheria and, out of budding affection for him, ensures his warm reception at her parents' palace.

Alcinous   The Phaeacian king who offers Odysseus hospitality in his island kingdom of Scheria. Alcinous hears the story of Odysseus's wanderings and provides him with safe passage back to Ithaca.

Arete   The Phaeacian queen, Alcinous's wife, and Nausicaa's mother. Arete is intelligent and influential. Nausicaa tells Odysseus to make his appeal for assistance to Arete.

ANALYSIS OF MAJOR CHARACTERS

ODYSSEUS

Odysseus has the defining character traits of a Homeric leader: strength, courage, nobility, a thirst for glory, and confidence in his authority. His most distinguishing trait, however, is his sharp intellect, which enables him to think his way out of difficult situations. Odysseus is also a convincing, articulate speaker and can win over or otherwise manipulate his audience with ease.

Like other Homeric heroes, Odysseus strives to win *kleos* (glory won through great deeds), but he also wishes to complete his *nostos* (homecoming). He enjoys his luxurious life with Circe in an exotic land, but only to a point. Eventually, he wants to return home, even though he admits that his wife cannot compare with Circe. Throughout the epic, Odysseus struggles to balance his desire for glory with his longing for home.

Homeric characters generally are static: though they may be complex and realistic, they do not change over the course of the work as many characters in modern novels and stories do. Odysseus and especially Telemachus, however, break this pattern. Early in his adventures, Odysseus's love of glory prompts him to reveal his identity to the Cyclops and bring Poseidon's wrath down on him. By the end of the epic, he is much more willing to temper pride with patience. Disguised as a beggar, he does not immediately react to the abuse he receives from the suitors. Instead, Odysseus endures it until the traps he has set and the loyalties he has secured enable him to strike back effectively.

PENELOPE

Penelope never loses faith in Odysseus, despite the fact that she has not seen him in twenty years and despite the pressure the suitors place on her to remarry. Her cares make her somewhat flighty and excitable, however. For this reason, Odysseus, Telemachus, and Athena often prefer to leave her in the dark about matters that might upset her. Athena must distract Penelope, for instance, so that she does not discover Odysseus's identity when Eurycleia is washing him. Athena often comes to her in dreams to reassure or comfort her, for Penelope would otherwise spend her nights weeping in her bed.

Though her love for Odysseus is unyielding, Penelope responds to the suitors with some indecision. She never refuses outright to remarry. Instead, she puts off her decision and strings the suitors along by promising to choose a new husband as soon as certain things happen. Her astute delaying tactics reveal her sly and artful side. Penelope displays her cleverness and buys herself time to wait for her husband by telling the suitors she cannot remarry until she finishes a burial shroud for her father-in-law; every day, she weaves the shroud, and every night, undoes her day's work. Similarly, some commentators claim that her decision to marry whomever wins the archery contest of Book 21 results from her awareness that only her husband can win it. Some scholars even claim that Penelope recognizes Odysseus before she admits it to him in Book 23.

TELEMACHUS

Just an infant when his father left for Troy, Telemachus is still maturing when the *Odyssey* begins. He is wholly devoted to his mother and to maintaining his father's estate but does not know how to protect them from the suitors. After all, it has only been a few years since Telemachus first realized the suitors' intentions. His meeting with Athena in Book 1 changes things. Aside from improving his stature and bearing, Athena teaches him the responsibilities of a young prince. Telemachus soon becomes more assertive. He confronts the suitors and denounces the abuse of his estate, and when Penelope and Eurycleia become anxious or upset, he does not shy away from taking control.

Telemachus never fully matches his father's talents, at least not by the end of the *Odyssey*. He has a stout heart and an active mind, and sometimes even a bit of a temper, but he never schemes with the same skill or speaks with the same eloquence as Odysseus. In Book 22, Telemachus accidentally leaves a weapons storeroom unlocked, a careless mistake that allows the suitors to arm themselves. While Odysseus does occasionally err in judgment over the course of the epic, it is difficult to imagine him making such a blunder. Telemachus has not yet inherited his father's brassy pride either. The archery scene captures the endpoint of his development perfectly, as Telemachus tries and tries to string the bow, and very nearly does, but not quite. He walks away feeling disappointment and exasperation but shows no signs of the rage or wounded pride that Odysseus would likely have felt under similar circumstances.

SUMMARY: BOOKS 1–3

The narrator of the *Odyssey* invokes the Muse, asking for inspiration as he prepares to tell the story of Odysseus. The story begins ten years after the end of the Trojan War, the subject of the *Iliad*. All the Greek heroes except Odysseus have returned home. Odysseus languishes on the remote island of Ogygia with the goddess Calypso, who has fallen in love with him and refuses to let him leave. Meanwhile, a mob of suitors is devouring Odysseus's estate in Ithaca and courting his wife, Penelope, in hopes of taking over his kingdom. Odysseus's son, Telemachus, an infant when Odysseus left but now a young man, is helpless to stop the suitors. Telemachus has resigned himself to the likelihood that his father is dead.

With the consent of Zeus, Athena travels to Ithaca to speak with Telemachus. Assuming the form of Odysseus's old friend Mentor, Athena predicts that Odysseus is still alive and that he will soon return to Ithaca. She advises Telemachus to assemble the suitors and banish them from his father's estate. Athena then instructs Telemachus to journey to Pylos and Sparta to try to find any news of his father.

At the assembly the next day, Telemachus confronts the suitors. One of the suitors, Antinous, blames the impasse on Penelope, who, he says, seduces every suitor but will commit to none of them. He reminds the suitors of a ruse that Penelope concocted to put off remarrying: she maintained that she would choose a husband as soon as she finished weaving a burial shroud for her elderly father-in-law, Laertes. But each night, she carefully undid the knitting that she had completed during the day, so that the shroud would never be finished. If Penelope can make no decision, Antinous declares, then she should be sent back to Icarius, her father, so that he can choose a new husband for her. The dutiful Telemachus refuses to throw his mother out and calls upon the gods to punish the suitors.

After the assembly, Telemachus and Mentor (Athena in disguise) set out for Pylos, the kingdom of Nestor. Unfortunately, Nestor has no information about Odysseus. He recounts that, after the fall of Troy, a falling-out occurred between Agamemnon and Menelaus, the two Greek brothers who had led the expedition. Menelaus set sail for Greece immediately, while Agamemnon decided to wait a day and continue to sacrifice to the gods on the shores of Troy. Nestor went with Menelaus, while Odysseus stayed with Agamemnon. Nestor has heard no news of Odysseus since. He says that he can only pray that Athena will show Telemachus the kindness that she showed Odysseus.

Telemachus then asks Nestor about Agamemnon's fate. Nestor explains that Agamemnon returned from Troy to find that Aegisthus, a coward who remained behind while the Greeks fought in Troy, seduced and married Agamemnon's wife, Clytemnestra. With Clytemnestra's approval, Aegisthus murdered Agamemnon. Aegisthus would have then taken over Agamemnon's kingdom had not Orestes, who was in exile in Athens, returned and killed Aegisthus and Clytemnestra. Nestor holds the courage of Orestes up as an example for Telemachus. Nestor sends his own son Pisistratus along to accompany Telemachus to Sparta, and the two set out by land the next day. Athena, who reveals her divinity by shedding the form of Mentor and changing into an eagle before the entire court of Pylos, stays behind to protect Telemachus's ship and its crew.

SUMMARY: BOOKS 4–6

In Sparta, the king and queen, Menelaus and Helen, celebrate the separate marriages of their son and daughter. They happily greet Pisistratus and Telemachus, the latter of whom they soon recognize as the son of Odysseus because of the clear family resemblance. As they all feast, the king and queen recount with melancholy the many examples of Odysseus's cunning at Troy. Helen recalls how Odysseus dressed as a beggar to infiltrate the city's walls. Menelaus tells the famous story of the Trojan horse, Odysseus's masterful gambit that allowed the Greeks to sneak into Troy and slaughter the Trojans. The following day, Menelaus recounts his own return from Troy. He says that, stranded in Egypt, he was forced to capture Proteus, the divine Old Man of the Sea. Proteus told him the way back to Sparta and then informed him of the fates of Agamemnon and Ajax, another Greek hero, who survived Troy only to perish back in Greece. Proteus also gave him news of Odysseus—that he was still alive but was imprisoned by Calypso on her island. Buoyed by this report, Telemachus and Pisistratus return to Pylos to set sail for Ithaca.

Meanwhile, the suitors at Odysseus's house learn of Telemachus's voyage and prepare to ambush him upon his return. The herald Medon overhears their plans and reports them to Penelope. She becomes distraught when she reflects that she may soon lose her son in addition to her husband. However, Athena sends a phantom in the form of Penelope's sister, Iphthime, to reassure Penelope. Iphthime tells Penelope not to worry, for the goddess will protect Telemachus.

As Book 5 begins, all of the gods except Poseidon gather again on Mount Olympus to discuss Odysseus's fate. Athena's speech in support of the hero prevails on Zeus to intervene. Hermes, messenger of the gods, is sent to Ogygia to tell Calypso that Odysseus must at last be allowed to leave so that he can return home. Calypso protests, but in the end, she submits to the supreme will of Zeus. By now, Odysseus alone remains of the contingent that he led at Troy, for his crew and the other boats in his force were all destroyed during his journeys. Calypso helps him build a new boat and stocks it with provisions from her island. With sadness, she watches as the object of her love sails away.

After eighteen days at sea, Odysseus spots Scheria, the island of the Phaeacians, which is the next destination the gods have appointed for him. Just then, Poseidon, returning from a trip to the land of the Ethiopians, spots Odysseus and realizes what the other gods have done in his absence. Poseidon stirs up a storm that nearly drags Odysseus under the sea, but the goddess Ino comes to Odysseus's rescue. Ino gives Odysseus a veil that keeps him safe after his ship is wrecked. Athena too comes to Odysseus's rescue as he is tossed back and forth, now out to the deep sea, now against the jagged rocks of the coast. After three days, a river up the coast of the island answers Odysseus's prayers and allows him to swim into its waters. He throws his protective veil back into the water as Ino commanded him to do and walks inland to rest in the safe cover of a forest.

That night, Athena appears in a dream to the Phaeacian princess Nausicaa, disguised as her friend. Athena encourages the young princess to go to the river the next day to wash her clothes so that she will appear more fetching to the many men courting her. The next morning, Nausicaa goes to the river, and while she and her handmaidens are naked, playing ball as their clothes dry on the ground, Odysseus wakes in the forest and encounters them. Naked himself, he humbly yet winningly pleads for their assistance, never revealing his identity. Nausicaa leaves Odysseus alone to wash the dirt and brine from his body, and Athena makes him look especially handsome, so that when Nausicaa sees him again, she begins to fall in love with him. Afraid of causing a scene if she walks into the city with a strange man at her side, Nausicaa gives Odysseus directions to the palace and advice on how to approach Arete, queen of the Phaeacians, when he meets her. With a prayer to Athena asking for hospitality from the Phaeacians, Odysseus sets out for the palace.

SUMMARY: BOOKS 7–9

Odysseus finds the palace residents holding a festival in honor of Poseidon. He is struck by the splendor of the palace and the king's opulence. As soon as he sees the queen, he throws himself at her feet, and the mist about him dissipates. At first, the king wonders if this wayward traveler might be a god. Without revealing his identity, Odysseus puts the king's suspicions to rest by declaring that he is indeed a mortal. He then explains his predicament, and the king and queen gladly promise to see him off the next day in a Phaeacian ship.

Later that evening, when the king and queen are alone with Odysseus, the wise Arete recognizes the clothes that he is wearing as ones that she herself had made for her daughter Nausicaa. Suspicious, she interrogates Odysseus further. While still withholding his name, Odysseus responds by recounting the story of his journey from Calypso's island and his encounter with Nausicaa that morning, which involved her giving him a set of clothes to wear. To absolve the princess for not accompanying him to the palace, Odysseus claims that it was his idea to come alone. Alcinous is so impressed with his visitor that he offers Odysseus his daughter's hand in marriage.

The next day, the king holds a feast and celebration of games in honor of his guest. There, a blind bard named Demodocus sings of the quarrel between Odysseus and Achilles at Troy. Everyone listens with pleasure except Odysseus, who weeps at the painful memories that the story recalls. The king notices Odysseus's grief and ends the feast so that the games can begin.

At dinner that night, Odysseus asks Demodocus to sing of the Trojan horse and the sack of Troy, but as he listens to the accomplished minstrel, he again breaks down. King Alcinous again notices and stops the music. He asks Odysseus at last to tell him who he is, where he is from, and where he is going.

Reluctantly, Odysseus tells the Phaeacians the sorry tale of his wanderings, and the narrative jumps back in time to follow his story. From Troy, the winds sweep Odysseus and his men to Ismarus, city of the Cicones, where he loses six men per ship during an attack. Then, a storm sent by Zeus sweeps Odysseus and his men along for nine days before bringing them to the land of the Lotus-eaters, where the natives give some of Odysseus's men the intoxicating fruit of the lotus. As soon as they eat this fruit, they lose all thoughts of home and long for nothing more than to stay there eating more fruit. Only by dragging his men back to the ship and locking them up does Odysseus get them off the island.

Odysseus and his men then sail through the murky night to the land of the Cyclopes, a rough and uncivilized race of one-eyed giants. After making a meal of wild goats captured on an island offshore, Odysseus and his men cross to the mainland, where they come upon a cave full of sheep and crates of milk and cheese. The men advise Odysseus to snatch some of the food and hurry off, but he decides to linger. The cave's inhabitant soon returns—it is the Cyclops Polyphemus, the son of Poseidon. Polyphemus makes a show of hospitality at first but soon turns hostile. He devours two of Odysseus's men on the spot and imprisons Odysseus and the rest of his men in his cave for future meals.

Although Odysseus wants to take his sword to Polyphemus immediately, he knows that only Polyphemus is strong enough to move the rock that he has placed across the door of his cave. Odysseus therefore devises a plan. The next day, while Polyphemus is outside tending to his sheep as they graze, Odysseus finds a wooden staff in the cave and hardens it in the fire. When Polyphemus returns, Odysseus gets him drunk on wine that he brought along from the ship. Feeling jovial, Polyphemus asks Odysseus his name. Odysseus replies that his name is "Nobody." As soon as Polyphemus collapses with intoxication, Odysseus and a select group of his men drive the red-hot staff into his single eye. Polyphemus wakes with a shriek, and his neighbors come to see what is wrong, but they leave as soon as he calls out, "Nobody's killing me." When morning comes, Odysseus and his men escape from the cave, unseen by the blind Polyphemus, by clinging to the bellies of Polyphemus's sheep as they go out to graze. Safe on board their ships and with Polyphemus's flock on board as well, Odysseus calls to land and announces his true identity. With his former prisoners now out of reach, the blind Cyclops lifts up a prayer to his father, Poseidon, calling for vengeance on Odysseus.

SUMMARY: BOOKS 10–12

The Achaeans sail from the land of the Cyclopes to the home of Aeolus, ruler of the winds. Aeolus presents Odysseus with a bag containing the winds of the world and then stirs up a westerly wind to guide Odysseus and his crew home. Within ten days, they are in sight of Ithaca. As they near home, however, Odysseus's shipmates, mistakenly thinking that the bag Aeolus gave Odysseus contains a fortune in gold and silver, jealously tear the bag open. The winds escape and stir up a storm that brings Odysseus and his men back to Aeolia. This time, however, Aeolus refuses to help them, certain that the gods hate Odysseus and wish to do him harm.

After several more brushes with death, Odysseus and his men travel to Aeaea, home of the beautiful witch-goddess Circe. Circe drugs a band of Odysseus's men and turns them into pigs. When Odysseus attempts to rescue them, Hermes approaches him in the form of a young man. He tells Odysseus to eat an herb called moly, which will protect him from Circe's drug, and then lunge at her when she tries to strike him with her sword. Odysseus follows Hermes' instructions, overpowers Circe, and forces her to change his men back to their human forms. Odysseus soon becomes Circe's lover, and he and his men live with her in luxury for a year. When his men finally persuade him to continue the voyage homeward, Odysseus asks Circe for the way back to Ithaca. She replies that he must sail to Hades, the realm of the dead, to speak with the spirit of Tiresias, a blind prophet who will tell him how to get home.

When Odysseus opens the portal to Hades, the first spirit to appear is that of Elpenor, a man from Odysseus's crew who broke his neck falling from Circe's roof. Elpenor begs Odysseus to return to Circe's island and give his body a proper burial. Odysseus then speaks with the Theban prophet Tiresias, who reveals that Poseidon has been punishing the Achaeans for blinding his son Polyphemus. Tiresias foretells Odysseus's fate—that he will return home, reclaim his wife and palace from the wretched suitors, and then make another trip to a distant land to appease Poseidon. Tiresias warns Odysseus not to touch the flocks of the Sun when he reaches the land of Thrinacia; otherwise, he will suffer more hardship and lose all of his crew before he reaches home.

After some pleading by the king and queen, Odysseus agrees to continue his tale. He then relates his encounters in Hades. In Hades, Odysseus meets Agamemnon, who speaks of his murder at the hands of his wife, Clytemnestra. Next, Odysseus meets Achilles, who asks about his son, Neoptolemus. Odysseus then tries to speak with Ajax—an Achaean who killed himself after he lost a contest with Odysseus over the arms of Achilles—but Ajax refuses to speak and slips away. Odysseus sees Heracles, King Minos, the hunter Orion, and others. But Odysseus soon finds himself mobbed by souls wishing to ask about their relatives in the world above. He becomes frightened, runs back to his ship, and immediately sails away.

Odysseus then returns to Aeaea, where he buries Elpenor and spends one last night with Circe. She describes the obstacles that he will face on his voyage home and tells him how to negotiate them. As Odysseus sets sail, he passes Circe's advice on to his men. When they approach the island of the lovely Sirens, Odysseus, as instructed by Circe, plugs his men's ears with beeswax and has them bind him to the mast of the ship. He alone hears their song flowing forth from the island, promising to reveal the future. The Sirens' song is so seductive that Odysseus begs to be released from his fetters, but his faithful men only bind him tighter.

Once they have passed the Sirens' island, Odysseus and his men must navigate the straits between Scylla and Charybdis. Scylla is a six-headed monster that eats one sailor for each head whenever ships pass. Charybdis is an enormous whirlpool that swallows ships whole. As instructed by Circe, Odysseus holds his course tight against the cliffs of Scylla's lair. As he and his men stare at Charybdis on the other side of the strait, the heads of Scylla swoop down and gobble up six of the sailors.

Odysseus then arrives on Thrinacia, the island of the Sun. He wants to avoid it entirely, but the outspoken Eurylochus persuades him to let the beleaguered crew rest there. A storm keeps them beached for a month, and at first, the crew is content to survive on its provisions in the ship. When these provisions run out, however, Eurylochus persuades the other crew members to disobey Odysseus and slaughter the cattle of the Sun one afternoon while Odysseus sleeps. When the Sun finds out about the death of his cattle, he asks Zeus to punish Odysseus and his men. Shortly after the Achaeans set sail from Thrinacia, Zeus kicks up another storm, which destroys the ship and sends the entire crew to its death beneath the waves. As Tiresias predicted, only Odysseus survives. Afloat on the broken timbers of his ship, he eventually reaches Ogygia, Calypso's island. Odysseus here breaks from his story, telling the Phaeacians that he sees no reason to repeat to them his account of his experience on Ogygia.

Analysis: Odysseus's Story

With the appearance of the various heroes and lesser divinities, Book 11 of the *Odyssey* gives the modern reader an extraordinary anthology of mythological lives. Homer's audience would already have been familiar with the stories of such figures as Heracles, Minos, Achilles, Agamemnon, Sisyphus, and Tantalus, and people turned to Homer's retellings for authoritative versions of the Greek myths even in the later ancient period. For the modern reader, Homer's stories provide invaluable insight into early Greek mythology. Again, by juxtaposing Odysseus's wanderings against the woes of these legendary figures, Homer both broadens the scope of his poem and further entrenches his hero in his culture's mythology. In even being allowed to enter Hades, Odysseus attains a privileged, transcendent status.

Odysseus's conversation with Achilles reveals a more complex view of warfare and kleos, or glory, than is found in the *Iliad*. Achilles' declaration that he would rather "slave on earth for another man . . . than rule down here over all the breathless dead," alludes to his dilemma, depicted in the *Iliad*, of choosing between earning glory on the battlefield but dying young and living out a long, uneventful life. Whereas the *Iliad*, which celebrates the glory of warfare, wholeheartedly endorses Achilles' choice of glory over long life, Achilles' lament in Book 11 of the *Odyssey* issues a strong caveat to this ethic of kleos. This change in Achilles' sentiment from one poem to the next is understandable, given that, as we have seen with Odysseus, the *Odyssey* tends to focus on characters' inner lives.

We must, however, take Odysseus's story cautiously and consider the consequences of it—for Odysseus's glory also is at stake. There several great Achaean warriors in the *Iliad*: Agamemnon, Achilles, Ajax, and Odysseus. Agamemnon, as we know, dies a shameful death at the hands of his wife. Ajax commits suicide—also ignoble—and shames himself further (according to Odysseus) by refusing to accept an apology when Odysseus journeys to Hades. Achilles dies a noble death by accepting his fate as a warrior, thus securing his legendary glory. But now, Odysseus tells us the story of his meeting with Achilles in Hades, where Achilles repents his life and death as a warrior. Suddenly, Odysseus is the only Greek captain who retains his glory and nobility. Knowing Odysseus's craftiness, the consequences of his tale ought to make us a little suspicious of his truthfulness.

Summary: Books 13–15

The account of his wanderings now finished, Odysseus looks forward to leaving Scheria. The next day, Alcinous gives Odysseus gifts, which are put on board the ship that will carry Odysseus to Ithaca. Odysseus sets sail as soon as the sun goes down. He sleeps the whole night, while the Phaeacian crew commands the ship. He remains asleep even when the ship lands the next morning. The crew gently carries Odysseus and his gifts to shore and then sails for home.

When Poseidon spots Odysseus in Ithaca, he becomes enraged at the Phaeacians for assisting his nemesis. He complains to Zeus, who allows Poseidon to punish the Phaeacians: the ship suddenly turns to stone and sinks to the bottom of the sea. The Phaeacian onlookers ashore immediately recognize the consummation of the prophecy and resolve to abandon their custom of helping wayward travelers.

Back in Ithaca, Odysseus wakes to find a country that he cannot recognize, for Athena has shrouded it in mist to conceal its true form while she plans his next move. At first, Odysseus curses the Phaeacians, whom he thinks have duped him and left him in some unknown land. But Athena, disguised as a shepherd, meets him and tells him that he is indeed in Ithaca. With characteristic cunning, Odysseus acts to conceal his identity from her until she reveals hers. Delighted by Odysseus's tricks, Athena announces that it is time for Odysseus to use his wits to punish the suitors. She tells him to hide out in the hut of his swineherd, Eumaeus, and gives him the appearance of an old vagabond so that no one will recognize him.

Odysseus finds Eumaeus outside his hut. Although Eumaeus fails to recognize the withered traveler as his master, he invites him inside. There, Odysseus has a hearty meal of pork and listens as Eumaeus heaps praise upon the memory of his former master—whom he fears is lost for good—and scorn upon the behavior of his new masters, the vile suitors. Odysseus predicts that Eumaeus will see his master again quite soon, but Eumaeus is disbelieving, for he has encountered too many vagabonds looking for a handout from Penelope in return for fabricated news of Odysseus. Still, Eumaeus takes a liking to his guest, puts him up for the night, and lets him borrow a cloak to keep out the cold. When Eumaeus asks Odysseus about his origins, Odysseus lies that he is from Crete. He says that he fought with Odysseus at Troy and made it home safely, but that a trip that he made later to Egypt went awry and reduced him to poverty. It was during this trip, he says, that he heard that Odysseus was still alive.

Then, Odysseus tests the limit of Eumaeus's hospitality by offering to leave in the morning—a false gesture that he hopes will prompt Eumaeus to offer to let him stay longer. He urges the old man not to go out of his way and says that he will earn his keep working for the suitors, but Eumaeus will have none of it. Eumaeus warns that to get mixed up with the suitors would be suicide. Odysseus and the swineherd then swap stories. Eumaeus explains how he first came to Ithaca: the son of a king, he was stolen from his house by Phoenician pirates with the help of a maid whom his father employed. The pirates took Eumaeus all over the seas until Laertes, Odysseus's father, bought him in Ithaca. There, Penelope brought him up alongside her own daughter.

The next morning, Telemachus returns to Ithaca from the kingdom of Menelaus. He disembarks while the crew heads to the city by ship. Telemachus entrusts Theoclymenus, a prophet he encountered on his journey, to a loyal crewman named Piraeus. As Telemachus and Theoclymenus part, they see a hawk fly by carrying a dove in its talons, which Theoclymenus interprets as a favorable sign of the strength of Odysseus's house and line.

Summary: Books 16–18

When Telemachus reaches Eumaeus's hut, he finds the swineherd talking with a stranger (Odysseus in disguise). Eumaeus recounts Odysseus's story and suggests that the stranger stay with Telemachus at the palace. Telemachus, however, worries about what the suitors might do if he and the stranger go to the palace. Eumaeus, therefore, goes to the palace alone to tell Penelope that her son has returned.

When father and son are alone in the hut, Athena appears to Odysseus and calls him outside. When Odysseus reenters the hut, his disguise is gone, and he stands in the pristine glory of his heroic person. At first, Telemachus cannot believe his eyes. The two embrace and weep. Odysseus recounts his voyage with the Phaeacians and then begins to plot the overthrow of the suitors. He formulates a plan to launch a surprise attack from within the palace: Odysseus will enter disguised as a beggar, and Telemachus will hide the palace's surplus arms where the suitors cannot easily reach them. The two of them will then seize the arms and slaughter the suitors.

Telemachus goes to the palace, where he dines with his mother and the suitors. He reveals only the fragments of news he heard about his father from Menelaus. Meanwhile, Eumaeus and Odysseus set out toward town, following Telemachus's path. On the way, they meet Melanthius, a subordinate of the suitors, who heaps scorn on Eumaeus and kicks his beggar companion. Odysseus receives a similarly rude welcome at the palace. The suitors give him food with great reluctance, and Antinous goes out of his way to insult him. When Odysseus answers insult with insult, Antinous gives him a blow with a stool that disgusts even the other suitors. Report of this cruelty reaches Penelope, who asks to have the beggar brought to her so that she can question him about Odysseus. Odysseus, however, does not want the suitors to see him going to the queen's room. Eumaeus announces that he must return to his hut and hogs, leaving Odysseus alone with Telemachus and the suitors.

Another beggar, Arnaeus (nicknamed Irus), saunters into the palace. He is rather brash for a beggar, as he insults Odysseus and challenges him to a boxing match. Irus thinks that he will make quick work of the old man, but Athena gives Odysseus extra strength and stature. Irus soon regrets challenging the old man and tries to escape, but by now the suitors have taken notice and egg on the fight for the sake of their own entertainment. The fight ends quickly as Odysseus floors Irus and stops just short of killing him.

The suitors congratulate Odysseus. One in particular, the moderate Amphinomus, toasts him and gives him food. Odysseus, aware of the impending bloodshed that will be visited upon the suitors, is overcome by pity for Amphinomus and pulls him aside. The disguised Odysseus predicts to Amphinomus that Odysseus will soon be home and gives him a thinly veiled warning to abandon the palace and return to his own land. But Amphinomus does not depart, despite being "fraught with grave forebodings," for Athena has bound him to death at the hands of Telemachus.

Athena now puts it into Penelope's head to make an appearance before her suitors. The goddess gives Penelope extra stature and beauty to inflame their hearts. When Penelope speaks to the suitors, she leads them on by telling them that Odysseus instructed her to remarry if he should fail to return by the time Telemachus began to grow facial hair. Penelope then tricks the suitors, to the silent delight of Odysseus, into bringing her gifts by claiming that any suitor worth his salt would try to win her hand by giving things to her instead of taking what is rightfully hers. The suitors shower Penelope with presents. As they celebrate, Odysseus instructs the maidservants to go to Penelope. The maidservant Melantho, Melanthius's sister, insults him as an inferior being and a drunk; Odysseus then scares them off with threats. Hoping to make Odysseus even more angry at the suitors, Athena now inspires Eurymachus to insult him. When Odysseus responds with insults of his own, Eurymachus throws a stool at him but misses, hitting a servant instead. Just as a riot is about to break out, Telemachus steps in and diffuses the situation, to the consternation of the suitors.

SUMMARY: BOOK 19–21

After Telemachus and Odysseus have safely disposed of the palace arms, Telemachus retires, and Odysseus is joined by Penelope, who has come from the women's quarters to question her curious visitor. She knows that he has claimed to have met Odysseus, and she tests his honesty by asking him to describe her husband. Odysseus describes the Greek hero—himself—and captures each detail so perfectly that his words reduce Penelope to tears. He then tells the story of how he met Odysseus and eventually came to Ithaca.

Penelope offers the beggar a bed to sleep in, but he declines, for he says he is used to the floor. Only reluctantly does he allow Eurycleia to wash him. As Eurycleia does so, she notices a scar on one of Odysseus's legs and immediately recognizes it as the scar that Odysseus received when he went boar hunting with his grandfather, Autolycus. Eurycleia throws her arms around Odysseus, but he silences her while Athena keeps Penelope distracted so that Odysseus's secret does not spread. The faithful Eurycleia recovers herself and promises to keep his secret.

Before Penelope retires, she describes to Odysseus a dream she had in which an eagle swooped down upon her twenty pet geese, killed them all, perched on her roof, and, in a human voice, said that he was her husband who had just put her lovers to death. Penelope declares that she has no idea what this dream means. Rising to the challenge, Odysseus explains it to her. But Penelope decides that she is going to choose a new husband nevertheless: she will marry the first man who can shoot an arrow through the holes of twelve axes set in a line.

As the palace springs to life the next day, Odysseus and Telemachus meet, in succession, the swineherd Eumaeus, the foul Melanthius, and Philoetius, a kindly and loyal herdsman who says that he has not yet given up hope of Odysseus's return. The suitors enter, once again plotting Telemachus's murder. Amphinomus convinces them to call it off, however, when a portent of doom appears in the form of an eagle carrying a dove in its talons. But Athena keeps the suitors antagonistic all through dinner in order to maintain Odysseus's anger. Ctesippus, a wealthy and arrogant suitor, throws a cow's hoof at Odysseus, and Telemachus, in response, threatens to run Ctesippus through with his sword.

Penelope gets Odysseus's bow out of the storeroom and announces that she will marry the suitor who can string it and then shoot an arrow through a line of twelve axes. Telemachus sets up the axes and then tries his own hand at the bow but fails in his attempt to string it. The suitors warm and grease the bow to make it supple, but one by one they all try and fail.

When Odysseus returns, Eurymachus has the bow. Eurymachus feels disgraced that he cannot string it because he knows that this failure proves his inferiority to Odysseus. Antinous suggests that they adjourn until the next day, when they can sacrifice to Apollo, the archer god, before trying again. Odysseus, still disguised, then asks for the bow. All of the suitors complain, fearing that he will succeed. Antinous ridicules Odysseus, saying that the wine has gone to his head and that he will bring disaster upon himself, just like the legendary drunken Centaur Eurytion. Telemachus takes control and orders Eumaeus to give Odysseus the bow. Odysseus strings it easily and sends the first arrow he grabs whistling through all twelve axes.

SUMMARY: BOOKS 22–24

Before the suitors realize what is happening, Odysseus shoots a second arrow, this one through the throat of Antinous. The confused suitors believe the shooting to be an accident. Odysseus finally reveals himself, and the suitors are terrified. They have no way out, as Philoetius has locked the front door and Eumaeus has locked the doors to the women's quarters. Eurymachus tries to calm Odysseus and insists that Antinous was the only bad apple among them, but Odysseus announces that he will spare none of them. Eurymachus then charges Odysseus, but he is cut down by another arrow. Amphinomus is the next to fall, to Telemachus's spear.

A full battle rages in the palace hall. Athena appears, disguised as Mentor, and encourages Odysseus but does not participate immediately, for she prefers instead to test Odysseus's strength. In a vicious battle with spears, Odysseus and his men kill several suitors but receive only superficial wounds themselves. Finally, Athena joins the battle, which then ends swiftly. Odysseus spares only the minstrel Phemius and the herald Medon, who have been unwilling participants in the suitors' profligacy. The priest Leodes begs unsuccessfully for mercy.

Odysseus brings out Eurycleia, who openly rejoices to see the suitors dead. Odysseus, however, checks her impropriety. Eurycleia rounds up the disloyal servant women and makes them clear the corpses from the hall and wash the blood from the furniture. Shortly thereafter, Odysseus tells Telemachus to execute the disloyal servant women with a sword, but Telemachus decides to hang them because hanging is a more disgraceful death. Last of all, Odysseus and his men torture and kill the traitor Melanthius. After the bloodbath, Odysseus cleans the house with sulfur.

Eurycleia goes upstairs to call Penelope, who has slept through the entire fight. Penelope does not believe Eurycleia's news and remains in disbelief even when she comes downstairs and sees her husband with her own eyes. Telemachus rebukes his mother for not greeting Odysseus more lovingly after his long absence, but Odysseus has other problems to worry about. He has just killed all of the noble young men of Ithaca, and their parents surely will be enraged. Odysseus decides that he and his family must lay low on their farm for a while. In the meantime, a minstrel strikes up a happy song so that no passersby will suspect what has taken place in the palace.

Penelope remains wary, afraid that a god is playing a trick on her. She orders Eurycleia to move her bridal bed, but Odysseus argues that the bed is immovable, for it was built from the trunk of an olive tree around which the house was constructed. Hearing him recount these details, Penelope knows that this man must be her husband. The couple gets reacquainted, and Odysseus gives his wife a brief account of his wanderings. He also tells her about the voyage that he must make to fulfill the prophecy of Tiresias in Book 11. The next day, Odysseus leaves with Telemachus for Laertes' orchard. On the way out, he gives Penelope instructions not to leave her room or receive any visitors. Athena cloaks Odysseus and Telemachus in darkness so that no one will see them as they walk through the town.

The scene changes abruptly. Hermes leads the souls of the suitors, crying like bats, into Hades. Agamemnon and Achilles argue over who had the better death. Agamemnon describes Achilles' funeral in detail. They see the suitors coming in and ask how so many noble young men met their end. The suitor Amphimedon, whom Agamemnon knew in life, gives a brief account of their ruin, pinning most of the blame on Penelope and her indecision.

Agamemnon contrasts the constancy of Penelope with the treachery of Clytemnestra.

Back in Ithaca, Odysseus travels to Laertes' farm. He sends Laertes' servants into the house so that he can be alone with his father in the gardens. Odysseus finds that Laertes has aged prematurely out of grief for his son and wife. He fails to recognize Odysseus, and Odysseus does not reveal himself immediately but instead pretends that he is someone who once knew and befriended Odysseus. When Laertes begins to cry at his son's memory, Odysseus throws his arms around Laertes and kisses him.

Laertes and Odysseus have lunch together. Dolius, the father of Melanthius and Melantho, joins them. While they eat, the goddess Rumor flies through the city spreading the news of the massacre at the palace. The suitors' parents hold an assembly and discuss how to respond. Halitherses, the elder prophet, argues that the suitors got what they deserved for their wickedness, but Eupithes, Antinous's father, encourages the parents to seek revenge on Odysseus. The small army of suitors' parents tracks Odysseus to Laertes' house, but Athena, disguised again as Mentor, decides to put a stop to the violence. Antinous's father is the only one killed, felled by one of Laertes' spears. Athena makes the Ithacans forget the massacre of their children and recognize Odysseus as king. Peace is restored.

ANALYSIS: ODYSSEUS AND PENELOPE REUNITED

The dramatic scene in which Odysseus effortlessly strings the bow is justly famous. The bow gives double meaning to the revelation scene, for the beggar's success not only implies his true identity as Odysseus but also reveals his inherent superiority to the suitors. Since the bow gives Odysseus a weapon in hand, it also allows for a seamless transition to the fighting of Book 22. Moreover, the bow's associations recall Odysseus's preeminence in Ithaca before the Trojan War. Homer tells us that Odysseus received the bow during a diplomatic trip to Messene, long before any of his hardships began, and that it has been seldom used since then. The bow thus recalls the good old days when there were no suitors and Odysseus's rule was unchallenged. Through his mastery of the bow, Odysseus comes full circle, once again the king and most powerful man in Ithaca.

The scene in which Penelope tests her husband's knowledge of the bed neatly brings together several ideas that the epic has touched on before. This subtle test reveals Penelope's clever side—the side we have seen in her ploy to use a never-to-be-finished burial shroud to put off remarriage for years. This test not only admits Odysseus to Penelope's arms but also sheds some light on why their love for each other is so natural in the first place. They are united by the commonality of their minds, by their love of scheming, testing, and out-maneuvering. They are kindred spirits because they are kindred wits. None of the suitors could ever replace Odysseus, just as Circe or Calypso could never replace Penelope. Literally and metaphorically, no one can move their wedding bed.

HESIOD

CONTEXT AND BACKGROUND

The poet Hesiod (born c. 700 B.C.), who made his home in Boeotia, a region in Greece north of the Gulf of Corinth, certainly was familiar with the *Iliad* and the *Odyssey* and may have been alive at the time of their written composition. Unfortunately, few details of Hesiod's life have survived. After Hesiod's father fled a destitute life in the sea trades, the family moved to Ascra, where Hesiod's father bought a farm. When their father died, Hesiod and his brother, Perses, were left in control of the farm. After a falling out between the brothers, Perses sued Hesiod for the greater share of the farm and won his case by bribing the nobles who acted as judges. In the end, however, this injustice may have inspired Hesiod's immortal text *Works and Days*, his instructional epic about living virtuously in ancient Greece. Hesiod dedicated *Works and Days* to his conniving brother in hopes of instilling in him some ethics.

Hesiod believed that he was living in the poorest of all ages—the Iron Age, when all humanity shared one, miserable lot. He attempted to use his poetry to transcend the hopelessness of everyday life and return, at least in spirit, to more glorious times. According to his own account, his career as a poet began when the Muses visited him on the hillside of Mt. Helicon, where they taught him the divinely inspired poem that became *Works and Days*.

Unlike Homer, whose works immortalize the exploits of a higher, godlike version of mankind, Hesiod's poems focus on the sober day-to-day life of the common man. His writings teach the importance of hard work, respect for virtue, and an acceptance of one's lot in life. Hesiod makes no promises of a glorious afterlife or immortal fame: unlike the characters of Homer's epics, Hesiod does not express any wish for a bard to remember his valiant deeds to future audiences. Avoiding the enraptured, dramatic strains used by Homer, Hesiod's poems are frank, pessimistic, and sometimes didactic. In their tone and subjects, his poems reflect the hard, toiling life he himself led.

WORKS AND DAYS

Hesiod begins his poem by meditating on the power of fate, which he asserts no man can ever understand. Nor can anyone know his own fate, for Zeus hides it from men proud enough to try to understand it. The discussion of fate leads Hesiod to explain two kinds of strife: one caused by natural competition, which is positive; and another caused by envy and pettiness, which is negative. Hesiod's own brother demonstrated the latter by suing him for the family farm. Hesiod says, however, that this conflict is not truly his brother's fault, and instead he blames the gods for causing strife among mankind.

Hesiod also blames the gods for withholding fire from humankind and forcing Prometheus, one of the Titans, to steal it for the human race. Zeus, angered by Prometheus's betrayal, commands Hephaestus to create the beautiful and teasing Pandora to seduce Prometheus's brother, Epimetheus. Epimetheus, forgetting Prometheus's warnings, accepts Pandora as a gift from Zeus. Pandora bears a box of gifts from the gods. When she removes the cover, the gifts all spill out—except Hope, who remains inside the box. Having thus lost the gods' blessings, mankind becomes eternally subject to the rule of Zeus.

As Hesiod continues his lamentable tale, he describes how humans have fallen from their once-blissful state. Before the reign of Zeus, human beings lived much as the gods did: never knowing wickedness or ailment, they died peaceful deaths at the end of their long lives. These men and women were called the golden race of humans.

Then, the Titans were overthrown, and the first race of humans was destroyed. To replace them, Zeus created a second race of men from silver. But this breed of humans was soon corrupted and incurred the wrath of heaven when they refused to honor the gods. Accordingly, Zeus destroyed this race as well.

The ruler of the gods then created a third version of humanity, this time from bronze. The lack of emotion in the hearts of this race reflected the material from which they were made. Rather than being destroyed by Zeus, they destroyed themselves and entered the underworld. When Zeus once again attempted to create humanity—his fourth try—he created men like gods. These men are the heroes of Homer's epics. Working for their survival, they were ruled by Cronos, Zeus's father.

These great men eventually gave way to the pathetic fifth generation of humanity, of which Hesiod unfortunately is a member. These men, constructed from iron, never know rest, sweat as they work the unfertile soil, and suffer constantly. Hesiod foretells that this race will eventually die off, its final days plagued by lying, deceit, and violence.

As Hesiod concludes his history of mankind, he addresses his brother, Perses, and begs him to give up his vile and corrupt lifestyle. He cautions him of the curses that plague the families of the sinful.

Here, the second part of *Works and Days* begins. Now that Hesiod has enumerated the pitiful lot of humanity, he offers a number of suggestions for improving life and making a better world. Above all, he recommends that one be virtuous and friendly and avoid enemies, the corrupt, and loose women. For longevity, Hesiod recommends avoiding the sea, especially during the stormy months.

For the bachelors in his audience, Hesiod recommends finding a good wife. Nothing, he says, is as good as a good wife, while nothing is as bad as a bad one. Hesiod finishes his poem by crying out against frequent stumbling blocks, like untrustworthy friends and slanderers.

THEOGONY

At the beginning of the text, Hesiod recounts his fateful meeting with the Muses on Mt. Helicon, during which he transforms from a shepherd into an inspired poet. The Muses instruct him to reveal to his fellow man the true nature of the Olympian gods. As Hesiod begins his mission, he pays homage to the Muses by recounting Zeus's tryst with Mnemosyne, mother memory. Mnemosyne gave birth to the nine Muses: Clio, the muse of history; Euterpe, the muse of music; Terpsichore, the muse of dance; Thalia, the muse of comedy; Erato, the muse of lyrical arts; Urania, the muse of astronomy; Melpomene, the muse of tragedy; Polyhymnia, the muse of sacred poetry; and Calliope, the muse of philosophy and epic poetry.

Hesiod then lists the gods in order of their births. In doing so, he recounts the formation of the world: from Chaos comes Erebus, Day, and Night. Then, the marriage of Gaia (Earth) and Uranus (Heaven) produces Oceanus, Hyperion, Iapetus, Phoebe, Rhea, the Hills, and Cronos. Cronos attacks his father, Uranus, at the behest of Gaia, castrating Uranus and hurling his testicles into the sea. Much later, the goddess Aphrodite rises from the foam made by the splash.

Cronos then has children by Rhea: Demeter, Hestia, Hades, Zeus, Hera, and Poseidon. Fearful that his children will betray him, Cronos swallows each of them as he or she is born. But Rhea, in a plot to save her youngest, Zeus, gives Cronos a stone swaddled in baby garments instead. Cronos is fooled and swallows the stone. Meanwhile, Rhea leaves Zeus in the care of Gaia, who rears him. Zeus saves his siblings, for which the Cyclopes reward him with the power of thunder and lightning.

Hesiod then relates the story of two Titans, Atlas and Prometheus, the sons of Iapetus. Zeus and the Titans battle for control over the heavens, and Zeus and his siblings once again emerge victorious. Zeus then grants powers to each of his siblings. After lying with Metis, Zeus remembers a prophecy that the son of Metis would challenge the Olympian gods. To save himself, Zeus swallows Metis. He then gives birth to the goddess Athena, who springs from his forehead fully grown and clad in armor.

LYRIC POETRY

SAPPHO

Scholars know few actual facts about Sappho and her life; most of what they do know comes from small pieces of information in what remains of Sappho's works and from the writings of other ancient writers. We do know that Sappho, who called herself Psappha in her own Aeolic dialect, was born on the island of Lesbos in the northeastern Aegean Sea around 612 B.C. Whether she was born in the city of Mytilene or Eresus is uncertain, but she lived most of her life in Mytilene. Sappho was born into a family of wealthy merchants and enjoyed a life of luxury, decorative ornaments, and beautiful clothing.

According to the historian Herodotus, Sappho's father died when she was six, so her mother raised her. She had three brothers, one of whom was a public cup-bearer in Mytilene—a position of great prestige in ancient Greece, which points to the family's wealth and prominence on Lesbos. According to a writer named Suidas, who compiled a Greek lexicon in the eleventh century, Sappho married a man named Cercylas, a wealthy merchant who sailed to Lesbos from Andros. Together, they had a daughter, Cleïs, whose name is mentioned in Sappho's poems.

There is no concrete record of Sappho's physical appearance, but scholars concur that she was short and of dark complexion. Nor is there any firm account of her occupation—for the lyric poets of the time, poetry was a vocation or hobby, not a career. The content of Sappho's poetry points to several occupational possibilities, none of which can be verified. Some fragments imply that Sappho was one of several priestesses to the goddess Aphrodite, while others suggest that she was a champion runner. She may have been a weaver and may even have invented a special garment called the *chlamys*. Other scholars conjecture that Sappho was a prostitute or courtesan. Whatever her occupation, she is famous for her poetry, which explores the deeper human emotions of love and desire rather than celebrating the glories of government, politics, and war.

It remains uncertain how long Sappho lived or where and how she died. One account reports that she threw herself from a promontory into the Ionian Sea because a boatman named Phaon would not return her love. This story, however, is unsubstantiated, and famous mostly because of the romantic fodder it provided later poets writing about Sappho. It is nearly certain, however, that Sappho was exiled to Sicily for a short time during her childhood due to political upheaval in Lesbos.

Three hundred years after Sappho's death, scholars in Alexandria, Egypt, collected her poetry in nine books. Sadly, however, little of her work now remains: in 380 A.D., St. Gregory of Nazianzus ordered the burning of all of Sappho's books due to their erotic content; then, in 1073 A.D., whatever escaped the first burning was destroyed when Pope Gregory VII issued a similar edict. Only fragments of Sappho's work remain, some of which were found in the early twentieth century wrapped around Egyptian mummies.

Sappho wrote extensively on love and desire in a variety of contexts. She examined the sheer magnitude of the emotions wrought by love, described the debilitating physical effect that those emotions can occasion, and theorized about the attainability of love at all. In Sappho's *Hymn to Aphrodite*, one of the more substantial of her remaining fragments, the poet invokes Aphrodite, the goddess of love, to come to her aid in seducing the object of her desire—an invocation that, the poet implies, she has summoned at other times in the past. Most hymns or prayers up to this time were addressed to gods of war or childbirth, so to pray to a deity for assistance in the achievement of sexual desire was unusual and bold, a true sign of the poet's fascination with the erotic.

Sappho frequently grapples with the debilitating force of passionate emotions. In certain fragments, she addresses the power of love: in fragments 8 and 9, for instance, she describes the power of love as shaking and overwhelming her soul. In other passages, her outlook is one of joyous, idealized romance:

Thou happy bridegroom! Now has dawned
That day of days supreme,
When in thine arms thou'lt hold at last
The maiden of thy dream.

Fragment 31, on the other hand, displays the difficult side of love, as it gives a detailed account of the physical and emotional breakdown the speaker experiences upon seeing her beloved in conversation with another. The poet's vision and hearing simply shut down, and she sweats, trembles, and is unable to speak. All she can do is utter the poem itself, and she uses short clauses and lists to describe her pain. The poem is simple and devoid of literary artifice—which in itself helps to convey the devastation the poet feels.

In some of her work, Sappho voices doubt about the attainability of love at all. The poem *Anactoria*, for example, invokes the story of Helen of Troy, who precipitated the Trojan War when she was abducted by Paris, her beloved. In this allusion, Sappho implies that an object of desire can be achieved, but only at a devastating price. Likewise, in fragment 17, the poet holds that the "best things" are always those that are hardest to attain. She uses the example of an unpicked apple at the farthest end of a bough, unpicked not because it has gone unnoticed but because of the spot in which it hangs, out of reach.

Another theme running through Sappho's poetry—albeit more subtly than her exploration of love—is a concern with the conflict between humans and nature. Nature appears in a number of the poet's fragments, in varying relationships with the poet herself and with humankind more broadly. Sappho's descriptions of natural scenes in fragments 1 and 2 are especially haunting and rendered with startling clarity. In each of these fragments, nature appears in personified terms: the stars "hide their faces," and the breeze, as if with a voice, "murmurs." Fragments such as these demonstrate the true lyricism of Sappho's poetry, as she endows the natural world with spirit and soul unique to classical poetry.

LYRIC POETRY

PINDAR

Pindar (518–438 B.C.) was born near Thebes, where he grew up in a renowned aristocratic family. Studying first under the poet Corinna, whom he quickly surpassed in skill, and later under Appolodorus, Pindar quickly established a reputation that allowed him to make a living writing poetry. His numerous paid jobs included the penning of verses to commemorate victors of the pan-Hellenic games, a sort of early Olympics. While he maintained a reputation for generous philanthropy, Pindar clearly took pride in his gifts as a poet and often showered himself with praise.

Although Pindar was married and had children, he also had a sexual affinity for young men. Indeed, some of his later writings express love for several young men in particular. While Pindar's homosexuality did constitute a large part of his love life, his poetry varies greatly in subject. For example, one of his favorite subjects was the Greek isle of Aegina, to which he dedicated eleven poems. He also wrote numerous poems for the nobility, addressing them as peers and intermingling advice with praise in the same verse.

Pindar's poems encompass many different forms and styles, including eulogies, hymns, dithyrambs, dirges, and paeans (hymns of praise or thanks, especially to Apollo). Unfortunately, most of Pindar's work is lost, aside from his forty-four victory odes. These odes, which he wrote for the pan-Hellenic games, were the building blocks for his prestigious reputation. The subject's friends performed Pindar's odes, probably during a procession or banquet in honor of the victorious athlete.

Although Pindar's victory odes vary in form like all of his poetry, they do feature certain recurring elements and patterns. For example, Pindar always is careful to mention the victor's lineage, from which the Greeks believed an athlete's skill was acquired. He also records the type of athletic event and the location of the victory, while scouring myth and history to find events that parallel the contest being commemorated. Pindar also injects praises and thanks to the gods in order to balance the pride of the victor with reminders of humility. Using variations on these standard formats, Pindar established an archetypal ode that many poets—Milton, Shelley, Wordsworth, and others—have imitated in the thousands of years since.

ALCAEUS

Alcaeus was born on the island of Lesbos in 620 B.C. Although Alcaeus knew Sappho and admired her work, his poems stand in stark contrast to hers. While Sappho's works are filled with sentiments of love and sadness, Alcaeus's works frequently assume a strong, masculine diction in describing the exploits of soldiers. His poems address a variety of subjects, from the gods to politics, from war to the beauty of both women and young men.

Alcaeus came from an aristocratic background and was fond of the diversions that his high rank provided—especially women, wine, and political rivalry. However, he fell into disfavor when he engaged in a politicized land dispute and subsequently was exiled to Egypt, where he wrote numerous poems expressing his distaste for his new land and his longing for home.

Unfortunately, much of Alcaeus's work has been lost, including an entire ten-volume collection that Aristophanes of Byzantium painstakingly edited. Only shreds of Alcaeus's two- and four-line stanzas exist today. Indeed, much of his renown stems from one fragment: several lines that portray the political state as a ship being tossed about in a stormy sea. Countless writers in ancient and modern literature—notably Sophocles in *Oedipus Rex*—have used this image of the "ship of state," a powerful metaphor that only hints at what could lie in the countless poems of Alcaeus's that have been lost.

ARCHILOCHUS

According to myth, Archilochus (c. 700–640 B.C.) met the nine Muses in person and received his poetic gifts from them in the form of a lyre. As the legend continues, Archilochus's father, Telesicles, consulted a prophetess about his son's encounter and learned that one of his sons—the first who saluted him upon his return—would go on to become an immortal poet. When Telesicles returned, Archilochus ran from the house to meet him, thereby fulfilling the prophecy.

The son of Telesicles and a slave girl, Archilochus was ineligible for an inheritance due to his low birth. Eventually, he and his family emigrated to the island of Thasos, where a better life awaited him. He fell in love with a young woman, Neoboule, but lost her hand when her father learned of Archilochus's low birth and broke off the engagement. In anger, Archilochus joined a band of mercenaries and dedicated his poetic gifts to depictions of combat and war. Ultimately, Archilochus himself lost his life in a battle between the armies of Thasos and Naxos.

Many scholars credit Archilochus with the invention of iambic meter, which countless poets—notably Shakespeare—went on to use. Archilochus's poems often were satirical and crude and, in general, less refined than the poems of Sappho, Pindar, and other later writers. Indeed, legend has it that Archilochus's invectives were so biting and destructive that two of his subjects hanged themselves out of shame.

LYRIC POETRY

THEOGNIS

Theognis of Megara (mid-500s B.C.) dedicated the bulk of his poetry to the aristocracy, for he did not trust the masses to handle the responsibilities of democracy. Theognis's poems emphasize his belief in a higher breed of man, while cynically attacking the rise of the lower, merchant classes. Theognis sets forth a rather joyless and unromantic view of marriage, stating that we should select our mates just as we select our horses and mules—with an eye toward noble blood.

ANACREON

In sharp contrast to Theognis, Anacreon (mid-500s B.C.) focused the bulk of his works on love. Scholars often describe him as a pleasure seeker, enjoying as he did the company of women, the life of the court, and the revelry of festivals. Anacreon did, however, recognize the danger of his own high-living ways, warning in one of his verses of the effects of wine on the tongue. The reputation of Anacreon's works as light-hearted and enjoyable persisted for thousands of years after his death, and his poetry influenced countless other writers after his death, especially during the Italian Renaissance.

LYRIC POETRY

SIMONIDES

Simonides (c. 556–468 B.C.) journeyed from his home in Ioulis to the court of Hipparchus, the ruler of Athens who became Simonides' patron. When Hipparchus was killed by a jealous rival, Simonides emigrated to Thessaly to find new patrons. Eventually, in old age, he settled in the court of Hieron in Sicily, where he worked alongside the poet Pindar.

Critics recognize Simonides for his mastery of a wide range of poetic forms. He wrote most of his poems on a commission basis, which enabled him to write as a career. Scholars credit Simonides with inventing the *eipinicion*, or victory ode—a form that Pindar later made famous.

DRAMA

INTRODUCTION TO
GREEK DRAMA

TRAGEDY AND COMEDY

According to modern scholars' best conjectures, Greek drama was born in 535 B.C., at one of the many annual festivals honoring Dionysus, the god of wine, revelry, and fertility. His name means "twice-born," alluding to his perilous birth, during which his father Zeus extracted the infant Dionysus from the belly of his dying mother and implanted him into his own thigh, out of which the boy later sprang. Because of this extravagant myth, the Greeks associated Dionysus with seasons and with the notion of rebirth. Seasonal festivals honoring him, therefore, took the form of fertility rites that were gradually formalized and ritualized. The festivals often featured rampant sexual revelry and drunkenness, as men gorged on wine while donning the skins of goats (animals renowned for strong sexuality) and long, fake phalluses.

Gradually, the performance of choral songs and hymns of praise, known as dithyrambs, came to dominate the Dionysian festivals. Although these songs frequently were playful, bragging, and robust in the sexual spirit of the god of revelry, the singers were not necessarily drunk with joy. Their songs also memorialized the pain of winter, the end of the harvest, and the death accompanied by the cold winter months. Initially, the songs were composed on the spur of the moment, but over time, a leader emerged from the chorus. This man's chants would be echoed by the other members of the chorus, so that the songs became call-and-response conversations. In this song and dance, the chorus—which would grow to be a staple of Greek drama—was created. Before long, the role of an actor was added to the arrangement. Finally, in 535 B.C., the Greek ruler Pisistratus called for a competition among the performers at the Dionysian festival. Theater was born, and Dionysus was its patron god.

Around 500 B.C., these tragedies began to gain complexity: plot attained importance over lyrics and dance, multiple actors were added, and stories became more complicated. By the time Sophocles entered the world of Greek drama, the debauched revelry that spawned the first chorus had all but disappeared. While the rowdiness of original Dionysian festivals was reserved mostly for comedies, major playwrights did write short, often vulgar comedies to provide occasional comic relief.

Over time, dramatic festivals swelled in status and importance to rival athletic contests, and playwrights enjoyed the social rank of the greatest athletes. Festivals in which the major playwrights competed drew large crowds. In such festivals, three hand-picked playwrights would present their best tetralogy—three tragedies and a comedy. The audiences easily suspended their disbelief as they watched stories from mythology and history portrayed time and again.

In addition to tragedy, the early Dionysian festivals proved fertile soil for the budding art of comedy. Comedy originated in processionals through towns during the Dionysian festivals. During these marches, the townsfolk and paraders exchanged good-natured insults, witticisms, jokes, and gossip similar to that which would later become the center of Greek comedy.

When the comedic art gained prominence, comic plays were performed at the end of festivals, after the tragedies had relinquished center stage. But over time, festivals developed in which comedies were the centerpieces. Unlike tragedies, which borrowed their material from widely known mythology, comedies were highly localized and put state and local officials on the receiving end of jokes.

Mythological Sources

The vast majority of tragic plots in ancient Greek drama were borrowed from Greek mythology, so Greek theatergoers undoubtedly would be familiar with the stories represented in most plays. The story Sophocles tells in *Oedipus Rex*, for example, was very familiar to Greeks and had been produced onstage numerous times by other playwrights before Sophocles wrote his masterpiece. Audiences enjoyed these familiar plots because they dramatized their society's major philosophical concerns—religious struggles, the undefined roles of the Greek gods, the desperate plight of mankind. In addition, because the dramatic festivals were religious in nature, tales from Greek mythology were perfectly suited to celebrations of the gods.

These reused plots maintained freshness because the playwrights were free to interpret myths as they saw fit. Thus, the story of Orestes told by Aeschylus greatly differs from the same story told by Euripides. Naturally, suspense was out of the question, for everyone in the audience knew how the story would turn out. In the place of suspense, then, the playwrights held the audience's attention with powerful dialogue, irony, and allusions to other tales and events. They used their choruses to provide fresh insights into the philosophical nature of the plays. The playwrights did not make any fundamental changes to the central characters of these well-known stories: Aeschylus presents the same Orestes as Euripides. Rather, the playwrights manipulated the story's presentation—changing, for example, how Oedipus discovers his true parents, or how Orestes decides to kill Clytemnestra. For, as Aristotle states in his *Poetics*, the unfolding of the plot is the most important element of a good tragedy.

Greek playwrights employed a set structure when retelling these mythological tragedies. A classic tragedy begins with a prologue, typically performed by one actor, that provides background about the story. Next, the chorus enters, typically chanting a song related to the plot or theme of the play. The tragedy progresses with a series of episodes, or scenes, that advance the plot through action and dialogue. At the conclusion of each episode, the chorus performs an ode that comments on the action that has taken place. In the final action of the play, the tragedy is fully revealed (e.g., the newly blind Oedipus appears onstage). At the very end, the actors exit the stage in procession.

THE CHORUS

The chorus is a staple of ancient Greek drama, especially in earlier works. A group of characters, usually cast as a group of elders or young women, the chorus comments or interprets the events of the story and expresses an opinion to the audience. Often, the chorus serves as an ideal spectator, articulating or clarifying the typical audience member's reaction to the play's events. The chorus never interferes with the action of the play, however. Occasionally, as in Euripides' *The Trojan Women*, the chorus appears as a central character in the play rather than merely a spectator or commentator. Whatever the role of the chorus in a particular play, the tragedians invariably used it to create the play's philosophic and emotional voice. Through its dances—the *strophe* and *antistrophe*—the chorus chants odes or laments based on the actions of the play. In these songs, the chorus moves above the world of the play, crying out to the gods or commenting on the plight of man.

As Greek tragedies grew more complex, the chorus lost its centrality. Initially, the chorus's job was large, as plays with only two or three characters and a simple plot required the chanting of the chorus to entertain the audience. When a new character arrived on stage or a major event occurred, the chorus asked questions, elucidated the situation, and stated its opinion—much like a narrator in a modern work of fiction. As Greek tragedies became more complex and the number of characters dramatically increased, the tragedies relied less on the chorus and more on character-to-character dialogue to shed light on the play's scenarios. Eventually, the chorus disappeared from tragedy.

ACTORS

As Greek dramatic festivals grew in popularity to rival major athletic contests, acting became a highly competitive field, and only the most talented men became successful performers. Women and children in ancient Greece were not allowed to pursue careers as actors. Acting required physical strength (in order to wield the costumes, which often were heavy) and singing talent, as many lines were chanted or sung.

Because the Greeks lacked the makeup available to us today, actors sometimes rubbed the sediments from a cask of wine on their faces to conceal their identities. Their large, heavy masks were designed to reveal characters' moods or traits. Inside these masks, the actors hid small megaphones, which allowed them to project their words. In addition to these masks, actors wore costumes designed to signify a character's role to the audience. Different costume colors and accessories linked the actors to different roles or professions. The tragic hero in each play, for instance, wore gloves and special platform shoes that elevated him above the other characters—so that his fall from grace symbolically would be that much greater.

The costumes of comic figures differed greatly from those of tragic heroes. Actors in comedies wore stylized garments, stockings, and large leather phalluses. Like tragic actors, they also wore masks, but comic masks were highly exaggerated. Because many Greek comedies involve talking animals—Aristophanes' *The Birds* and *The Wasps*, for instance—the actors in these plays frequently donned furs, wings, tails, and other animal features.

VENUES AND SETS

The first major theater venue in ancient Greece, the Theater of Dionysus, was built into a hillside near Athens. Begun by Pericles in 435 B.C., it was not completed until 360 B.C. When it was finished, it had seating for twenty thousand and nearly perfect acoustics. Despite its immense size, actors where able to whisper their lines and still be heard by everyone in the theater. Typical Greek theaters were U-shaped, with bleachers rising up on three sides. The seats closest to the stage were reserved for state officials and high-ranking officers. Directly in front of these seats was the chorus. Behind the chorus was the stage, which included an altar to Dionysus. This monument, which stood in the center of the stage, became a prop for the actors. With the audience's imagination, the altar could become a ship, a statue, or any number of other things.

As plays were performed during the day, artificial lighting was neither needed nor used. In fact, Greek theater relied very little on contrivances and special effects. The same scenery would remain on stage throughout the play. Only occasionally, when it was necessary that gods appear from above, would the stagehands use ropes and pulleys to raise an actor to the level of the roof. From this practice comes *deus ex machina*, the familiar theatrical term for a miraculous ending—"god from a machine," that is, from ropes and pulleys.

AESCHYLUS

CONTEXT AND BACKGROUND

The great tragedian Aeschylus was born in 525 B.C. in Eleusis, a place renowned for its mystical rituals of worship to the goddess Demeter. Biographers often attribute the mysticism of Aeschylus's plays to this early influence. According to legend, the god Dionysus appeared to Aeschylus in a dream and told him to write tragedies, which the then-seventeen-year-old proceeded to do.

Aeschylus spent much of his life in Athens, where he witnessed political and social changes that almost certainly influenced his plays. *Prometheus Bound*, Aeschylus's account of the rebellion of Prometheus against tyranny, likely stemmed from Aeschylus's first-hand witnessing of the collapse of tyranny, the introduction of a constitution, and the slow maturation of the world's first democracy in Athens. Aeschylus's tragedies also reflect cultural shifts in Athens, especially new scientific and philosophical ideas of the time that threatened to supplant traditional faith in the gods.

As all male Athenian citizens were required to perform military service, Aeschylus was a soldier as well as a playwright. Athens, at the time, was part of a federation of small Greek states allied against the enormous forces of the Persian army, led by Xerxes. Aeschylus's military experience included fighting against the Persians at Marathon in 490 B.C. and again at Salamis and Platea in 480 B.C. Aeschylus's play *The Persians* extensively draws on this experience.

As the classical scholar Robert Fagles maintains, the Greeks saw their victory over the Persians as a "triumph of right over might, courage over fear, freedom over servitude, moderation over arrogance." Indeed, the cultural flowering that followed the Greek victory celebrated these values and established them as the principles upon which Athens stood. Athens entered an era of optimism in which Athenians felt that a new religious, political, and personal harmony could arise from the primitive savagery of past wars. It is in this context that Aeschylus, at the age of sixty-seven and after producing at least eighty plays, wrote his masterpiece, the trilogy of plays collectively known as the *Oresteia*.

In many respects, the *Oresteia* exemplifies the new charter myth of Athens. After spearheading the defense of Greece against the Persians, Athens took a strong leadership position among its neighbors and quickly began redefining itself as an empire. In celebration of its new status, Athens set about redefining itself and its history. From a broad perspective, Aeschylus's Oresteia chronicles the transition of the rule of law from the old tradition of personal vengeance, which was bound to a cycle of bloody violence, to the new system of law courts, wherein the state assumed responsibility for meting out just punishments.

After a long and prolific career, Aeschylus died honored and revered as a poet and as a man who had reinvented drama. Indeed, contemporary theater has more in common with the tragedies of Aeschylus than Aeschylus himself had with the drama that came before him. Before Aeschylus, drama involved a single actor on stage speaking in monologues while a chorus offered extensive commentary. Aeschylus introduced a second actor on stage, allowing for action and interaction to take place and establishing a caste of professional actors. He allowed the chorus to converse with the characters, introduced elaborate costumes and stage designs, and wrote a significant body of material for the stage himself. Scholars credit over eighty plays to Aeschylus's name, of which only seven have been preserved in full—primarily by the efforts of ancient grammarians who considered these particular seven tragedies appropriate for teaching in schools.

AGAMEMNON

Agamemnon is the first play in the *Oresteia*, Aeschylus's trilogy about the house of Atreus (the father of Agamemnon). *The Libation Bearers* and *The Eumenides* complete the trilogy.

MAJOR CHARACTERS

Agamemnon The king of Argos, husband of Clytemnestra, and commander of the Greek armies during the siege of Troy. Agamemnon is also the son of Atreus and older brother of Menelaus, whose wife, Helen, was stolen by a Trojan prince, thus igniting the decade-long Trojan War. A great warrior, Agamemnon sacrificed his daughter Iphigenia in order to obtain a favorable wind to carry the Greek fleet to Troy. During the ten-year conflict, his queen, Clytemnestra, has plotted his death in order to avenge the killing of their daughter.

Clytemnestra Agamemnon's wife, who rules Argos in his absence. Clytemnestra plans her husband's murder with ruthless determination and feels no guilt after his death, for she is convinced of her own rectitude and of the justice of killing the man who killed her daughter. Although Clytemnestra is a sympathetic character in many respects, her entanglement with her lover, Aegisthus, taints the righteousness of her crime.

Cassandra A Trojan princess and a war prize for Agamemnon, who carried her to Argos as his slave and mistress. Cassandra is the lover of Apollo, who gave her the gift of prophecy; however, when she refused to bear him a child, he punished her by making all those around her disbelieve her predictions. A voice of reason in tempestuous play, Cassandra sees the ancestral curse afflicting Agamemnon's family and predicts both his death and her own, as well as the vengeance brought by Orestes in the next play.

Aegisthus Agamemnon's cousin and Clytemnestra's lover. Aegisthus's father, Thyestes, and Agamemnon's father, Atreus, were brothers and rivals for the throne. Atreus boiled two of Thyestes' children—Aegisthus's brothers—and served them to the unwitting Thyestes for dinner. Since that time, Aegisthus has been in exile, awaiting a chance to seek revenge for the terrible crime.

SUMMARY

The events of *Agamemnon* take place after King Agamemnon returns from ten years of fighting in the Trojan War. Although trouble arose soon after Agamemnon departed, the tragedies depicted in the play also occur as a result of crimes that members of Agamemnon's family committed while he was away. First, Agamemnon's father, Atreus, boiled the children of his own brother, Thyestes, and served them to him as a meal—prompting Clytemnestra's lover,

Aegisthus (Thyestes' only surviving son), to desire vengeance against Atreus. Moreover, on the way to Troy, Agamemnon chose to sacrifice his own daughter, Iphigenia, in order to gain a favorable wind to push the Greek ships along—prompting Clytemnestra to desire vengeance against her husband. Ultimately, the family cannot escape the weight of this cycle of bloodshed and vengeance in *Agamemnon*, or indeed in the entire *Oresteia*.

As *Agamemnon* opens, a watchman is on duty on the roof of the palace at Argos, waiting for a signal announcing the fall of Troy to the Greek armies. A beacon flashes, and the watchman joyfully runs to relay the news to Queen Clytemnestra. When the watchman leaves, the chorus, made up of the old men of Argos, enters and tells the story of how the Trojan prince Paris stole Helen, the wife of the Greek king Menelaus, leading to ten years of war between Greece and Troy. The chorus recalls how Clytemnestra's husband, Agamemnon (Menelaus's brother), sacrificed their daughter Iphigenia to the goddess Artemis in order to obtain a favorable wind for the Greek fleet.

The queen appears, and the chorus asks her why she has ordered sacrifices of thanksgiving. Clytemnestra replies that a system of beacons has brought word that Troy fell the previous night. The chorus gives thanks to the gods but wonders if her news is true. A herald appears, confirms the tidings, describes the army's sufferings at Troy, and gives thanks for a safe homecoming. Clytemnestra instructs him to go back to Agamemnon to tell her husband to come swiftly. Before the herald departs, however, the chorus asks him for news of Menelaus. The herald answers that a terrible storm seized the Greek fleet on the way home, leaving Menelaus and many others missing.

The chorus sings of the terrible destructive power of Helen's beauty. Agamemnon enters, riding in his chariot with Cassandra, a Trojan princess whom he has taken as his slave and concubine. Clytemnestra welcomes her husband and professes her love. She announces that, out of fear of revolt, she sent Orestes, their young son, to stay with friends in another country. Clytemnestra orders a carpet of purple robes spread in front of Agamemnon as he enters the palace. But Agamemnon, reluctant to anger the gods and longing only for a hot bath, says that to walk on the carpet would be an act of hubris, or dangerous pride. Only after insulting Agamemnon's bravery and praising his enemy, King Priam of Troy, does Clytemnestra convince him to walk on the carpet into the palace.

The chorus expresses a sense of foreboding as Clytemnestra orders Cassandra inside. Cassandra is silent, and Clytemnestra leaves her in frustration. When Cassandra begins to speak, she utters incoherent prophecies about a curse on the house of Agamemnon. She tells the chorus that she and Agamemnon will die at the hands of "a woman-lioness, who goes to bed / with the wolf," and predicts that an avenger will come. After these bold prophecies, Cassandra resigns herself to her fated death and enters the house.

Suddenly, Agamemnon cries out in pain from inside. As the chorus debates what to do, the doors open, and Clytemnestra, axe in hand, stands over the corpses of her husband and Cassandra. Clytemnestra is joined by her lover, Aegisthus, Agamemnon's cousin, whose brothers Agamemnon's father cooked and served to Aegisthus's father. Clytemnestra declares that she has killed Agamemnon to avenge their daughter, Iphigenia. The lovers assume control of the government, and the chorus declares that Clytemnestra's son Orestes will return from exile to avenge his father.

ANALYSIS

The events in *Agamemnon* compose only a small part of a much larger story, as the chorus makes clear in a lengthy speech at the beginning of the play. Two women who do not appear in the play have a profound effect upon the events in Argos: Helen (Menelaus's wife and Clytemnestra's daughter) and Iphigenia (Agamemnon and Clytemnestra's daughter). Paris's abduction of Helen sparks the entire Trojan War and its aftermath. Indeed, throughout *Agamemnon*, the chorus comments on how much suffering has occurred "for one woman's promiscuous sake." Meanwhile, the sacrifice of Iphigenia—despite being a command from the gods—forms a cloud over the marriage of Agamemnon and Clytemnestra and ultimately leads to Agamemnon's murder.

After further discourse on Helen's guilt, the chorus focuses on what becomes a recurring theme in the play: the danger of hubris. Hubris refers to mortal pride or arrogance: a human who is guilty of hubris aspires to be and do more than the gods allow, and therefore must be thwarted and punished. When the chorus says "the vaunt of high glory / is bitterness; for God's thunderbolts . . ." they refer to the idea that too much success leads inevitably to a fall—which, ultimately, is Agamemnon's fate.

Despite his reputation as a great warrior, Agamemnon does not make a heroic impression; rather, the play belongs to Clytemnestra, his fierce, intelligent, and daring wife. Although the king is a mighty soldier, the story of Iphigenia's death biases the audience against him from the start. His arrogant account of his triumph at Troy reinforces this unpalatable side of Agamemnon's character, as does his dismissive attitude toward his wife. Agamemnon flaunts Cassandra, his mistress, before Clytemnestra's eyes, and after the queen's lengthy welcome speech, his reply comes across as brusque and disrespectful.

As the first play ends, however, the sordid aspects of Clytemnestra's crime begin to surface. When her lover, Aegisthus, appears, Clytemnestra begins the transformation from vengeful mother to adulterous murderess—a role that she carries out fully in the next play, *The Libation Bearers*. Indeed, we receive foreshadowing of Clytemnestra's doom when she boasts about ending the ancestral curse on her family: "I swept from these halls / the murder, the sin, and the fury." This arrogant declaration makes her guilty of the same deadly hubris that plagued her husband.

THE LIBATION BEARERS

The Libation Bearers (also known as *The Choephore*) is the second play in the *Oresteia*.

MAJOR CHARACTERS

Orestes Clytemnestra and Agamemnon's son and Electra's brother. The infant Orestes is sent away before the murder of his father in *Agamemnon*. He reemerges as the protagonist of *The Libation Bearers* and spends the course of the play preparing to avenge his father's murder. In doing so, Orestes overcomes familial bonds and sentimentality and commits himself to the command of Apollo, who orders him to avenge his father. Despite this divine order, however, Orestes knows that he will have to face the consequences of his revenge.

Pylades A companion to Orestes. Pylades is present for much of the play, although he does not speak a word until the climax of the action. He is a representative of and the mouthpiece for Apollo. Pylades' only lines come at the moment when Orestes hesitates to kill Clytemnestra. At this point, Pylades reminds Orestes of his duties to Apollo and says that one should rather make enemies of all men than anger the gods.

Electra   Orestes' older sister. Electra cared for Orestes as a child and loves him dearly. Since Agamemnon's death, people in the palace have treated Electra like a slave, and she is aware that Clytemnestra is about to marry her off in order to break her bond with the house. Fiercely devoted to her father's memory, Electra loathes her mother and is quick to transfer all of her love to Orestes when he reappears. After going into the palace in silence at Orestes' command, Electra does not reappear in the play.

DRAMA

SUMMARY
Several years after Agamemnon's murder at the hands of his wife, Clytemnestra, and her lover, Aegisthus, Agamemnon's son Orestes returns home with his companion, Pylades, to mourn at Agamemnon's grave. Orestes, who has been living in exile, has come back to Argos in secret, sent by an oracle of Apollo. His mission is to exact vengeance for Agamemnon's death upon his murderers. Apollo has threatened Orestes with horrible punishments, including leprosy and further exile, if he does not agree to accept this task of vengeance.

While performing rituals at Agamemnon's grave, Orestes reunites with his sister, Electra, whom he has not seen since he was a child. Electra explains that their mother, Clytemnestra, sent her to the grave to bring libations to Agamemnon in the hopes that they would quiet the source of Clytemnestra's terrible dreams. Clytemnestra dreamed she bore a snake, wrapped it like a baby, and tried to feed it from her breast. However, the snake bit her, and blood curdled the milk. Clytemnestra awoke with a scream and sent the libations in the hope that they would appease whoever sent the vision. Orestes interprets the dream, saying that he will be the snake, saying that just as Clytemnestra bred this violent sign, so she will die by violence.

Orestes and Electra engage in wishful thinking about how their father could have lived, but the chorus urges them to focus on the present and to act on their anger. Together, Orestes and Electra plot to avenge Agamemnon's death. With the eager support of the chorus, Orestes concocts a plan wherein he will gain admittance to the palace and kill Aegisthus on the throne. Complicit, Electra and the chorus disappear back into the palace.

Unexpectedly, Clytemnestra comes to the door when Orestes knocks, thus forcing him to fabricate a story about his origins. He claims to be a stranger bearing sad news of the death of Orestes. Clytemnestra laments, citing Orestes' death as evidence that the curse is still at work upon the house of Atreus. She sends Cilissa, Orestes' old nurse, to tell Aegisthus to come with his bodyguard to hear the news.

The chorus intervenes, intercepts Clytemnestra's message, and tells Cilissa to compel Aegisthus to come alone, without his guard. Although Cilissa does not understand why the chorus seems so gleeful—as she assumes Orestes is dead—she does as she is told. Aegisthus appears briefly on stage, after which he goes back into the palace to meet Orestes. Moments later, Aegisthus's servant announces his master's death and cries out for Clytemnestra to come and see what has happened.

Alarmed at the shouting, Clytemnestra appears and immediately realizes that something is horribly wrong. The doors open, and she sees Orestes over the fallen body of Aegisthus. The climax of the play follows, as Orestes resolves to carry out his vengeance on his mother as well. He hesitates at the crucial moment, however, when Clytemnestra bares her breast to him and implores him to respect their filial bonds. She warns him of her curse and then recognizes him as the snake from her dream. Orestes pronounces that she has killed her husband in an outrageous manner and that she will suffer the same outrage now. Orestes pulls his mother over the threshold, and they disappear behind the palace door. He wraps the two bodies in the same shroud in which Agamemnon was killed and announces to the world that he has carried out the commands of justice.

However, with the deed finally done, Orestes falls victim to the Furies' retributive violence. He goes mad and flees the stage in the direction of Delphi, where he will seek refuge at Apollo's shrine. As the play ends, the chorus despairs that the cycle of bloodshed has not stopped with Orestes' action but continues ever still.

THE EUMENIDES

The Eumenides, the final play in Aeschlyus's *Oresteia* trilogy, resolves the curse of violence that begins with Atreus, Agamemnon's father. The family's legacy of vengeance eventually ensnares Agamemnon's son Orestes, who, as the protagonist of *The Libation Bearers*, avenges the murder of his father by killing his mother and her lover.

The play opens outside Pythia's shrine at the temple of Apollo, the god of truth, who favors Orestes and urged him to avenge Agamemnon's death. The priestess of the temple relates to the audience her terrifying vision of Orestes being hounded by the Furies, a group of monstrous women who torment those who have committed crimes against family members. The temple doors open, exposing Hermes (Apollo's brother), Apollo, Orestes, and the slumbering Furies. Within the temple of Apollo, Orestes is safe from the tortures of Furies, but upon his departure, they will once again begin their torment. To free himself from them fully, Orestes must make a plea before Athena at the Acropolis in Athens, for only Athena has the power to find Orestes innocent of wrongdoing.

Orestes sneaks away from the temple of Apollo, leaving the sleeping Furies behind him. The angry ghost of Clytemnestra enters and wakes the Furies, who chant, "seize him, seize him, seize him" even in their sleep. Upon waking, the Furies lambaste Apollo both for persuading Orestes to commit matricide and for interfering in their work. Apollo argues that Agamemnon's murder was inexcusable and that Orestes acted justly by slaying his mother. The Furies disagree, and the two parties exit separately to make their case before Athena at the Acropolis.

Orestes reaches the Acropolis exhausted. As he cries out for Athena, the Furies close in around him, curse him, and call him to Hades. Athena finally appears, clad in full armor, and calmly demands that both sides present their case. The Furies scream that Orestes slew his mother and that, just or unjust, the crime calls for damnation. But Athena, slow to judge, commands Orestes to tell his side of the story. Orestes reveals his ancestry—the cursed house of Atreus—and explains the events preceding the murders of his father and mother. Above all, he says, he acted upon the guidance and advice of Apollo. After hearing both sides, Athena determines the matter too weighty to judge on her own. She exits and returns accompanied by a jury of twelve Athenian citizens.

During the ensuing trial, Apollo enters to testify his case, despite cries from the chorus that the realm of Athena lies outside Apollo's rightful place. Nonetheless, Apollo serves as counsel to the bewildered and exhausted Orestes. Making a case against the Furies' right to pursue Orestes, Apollo argues that Clytemnestra technically is not Orestes' parent, since a mother is merely a container to incubate a developing child, which is produced by the father alone. To support his argument, Apollo cites Athena, who was born from Zeus's forehead. Under this logic, the Furies have no right to Orestes, as they may pursue only those who kill blood relations.

After a brief pause in the trial to establish the Acropolis as the future court of Athens and to encourage all Athenians to eschew tyranny and love justice, Athena calls for the jurors to cast their votes. At the same time, she announces her vote in favor of Orestes, explaining that she always sides with the male and was swayed by Apollo's argument against the mother being a true parent. Athena declares that if the jurors' votes are tied, her vote will be decisive. After a moment of suspense, Athena announces that the ballots are tied. Orestes is free.

The outraged Furies curse Athena and the other children of Zeus who have trampled on the ways of the old gods. In their anger, they promise to destroy the land in revenge for Athena's slight. Athena, however, refuses to be drawn into the argument and reminds the Furies that Zeus and his thunderbolts protect her. Rather than take up arms against the Furies, Athena offers them a place in Athens if they will relinquish their fiery hatred of the world. At first incredulous, the Furies gradually soften with every praise and invitation Athena offers them: she reminds them that they have wisdom, that Athens will be a great city, and that she offers peace and position. At last, the Furies accept Athena's offer and quit their role as the tormenters of murderers. They become the Eumenides, or "kind ones."

PROMETHEUS BOUND

SUMMARY
Of the Aeschylean tragedies passed down to us, *Prometheus Bound* may be the most significant to the intellectual history of Western civilization, for it displays a rebellious spirit and a remarkable faith in human progress. The play also presents the greatest number of difficulties for scholars. First and foremost is the problem of authorship. Recent examination of the play has shown that the style and meter of *Prometheus Bound* differs substantially from Aeschylus's other plays. Some have gone so far as to argue that certain linguistic turns and philosophical ideas expressed in the tragedy simply were not available to playwrights before 456 B.C., the year of Aeschylus's

death. In addition to these problems, the other plays in the trilogy—
Prometheus Unbound and *Prometheus the Fire Bringer*—are frag-
mented and completely lost, respectively. Without understanding
the conclusion to the story of Prometheus, presenting a critique of
this first part is difficult.

As the play opens, Kratus (Force) and Bia (Strength), two servants of Zeus, carry in the Titan Prometheus and hold him against a
rock in the Caucasus Mountains. The god Hephaestus, whose job is
to chain Prometheus to the rock, follows them. Kratus states that
Prometheus is being punished for giving fire to human beings and
that Prometheus must learn to like Zeus's rule. Hephaestus
expresses his pity for Prometheus and laments the fact that he must
bind his friend to the rock. Kratus urges Hephaestus on and insists
that pity for Zeus's enemies is both useless and dangerous. Hephaestus finishes his task and leaves with Kratus and Bia.

Prometheus calls on nature to witness the suffering of a god at the
hands of other gods, specifically the new ruler of the gods, Zeus.
Prometheus mentions that he has the gift of prophecy and knows all
that will happen. He must live with his suffering because no one can
fight fate. Prometheus hears the sound of wings and discovers that
the sound is coming from the chorus of Oceanids, daughters of
Oceanus, arriving on winged chariots. The Oceanids express their
sympathy for Prometheus's suffering and explain that the new ruler
of Olympus follows only his own laws. Prometheus prophesies that,
one day, Zeus will be in danger and will be forced to befriend
Prometheus to avoid it.

Asked what crime he has committed to deserve this punishment,
Prometheus recounts the war between Zeus and the Titans.
Prometheus had tried to help the Titans, but they refused his guile
and decided to use force. Prometheus then offered his guile to Zeus
and helped him win. Now, Zeus punishes Prometheus because, like
all tyrants, he distrusts his friends. Zeus had planned to destroy
humanity, but Prometheus stood in his way. Questioned further,
Prometheus recounts that he gave humanity blind hope and also the
gift of fire. The chorus responds to this last admission, saying that
Prometheus has sinned, but Prometheus replies that he did so willingly and will not renounce his action. He asks the chorus to come
down to earth so he can tell them the whole story.

Oceanus flies in on a winged beast and says that Prometheus
should stop provoking Zeus while he himself goes to Zeus to have
Prometheus freed. Prometheus responds that talking to Zeus would

be useless and that Oceanus should not place himself in danger by getting involved. Oceanus argues that words are needed for healing, but Prometheus counters that the medicine must be applied at the proper time. Convinced by Prometheus's categorical refusal of his help, Oceanus departs.

The chorus sings that the entire old world mourns for Prometheus and his brothers, who also suffer at the hands of Zeus—especially Atlas, who must hold the world. Prometheus summarizes everything he has done for humanity. He taught human beings agriculture, language, mathematics, harnessing of animals, and sailing. He also taught medicine, divination, and mining. He insists that all human arts come from him. Prometheus almost reveals his prophecy to the chorus but stops himself, saying only that it will free him because Zeus is a slave to necessity like all others. The Oceanids affirm their piety to Zeus and chide Prometheus for helping mortals who cannot help him in return.

The young woman Io enters wearing cow horns, screaming that a gadfly is biting her and that the ghost of the hundred-eyed monster Argos is pursuing her. She calls on Zeus and asks him why he tortures her so. In response to Io's questions, Prometheus reveals who he is and why he is being punished. Io asks him to tell her about her future wanderings, but first the chorus asks to know of her past suffering. Io tells how Zeus became infatuated with her and forced her father to drive her out of his house. Zeus turned Io into a cow and put her under the guard of Argos. Argos was killed but returned as a ghost, along with a gadfly that drove Io around the world. Prometheus tells Io of her future wanderings through Europe, Asia, and Africa, where she must constantly avoid dangerous peoples and monsters.

Prometheus reveals that Zeus, who makes Io suffer, will one day choose a mate whose son will depose his father. Only Prometheus can help Zeus prevent this. Prometheus reveals also that, one day, Io's descendant will free him. He then concludes the story of Io's journey and says that, at the end of her suffering, Zeus will cure and impregnate her with a gentle touch of his hand. Prometheus talks about Io's descendants, who will become kings of the city Argos. Io runs off, again tortured by the gadfly. The Oceanids chant about the dangers of marrying above one's rank and express the hope that Zeus never takes an interest in them.

Angered by Io's suffering, Prometheus shouts out that Zeus's own son will topple him. This outburst prompts Zeus's messenger,

Hermes, to enter and order Prometheus to reveal the identity of this son's mother. Prometheus says mockingly that he will tell Hermes nothing. Hermes accuses Prometheus of being overly obstinate, disobedient, even insane. Prometheus deflects each accusation with direct insults or sarcasm. Hermes warns that if Prometheus does not yield, a storm will send him to Tartarus. He will emerge only to have an eagle eat his liver every day—a torment that will not end until a god agrees to die for him. Although the chorus advises Prometheus to yield, he shows no fear of his destiny. Hermes orders the Oceanids away, but they reply that betrayal of a friend is the worst crime of all and vow to stay with Prometheus. As the earth begins to shake and thunder gathers around him, Prometheus calls on the elements to witness his suffering.

ANALYSIS

Prometheus's crime is not as simple as it first appears. It is true that he is punished primarily for stealing fire and giving it to mortals. Comments by all three speakers here make clear that Prometheus is also being punished for loving humanity. Mythical accounts differ, but some suggest that Prometheus actually created human beings. As he reveals later in the play, he has also taught them almost everything of value. According to Hesiod, one of the earliest known writers of Greek myth, Zeus planned to destroy humanity by demanding that parts of animals slaughtered for food be sacrificed to him. Prometheus, however, wrapped the bones of the animals in fat to make them look appetizing, thereby tricking Zeus into accepting this portion as his sacrifice while allowing human beings to keep the meat. This support for human beings in clear opposition to Zeus is the underlying reason for Prometheus's punishment. Finally, as Hephaestus emphasizes, Prometheus betrayed his fellow gods by stealing the power of fire from them and giving it to undeserving mortals. In addition to violating the laws of the gods, Prometheus also has disturbed the universal balance of power.

Aeschylus emphasizes the power of necessity and the relationship between necessity and time. He refers to human beings as "creatures of a day" and therefore clearly inferior to the immortal gods. Yet while Zeus is immortal, he is not an eternal ruler. Zeus's father, Cronos, overthrew his own father, Uranus, and Zeus, in turn, overthrew Cronos. Cronos, like Prometheus, was one of the Titans and belonged to the older ruling class. Zeus is one of the younger gods, and the fact that he is a "new" ruler is mentioned repeatedly in

Prometheus Bound. The newness of Zeus's reign suggests that his position is not as stable as he would like to believe. Prometheus reveals that he has knowledge of the future and can see the extent of Zeus's power through time. As Prometheus tells us, the ultimate power is not Zeus but necessity. Even the gods must live out their fate, and all they do is preordained. Aeschylus's central message is that the passage of time is governed by necessity, by which both the mortals and the immortals are trapped. The gods may be superior to human beings, but the gap between them is not as wide as Zeus believes.

THE PERSIANS

The Persians, first performed in 472 B.C., is the only surviving Greek tragedy based upon events contemporaneous with the playwright's world—the Greek naval victory over the Persians at Salamis in 480 B.C. Aeschylus undoubtedly drew on his own wartime experience at the famous battle of Marathon, in 490 B.C., where the Greeks enjoyed their first major victory over the invading Persians.

The play opens before the Persian council hall. Xerxes, the king of Persia, has taken all his country's youth with him to do battle against the Greeks, leaving the affairs of state in the hands of a group of elder statesmen. The statesmen compose the chorus of the play. In the opening scene, the chorus of elders chants about Persia's great strength and Xerxes' strong leadership. They confess, however, that after months without hearing any news from the war, they have grown worried over the fate of their king.

Atossa, the queen of Persia, Xerxes' mother and King Darius's widow, shares these fears. She has been plagued by strange, foreboding dreams ever since her son departed for Greece. She is further troubled to learn from the chorus that the Greeks possess a strong army, are a free people, and in the past rebuffed her late husband Darius's attacks.

In the midst of the queen's fretting, a herald arrives with solemn news: Xerxes' navy has been defeated at Salamis, and many men have died, although Xerxes himself has survived. The herald explains the battle in detail: the outnumbered Greek host encircled the larger Persian fleet, the Persian troops on the shore were slaughtered, and Xerxes was filled with shame.

Deep in lament, Queen Atossa seeks the counsel of her dead husband by pouring libations and summoning his spirit from Hades.

Upon seeing evidence of mourning everywhere, the spirit of Darius quickly gathers that some great tragedy has occurred. He is surprised to learn, however, that his son tried to conquer the Greek empire—their defeat of his army makes him well aware of their tenacity. Accordingly, Darius commands that the Persians never again send their armies in Greece.

Finally, Xerxes returns, full of woe and self-loathing. He recounts how he tore off his royal robes as he watched his army fall to the Greeks. He ends the play by acknowledging his disgrace and the bravery of the Greeks.

THE SEVEN AGAINST THEBES

This play, which Aeschylus composed around 467 B.C., retells one of the Athenian playwrights' favorite legends. Fifty years after Aeschylus presented his version of the story, Euripides composed a similar play: *The Phoenician Women. The Seven Against Thebes* was originally part of a tetralogy (four-part cycle) of the Oedipus story that Sophocles made famous.

Oedipus has two sons, Eteocles and Polynieces. After Oedipus uncovers his terrible fate, he leaves Thebes in the hands of Eteocles. At the same time, however, Oedipus curses both of his sons for their lack of love and makes a prophecy for their future: "They shall divide their inheritance with the sword in such a manner as to obtain equal shares." *The Seven Against Thebes* is the story of Eteocles and Polynieces trying to divide their inheritance, which Polynieces does by waging war against his brother and the city of Thebes.

The play opens as Eteocles spurs on the men of Thebes to stand on high alert, for the seers have foretold that the Achaeans will attack the city. A spy enters and confirms the seers' vision: he tells of an Achaean council of seven warriors, including Polynieces, who have sworn to raze Thebes through its seven gates or die trying. The spy even has witnessed the Achaeans cast lots to determine who will lead the assaults on the city. As he speaks, the chorus of Theban women cries out that the Achaean army has begun its approach.

Eteocles realizes that he must beg Zeus for his support if he is to stand any chance of winning the battle. However, because of his father's terrible fate (Oedipus married his mother and killed his father), Eteocles knows that his family has been cursed. Therefore, rather than pray for Zeus to protect his own life, he beseeches Zeus to protect, above all, the city of Thebes.

The spy returns to report in greater detail the formation of the Achaean host. He gives detailed information about which warriors will lead the charge on which gates to the city. With each name and location, Eteocles assigns one of his brave commanders to meet the besieging warriors. But when he hears that his own brother, Polynieces, will attack the seventh gate, Eteocles decides to lead that defense himself—despite protests from the chorus of Theban women.

After Eteocles departs, the chorus continues to lament his decision, sensing that nothing but destruction can come from the war between the brothers. They turn their anger against Laius, Oedipus's father, who impregnated his wife despite the prophecy that his offspring would doom the house of Cadmus. The chorus recounts how, after Oedipus's sins were revealed and his children banished from the city, Oedipus cursed his sons for their loveless treatment of their father.

It seems as though things have turned for the better, when a messenger arrives and reports that the enemy has been repelled and Thebes is safe. Eteocles and Polyneices, however, have slain each other. Thus do the sons of Oedipus divide their inheritance—each gains an equal share of death. As Antigone and Ismene, the daughters of Oedipus, enter bearing their brothers' bodies, they join the chorus in bemoaning the fate of their family, whose destruction was sealed by their forefathers' sins.

The tragedy deepens when a herald arrives to announce that, while Eteocles will receive a proper funeral, Polynieces is to be cast out, unburied, for the dogs to tear apart. In Greek culture, such treatment constituted more than disrespect—it was a way to punish the spirit of the deceased by preventing him from finding peace in the underworld. Antigone, however, refuses to let her brother suffer this punishment, so she vows to give him a proper burial even if it means angering the council of Thebes. (See section on Sophocles' *Antigone*.)

THE SUPPLIANTS

The oldest of the extant Greek tragedies (c. 490 B.C.), *The Suppliants* reveals a young Aeschylus just beginning to find his style. The play is partly in the style of the traditional choral dithyramb, which preceded the great Greek playwrights, and partly in the tragic style established by Aeschylus, Sophocles, and Euripides. The chorus of fifty maidens in *The Suppliants* is the central character in the story—not simply a bystander and commentator, as the chorus usually is. Much of the play consists of the chorus simply telling its stories or invoking gods, leaving little room for real action.

The play opens on the shores of Argos, where Danaus and his fifty daughters have escaped from his brother Egyptus, who wishes for his sons to marry Danaus's daughters. Danaus's daughters, however, want to marry for love and do not love Egyptus's sons. After the daughters pray to Zeus and Artemis to protect them, Danaus spots a group of men approaching their altar. He tells his daughters that they must tell their story to the strangers and explain why they have landed on the shore of Argos. The men enter, and among their number is King Pelasgus. They are surprised to learn that Danaus and his daughters are Argives. The daughters explain that they are descendants of Io, whom Hera turned into a cow out of jealously (see section on *Prometheus Bound*). Zeus, in the semblance of a bull, seduced Io, and then Hera, upon her discovery of Zeus's infidelity, turned Io into a heifer. Hera goaded Io constantly with a nagging gadfly and commanded Argus, the hundred-eyed herdsman, to follow and watch her.

The maidens explain that they have fled from their uncle Egyptus and his fifty sons. They beseech Pelasgus for his help, but he hesitates, saying that he must deliberate with his citizens before he can offer protection, for he fears starting a war in his peaceful country. The maidens continue their arguments against Egyptus's sons, saying they want to be married for love. They remind Pelasgus that he is king and that he does not have to consult his people about his decisions. Despite the continued pleas of the chorus of maidens, however, Pelasgus refuses to promise protection. Pelasgus suggests that Danaus go ahead of him to the city to arouse piety in the citizens. The king then tells the maidens to go to a nearby cove where he believes they will be safe. Alarmed as they are to leave the safety of their altar, they consent, and Pelasgus departs for the city to confer with his citizens.

Soon, Danaus returns with the good news that the citizens support the maidens' cause. But Danaus spies an Egyptian ship quickly approaching the shores of Argos. He leaves to get help and promises to return in time to save his daughters. Not long after Danaus leaves, however, a herald from the ship enters and orders the maidens to submit or be forced to board the ship. Fortunately, Pelasgus arrives just in time. Without revealing his identity, he tells the herald that he has many men ready to fight should Egyptus and his sons try to seize the daughters. The herald leaves, and Pelasgus invites the maidens to the city, where they may stay to live.

SOPHOCLES

CONTEXT AND BACKGROUND

Sophocles was born in 496 B.C. in Colonus, a village a mile north of Athens. His father was a man of wealth and stature and was, accordingly, able to provide his son with the benefit of a rounded and far-reaching education. That education included instruction in the arts of poetry, music, and dance. Sophocles' education produced immediate results: at the age of sixteen, he was chosen to lead with dance and lyre the chorus that celebrated the Greek victory at Salamis. Then, at twenty-eight, in his first competition, his play took first prize, defeating even the renowned dramatist Aeschylus, who was thirty years Sophocles' senior. This victory marked the commencement of a dramatic career that produced 123 plays, of which only seven have survived intact.

Sophocles proved himself one of the great innovators of theater, adding to the improvements that Aeschylus had already made in the field of tragedy. He introduced a third actor to the stage, abbreviated the choral components of Greek drama, and more fully developed the tragedy's moments of dialogue. In addition, Sophocles was the first to abandon the trilogy form. Other dramatists, such as Aeschylus, had previously used three tragedies to tell a single story. Sophocles, however, chose to make each tragedy its own entity. As a result, he had to pack the complete action of a story into a compressed form, which afforded new and uncharted dramatic possibilities.

Sophocles was a deeply sensual dramatist. His language, though sometimes characterized by harsh words or complicated syntax, was for the most part grand and majestic. He was careful to avoid both the colossal phraseology that typified the work of Aeschylus and the ordinary diction of Euripides. He paid unprecedented attention to the spectacular effects of the play, insisting upon meticulously painted scenery that was properly and purposefully placed. Sophocles was also of a profoundly religious temperament, filled with a deep reverence for his country's gods but without any strains of crude superstition. In many of his plays, he grapples with his country's sacred myths, examining them from the point of view of the diligent artist and pondering their relation to the struggles of humanity.

Sophocles did not devote his life exclusively to drama. During the Peloponnesian War, he was among the ten Athenian generals who suppressed the revolt of Samos. An ordained priest in the service of Alcon and Ascelpius, the god of medicine, Sophocles was also for a time the director of the Treasury, responsible for the funds of a group of states known as the Delian Confederacy, and he served on the Board of Generals in administration of the civil and military affairs of Athens. Sophocles died in 406 B.C., at the age of ninety.

OEDIPUS REX

MAJOR CHARACTERS

Oedipus   The protagonist of *Oedipus Rex* and *Oedipus at Colonus*. Oedipus becomes king of Thebes before the action of *Oedipus Rex* begins. He is renowned for his intelligence and his ability to solve riddles: he saved the city of Thebes and was made its king by solving the riddle of the Sphinx, the supernatural being who had held the city captive. Nonetheless, Oedipus is stubbornly blind to the truth about himself. His name's literal meaning ("swollen foot") is a clue to his identity—he was taken from the house of Laius as a baby and left in the mountains with his feet bound together. On his way to Thebes, Oedipus killed his biological father, King Laius, not knowing who he was, and proceeded to marry Jocasta, his biological mother. As the play opens, Oedipus sends Creon, his brother-in-law, to the Oracle at Delphi to seek information regarding the plague that has stricken Thebes.

Jocasta   Oedipus's wife and mother and Creon's sister. Jocasta appears only in the final scenes of *Oedipus Rex*. In her first words, she attempts to make peace between Oedipus and Creon, pleading with Oedipus not to banish Creon. She is comforting to her husband and calmly tries to urge him to reject Tiresias's terrifying prophecies as false. Jocasta solves the riddle of Oedipus's identity before Oedipus does and expresses her love for her son and husband in her desire to protect him from this knowledge.

Tiresias   A blind soothsayer who appears in both *Oedipus Rex* and *Antigone*. In *Oedipus Rex*, Tiresias tells Oedipus that Oedipus himself is the murderer he hunts, but Oedipus does not believe him. In *Antigone*, Tiresias tells Creon that Creon himself is bringing disaster upon Thebes, but Creon does not believe him. Despite their disbelief, both Oedipus and Creon claim to trust Tiresias deeply. The literal blindness of the soothsayer points to the metaphorical blindness of those who refuse to believe the truth about themselves when they hear it spoken.

DRAMA

SUMMARY

A plague has stricken the city of Thebes. The citizens gather outside the palace of their king, Oedipus, and ask him to take action. Oedipus replies that he already sent his brother-in-law, Creon, to the Oracle at Delphi to learn how to help the city. Creon returns with a message from the Oracle: the plague will end when the murderer of Laius, former king of Thebes, is caught and expelled. The murderer apparently is within the city. Oedipus questions Creon about the murder of Laius, who was killed by thieves on his way to consult an oracle. Only one of Laius's fellow travelers escaped alive. Oedipus promises to solve the mystery of Laius's death and vows to curse and drive out the murderer.

Oedipus sends for the blind prophet Tiresias and asks him what he knows about the murder. Tiresias responds cryptically and laments his ability to see the truth when the truth brings nothing but pain. At first, he refuses to tell Oedipus what he knows. Oedipus curses and insults the old man, going so far as to accuse him of the murder. These taunts provoke Tiresias into revealing that Oedipus himself is the murderer. Oedipus naturally refuses to believe Tiresias's accusation. He accuses Creon and Tiresias of conspiring against his life and charges Tiresias with insanity. Oedipus asks why Tiresias did nothing when Thebes suffered under a plague once before. At that time, a Sphinx held the city captive and refused to leave until someone answered her riddle. Oedipus brags that he alone was able to solve the puzzle. Tiresias defends his skills as a prophet, noting that Oedipus's parents found him trustworthy. At this mention of his parents, Oedipus, who grew up in the distant city of Corinth, asks how Tiresias knew his parents. Tiresias again answers enigmatically. Before Tiresias leaves, he puts forth one last riddle, saying that the murderer of Laius will turn out to be both father and brother to his own children, and the son of his own wife.

Oedipus threatens Creon with death or exile for conspiring with Tiresias. Oedipus's wife, Jocasta (also the widow of King Laius), enters and asks why Oedipus and Creon are shouting at one another. Oedipus explains to Jocasta that Tiresias has charged him with Laius's murder, and Jocasta replies that all prophecies are false. As proof, she notes that the Oracle at Delphi once told Laius he would be murdered by his son, when in fact his son was cast out of Thebes as a baby and Laius was murdered by a band of thieves. Her description of Laius's murder, however, sounds familiar to Oedipus, and he asks further questions. Jocasta tells him that Laius was killed at a three-way crossroads, just before Oedipus arrived in Thebes. Oedipus, stunned, tells his wife that he may be the one who murdered Laius. He tells Jocasta that, long ago, when he was the prince of Corinth, he overheard someone mention at a banquet that he was not really the son of the king and queen. He therefore traveled to the Oracle at Delphi, who did not answer him but did tell him he would murder his father and sleep with his mother. Hearing this, Oedipus fled his home, never to return. It was then, on the journey that would take him to Thebes, that Oedipus was confronted and harassed by a group of travelers, whom he killed in self-defense. This skirmish occurred at the very crossroads where Laius was killed.

Oedipus sends for the man who survived the attack, a shepherd, in the hope that he will not be identified as the murderer. Outside the palace, a messenger approaches Jocasta and tells her that he has come from Corinth to inform Oedipus that his father, Polybus, is dead, and that Corinth has asked Oedipus to come and rule there in his place. Jocasta rejoices, convinced that Polybus's death from natural causes has disproved the prophecy that Oedipus would murder his father. At Jocasta's summons, Oedipus comes outside, hears the news, and rejoices with her. He now feels much more inclined to agree with the queen in deeming prophecies worthless and viewing chance as the principle governing the world. But while Oedipus finds great comfort in the fact that one-half of the prophecy has been disproved, he still fears the other half—the half that claimed he would sleep with his mother.

The messenger remarks that Oedipus need not worry, because Polybus and his wife, Merope, are not Oedipus's biological parents. The messenger, a shepherd by profession, knows firsthand that Oedipus came to Corinth as an orphan. One day long ago, he was tending his sheep when another shepherd approached him carrying a baby, its ankles pinned together. The messenger took the baby to the royal family of Corinth, who raised him as their own. That baby was Oedipus. Oedipus asks who the other shepherd was, and the messenger answers that he was a servant of Laius.

Oedipus asks that this shepherd be brought forth to testify, but Jocasta, beginning to suspect the truth, begs her husband not to seek more information and runs back into the palace. The shepherd then enters. Oedipus interrogates him and asks who gave him the baby. The shepherd refuses to disclose anything, and Oedipus threatens him with torture. Finally, the shepherd answers that the child came from the house of Laius. Questioned further, he answers that the baby was in fact the child of Laius himself, and that it was Jocasta who gave him the infant, ordering him to kill it, as it had been prophesied that the child would kill his parents. But the shepherd pitied the child and decided that the prophecy could be avoided just as well if the child were to grow up in a foreign city, far from his true parents. The shepherd therefore gave the boy to the shepherd in Corinth.

Realizing who he is and who his parents are, Oedipus screams that he sees the truth and flees back into the palace. The shepherd and the messenger slowly exit the stage. A second messenger enters and describes scenes of suffering. Jocasta has hanged herself, and Oedipus, finding her dead, has pulled the pins from her robe and stabbed out his own eyes. Oedipus now emerges from the palace, bleeding and begging to be exiled. He asks Creon to send him away from Thebes and to look after his daughters, Antigone and Ismene. Creon, who covets royal power, is all too happy to oblige.

ANALYSIS

Sophocles did not invent the story of Oedipus himself, and in fact, the play's most powerful effects depend to some degree on the fact that the audience already knows the story. Since the first performance of *Oedipus Rex*, the story has fascinated critics just as it fascinated Sophocles. Aristotle used this play and its plot as the

DRAMA

supreme example of tragedy: an above-average, fortunate man ensnared by a terrible, unavoidable fate. Sigmund Freud famously based his theory of the "Oedipus complex" on this story, claiming that every boy has a latent desire to kill his father and sleep with his mother. The story of Oedipus has given birth to innumerable fascinating variations, but we should not forget that *Oedipus Rex* is one of the variations, not the original story itself.

Sophocles' audience knew the ancient story of Oedipus well and therefore would interpret the greatness Oedipus exudes in the beginning of the play as a tragic harbinger of his fall. Sophocles seizes every opportunity to exploit this irony. Oedipus frequently alludes to sight and blindness, creating many moments of dramatic irony, as the audience knows that it is Oedipus's metaphorical blindness to the relationship between his past and his present situation that brings about his ruin. For example, when an old priest tells Oedipus that the people of Thebes are dying of the plague, Oedipus says that he could not fail to "see" this. Oedipus eagerly attempts to uncover the truth, as he acts decisively and scrupulously refuses to shield himself from the truth. Although we see him as a mere puppet of fate, at some points the irony is so magnified that it seems almost as if Oedipus brings catastrophe upon himself willingly. One such instance of this irony is the scene in which Oedipus proclaims proudly—but, for the audience, painfully—that he possesses the bed of the former king, and that marriage might have even created "blood-bonds" between him and Laius had Laius not been murdered.

As the play progresses and tragedies approach, Jocasta becomes both careless and maternal as she, like Oedipus, becomes blind to the increasingly apparent truth of Tiresias's statements. She tells him that prophecies do not come true, and as evidence, she asserts that an oracle incorrectly prophesied that Laius would be killed by his own son. Jocasta's mistake is similar to Oedipus's in the previous section, as she confuses conclusions and evidence. Just as Oedipus assumes that Tiresias's unpleasant claims could only be treason, so Jocasta assumes that because one prophecy has apparently not come to pass, all prophecies must be lies. But whereas Oedipus's hasty and imperfect logic in the second section has much to do with his pride, Jocasta's in this section seems to stem from an unwitting desire to soothe and mother Oedipus. When Jocasta is not answering Oedipus's questions, she is calming him down, asking him to go into the palace, telling him that he has nothing to worry about—no need to ask more questions—for the rest of his life. Jocasta's casual attitude upsets the chorus, which continues to be loyal to Oedipus throughout this section. One chorus's ode serves as a reminder that neither Oedipus, Jocasta, nor the sympathetic audience should feel calm, for oracles speak to a purpose and are inspired by the gods who control the destiny of men. Throughout the play, the chorus is miserable, desperate for the plague to end and for stability to be restored to the city. Nevertheless, the chorus holds staunchly to the belief that the prophesies of Tiresias will come true. For if they do not, there is no order on earth or in the heavens.

Oedipus at Colonus

Summary

After years of wandering in exile from Thebes, a blind, frail Oedipus arrives in a grove outside Athens, walking with the help of his daughter, Antigone. A citizen tells Oedipus and Antigone that they are standing on holy ground reserved for the Eumenides, goddesses of fate. Oedipus sends the citizen to fetch Theseus, the king of Athens and the surrounding lands. Oedipus tells Antigone that, earlier in his life, when Apollo prophesied his doom, the god promised Oedipus that he would come to rest on this ground.

In a brief interlude, Oedipus tells the chorus who he is. Then, Ismene, Oedipus's second daughter, enters, having come from the Oracle at Delphi. Ismene tells Oedipus that, back in Thebes, Oedipus's younger son, Eteocles, has overthrown Oedipus's elder son, Polyneices. Polyneices apparently has amassed troops in Argos for an attack on his brother and on Creon, who rules along with Eteocles. The Oracle has predicted that the burial place of Oedipus will bring good fortune to the city in which it is located. Both of Oedipus's sons, as well as Creon, know of this prophecy. Both Polyneices and Creon are currently en route to try to take Oedipus into custody and thus claim the right to bury him in their kingdoms. Oedipus swears he will never give his support to either of his sons, for they did nothing to prevent his exile years ago.

King Theseus arrives and says that he pities Oedipus for the fate that has befallen him. He asks how he can help, and Oedipus asks Theseus to harbor him in Athens until his death. However, Oedipus warns that by doing him this favor, Theseus will incur the wrath of Thebes. Despite the warning, Theseus agrees to help Oedipus. Creon arrives to abduct Oedipus, but, as Oedipus is under Theseus's protection, Creon kidnaps Antigone and Ismene instead. Theseus promises Oedipus that he will get his daughters back, and does in fact return with Oedipus's daughters shortly.

Soon after, Polyneices arrives, seeking his father's favor in order to gain custody of his eventual burial site. Oedipus asks Theseus to drive Polyneices away, but Antigone convinces her father to listen to his son. Polyneices insists that he never condoned Oedipus's exile and that Eteocles is the bad son, for he has bribed the men of Thebes to turn against Polyneices. Oedipus responds with a terrible curse, upbraiding Polyneices for allowing him to be sent into exile and predicting that Eteocles and Polyneices will die at one another's hands. Polyneices, realizing he will never win his father's support, turns to his sisters and asks that they provide him with a proper burial should he die in battle. Antigone embraces Polyneices and says that he is condemning himself to death, but he responds resolutely that his life remains in the hands of the gods. Polyneices prays for the safety of his sisters and then leaves for Thebes.

Terrible thunder sounds, and the chorus cries out in horror. Oedipus says that his time of death has come. He sends for Theseus and tells him that he must carry out certain rites on Oedipus's body in order to assure divine protection for his city. Theseus states that he believes Oedipus and asks what he must do. Oedipus answers that he will lead the king to the place where he will die, and that Theseus must never reveal that location to anyone. He must pass on the knowledge of the location to his son at his own death, who in turn must pass it on to his own son. In this way, Theseus and his heirs may always rule over a safe city. Oedipus then strides off with a sudden strength, taking his daughters and Theseus to his grave.

A messenger enters to narrate the mysterious death of Oedipus: his death seemed a disappearance of sorts, "the lightless depths of Earth bursting open in kindness to receive him." Just as the messenger finishes his story, Antigone and Ismene come onstage, chanting a dirge. Antigone wails that she and her sister will cry for Oedipus for as long as they live. Not knowing where to go, Antigone says that they will have to wander forever alone. Theseus returns to the stage and asks the daughters to stop their weeping. They plead to see their father's tomb, but Theseus insists that Oedipus has forbidden it. Antigone and Ismene give up their pleas but ask for safe passage back to Thebes so that they may prevent a war between their brothers. Theseus grants them this request, and the chorus tells the girls to stop their weeping, for all rests in the hands of the gods. Theseus and the chorus exit toward Athens, and Antigone and Ismene head for Thebes.

ANALYSIS

Oedipus at Colonus is set many years after *Oedipus Rex*, and the long-wandering Oedipus has changed his perspective on his exile. First, he has decided that he was not responsible for his fate, despite the fact that, at the end of the previous play, Oedipus claims responsibility for his actions, blinds himself, and begs for exile. Since that time, Oedipus also has decided that his sons should have prevented his exile, though in *Oedipus Rex*, his sons never even appeared onstage. We do not yet know what to make of Oedipus's revised sentiments: he may simply be a broken man making excuses, or perhaps his many years of wandering have imbued him with a new kind of wisdom.

Like that of *Oedipus Rex*, the central theme of *Oedipus at Colonus* is self-knowledge, but in the latter play, Oedipus's self-knowledge may be too great rather than too scant. In *Oedipus Rex*, the distance between Oedipus and the audience is an ironic one: we know the truth about Oedipus, but he does not understand it himself. In *Oedipus at Colonus*, Oedipus's actions all are sanctified by his divine knowledge, and Oedipus has knowledge and understanding of his own plight that the rest of the characters do not. Throughout the Theban plays, Sophocles distances the audience from real events, especially violent ones. Because many of the play's events are reported after they occur, in narrative, the distance between the reader and Oedipus in this final play is doubled. Not only do we not see Oedipus die, no one in the play—aside from Theseus—does either.

ANTIGONE

MAJOR CHARACTERS

Antigone Daughter of Oedipus and Jocasta, and therefore both Oedipus's daughter and his sister. Antigone appears briefly at the end of *Oedipus Rex*, when she bids farewell to her father as Creon prepares to banish him. She appears at greater length in *Oedipus at Colonus*, leading and caring for her old, blind father in his exile. But Antigone does not come into her own until *Antigone*. As that play's protagonist, she demonstrates a courage and clarity of sight unparalleled by any other character in the three Theban plays. Whereas other characters—Oedipus, Creon, Polyneices—are reluctant to acknowledge the consequences of their actions, Antigone is unabashed in her conviction that she has done right.

Creon   Oedipus's brother-in-law. Creon appears more than any other character in the three plays combined. In him, more than in any other character, we see the gradual rise and fall of one man's power. Early in *Oedipus Rex*, Creon claims to have no desire for kingship. Yet when he has the opportunity to grasp power at the end of that play, Creon appears quite eager. We learn in *Oedipus at Colonus* that Creon is willing to fight with his nephews for this power, and in *Antigone*, Creon rules Thebes with a stubborn blindness that is similar to Oedipus's during his rule. However, Creon never wins our sympathy in the way Oedipus does, for he is bossy and bureaucratic and intent on asserting his own authority.

SUMMARY

Antigone and Ismene, the daughters of Oedipus, discuss the disaster that has just befallen them. Their brothers, Polyneices and Eteocles, have killed one another in a battle for control over Thebes. Creon, who now rules the city, has ordered that Polyneices, who brought a foreign army against Thebes, not be allowed proper burial rites. Creon threatens to kill anyone who tries to bury Polyneices and stations sentries over his body. Antigone, in spite of Creon's edict and without the help of her sister, resolves to give their brother a proper burial. Soon, a nervous sentry arrives at the palace to tell Creon that someone gave Polyneices burial rites while the sentries slept. Creon says that he thinks some of the dissidents of the city bribed the sentry to perform the rites, and he vows to execute the sentry if no other suspect is found.

The sentry exonerates himself by catching Antigone in the act of attempting to rebury Polyneices after the sentries have disinterred his body. Antigone freely confesses her act to Creon and says that he himself defies the will of the gods by refusing Polyneices a proper burial. Creon condemns Antigone and Ismene to death. Haemon, Creon's son and Antigone's betrothed, enters, and Creon asks him his opinion on the issue. Haemon at first seems to side with his father but gradually admits his opposition to Creon's stubbornness and petty vindictiveness. Creon curses Haemon and threatens to slay Antigone before his very eyes. Haemon storms out. Creon decides to pardon Ismene but vows to kill Antigone by sealing her alive in a tomb.

The blind prophet Tiresias arrives, and Creon promises to take whatever advice he gives. Tiresias advises that Creon allow Polyneices to be buried, but Creon refuses. Tiresias predicts that the gods will bring down curses upon the city. The words of Tiresias strike fear into the hearts of Creon and the people of Thebes, and Creon reluctantly goes to free Antigone from the tomb where she has been imprisoned. But his change of heart comes too late. A messenger enters and recounts the tragic events: Creon and his entourage gave proper burial to Polyneices and then heard what sounded like Haemon's voice wailing from Antigone's tomb. Upon entering, they saw Antigone hanging from a noose and Haemon raving. Creon's son then took a sword and thrust it at his father. Missing, he turned the sword against himself and died embracing Antigone's body.

Creon's wife, Eurydice, hears this terrible news and rushes away into the palace. Creon enters carrying Haemon's body and wailing against his own tyranny, which he knows has caused his son's death. The messenger tells Creon that he has another reason to grieve: Eurydice has stabbed herself, and, as she died, she called down curses on her husband for the misery his pride had caused. Creon kneels and prays that he, too, might die. His guards lead him back into the palace.

ANALYSIS

Antigone probably was the first of the three Theban plays that Sophocles wrote, although the events dramatized in it are chronologically last in the story. Antigone is one of the first heroines in literature, a woman who fights against a male power structure and exhibits greater bravery than any of the men who scorn her. *Antigone* is not only a feminist play but a radical one as well in that it depicts rebellion against authority as splendid and noble.

In the struggle between Creon and Antigone, Sophocles' audience would have recognized a genuine conflict of duties and values. In their ethical philosophy, the ancient Athenians clearly recognized that conflicts can arise when two separate but valid principles clash, and that such situations call for practical judgment and deliberation. From the Greek point of view, both Creon's and Antigone's positions are flawed, because both oversimplify ethical life by recognizing only one kind of "good" or duty. By oversimplifying, each ignores the fact that a conflict exists at all, or that deliberation is necessary. Moreover, both Creon and Antigone display the dangerous flaw of pride in the way they justify and carry out their decisions. Antigone admits from the beginning that she wants to carry out the burial because the action is "glorious." Creon's pride, meanwhile, is that of a tyrant. He is inflexible and unyielding, unwilling throughout the play to listen to advice. The danger of pride is that it leads both these characters to overlook their own human finitude—the limitations of their own powers.

Throughout the play, Creon emphasizes the importance of "healthy" practical judgment over a twisted mind, but Tiresias informs Creon that practical judgment is precisely what he lacks—indeed, Creon himself has a twisted mind. When the catastrophes occur, the messenger boldly summarizes the problem of the play: the worst ill afflicting mortals is a lack of judgment. We may wonder whether judgment really means anything given the limitations of human beings and the inescapable will of the gods. Perhaps the best explanation is that possessing wisdom and judgment means acknowledging human limitations and behaving piously so as not to actually call down the gods' wrath. Humans must take a humble, reverential attitude toward fate, the gods, and the limits of human intelligence. At the end of the play, Creon shows he has learned this lesson at last when, rather than mock death as he has throughout the play, he speaks respectfully of death heaping blows upon him.

AJAX

Composed around 440 B.C., *Ajax* relates some of the events that take place after Odysseus wins the fallen Achilles' prized armor. After Achilles' death, Ajax and Odysseus are undoubtedly the two most fearsome warriors in the Achaean army, and both covet the near-perfect armor that the god Hephaestus made for Achilles. When the armor is awarded to Odysseus, Ajax, blind with fury, plots to kill the commanders of the Achaean army as they sleep. Athena, however, who is always protective of the shrewd Odysseus, punishes Ajax by sending delusions and hallucinations into his mind. Rather than kill the leaders of the army, he attacks dogs, goats, and bulls.

SUMMARY

Sophocles' play opens outside Ajax's tent, to which Odysseus has followed a mysterious trail of blood and footprints. Athena tells Odysseus that she has saved him and the other leaders by making Ajax delusional. Athena calls Ajax forth from his tent and shrouds Odysseus from Ajax's sight. Ajax brags that he has killed Agamemnon, Menelaus, and the others but says he has spared Odysseus, whom he believes he holds captive inside his tent. Athena, having fun at Ajax's expense, encourages him to finish his vengeance and slaughter Odysseus—in reality, the goat that Ajax believes is Odysseus. Odysseus, in a rare show of emotion, confesses that he pities Ajax.

After Odysseus and Athena depart, Tecmessa, Ajax's mistress, joins the chorus on stage to bemoan her fate and that of her husband. She realizes that nothing can save Ajax now that the gods have risen against him. She recounts how Ajax entered the tent the previous night, driving before him the Achaean army's livestock. Ajax had called the animals by the names of the Greek commanders, threatened them, and finally slaughtered them. As Tecmessa speaks, however, Ajax's sanity finally returns. Terrified, he finds himself sitting amid a throng of slaughtered animals and cries out from inside his tent.

Ajax emerges, calling out in shame for his son, Eurysaces; his brother, Teucer; and his shipmates, all of whom he has dishonored. Despite Tecmessa's attempts to ease his self-hatred, Ajax cries out for his homeland. Still sitting amid the carcasses of the butchered animals, Ajax laments how he has shamed his noble father, Telamon. His only hope of salvaging his honor lies in a noble death.

When his brother Teucer arrives with Eurysaces, Ajax directs Teucer to show the child the carnage within the tent so that Eurysaces might have some remembrance of his father's downfall. Ajax implores Teucer to escort Eurysaces safely home to his grandparents and to ensure that, when Eurysaces comes of age, he inherits Ajax's sturdy spear-proof shield.

With these final requests, Ajax exits. He then reenters, bearing his sword, and goes off in search of solitude. A messenger reports the cruelty with which the Greek host has treated Teucer: unable to taunt Ajax, they aim their invectives against his innocent brother instead. When Teucer attempts to leave, Calchas, a prophet, stops him. Calchas says that if Teucer wants Ajax to live, he must detain

Ajax in his tent throughout the day. Meanwhile, Ajax's companions grow increasingly concerned over his long absence.

Alone on the seashore, Ajax beseeches the gods one last time for their forgiveness. He asks Zeus to send Hermes to speed him to the underworld after he has fallen upon his sword. He implores the Furies to hound the Greek generals for their part in his shame. Bidding farewell to all who have sustained his life, Ajax falls upon his sword and dies.

Tecmessa, Teucer, and the chorus discover Ajax's body. Menelaus enters and declares that Ajax, as a traitor, will not receive a proper burial—which will prevent his soul from reaching the underworld. The chorus and Teucer are outraged, for they believe that Ajax has suffered enough and has inflicted no harm upon the Greek commanders. Menelaus, verbally outmatched by Teucer, departs, leaving the argument unresolved. Eventually, Odysseus enters and defends Teucer's cause, saying that Ajax deserves a proper burial despite the wrongs he committed. With this, the only kind gesture to Ajax, Teucer begins to dig his brother's grave, and the play ends.

ELECTRA

SUMMARY

Electra, set several years after the murder of Agamemnon, opens as Pylades, Orestes, and the Old Man, Orestes' keeper, arrive at Mycenae at daybreak. They have come to exact revenge for the murder of Agamemnon, Orestes' father, as instructed by an oracle of Apollo. Electra, Orestes' sister, sobs audibly from within the house, outside of which the three stand discussing how to execute their plan. Orestes wishes to greet Electra, but the Old Man instead leads Orestes away to present an offering at his father's grave as Apollo's oracle has instructed. Electra emerges from inside the palace gates, pours forth her grief in a mournful address to the heavens, and prays to the deities to help her exact revenge for her father's death.

Chrysothemis, Electra's younger sister, emerges from the palace with a funeral offering and finds Electra mourning as usual outside the palace gates. Chrysothemis scolds her sister for her excessive mourning and urges her to get on with her life. Chrysothemis explains that Clytemnestra has sent her to make an offering at Agamemnon's grave. The previous night, Clytemnestra had a terrifying dream in which that Agamemnon, the husband she murdered, returned and planted his scepter in the floor of the house. The scepter grew branches from which leaves grew and overshadowed the land.

Clytemnestra enters and chastises Electra for mourning in the streets, and the two have an argument about Agamemnon's murder. Clytemnestra maintains that it was a just murder, done as revenge for Agamemnon's sacrifice of their daughter, Iphigenia. Electra holds that the sacrifice of Iphigenia was necessary and that, in any case, the real reason Clytemnestra murdered Agamemnon was her lust for Aegisthus. After this angry confrontation, Clytemnestra, standing beside an altar, prays to Apollo for wealth, longevity, and, in guarded terms, for the death of her son, Orestes, so that he might not return and disrupt her life. As soon as Clytemnestra has finished praying, the Old Man enters in the character of a Phocian, bearing a false account of Orestes' death. Clytemnestra is briefly touched by maternal feelings but delighted that her prayer has been answered. Electra, meanwhile, is overcome with grief. Clytemnestra ushers the Old Man inside to receive her hospitality.

Chrysothemis returns from Agamemnon's grave full of joy because she found a fresh offering of flowers and a lock of hair at the grave—signs that she takes to mean Orestes has returned. Electra informs Chrysothemis that, to the contrary, Orestes is dead. After Chrysothemis departs, Orestes and Pylades arrive disguised as Phocians, carrying an urn that they claim contains Orestes' ashes. Electra plunges deeper into despair, takes the urn, and laments over it at length. Orestes, visibly affected by the sight of his sister's suffering, reveals his identity to her. Electra's grief gives way to joy, and she is in the middle of celebrating when the Old Man emerges from within the palace. He chastises the two for their imprudence and indiscretion, saying that anyone could have overheard them. He urges immediate action in accordance with Apollo's oracle. As the Old Man ushers Orestes inside to kill Clytemnestra, Electra recognizes him as the faithful servant to whom she entrusted Orestes as a young boy to smuggle off to Phocia after Agamemnon's murder.

Electra remains outside, watching for Aegisthus so that he might not return unobserved. She listens excitedly to the sounds of Orestes killing Clytemnestra. Orestes, having successfully killed his mother, returns to Electra to tell her the news but hurries back inside as they see Aegisthus approaching. Aegisthus asks Electra to direct him to the Phocians who came with news of Orestes' death, and she points inside the house. Aegisthus demands that the doors and gates of the palace be opened so that the citizens can see what he believes to be

Orestes' corpse. Electra complies, and a shrouded corpse becomes visible, with Orestes and Pylades standing beside it in disguise. Orestes tells Aegisthus to uncover the corpse himself. As Aegisthus does so, he orders Orestes to call for Clytemnestra. As Aegisthus uncovers the body, he sees that it belongs to Clytemnestra herself.

Denying his victim permission to speak, Orestes denies Aegisthus permission to speak orders Aegisthus inside so that he might kill him in the exact spot where, years before, Aegisthus killed Agamemnon. Orestes, Aegisthus, and Electra enter the house, where Aegisthus will be killed in a manner supposedly so gruesome that it must be left to the audience's imagination.

ANALYSIS

Many scholars consider *Electra* to be Sophocles' best character drama due to the thoroughness of its examination of the morals and motives of Electra herself. Rather than follow Aeschylus in focusing on the moral issues of matricide and revenge, Sophocles plunges into the tormented soul of his tragic title character. He questions what kind of woman would want so keenly to kill her mother. Sophocles' Electra prevails and triumphs, rendering his play both a highly satisfactory revenge drama and an interesting study of the psychology of Electra herself.

The motives and psychology behind Electra's drive for revenge are indeed complex. In the Prologue, Electra suggests that her desire for revenge and her constant mourning are not so much self-willed and self-approved as they are forced upon her. She expresses a certain level of self-doubt that seems healthy and rational given the extreme nature of her desires and actions. Toward the end of the play, however, Electra's rationality and self-awareness disappear. She displays excessive enthusiasm at the prospect of a murder that some might consider morally repugnant. She delights in the sounds of her mother's cries as Orestes kills her and urges Orestes to strike Clytemnestra again. Electra baits Aegisthus as he returns home, feigning a humbleness and servitude that barely conceal her excitement at the murder she knows to be imminent.

Aegisthus himself shows a touch of humanity, for he worries not to offend the gods and offers to undo potentially offensive remarks. This human touch is similar to the one that Sophocles gives to Clytemnestra in her (albeit brief) grief and guilt over Orestes' death. Sophocles' effort to humanize the play's supposed villains and vilify the play's supposed heroine lend the ultimate revenge a degree of complexity.

THE TRACHINIAE

Written around 430 B.C., *The Trachiniae* opens as Deianeira, the forlorn wife of Heracles, fondly remembers how her husband saved her from Achelous, an oppressive river god who tried to force marriage upon her. After her rescue, Deianeira wedded Heracles and bore his children, including his son, Hyllus. Deianeira reports that the marriage has not been easy: ever since Heracles killed Iphitus, the family has been in exile. Heracles, meanwhile, has been fighting to free himself from his obligation to Queen Omphale, who has ordered him to complete a number of nearly impossible tasks.

Hyllus reports that he has heard a rumor that Heracles has freed himself from Queen Omphale and that he has begun a war against Euboea, the realm of Eurytus. Hyllus decides to set out in search of more news concerning his father's fate. Deianeira, however, remains anxious about Heracles' fate. She reveals that Heracles, when he left on his last adventure, wrote a will. He said that if he were still gone fifteen months after he left, then he was fated to die; but that if he survived that period, he would live a prosperous life afterward.

A messenger enters bearing good tidings: Lichas, a herald, has proclaimed that Heracles is alive and returning home. Lichas would have announced the news himself, the messenger says, but the Malian townsfolk have surrounded him and are besieging him with questions. Soon, however, Lichas enters, leading maidens whom Heracles has captured from Euboea. Lichas says that Heracles, after winning his freedom from Queen Omphale, went to look for Eurytus, who Heracles claimed was responsible for all his misfortune at the hands of the queen. According to the herald, Eurytus cast Heracles from his home, and Heracles, in anger, flung Eurytus's son Iphitus from a cliff. Zeus decided to punish Heracles for his wanton vengeance by enslaving him for a year. At the end of the year, Heracles returned to Euboea to kill Eurytus and capture his daughter, Iole. Iole is present in Lichas's company of maidens but refuses to answer Deianeira's questions.

When Lichas leads the captive maidens away, Deianeira starts to follow, but the messenger, who has been present all the while, detains her. He tells her that most reports contradict the herald's story: they say that Heracles toppled Eurytus not for revenge but for lust, and that he invented a pretext to fight Eurytus so that he could abduct Iole. When Lichas returns, Deianeira interrogates him, and he finally confirms the messenger's story and admits Heracles' adoration for Iole.

Although Deianeira concedes Iole's superior beauty, she also reveals a means of keeping Heracles' love for herself. Long ago, Heracles slew the centaur Nessus, who was ferrying Deianeira across a river. As Nessus lay dying, he made a gift of his blood to Heracles' wife, telling her that his blood would serve as a charm to prevent Heracles from ever loving any woman more than Deianeira.

Deianeira anoints a robe with the potion from Nessus and asks Lichas to deliver it to Heracles. Soon afterward, however, Deianeira emerges from the house in great agitation and recalls how a tuft a wool that was anointed with the blood disintegrated when exposed to sunlight. She fears that she may have accidentally sent Heracles to his doom by sending him the cloak. Hyllus enters and accuses his mother of trying to kill Heracles. Deianeira listens in shock as Hyllus recounts how Heracles donned the robe and soon entered a state of agonized frenzy. His company laid him on his ship and set sail for home, but it remained uncertain whether or not he would survive the voyage.

Deianeira, devastated by sorrow, retreats into her house. Soon enough, her nurse emerges with the news that Deianeira lay down on her husband's bed and stabbed herself in the heart. Heracles is carried in upon a table, writhing in pain and beseeching his son to kill him. Hyllus, unable to kill his father, reports the news of Deianeira's death. Heracles refuses to forgive his late wife until he learns of Nessus's part in the potion. Heracles realizes the fulfillment of a prophecy—that he would be killed by a creature already in Hades.

Heracles then persuades Hyllus to fulfill a filial oath. Although Hyllus initially hesitates, he gives Heracles his hand and promises to carry him to the peak of Mt. Oeta and prepare a funeral pyre for him. Hyllus refuses, however, to light the fire for his father. Heracles also requests that Hyllus marry Iole, to which Hyllus also reluctantly agrees.

PHILOCTETES

Odysseus and Neoptolemus, Achilles' son, stand on a lonely shore on the island of Lemnos. By command of the Greek commanders

Agamemnon and Menelaus, they undertake a search for Philoctetes, a once formidable hero who has degenerated into a wretched man ever since Odysseus stranded him on the island years before. The clever Odysseus recounts how he had to abandon Philoctetes on the island after the wretch suffered a serpent bite, leaving him in terrible pain and omitting a foul odor that terrified the Greek army and disrupted sacrifices. Philoctetes now haunts the island, carrying a bow and magical arrows. By order of the Greek commanders, Odysseus and Neoptolemus must convince Philoctetes to return with them to Troy.

Odysseus, wary that Philoctetes despises him for abandoning him, convinces Neoptolemus to go alone to find Philoctetes. Odysseus instructs Neoptolemus to pretend to hate Odysseus and the other Greek leaders in order to earn Philoctetes' trust. As Neoptolemus approaches, Philoctetes greets him warmly, relieved to be freed from his oppressive solitude. After learning that Neoptolemus is Achilles' son, Philoctetes begins to trust him and gives a long, woeful account of his mistreatment at the hands of the Greeks. Neoptolemus relates the recent news from Troy—victories, losses, leaders fallen—and recounts with feigned rage how Odysseus stole his father's divine armor from him.

As Neoptolemus pretends to prepare his departure for his native land, Scyros, Philoctetes beseeches him to save him from his solitude. The chorus too joins Philoctetes in his plea. Neoptolemus, of course, relents—the entire setup is all by Odysseus's design. Before Neoptolemus and Philoctetes can make their departure, a spy enters and relays to Neoptolemus some information about the Greeks: a fleet, lead by Phoenix, has set sail from Troy to fetch Neoptolemus back to the war. The spy also reveals what Neoptolemus already knows—that Odysseus has landed on Lemnos in search of Philoctetes and his magical arrows. The spy recounts the prophet Helenus's prediction that Troy will not fall until Philoctetes returns to the Greeks.

Upon hearing this news, Philoctetes grows agitated and wants to leave as quickly as possible to avoid Odysseus. Philoctetes collects his arrows, bow, and some herbs and is ready to depart. As the two make their way to the ship, however, Philoctetes is overcome by the terrible pain in his foot. Incapacitated, he hands his arrows to Neoptolemus while he nurses his wound.

As Philoctetes falls asleep, Neoptolemus's conscience troubles him. He considers stealing the arrows but realizes that, according to the prophecy, all would be in vain if Philoctetes did not accompany him. When Philoctetes awakes, he thanks Neoptolemus for his faithfulness. But the son of Achilles no longer can bear the burden of his deceit, so he confesses the truth to Philoctetes: by command of Agamemnon and Menelaus, he and Odysseus are on their way back to Troy.

Philoctetes, initially heartbroken and enraged by the deceit, forgives Neoptolemus when he realizes that the son of Achilles is not truly wicked but rather has been misguided and manipulated. When Odysseus arrives unexpectedly, Philoctetes flies into a frenzy of hatred and self-pity and is about to hurl himself upon the rocks when Neoptolemus and Odysseus seize him. Despite his pleas, they depart with his bow and arrows and leave him behind.

Neoptolemus, however, is unable to escape his conscience. He returns, with bow in hand and Odysseus berating him, to make amends with Philoctetes. This time, Philoctetes tries to kill Odysseus and stops only upon hearing the counsel of Neoptolemus, who argues that it would be best for everyone, including Philoctetes, if they all returned to Troy. Philoctetes is convinced only when Heracles suddenly appears from above, commanding Philoctetes to obey the will of the gods and return to Troy, where he will fight alongside Neoptolemus.

EURIPIDES

CONTEXT AND BACKGROUND

Euripides was born c. 485 B.C. at Phyla in Attica, probably of a good family. He made his home in Salamis, where he lived at the estate of his father and, according to some accounts, composed his works in a cave by the sea. Euripides also held a position in the lay priesthood of the cult of Zeus. Evidence in his own plays and other documents connects him with leading philosophical circles and thinkers of his day, including Protagoras and Socrates. Considered something of a loner, Euripides spent his entire life upon his estate, living with family. In 408 B.C., he left Athens to go north all the way to Macedonia; historians speculate that hostility to his intellectual beliefs and associations prompted him to leave his homeland so late in life. Euripides wrote his last play, *The Bacchae*, in Macedonia and was buried there upon his death in 406 B.C.

Euripides wrote for audiences in Athens and the surrounding Attica, and these geographical and historical limits lend his plays an intense, narrow focus. Euripides generally is considered the most tragic and least polite of the major dramatists, and his writings in some ways foreshadow the individualism of the coming Hellenistic age.

Although various accounts attribute ninety-two plays to Euripides, of which seventeen—more than any other classical playwright—survive, his standing as a dramatist is disputed, and was so during his lifetime. While Aristotle heralded Euripides as "the most tragic of poets," he also criticized Euripides' confused handling of plot and the less-than-heroic nature of his protagonists. The comic dramatist Aristophanes frequently mocked Euripides' fondness for wordplay and paradox. Euripides' role as a dramatic innovator, however, is unquestionable: the simplicity of his dialogue and its closeness to actual speech patterns paved the way for dramatic realism, while the emotional vacillations in many of his works created our understanding of melodrama.

Admired by Socrates and other philosophers, Euripides also distinguished himself as a free thinker. Criticisms of traditional religion and defenses of oppressed groups, especially women and slaves, permeate his plays with an explicitness unheard of before him. More than edifying pieces of art, works such as *The Bacchae, The Trojan Women, Iphigenia at Aulis, Alcetis,* and *Electra* became basic components of the Athenian citizen's political education.

ELECTRA

In *Electra* (413 B.C.), Euripides presents his version of the story of Agamemnon's cursed children. Upon returning from the Trojan War, Agamemnon was murdered by his wife, Clytemnestra, and her lover, Aegisthus. Euripides' play opens with a monologue by a peasant, who, at Aegisthus's command, is now the husband of Electra, Agamemnon's daughter. The peasant explains how, after the murder of Agamemnon, Aegisthus feared revenge from Agamemnon's children and their offspring. To protect himself from Agamemnon's son Orestes, who escaped to another country, Aegisthus set a price on Orestes' head.

The peasant goes on to recount how Aegisthus wanted to kill Electra as well. Although Electra was only an infant when her father was murdered, Aegisthus feared that she would grow up to bear a son who could challenge Aegisthus's claim to the throne. Clytemnestra, however, though able to justify the murder of her husband, could not accept the murder of her daughter as well. Shrewdly, Aegisthus instead arranged for Electra to marry a peasant: by this move, Electra's children would be of low birth and therefore unable to challenge Aegisthus. The peasant goes on to say that he understands Electra's position and has respected her maidenhood—he swears by the gods that Electra is not truly his wife.

Electra enters carrying a pail of water and bemoaning her sad fate. Although she subjects herself to the hard labor of a peasant, she makes it clear that her toil is not out of necessity—she does it to underscore to the gods the extent of Aegisthus's cruelty. Electra and her peasant husband depart to tend to their work.

Orestes enters with his companion, Pylades, and recounts how he has come from Apollo's shrine, where he steeled his determination to avenge his father's death by killing his mother and Aegisthus. After performing the appropriate rituals at his father's unmarked grave, Orestes has arrived at the town walls. He plans to make inquiries after his sister, for he has heard about her recent marriage. Orestes and Pylades catch a glimpse of Electra approaching but mistake her for a peasant. They retire to spy on her and learn if she can be trusted.

DRAMA

The chorus of Argive peasant women sings to Electra about an upcoming feast and sacrifice in honor of Hera. Electra confesses to them that her misery and low position put her in no mood for festivities. Electra reveals her identity to the eavesdropping Orestes as she reminds the chorus of Agamemnon's recent death and Aegisthus's subsequent cruelties.

Although Orestes is satisfied of the peasant maid's identity, he remains suspicious. The chorus and Electra break off their singing as the two strangers approach. Orestes and Pylades know that Electra will not recognize them but decide to keep their identities concealed nonetheless. Electra, alarmed at first, calms down when Orestes announces that he has news about her brother. He reveals that Orestes lives still, at which news Electra rejoices. She bristles as she recounts once more how Aegisthus forced her out of her home and wed her to a peasant, albeit a noble one. Orestes, his identity still concealed, asks whether Electra would help him kill Clytemnestra and Aegisthus. Electra responds with a resounding yes and implores the stranger to relay her message to Orestes and beg him to come avenge his father's death.

Not long after, Electra's husband returns, sees her conversing with the two strangers, and learns the reason for their visit. He is quick to invite them into his house and offer them whatever they need. Orestes, impressed with the peasant's innate nobility, remarks that there is no sure mark of a man's worth—suggesting that men be judged by their conversation and habits, not by their rank or wealth.

An old servant, one still loyal to Agamemnon and his children, arrives bearing provisions for the strangers. He says that on his way to the house, he stopped at Agamemnon's tomb, where he discovered evidence—bull's blood and a lock of hair—of a recent sacrifice. The hair, he adds, matches Electra's. The servant then grows excited that perhaps Orestes has returned in stealth to avenge his father's death. Electra discounts this theory and says that Orestes would never fear Aegisthus enough to make a secret of his return.

The old servant's curiosity is further piqued when he spies Orestes himself. Orestes, of course, recognizes the old servant immediately, for it was this servant who helped Orestes escape the clutches of Aegisthus. Much to Orestes' discomfort, the old servant begins to examine him closely. At last, the servant lets out praise to the gods and reveals Orestes' identity, pointing at a scar above the man's eye as proof.

With Orestes' identity known, Electra, Orestes, and the old servant immediately concoct a plan to kill Aegisthus and Clytemnestra. The old servant remembers that on his way to Electra's house he saw Aegisthus at the stables, attended by only his slaves, preparing a sacrifice for the nymphs. Because Aegisthus is practically alone at such moments, Orestes decides that would be a perfect time to strike. The three then devise a plan to kill Clytemnestra. They decide that the old servant will go with news that Electra has just given birth; Clytemnestra, though she has little love for Electra, will want to weep over her granddaughter's low birth. Electra plans to kill Clytemnestra when she approaches.

Later, Electra waits impatiently for news from Orestes. When a messenger finally arrives, she fears the worst. The messenger brings good news, however: he relates how Aegisthus, seeing the two strangers, invited Orestes and Pylades to his sacrifice. Orestes graciously accepted and helped Aegisthus slaughter calves for the nymphs. As Aegisthus examined the entrails of one calf, searching for portents of the future, Orestes snuck up from behind and struck him in the spine with an axe. When Aegisthus's servants took up their arms, Orestes revealed his identity, and the servants quickly sheathed their swords and bestowed the crown upon him.

Before Clytemnestra arrives at Electra's hut, an overwhelming sense of guilt strikes Orestes: how can he slay his mother, who birthed and suckled him? Electra chides him for his hesitation and reminds him that if he does not slay Clytemnestra, he will have failed in his duty. Orestes retires to the hut as Electra waits outside for their mother. When Clytemnestra finally arrives, Electra initiates an argument with her, berating her for casting her children out of her house, for her loyalty to Aegisthus, and for the murder of Agamemnon. Clytemnestra maintains that Agamemnon deserved to die for his treatment of their daughter Iphigenia, whom she offered as a sacrifice (see section on Euripides' *Iphigenia in Aulis*). When the argument finally reaches a stalemate, Electra leads Clytemnestra into her hut, where Orestes waits in ambush. The chorus laments the sad fates of Agamemnon's children as Clytemnestra's cries of distress issue from the house.

MEDEA

Medea (431 B.C.) tells the story of the tragic romance between Medea, daughter of Aeëtes, and her husband, Jason. Before the start of Euripides' play, Jason went in search of the famed Golden Fleece in the land of Colchis. In the midst of his quest, he met Medea, whose father, Aeëtes, stood guard over the Golden Fleece. Overcome by passion for Jason, Medea used black magic to trick her father and kill her brother in order to secure the Golden Fleece for Jason. Jason and Medea then fled together and stayed with Pelias, Jason's uncle. Medea again let loose her magic upon Pelias and his family, casting a spell on Pelias's sons to make them kill their father. Finally, Jason and Medea fled to Corinth, where they found refuge in the kingdom of Creon.

Medea opens near Creon's palace in Corinth, as Medea's nurse laments her mistress's lot in life: despite all that Medea has done to help Jason, he has fallen hopelessly in love and wedded another woman—Creon's daughter. More bad news arrives when the children's attendant announces that Creon, aware of Medea's dangerous reputation, plans to banish her and her children out of Corinth.

The chorus of Corinthian women makes a long, wailing lament of life, and then Medea enters the stage. She joins the chorus as they bemoan the hapless lot of women—sacrifices for their husbands, who become their tyrants; the shame of divorce; unrequited love; and general powerlessness. As Medea closes her misanthropic tirade, Creon enters and abruptly casts Medea out of his kingdom. He knows she is a witch and fears that she is planning some evil scheme against his children or his city. Medea protests that she hates Jason, not Creon, and that she would never consider inflicting harm upon the royal family. Creon, however, remains resolved in his decree—thereby adding himself to the list of Medea's enemies. After Creon exits, Medea, struggling to suppress her fury, considers the best way to kill all three: whether by poison, fire, or sword. The only idea that tempers her rage is the consideration of which country would receive her after committing such an atrocious crime.

Jason enters, chides Medea for her foolish treatment of Creon, and suggests that she could have averted exile by behaving better. Medea lashes out against Jason, reminding him of all the ways she helped him overcome adversity and rise to power. Jason, however, sees the story differently: trouble has followed him constantly ever since he met Medea. Moreover, the protection he has offered her is more than compensation for her magic favors. Jason goes on to offer justification for a marriage to Creon's daughter—it strengthens his political stature by allying him with Creon and offers the chance of more progeny.

DRAMA

After Jason exits, Aegeus, the king of Athens, passes through on his way home from visiting an oracle. Upon hearing of Medea's tribulations, he grants her request for shelter in Athens after her banishment from Corinth. Aegeus's only condition is that Medea must arrive in Athens on her own; he cannot take her there. He also promises never to banish her from his kingdom, upon pain of a cursed existence.

Aegeus makes his departure, and Medea reveals to the chorus her plans for revenge. She will send a messenger to ask for an interview with Jason and then will beg Jason to let the children stay in Corinth. To support her cause, she will send the children with gifts—a wool robe and a garland made of gold—to Jason's new bride. But the robe and garland will be smeared with a deadly poison that will kill Jason's bride, along with everyone who touches her, as soon as she dons her new clothes. Medea chills even her own blood as she continues to describe her sinister plan: after she has killed the bride, she will murder her own children (whom she had by Jason), to inflict pain on Jason and to keep him from having heirs.

Jason arrives, and Medea's scheme works perfectly, as Jason foolishly pities Medea's premeditated tears and agrees to let the children stay. Medea offers the poisoned clothes as tokens of thanks and sends her unknowing sons to deliver the gifts. Soon, a messenger arrives with news that both Creon and his daughter have died. Jason's bride, overjoyed with the children's gifts, quickly donned the new clothes. But her joy quickly turned to terror as the poison consumed her body. To Medea's delight, the messenger reports how her flesh fell away as her blood mixed with fire. Creon, hearing his daughter's cries, rushed into the room and stumbled over the corpse. He fell upon her, weeping for his daughter, but soon found he could no longer rise, for some magic had fastened to his daughter's dead body. Soon, the poison consumed him too, and father and daughter lay dead on the floor of her bedroom.

After Medea completes this fateful act, she wavers in her determination to kill her children. She steels herself, however, and enters the house where her children wait. The chorus listens passively to the helpless cries of Medea's sons, who call out for the protection of the gods as Medea menaces them with a sword. Jason comes rushing in only to learn from the chorus that he is too late, for Medea has already killed his children. Medea suddenly rises above the house, holding the reins of a chariot drawn by dragons. She taunts Jason from her high and safe position, refusing to let him bury his dead sons. She predicts a lonely and inglorious death for him beneath the wreckage of his ship, the *Argo*.

HIPPOLYTUS

Hippolytus, first performed in 428 B.C., tells the story of Aphrodite's revenge on Hippolytus, the illegitimate son of Theseus and a worshipper of Artemis, goddess of the hunt. The play opens before the altar of Artemis at Theseus's palace. Aphrodite, alone on the stage, says that Hippolytus scorns her and calls her the vilest of deities. For this offense, she promises revenge. Aphrodite already has willed Phaedra, Theseus's wife and Hippolytus's stepmother, to fall in love with her stepson. Aphrodite says that Theseus, upon discovering Phaedra's love for Hippolytus, will fly into rage, invoke the three wishes that the god Poseidon has granted him, and command Poseidon to kill Hippolytus.

Aphrodite vanishes as Hippolytus and his attendants return from a hunt. Hippolytus prays at the altar of Artemis. The leader of his attendants, concerned that his master gives Artemis too much of his devotion, advises him to remember the goddess Aphrodite. Scorning the weakness inherent in love and marriage, Hippolytus dismisses his attendant's advice, asserts his devotion to Artemis, and exits to attend to his horses.

A chorus of women enters, brooding over the frenzy that has gripped their mistress, Phaedra. The ranting Phaedra speaks wildly of the hunt and of driving steeds across the desert. After recovering her senses, she is still too overcome with shame to confess her passion for Hippolytus. When the nurse mentions Hippolytus, Phaedra's attention is piqued, and the nurse becomes suspicious. Finally, the nurse's questions elicit the truth. Outraged, the nurse expresses her shock that Phaedra could become the toy of cruel Aphrodite. The chorus joins her in lamenting the hopelessness of the situation.

Phaedra decides to follow the course she has been on ever since she was smitten by love—to remain silent on the matter and suffer in silence even if it kills her. The nurse, fearing Phaedra's self-destruction, suggests that a better course would be to confess her love to Hippolytus. This idea repulses Phaedra, so the nurse suggests using a charm to battle Aphrodite's power. While Phaedra remains skeptical that a charm would work, the nurse insists and exits to find a charm within the house.

DRAMA

Moments later, cries from the within the house signal that something has gone wrong. Hippolytus bursts forth, followed closely by Phaedra's nurse, who pleads for his forgiveness: she has confessed Phaedra's love to Hippolytus, but only after binding Hippolytus to an oath of secrecy. Nonetheless, Hippolytus is disgusted. He announces his plans to leave home until his father returns from abroad and says he will return only to see how Phaedra and her nurse face Theseus.

Phaedra, destroyed by shame, berates her nurse for her carelessness and banishes her from her presence. The chorus asks Phaedra what action she will take now that her shame has been exposed, and Phaedra announces her plan for suicide. She exits the stage and enters the house. Moments later, cries pour from the house, and the nurse brings news of Phaedra's death—she has hanged herself in shame.

Meanwhile, Theseus and his retinue have entered the stage unnoticed. Theseus questions the chorus about the uproar in the palace. The palace doors swing open, revealing Phaedra's corpse. In Phaedra's hand, Theseus notices a note accusing Hippolytus of trying to destroy their marriage. Without hesitation, Theseus calls upon Poseidon to slay his son, despite the chorus's warnings to retract his request.

When Hippolytus enters, Theseus flies into a rage and banishes his son from his kingdom. Hippolytus, unaware of the note his father has found, tries in vain to defend himself. Bound as he is to his oath of silence, however, he cannot reveal Phaedra's confession to his father. Instead, Hippolytus calls upon the gods to be witness to his innocence or to strike him down where he stands. Theseus discounts this move by insisting that his son must be a conjurer or magician to avoid the wrath of the gods. Finally, with neither son nor father relenting, Theseus retires to the palace, and Hippolytus departs with his entourage.

Soon, one of Hippolytus's messengers arrives and relates the news of a terrible fatal accident Hippolytus has had near the coast. The chorus laments, but Theseus, his curiosity piqued, asks for the details of his son's death. The messenger relates that Hippolytus had just entered his chariot when he implored the gods to strike him down if he was in the wrong. At that moment, the group heard something like an earthquake, and a giant wave grew from the ocean and towered over their heads. An enormous bull emerged from the wave, and Hippolytus and his horses took flight. Despite

Hippolytus's attempts to rein his horses in, they would not be controlled and, in their flight from the watery bull, led Hippolytus and his chariot into the rocks.

As Theseus rejoices, Artemis appears above him and chides him for his foolishness and impiety. She tells him that he judged his son unjustly and sentenced him for a crime he did not commit. Artemis tells Theseus how Phaedra was cruelly struck by love's arrow and wrote the incriminating note in a blind fit of passion. The dying Hippolytus is brought in, and Artemis reminds him that he too committed sins of pride. Before dying, Hippolytus forgives his father of his sins and begs him to have only legitimate children in the future.

ANDROMACHE

First produced at a rural festival outside Athens sometime between 428 and 424 B.C., scholars do not consider *Andromache* one of Euripides' finest plays. Although the play ostensibly concerns the plight of Andromache, the play ultimately loses its focus and shifts its attention to Orestes, who acts as both hero and villain.

The play opens before the temple of Thetis, near the palace of Achilles, sometime after the Trojan War. Andromache, Hector's widow, recounts that after her husband's death, she became a spoil of war and was awarded to Achilles' son, Neoptolemus. Neoptolemus has brought Andromache to his home in Thessaly, where her life again is in danger. Andromache's relationship with Neoptolemus has filled Hermione, daughter of Menelaus and wife of Neoptolemus, with jealous hatred. Hermione believes that Andromache, in an effort to force her way into Neoptolemus's heart, has cast a spell to make Hermione barren.

Hermione, meanwhile, has enlisted her father, Menelaus, to help her unburden herself of the troublesome Andromache. After Andromache's prologue, the maid warns Andromache that Menelaus has gone to kill her only son, Molossus, whom Andromache has sent away out of fear for his life. The absence of Neoptolemus—who has gone to Delphi to seek forgiveness for his sins at Troy—leaves Andromache without an ally. She finally decides to send her maid for Peleus, the aging father of Achilles.

After the maid departs and the chorus recounts Andromache's many troubles, Hermione and her entourage make their entrance. Hermione commands Andromache to lower herself before her, accuses her of being descended from a savage race, and scorns her for sharing a bed with the son of the man who slew Hector. Without avail, Andromache tries to demonstrate her utter lack of power. She lectures Hermione on the qualities of a good wife—how can Hermione expect her husband to revere her when she alienates Neoptolemus by esteeming Menelaus more than Achilles? Andromache's words incite an bitter argument that culminates when Hermione threatens to burn down the temple of Thetis in order to flush Andromache outside, where Hermione can kill her with impunity. Andromache reminds Hermione that the gods would surely punish her for burning down a temple.

Menelaus enters the temple next, dragging the young Molossus by the arm. The boy will die, he says, if Andromache does not quit the temple of Thetis. Andromache tries to show Menelaus the pettiness of the argument, but Menelaus stands firm in his resolve to avenge whatever insult his daughter has received. Menelaus makes a final offer: either he kills Andromache or kills Molossus. Andromache relents, but to her horror, Menelaus's henchmen seize both her and her son. Menelaus decides that Hermione will decide the boy's fate.

As Molossus clings to her arms, Andromache laments her tragic end, and Menelaus repeatedly ignores her pleas for her life. Suddenly, when all hope seems lost, old Peleus arrives and condemns Menelaus for his evil scheming. Menelaus challenges Peleus, but the old man is quick to lambaste his adversary with reminders of Helen's unfaithfulness. The old king stands firm over his right to Andromache. Menelaus finally retreats, exiting under the pretext of having a war to fight in another town.

Hermione, destroyed by Andromache's victory, decides to kill herself. She escapes the watchful eyes of her servants and enters the stage bearing a sword, but her nurse wrests it away from her. Hermione bewails her failed attempts on Andromache's life. Certain that Neoptolemus will never forgive her, Hermione contemplates various ways to kill herself and considers self-imposed exile.

After the nurse departs, Orestes, Agamemnon's son, enters looking for his cousin Hermione. He quickly learns about her current hardships and offers to return her to Menelaus. Hermione worries that Peleus will interfere, but Orestes, confident that he can rightfully claim Hermione as his bride, insists that there will be no problems. They depart, and Peleus arrives again, seeking the veracity of a rumor about Hermione's flight. The leader of the chorus confirms the rumor and adds that Orestes intends to slay Neoptolemus.

Before Peleus has time to act, news arrives that Orestes has slain Neoptolemus. According to the messenger, Orestes incited a mob with a rumor that Neoptolemus planned to steal treasures from Apollo's temple at Delphi. As Achilles' son made his prayers for forgiveness, a group of armed men assailed him and stabbed him in the back. Rousing himself, Neoptolemus bravely fought off the band of misinformed vigilantes. But a voice from within the temple—no doubt the voice of Orestes—continued to provoke the mob, and Neoptolemus eventually succumbed.

Thetis, Achilles' mother and Peleus's former wife, appears and tries to console Peleus. She foretells that Andromache will marry the prophet Helenus and that Molossus will produce noble progeny. Still filled with tenderness for Peleus, Thetis promises to make him a deity and reunite him with Achilles.

THE TROJAN WOMEN

The Trojan Women, which was presented as part of a tetralogy in 415 B.C., recounts the hardships the women of Troy face when their husbands go off to the Trojan War. At the time of the play's production, Athens and Sparta still were locked in a fierce struggle for power. By 415 B.C., the tide had turned against Athens, as a plague had decimated the city, the Athenian armies were ragged and hungry, and the great Athenian statesman Pericles had died. From the picture of war that Euripides paints in *The Trojan Women*, we can infer that the Athenians had grown tired of war. Those who watched the play—the citizens free from the armed service who had no part in the war—undoubtedly could sympathize with the plight of the Trojan women, who were left behind to suffer the consequences of their country's war.

Euripides' play opens on the fields of Troy, near Agamemnon's tent, only a few days after the fall of Troy. As the god Poseidon delivers the prologue, he surveys the destruction around him and recounts how he and Apollo built the city. He tells how the Greeks finally broke through the walls by hiding in a large wooden horse offered as a gift to the Trojans. After the Trojans accepted the gift, the Greeks burst forth from the horse and took the city by storm. Poseidon defers to Athena and Hera, who waged divine battle against Troy, and then turns to Hecuba, widow of Priam, who sleeps on the floor with the other prizes of war. Hecuba's husband and all of her sons have died at the hands of the Greeks. Her only remaining children are her daughters Polyxena and Cassandra, who is a raving priestess of Apollo. By the end of the day, only one of the queen's daughters will remain.

Athena enters and sides with Poseidon in his rage against the Achaeans. She explains that she will punish the Greeks because of Ajax's cruelty toward Cassandra, the cursed daughter of Priam. Ajax, in a moment of sin, raped Cassandra in the temple of Athena—a great sacrilege. Poseidon agrees to help Athena torment the Achaeans.

Hecuba awakens and mourns the fall of her city. The other captured women around her, who also will become concubines, lament their fate as they join to form the chorus. Hecuba begs the other women not to wake Cassandra, the cursed prophetess whose prophecies, while true, are never believed. Soon, the Greek herald Talthybius enters, bearing the news that the women have been dreading: the Greek leaders have cast lots for ownership of the Trojan women. Talthybius announces that Cassandra has gone to Agamemnon; her sister, Polyxena, to the dead Achilles; their mother, Hecuba, to Odysseus; and Hector's widow, Andromache, to Achilles' son, Neoptolemus.

Talthybius then attempts to deliver Cassandra to Agamemnon, but the priestess wanders from her hut, oblivious to the world and the herald who is trying to stop her. Overcome with the powers of Apollo, she foresees Agamemnon's death and the continued blight on the house of Atreus. Cassandra predicts, one by one, the travails of the Greek heroes: long and dangerous journeys home await them, and many of them will die before embracing their wives and seeing their children again. Cassandra compares the lot of the Greeks with the relatively better lot of the Trojan heroes—at least they had the privilege of dying at home, giving their families the chance to bury them properly. As soldiers lead Cassandra away, she foresees the endless wanderings of Odysseus and grieves over her new role as Agamemnon's concubine.

A chariot arrives bearing Andromache and her young son, Astyanax. The two widows mourn their fates as Andromache recounts the fate of Polyxena: she was sacrificed over Achilles' grave. Hecuba suddenly understands the meaning of the edict—that Polyxena would keep watch over Achilles' tomb—and crumbles at the news of her daughter's death. Now, left alone, she foresees the bitterness of her life with Odysseus. The herald interrupts and compounds her suffering: Odysseus has ordered that Astyanax, Andromache's son, shall be thrown from the tower to prevent the boy from seeking revenge on the Greeks when he comes of age.

After the chorus laments Andromache's sad state of affairs, Menelaus arrives and searches for his wife, Helen—the woman whose kidnapping ignited the Trojan War in the first place. Hecuba detains Menelaus with a plea that he kill Helen for bringing about the destruction of Troy. When the beautiful Helen appears, Menelaus informs her that all the Greek commanders have refused her. Helen defends herself by blaming the gods for her bad decisions and for her loyalty to Paris, prince of Troy. She claims that she desperately tried to escape after Paris's death. Hecuba, however, silences Helen and says that a good wife would have killed herself. Hecuba again begs Menelaus to kill the traitor Helen, but Menelaus is overwhelmed by Helen's beauty, turns on Hecuba, and chooses to take Helen home.

Just before the herald Talthybius returns to lead the women to their ships, Hecuba has a happy vision of the future. Nonetheless, she attempts to throw herself into a fire as she is pushed toward Odysseus's soldiers. The soldiers prevent Hecuba's self-immolation and herd her and the rest of the Trojan women offstage.

ALCESTIS

Alcestis, first performed at a festival in 438 B.C., is one of Euripides' earliest plays. It recounts Apollo's exile from Olympus to serve Admetus, the king of Thessaly; Queen Alcestis's willingness to die for her husband; and Heracles' rescue of Alcestis from the clutches of Thanatos, the god of death.

The play begins outside Admetus's palace while Queen Alcestis lies inside, on the brink of death. Apollo enters and recounts how he slew the Cyclopes, incurring the wrath of Zeus, who cast him from Olympus. As part of his exile, Apollo was condemned to serve a mortal for one year. He fell into the service of Admetus, a just man who is now fated to die. Apollo, filled with gratitude for his gentle master, tricks the Fates into agreeing to allow Admetus to go on living if someone else volunteers himself or herself to die instead. Admetus's wife, Alcestis, has agreed to die for her husband, and the day of her fated death has arrived.

As Apollo exits, he encounters Thanatos, the god of death, and argues for Alcestis's life. Thanatos, however, refuses to relinquish his hold on Admetus's wife, saying that the death of the young yields a greater reward than the death of the elderly. At the end of their argument, Apollo predicts the arrival of Heracles, whom he promises will tear Alcestis from Thanatos's grip.

The chorus notes the absence of moans coming from inside the palace. One of the queen's servants enters to report on her lady's condition, which grows worse by the minute. Soon, Admetus escorts his ailing wife outside into the sun for the last time. Together, the couple mourns Alcestis's imminent departure into Hades. With the last of her strength, Alcestis asks Admetus never to remarry, and Admetus agrees as a token of honor to his generous wife. He vows to spend the rest of his life mourning the loss of his noble bride. With this, the last of Alcestis's strength departs, and she falls to the ground dead.

Admetus and his children bear Alcestis's body back into the palace. During their absence, Heracles arrives, having been commanded by Eurystheus to bridle four wild, rage-filled horses to the chariot of Diomedes. When Admetus appears, Heracles sees his mourning garb and realizes that someone has died. The king elaborates only a little, saying only that a woman, a visitor, has died. Seeing Admetus's obvious grief, Heracles tries to excuse his poorly timed entrance and take his leave. The king, however, insists that the heroic visitor stay for the funeral.

The funeral begins. Admetus's father, Pheres, gives a eulogy and offers gifts, but Admetus, unwilling to forgive his elderly father for refusing to die in his place, rejects the gifts. The old man, in turn, accuses his son of cowardliness for letting a woman die in his place. An argument ensues, despite the chorus leader's cries for calm. Admetus ends the funeral by cursing his parents.

Heracles, in the meantime, has gotten drunk. After the rest of the company clears away, he stumbles up to a servant and demands to know the cause of everyone's grief. The servant finally reveals the queen's death, the news of which quickly sobers Heracles. Embarrassed by the scene he has caused and the awkwardness of his visit, Heracles promises to retrieve Alcestis from Hades. With this promise, Heracles rushes to the underworld.

Soon afterward, Heracles reappears and finds the chorus and Admetus at Alcestis's grave. Admetus bemoans his lonesome life as a widower and admits that he has compounded his isolation by turning against his father. As the chorus muses on the inscrutable nature of fate, Heracles leads a veiled woman toward the tomb. After apologizing for his insensitive behavior, he offers the woman as a gift. Admetus, however, remembers his promise of fidelity to his departed wife and is quick to reject Heracles' offer. Looking closer, however, he notices that the veiled woman vaguely resembles his departed wife. Heracles continues to insist that Admetus take the woman. Admetus finally accepts, and upon lifting her veil, discovers his dear Alcestis.

THE HERACLEIDAE

Euripides probably wrote *The Heracleidae* (430 B.C.) in the midst of the Peloponnesian War. The play brims with nationalism, emphasizing the nobility, piety, and charity of Athens. It is no accident that the play is set in Marathon, where the outnumbered Greek armies, led by Athens, repelled the charge of Xerxes' enormous Persian forces.

The play begins before the altar of Zeus at Marathon. Heracles' old friend Iolus recounts how he; Heracles' mother, Alcmena; and Heracles' children fled from Argos and the rage of King Eurystheus (see section on Sophocles' *The Trachiniae*). Before Heracles died, he engaged in a battle with Eurystheus and, in a rage, cast Eurystheus's son from a cliff. For this transgression, Eurystheus continues to persecute Heracles' friends and family even after his death. Iolus, Alcmena, and the children now find themselves in Marathon, suppliants at the altar of Zeus.

Their prayers are interrupted when Copreus, a messenger of Eurystheus, rushes in and seizes the children. As the chorus cries foul, the messenger commands Iolus back to Argos to receive his punishment—death by stoning—for his part in Heracles' crimes. The chorus berates the messenger for acting with such cruelty at the sacred altar of Zeus.

Theseus's sons Demophon and Acamas come to the rescue and reproach Copreus for his ignoble actions. Unmoved by Copreus's accusations against Iolus, Demophon questions old Iolus himself. Iolus explains that he and Alcmena are companions of Heracles and that Alcmena is a distant relative of Theseus and his family. Iolus begs Demophon to rescue them from the vengeance of Eurystheus. Demophon, invoking Athens's reputation as a pillar of democracy and a defender of the weak, promises his help.

Copreus makes vague threats to attack and then exits. Demophon goes to prepare his citizens for battle. After leading the children to the safety of his palace, Demophon returns to Zeus's altar looking troubled. For reasons he cannot understand, the oracle has commanded him to sacrifice a maiden to the goddess Demeter. Iolus offers to give himself up to Eurystheus to end the trouble, but Demophon refuses. Just as the situation appears insoluble, Macaria, one of Heracles' daughters, offers herself as a sacrifice. Despite Iolus's insistence that the daughters draw lots for the sacrifice, Macaria remains resolute in her desire to give herself up to Demeter.

Hyllus, Heracles' son, arrives with news of his army close behind him. Iolus and Alcmena rejoice at the large force coming to protect them. Iolus, excited over the prospect of battle, demands that his servant go to the temple to retrieve his armor. Drunk on his fond memories of fighting alongside Heracles, the old man ignores everyone's pleas that he stay away from the battle.

The battle begins, and soon, Iolus's servant returns to Alcmena with a message of victory: as the battle began, Hyllus challenged Eurystheus to a duel in order to end the battle with minimal bloodshed. Eurystheus, however, declined, realizing he would be no match for the son of Heracles. The messenger then recounts how Iolus, against all expectation, stormed the battlefield, leaving a wake of slain Argives behind him. When the Argives seemed to gain the upper hand, Heracles transformed Iolus into a youth again, allowing him to capture Eurystheus.

While Alcmena celebrates her son Heracles' rank among the deities, she remains unsatisfied with the outcome of the battle: Iolus, she thinks, should have slain Eurystheus. She holds out hope that the Athenians will execute their hostage, but the Athenian leaders rule against it. As a herald leads Eurystheus onstage, the king apologizes for his wrongs. He defends his persecution of Heracles' children by asserting the danger they pose to his kingdom: as grown men, they undoubtedly would finish the wars their father began.

Eurystheus's shallow defense only increases Alcmena's rage, and she openly wishes for his death. Eurystheus warns her, however, that if she kills him, she will be killing a relative—a crime that incurs a curse. But these threats are not enough to stop Alcmena: she commands the servants to kill Eurystheus and cast his corpse to the dogs.

HECUBA

First produced around 424 B.C., *Hecuba*, like *The Trojan Women*, tells the story of the Trojan queen after the death of her husband, King Priam, and the fall of Troy. Written during the Peloponnesian

War, it is another of Euripides' dramas that questions the merits of war by depicting the plight of its survivors.

The play opens before Agamemnon's tent in Thrace, where the Greeks hold Hecuba and other Trojan women captive. The ghost of Polydorus, the youngest son of Priam and Hecuba, recounts how his father, fearing for his city and his children, sent him secretly to Polymestor, king of Thrace, with gold to provide for his brothers and sisters after the fall of Troy. When Polymestor learned of Hector's death and the inevitable fall of Troy, he killed Polydorus for his gold and cast his body into the sea. For three days, Polydorus's ghost lingers over the Trojan captives, but they remain unaware that he has died, for his body has not been found. Polydorus foresees that his corpse will wash up on shore the same day as his sister's sacrifice and bemoans the fact that his mother will have to face two tragedies on the same day.

Achilles' ghost, meanwhile, visits the Greeks and commands them to sacrifice Polyxena, daughter of Hecuba and Priam, over his grave as a tribute to his valor. Hecuba staggers from Agamemnon's tent as she learns of Achilles' demand. The chorus of Trojan women recounts how Agamemnon tried to dissuade Achilles from his request, but Odysseus, longing to return home, argued in favor of Achilles and succeeded in convincing the captains to carry out the sacrifice.

Although Polyxena is shocked to learn her fate, she mourns more for the double loss her mother will suffer. Soon, Odysseus comes to claim Polyxena. In a final effort to save her daughter, Hecuba reminds Odysseus how she once spared his life when he snuck into Troy disguised as a beggar. She begs Odysseus to offer Helen as a sacrifice in Polyxena's place. But Odysseus, with his coldhearted logic, denies Hecuba's request.

Hecuba then begs Odysseus to sacrifice her, not Polyxena—she is the mother of Paris, the one who stole Helen from Menelaus, and therefore is more guilty than her daughter. Once again, however, Odysseus remains steadfast in his obedience to Achilles' ghost. Mother and daughter bid each other a final, tender farewell. Polyxena promises to bear her mother's love to her brother, Hector, who already dwells in the underworld.

Soon, Talthybius, Agamemnon's messenger, arrives with news of Polyxena's death. As gently as he can, he describes how Neoptolemus, Achilles' son, poured the sacrificial wine and prepared his victim. Polyxena, maintaining her nobility to the end, calmly asked

Neoptolemus to remove her bonds. Her request granted, she bared her breast, fell to her knees, and awaited the thrust of the sword. Upon completing the sacrifice, Neoptolemus commended the dead Polyxena for her incredible courage. The responsibility of burying Polyxena now falls upon Hecuba.

As Hecuba and the chorus busy themselves making the preparations for the funeral, a procession enters, lead by Hecuba's handmaid, bearing a veiled corpse. When Hecuba lifts the veil, she sees the body of her son, Polydorus, which finally has been discovered. As Hecuba relates to the chorus her vision of Polydorus's death, Agamemnon enters to ask why Hecuba has delayed attending to the burial of her daughter. Surprised to find the body of the dead Trojan youth before him, Agamemnon displays a rare pity and respect for Hecuba.

Seizing upon Agamemnon's pity, Hecuba begs him to avenge Polydorus's death by killing Polymestor. For not only did Polymestor kill Polydorus, the last son of Priam, he also cast him into the ocean, thereby keeping Polydorus's soul from reaching the underworld. Fearing the reproach of the other Greek captains, Agamemnon hesitates to help the Trojan queen. However, since the gods continue to deny wind for the Argive fleet, Agamemnon allows Hecuba to seek revenge on her own. Hecuba sends a servant to summon Polymestor and his children to Troy.

Polymestor makes a show of great sympathy when he and his children arrive. When Hecuba asks about her son, Polymestor promises her that Polydorus and his gold are well-protected in Thrace. Hecuba says that she has hidden more gold in her tent and asks Polymestor and his children to enter. They do so, and cries of pain soon resound from the tent. As Polymestor stumbles out, blood and tears pour from his now blinded eyes. In his agony, Polymestor recounts the horrors that awaited his family within Hecuba's tent. While Hecuba pretended to fetch the gold, some among the chorus of Trojan women slaughtered Polymestor's children with daggers, while others stabbed out his eyes with their brooches.

Desperate to strike back against the old Trojan queen, Polymestor appeals to Agamemnon for help, arguing that he helped Agamemnon by protecting him from future threats from Polydorus. Hecuba counters this argument, saying that if Polymestor were truly a friend of Greece, he would have shared his gold with the Greek forces to help in the war against Troy. Agamemnon agrees with Hecuba and deems Polymestor worthy of Hecuba's vengeance.

In his humiliation, Polymestor recounts the words of a Thracian prophet who foresaw that Hecuba would leap from a mast on her way to Greece and that Cassandra would die with Agamemnon at Clytemnestra's hands.

THE SUPPLIANTS

The Suppliants (c. 422 B.C.) recounts the final part of the Theban legend presented in Sophocles' Oedipus plays—the burial of the seven warriors who attacked Thebes in an effort to topple the ruler Creon. Euripides wrote the play during the Peloponnesian War, when a series of serious Athenian defeats, along with a plague in Athens and the death of the great statesman Pericles, caused Athenian morale to tumble. Some scholars postulate that these gloomy times inspired Euripides to compose a play that would remind the Athenians of their country's nobility, strength, and bravery.

The Suppliants opens in Eleusis at the temple of Demeter. Theseus's widowed mother, Aethra, sits by the altar with the grief-stricken Adrastus, the defeated king of Argos and leader of the seven who challenged Thebes. Aethra begs Demeter to take pity on her family and the families of the other mothers at the altar, all of whose sons lie still unburied at the gates of Thebes. Adrastus begs Aethra to persuade Theseus, king of Athens, to fight against Thebes for the warriors' right to proper burials.

When Theseus arrives, Adrastus pleads him to use his powerful voice to convince Thebes to release the bodies of his comrades. Theseus demands an explanation for the war. Adrastus replies that he sought to help his outcast sons-in-law, Polyneices and Tydeus: Oedipus cursed Polyneices after Jocasta's death, while Tydeus murdered one of his relatives. Although Theseus pities Adrastus's guilt for instigating the foolish war, he declines to intervene on the king's behalf. Overhearing Theseus's rejection, Aethra upbraids her son and reminds him that generosity toward the unprotected is what has made Athens great. Moved by his mother's sentiments, Theseus promises to present Adrastus's case before the assembly and implore Creon to hand over the bodies of the warriors.

Just as Theseus begins to dictate a message for Creon, a Theban messenger arrives seeking the tyrant who governs Athens. Theseus, proud of his democracy, replies that Athens has no tyrant. The messenger boasts of Thebes while belittling Athens. Theseus refuses to let this foreigner insult his city, saying that Athens stands strong as a pillar of democracy and that, through democracy, Athens fosters a race of truly happy men. According to the messenger, Creon demands that the Athenians expel Adrastus and rebuff the suppliants' foolish pleas for justice. Moreover, Creon threatens to attack Athens should it refuse his request. Theseus, however, is quick to deny Creon province over Athens, stressing also that actions against the dead go beyond the limits of just revenge. Theseus promises to see the dead buried, through the use of force if necessary. With this, the messenger departs, and Theseus and his army set out for Thebes.

A messenger arrives at Demeter's altar with news of the Athenian victory over Thebes. Before the battle began, the messenger says, Theseus called to Creon from a hill overlooking Thebes. The Theban king did not answer Theseus's final offer to avoid war by burying the bodies. Theseus and his army fought their way to the city gates, where the Athenian king, wary of too much bloodshed, stopped his own advance and sought his enemy's surrender.

Theseus enters with his troops bearing seven corpses. Upon viewing the corpses, Adrastus gives a eulogy for each fallen warrior. Their bodies are taken to the funeral pyre as the women sing songs of remorse. Evadne, the widow of Capaneus, emerges on a rock above the pyre, heartbroken by her husband's death. Despite the pleas from her father, Isphis, Evadne hurls herself into the flames.

Theseus makes a gift of the fallen seven's bones to their bereaved mothers and reminds them to honor Athens. Athena appears and orders Adrastus to swear an oath never to take up arms against Athens, or Argos will be destroyed.

HERACLES

Written sometime between 421 and 417 B.C., Euripides' retelling of the Heracles myth opens before the altar of Zeus at Heracles' palace in Thebes. Heracles' father, Amphitryon, accompanied by Megara, Heracles' wife, and her sons, recounts Heracles' family history. Amphitryon notes Megara's distant kinship with Creon, the king of Thebes, and the tryst between Alcmena, Heracles' mother, and Zeus, which produced the mighty Heracles.

As Amphitryon continues his brief history, he recounts how the duplicitous Lycus murdered Creon and usurped the Theban throne while Heracles was away fulfilling superhuman missions for Eurystheus. Filled with hatred for Heracles and his family, Lycus has forced Megara, Amphitryon, and the children to seek refuge at the temple of Zeus. The group anxiously awaits Heracles' return, but no one has seen him since he ventured into the underworld to capture Cerberus, the three-headed hound guarding Hades.

Lycus, filled with pride and drunk on his own power, enters and mercilessly taunts Heracles' family, calling Heracles a coward and his family fools for respecting him. Only a coward, Lycus says, fights with a bow rather than in close battle with a sword. Moreover, only a fool like Amphitryon would embrace a child that was not his but rather was fathered through an adulterous tryst. Amphitryon rages against Lycus's insults but admits that his old age prevents him from offering resistance. Lycus then threatens to burn Heracles' family alive as they hide at Zeus's altar. Amphitryon, too old to make a defense, begs that he and Megara be killed before the children. Megara adds another request: that the children be allowed to don robes proper for execution.

As the family members anxiously await their execution, Heracles makes his entrance, finally having completed the twelve superhuman tasks assigned to him by Hera, Zeus's bitter, jealous wife. Megara quickly explains to Heracles how Lycus has usurped the throne of Thebes. Amphitryon advises his son to control his rage, for Lycus has friends who back his power. Before Heracles departs, he explains his tardiness: he captured the hound Cerberus but was detained in Hades to release his dear friend, Theseus, king of Athens. Heracles, Megara, and their children exit into the palace.

Lycus enters, demanding that Amphitryon tell him the location of his victims. Amphitryon follows Lycus into the palace, where Heracles lies in ambush. Soon, the cries of the dying Lycus come from offstage. Iris, accompanied by the spirit of madness, enters and reminds the chorus that Lycus was a relative of Heracles. Despite the hero's legendary status, he cannot be excused for the murder of a relative. His punishment, as decreed by Hera, will be a fit of murder-inducing madness.

A messenger enters and reports terrible news from within the palace: madness gripped Heracles just as he and Megara were preparing a sacrifice to Zeus. Heracles raged through the house in a frenzy, hallucinating that he was about to kill his old enemy, Eurystheus. Mistaking his wife and children for enemies, he savagely struck them down with his bow and club. He then turned his rage against Amphitryon, who had helplessly stood by and watched his son murder his grandchildren. Just as Heracles raised his club to smite his

DRAMA

father, a messenger from Athena struck him with a rock, knocking him to the ground.

When Heracles awakes, he has no recollection of his terrible crime, and he supposes that he has entered Hades a second time. As Amphitryon tests Heracles' memory and gradually reveals the atrocity to his son, Heracles longs for his death. He pleads for Amphitryon's forgiveness and bemoans the plight of man and the wrath of Hera, who has forever persecuted Heracles.

Soon, Theseus arrives to help Heracles in his fight against Lycus. Amphitryon explains the recent catastrophe, but Theseus feels nothing but compassion for his old friend. He offers Heracles asylum and great fortunes in Athens, but Heracles accepts only the offer of refuge. Heracles bids Amphitryon a final farewell and departs with Theseus for his new home.

ION

While the exact date of *Ion*'s production remains uncertain, Euripides probably wrote it toward the end of his career, around 410 B.C. Set at sunrise before the temple of Apollo in Delphi, the story that Euripides presents is a rare one: the childless marriage of Creusa, queen of Athens, to Xuthus, an Achaean.

As *Ion* opens, Hermes, messenger of the gods, reveals both the background and the outcome of the story. We learn that the god Apollo seduced Creusa, the daughter of Erechtheus, and that Creusa later gave birth to his illegitimate son. To keep the shameful son a secret from her father, the king of Athens, Creusa abandoned the boy in the wilderness. On Apollo's orders, however, Hermes went to rescue the boy and preserve him at Apollo's shrine, where Apollo's priestess reared and cared for him. When the child grew up, he became caretaker of the temple of Apollo. Meanwhile, Creusa married Xuthus, a war hero. At the opening of the play, Xuthus has arrived at Delphi to seek advice from the Oracle about his childless marriage. According to Hermes, although Xuthus arrives in Delphi childless, he will leave with a son—Apollo's own illegitimate boy, Ion.

Inside the temple, Ion cares for the treasures and praises Apollo. The chorus of handmaidens introduces Ion to Creusa, who appears on the verge of tears. Ion presses her to reveal her family history, so she recounts how her father slaughtered her sisters when she was born. Poseidon then struck down her father. Ion continues asking questions, so Creusa tells him about her husband, Xuthus, and their childless marriage. She, in turn, questions him about his family, and he confesses that he does not know the identity of his parents and has no way of finding them.

As Creusa begins to feel comfortable with Ion, she confesses that she has a question for the Oracle also. Creusa claims to have a friend who was seduced and impregnated by Apollo. Her "friend" abandoned the baby boy, but when she returned to learn of his fate, the cradle and the baby were gone, although there were no signs that an animal had dragged the child away. Tortured by the unknown fate of her child, Creusa's "friend" seeks advice from the Oracle.

In due time, Xuthus approaches with news from the Oracle: he and Creusa will have a child before returning home. He and his wife depart to pray to Apollo. Later, as Ion tends to his duties around the temple, Xuthus rushes in and greets Ion with a warm embrace. Ion, confused and angry that Xuthus, in his excitement, has trampled on the ceremonial wreaths, threatens to kill him on the spot. But Xuthus, still glowing with happiness, explains that he must be Ion's father: in answer to his pleas to Apollo, Xuthus learned that the first person he met after leaving the temple would be his son. That person is Ion.

Ion concurs with Xuthus's interpretation of the Oracle's message and, resolving to search for his mother's identity, questions Xuthus about his love affairs. Xuthus insists that he has been with no other women since his marriage to Creusa. He does confess that he did have several love affairs during his youth, about the time Ion might have been conceived.

Creusa, meanwhile, asks her aged tutor to consult the Oracle to determine whether Creusa ever will bear children. He returns to inform Creusa that the Oracle says that Xuthus has received a grown son from Apollo. The tutor tries to turn Creusa against her husband, painting Xuthus as a foreigner interested only in her kingdom now that he has a foundling son. The tutor insists that Creusa strike against her husband and Ion before they can return to Athens and usurp her kingdom.

Creusa, no longer able to contain her sordid past, confesses to the tutor and the chorus her tryst with Apollo. The tutor urges her to take immediate action and kill her husband and Ion. Deciding that a nearby grotto would be a good setting for the murder, Creusa entrusts the tutor with a vial of lethal gorgon's blood with which to poison the father and son.

Soon afterward, an attendant warns Creusa that the Delphian leaders plan to stone her for the attempted murder of her husband and son. While Ion and Xuthus were making a sacrifice to Dionysus, Ion sensed trouble and poured all the wine onto the ground. A flock of birds drank from the wine and died immediately, alerting Ion to a plot against his life. The tutor, caught in his deception, admitted everything and placed the blame squarely on Creusa. Creusa now faces a death sentence.

Ion comes to seize Creusa, who has taken refuge near the altar of Apollo. After an argument over the nature of the crime, Ion loses patience and seizes Creusa. At that moment, however, Apollo's priestess rushes in and shows Ion the basket in which he was brought to the temple as a baby, thus giving the boy some clue to his mother's identity. Inside the basket, Ion finds the embroidered clothing in which Creusa swaddled him. Creusa staggers as she recognizes the embroidered gorgon on the baby clothes.

Overcome with joy, Ion embraces his mother, and she assures him that he is the child of Apollo. Athena appears to defend Apollo's actions and foretell Ion's future greatness.

IPHIGENIA IN TAURIS

In this variation on the traditional story of Iphigenia, Euripides gives this tale of Agamemnon's sacrificial daughter a happier ending. Whereas in most versions of this myth Agamemnon sacrifices his daughter on his way to Troy, Euripides here employs a *deus ex machina* to save Iphigenia from her fate. The reason for this decision remains unclear. In any case, Euripides' twist on the story of Iphigenia forces us to reconsider the end of his later play Iphigenia at Aulis (see below).

Composed around 414 B.C., *Iphigenia in Tauris* opens at the temple in Tauris, an area on the Black Sea. Iphigenia, daughter of Agamemnon, stands alone in the temple, a blood-covered altar in prominent view. She explains how her father, at the behest of the seer Calchas, attempted to sacrifice her in Aulis in order to rescue Helen. Iphigenia blames Odysseus for luring her from her mother and recounts how Artemis saved her from her doom at the last moment, putting a deer in her place just as the knife was about to strike. Now, Iphigenia serves Artemis in Tauris, where she prepares foreigners to be sacrificed.

Iphigenia recounts a dream from the night before, in which she was at home in her bed at Argos when thunder sent her fleeing from the house as the royal palace crumbled. The one pillar that remained standing transformed into her brother, Orestes. Iphigenia confesses her fear that her dream symbolizes the death of Orestes.

Meanwhile, Orestes and his companion Pylades arrive in Tauris. We learn that the Furies hounded Orestes after he killed his mother to avenge his father's murder. To atone for his sin, Apollo sent Orestes to Tauris to steal the statue of Artemis. Fearing capture and daunted by their task, Orestes and Pylades withdraw to cover and wait for nightfall.

As Iphigenia and the temple maidens perform the rituals of Artemis, a herdsman enters and announces the arrival of a Greek ship that has evaded the deadly rocks off the shores of Tauris. The crew—two young men—has been captured. The herdsman relates the name of one of the men, Pylades, but regrets not to know the name of the other. He also recounts how the unknown captive battled fiercely against his captors until his sword was knocked from his hand. Iphigenia, her curiosity piqued by the news of the Greeks, sends the herdsman for the captives.

As the captives are led in and prepared for sacrifice, Iphigenia questions them about their identities and families. Orestes refuses to name himself and reveals only the name of his home: Mycenae, in Argos. Their talk eventually turns to the murdered Agamemnon and to Clytemnestra, his deceptive wife, whom Orestes killed. Orestes, still concealing his identity, insists that Agamemnon's son still is alive, at which point Iphigenia denounces her dream as a lie and offers to free Orestes if he will take a letter back to Argos. Orestes, however, refuses to leave Pylades behind and insists that if only one may live, it should be Pylades. Iphigenia agrees.

To ensure the safety of the contents of the letter, Iphigenia relates its subject to Pylades. As Orestes listens in, he recognizes his sister. She also recognizes him and begs him to make an escape. Before he and Pylades plan their escape, Orestes relates the tragic news to his sister: Clytemnestra killed Agamemnon, Orestes in turn killed Clytemnestra, Menelaus usurped the throne of Mycenae from Orestes, and the Furies now chase Orestes as punishment for killing his mother. Orestes begs Iphigenia to help him steal the statue to appease the Furies, but his sister fears that Thaos, the king of Tauris, will kill her if she is caught.

Orestes proposes that they kill Thaos. Iphigenia has a better plan: she will denounce Orestes for murdering their mother. She decides that they must cleanse the altar in the temple, so Orestes, Pylades, and the statue of Artemis need to be bathed in seawater. When Thaos arrives, Iphigenia puts her plan in motion by stopping him at the door and telling him of Orestes' sin. She commands the Taurians to stay indoors until the temple is cleansed. Iphigenia instructs the king to purify the temple while she leads the victims and the statue toward the sea. Soon afterward, soldiers rush back to the temple with news that Iphigenia, Orestes, and Pylades have escaped.

Upon hearing the news, Thaos bursts into a rage and sets out after the group. Athena stops him, defends Orestes' theft of the statue, and secures a safe escape for Iphigenia and the captives.

HELENA

Helena (c. 412 B.C.) develops a precedent set by the earlier Greek poet Stesichorus, who, legend has it, was struck blind after writing poems that disparaged Helen, the wife of Menelaus. As the myth goes, it was only after Stesichorus retracted his insults against Helen in another poem, Palinode, that his eyesight returned. In Palinode, Stesichorus unburdens Helen of blame for the Trojan War by having the gods send her to Egypt, far from the scene of the battle, and putting a phantom Helen in her place at Troy—a twist that Euripides uses as the starting point of Helena.

Like many of Euripides' extant plays, *Helena* cannot necessarily be called a tragedy. Whereas many of the Greek dramas, like Sophocles' *Oedipus Rex*, create tragedy through one character's recognition of something or someone, Euripides frequently uses recognition to avoid tragedy. Such is the case in *Helena*, in which Helen's recognition of the forlorn Menelaus saves the separated couple from a bleak existence. Also in *Helena*, Euripides employs *deus ex machina*—a dramatic effect Greek playwrights frequently used to achieve miraculous turns of events within plays. But rather than use *deus ex machina* at the end of the play, where it typically appears (as, for example, in *Iphigenia at Aulis*), Euripides uses it before the play begins—by transporting Helen to the safety of Egypt, away from the dangers of the Trojan War.

Helena opens near the palace of the king of Egypt, by the tomb of Proteus, where Helen prays for protection. She relates the source of her sadness, telling how Aphrodite awarded her to Paris, a prince of Troy, after he deemed Aphrodite more beautiful than Hera and Athena. When Zeus complicated the events by inciting the Trojan War, he removed Helen to Egypt to save her from ill repute and allow her to wait for Menelaus in safety. However, Helen has found only trouble in Egypt: the good king Proteus has died, ceding his throne to Theoclymenus, who presses Helen for her hand in marriage.

Teucer, a Greek warrior and brother of Ajax, enters and is surprised to find Helen. He openly expresses his wish that he could kill her for all the trouble she has caused. Soon, however, her beauty softens him, and he describes the fall of Troy. Teucer says that Menelaus supposedly left Troy with his wife but never reached home. Most presume he is dead. Teucer also tells Helen about the death of her mother, Leda, who hanged herself out of shame for her daughter. Furthermore, her brothers, Castor and Pollux, have ascended to heaven after killing themselves out of shame for their sister. Teucer departs after exchanging kind words with Helen. When Teucer takes his leave, however, the leader of the chorus urges Helen not to believe Teucer's account of Menelaus's death. She advises Helen to consult the seer Theonoe to learn the truth about Menelaus's fate.

After Helen and the chorus retire into the palace, the beleaguered Menelaus enters and recounts his adventures after the fall of Troy. After the gods shipwrecked Menelaus in a strange land, he set out in search of help, leaving the woman he thought to be Helen—actually the phantom Helen—in a cave with his men. Since then, Menelaus has wandered desperately in search of safety, food, and water. When the woman at the palace gates learns his nationality, she urges him to leave quickly. Before Menelaus leaves, however, he discovers that a woman named Helen abides in the palace.

Helen enters after learning from the seer that Menelaus still lives. In her excitement, she fails to notice the wretch at the city gates. Menelaus, however, detains her, and they recognize each other. Even though Helen explains the gods' plot to give him a phantom Helen, Menelaus still believes that the true Helen is hiding with his men in a cave. Soon, a messenger to Menelaus arrives with strange news: the phantom Helen in the cave has disappeared into the air. Menelaus and Helen embrace in happiness.

Her curiosity piqued, Helen begs Menelaus for news from Troy. Menelaus relates how Troy fell after ten years of fighting. Since then, seven years have passed, during which he has wandered helplessly, searching for his home. Helen entreats Menelaus to hide his identity to avoid the vengeance of Theoclymenus, the king of Egypt. Menelaus leaves the arrangements to Helen. She entreats him to ally himself with the seer Theonoe, who already knows that Menelaus has come. Theonoe also reveals that the gods are again at war. The once-jealous Hera now champions Helen's cause, while Aphrodite fears that Helen will return to Greece and reveal the bribery that occurred in the beauty contest that ignited the Trojan War in the first place.

Helen earns a pledge of secrecy from Theonoe. The reunited Helen and Menelaus plan their escape and decide to maintain that Menelaus has died at sea: Helen will request a ship so that she can scatter funeral offerings into the water, while Menelaus will pretend to be the only survivor of Menelaus's crew. Helen retires to the palace to cut her hair and don funeral attire to convince Theoclymenus of her grief.

King Theoclymenus returns from the hunt prepared to kill the strange Greek—actually Menelaus—but sees Helen in her robes of mourning. Her eyes brimming with feigned tears, Helen invents a painful tale about Menelaus's shipwreck and requests that she be allowed to perform the funeral rituals before she marries Theoclymenus. Menelaus enters, playing the part of the forlorn soldier, and describes in detail how only a wife, mother, or child may carry out funeral rituals for a deceased person. Theoclymenus promises to let Helen pay her respects to the allegedly dead Menelaus. Helen and Menelaus set out for the fake funeral.

Not long after, a messenger arrives at the palace with news of Helen's escape. Other "survivors" joined Helen and Menelaus at the shore as suspicion grew among the Egyptian guards. When safely out to sea, the messenger says, the Greeks assailed the Egyptian crew. Theoclymenus vows to punish Helen for her treachery, but Helen's brothers appear from above and calm his anger. They predict that after her death, Helen will join the ranks of the gods, and Menelaus will gain admittance to the blessed Elysian Fields.

THE PHOENICIAN WOMEN

The Phoenician Women, presented to Athenian audiences around 409 B.C., depicts the entire myth of Oedipus in one play. As the play opens before the royal palace in Thebes, Jocasta, wife of King Oedipus, details the events that have already taken place. She begins with the story of her marriage to her first husband, Laius. Even after the Oracle at Delphi warned him that his son would spell doom for his family, Laius impregnated Jocasta during a moment of inebriated carelessness.

Fearing his own infant, Laius ordered a group of shepherds to expose the child to the elements on Mt. Cithaeron, impaling the babe's ankles with metal spikes and naming him Oedipus, or "swollen foot." Several servants of King Polybus, however, rescued the infant and brought him to Polybus, who took in Oedipus as one of his own. Later in life, however, the boy Oedipus began to question his identity and journeyed to the temple of Apollo for answers. By coincidence, Laius made the same journey at the same time, hoping to learn the fate of his abandoned child. The two met on the road, Laius commanded Oedipus to yield, an argument ensued, and Oedipus killed Laius, unaware of his identity.

Then, a monster called the Sphinx inflicted a plague upon Thebes. Creon tendered his sister, Jocasta, as a reward to whomever could solve the Sphinx's riddle. Oedipus solved the puzzle, married Jocasta, and ascended to the throne of Thebes. Unaware that her husband was also her biological son, Jocasta unwittingly committed incest with Oedipus and gave birth to two sons, Polyneices and Eteocles, and two daughters, Antigone and Ismene. After discovering his heinous crimes, Oedipus put out his own eyes. (Although most versions of the story maintain that Jocasta hanged herself, Euripides has her live on.) Oedipus continued to dwell inside the Theban palace, consumed by an uncontrollable rage. In the ensuing confusion, Eteocles seized the Theban throne and banished his brother, Polyneices.

As the action of *The Phoenician Women* begins, Polyneices and his six fellow warriors approach the gates of Thebes, for the banished Polyneices has decided to claim his share of his father's inheritance. When Jocasta hears of his approach, she tries to negotiate a truce between the brothers. Polyneices, however, enters the palace. A chorus of Phoenician women who have traveled from Tyre to the temple of Apollo demands an explanation for the battle.

Jocasta appears and greets Polyneices. Pleading with her sons, she convinces them to discuss the rightful fate of Thebes. Eteocles maintains that he never can abdicate the throne if Polyneices and his fellow warriors are menacing the city. Polyneices counters, declaring that he agreed to leave the city for one year and has now returned to take his throne. The negotiations break down as the brothers trade insults. They exit, reasserting their hatred and vowing murderous revenge.

As Polyneices leaves to attend to his army, Creon and Eteocles discuss strategy. They decide to counter Polyneices' seven-pronged attack with seven warriors, one at each of the seven gates of Thebes. Eteocles senses his own death in the battle ahead. His foresight sharpened by his sense of doom, Eteocles places Jocasta in Creon's care and consents to the marriage of Creon's son, Haemon, to Antigone.

The blind prophet Tiresias further darkens the picture of Thebes' future by predicting a tragic end to war—death for both of Oedipus's sons. After many demands, Tiresias reveals the rest of the prophecy: war can be averted, but only if Creon sacrifices his son, Menoeceus. Creon begs Tiresias to keep the second half of the prophecy secret. Tiresias, however, declares that the curse over Thebes will never be lifted without the sacrifice.

Despite the prophet's prediction, Creon proves unable to carry out the sacrifice and sends his son abroad instead. Nonetheless, after taking leave of his father, the boy contrives to sacrifice himself in order to save the city. A messenger arrives and announces to Jocasta that Menoeceus has killed himself. The messenger also describes the beginning of the battle and mentions that Eteocles and Polyneices still live. Zeus, it seems, showed his favoritism toward the Thebans when he slew Capaneus, an Argive leader, with a thunderbolt. Yet the news is not all good: the messenger reveals also that Eteocles challenged his brother to a duel in order to end the fighting. Jocasta and Antigone rush to stop them.

Creon enters, searching for Jocasta and bearing the body of his dead son, Menoeceus. A messenger arrives with terrible news: the sons of Oedipus are dead. Both men traded wounds until they met their deaths. Polyneices fell first, but as Eteocles lorded over him, preparing to desecrate his brother's body, he dropped his guard and was struck in the chest. As Polyneices died, he lamented his war against his brother and begged to be buried in Thebes. Furthermore, Jocasta, in a frenzy of grief, picked up her son's sword and plunged it into her chest.

Antigone arrives bearing the corpses of her family members. At Oedipus's request, Antigone retells the painful story of their deaths. Here, Creon takes charge, declaring that Haemon is the new king of Thebes and that Oedipus is to be exiled from the city before he can bring more destruction to it. Creon continues, declaring that Polyneices, being a traitor, shall lie unburied outside the city limits.

Antigone argues against this decree and, in protest, abandons her marriage to Haemon. Before Oedipus departs for exile, he recalls the prediction of an oracle who said he would die in Colonus after a life of banishment. Antigone promises to entomb her brother.

ORESTES

Euripides continued his exploration of the fall of the house of Atreus with another play, *Orestes* (408 B.C.), concerning the destruction of the cursed family. The play opens before the palace of Argos, six days after Orestes and his sister, Electra, conspired to kill their mother, Clytemnestra, and her lover, Aegisthus, for the murder of their father, Agamemnon. As Electra speaks the prologue, she dwells painfully upon her family's tortured history. She recalls Tantalus, her great-great-grandfather, a favorite of the gods until he betrayed their secrets to the mortals. Since then, he has passed a tormented afterlife in Hades. Electra then remembers Atreus, her grandfather, who feasted upon his brother's children. Atreus fathered Agamemnon and Menelaus—the latter murdered by his wife, the former cursed in his marriage to Helen. Now Clytemnestra lies dead. Electra acknowledges her role in the murders and defends Orestes, who carried out the crimes, by blaming Apollo for dubious guidance.

Electra tells how the gods have driven Orestes insane. Since slaying his mother, he has neither bathed nor eaten. Plagued by madness and fever, he sleeps only in rare moments of lucidity. Meanwhile, Orestes and Electra have been ostracized from the city while the council members decide whether to kill them by stoning or decapitation. Electra's hopes rest on the arrival of Menelaus, her uncle, from Troy. Menelaus's wife, Helen, has taken refuge in the palace, hiding to avoid blame for the Trojan War.

As Helen enters, she coolly comforts Electra and asks about Orestes. Clearly insensitive to the siblings' plight, Helen asks a favor from Electra: she begs Electra to take a sacrificial offering to Clytemnestra's tomb, being too afraid herself to face the hatred of the citizens. Electra, who has no interest in such a task, proposes that Hermione, Helen's daughter, pour the libations instead. As Helen departs, Electra quietly confesses her disdain for her aunt.

Orestes wakes from his deep slumber and questions his sister about his madness. She tells him the events of the past days and relates that Menelaus has landed in Nauplia. Orestes takes comfort in this fact before the Furies and his frenzy again return.

Menelaus arrives, saddened to learn of Agamemnon's death. Orestes warmly greets his uncle, as Menelaus demands to know the symptoms of his nephew's madness. Orestes explains that three raging shadows besieged his mind as he watched his mother burn upon her funeral pyre. Since then, constrained by his madness and by armed guards, he has been unable to wash his mother's blood off his hands.

Tyndareus, Orestes' grandfather, arrives, berates Orestes for his foul sin. Tyndareus laments the tragedy that has gripped his house and wishes that Agamemnon had banished Clytemnestra with his last breath in order to avoid the terrible chain of events that has followed. Tyndareus then sets out for the village to advise against clemency for Orestes and Electra. Orestes defends himself by citing the duplicitous alliance that Clytemnestra formed with her lover, Aegisthus. Unable to sway his grandfather, Orestes turns to Menelaus, and his arguments have an effect. Menelaus follows Tyndareus into town, hoping to bring some sympathy to the debate over Orestes' and Electra's punishments.

Orestes' friend and accomplice, Pylades, expresses his concern that the deliberations are going against the murderous siblings. Orestes voices his hatred of Menelaus, whom he considers a traitor and a coward, and of his spiteful, unsympathetic grandfather. Pylades sympathizes with Orestes, for his own father, Strophius, cast him from home for his role in the murders. Pylades decides that the best course of action would be to lead Orestes through town so that everyone may see his pitiable state.

A messenger arrives and tells Electra about Orestes' trip into town. He recounts how he heard Talthybius, an old veteran, urging capital punishment. Diomedes, another old soldier, considered exile a more reasonable punishment. Talthybius, anxious to see the end of Electra and Orestes, pressed his case on a foreigner, who called out for death by stoning. Then, a laborer offered his opinion: Orestes should be awarded the throne of Argos for avenging Agamemnon and ridding the land of the treacherous Clytemnestra and Aegisthus. The laborer accused Aegisthus of supreme cowardice and said that any man who seduces the wife of man at war deserves the same fate. Orestes took this moment to defend himself, reminding the crowd that his actions cleansed the land of two murderers. But his defense fell upon deaf ears, and Orestes tottered home weeping, with suicide the only option.

When Orestes returns, Electra begs him to help her take her own life, but Orestes cannot bear the idea of taking the life of yet another family member. He announces that Menelaus has abandoned them in favor of his ambition to win the throne of Argos for himself. Desperate and driven to rage, Pylades and Orestes begin to plot against Menelaus, thinking that perhaps they should kill Helen. Electra has a better idea: they should kill Helen and intercept Hermione on her way back from Clytemnestra's tomb. As Hermione enters, Helen's screams are audible from within the palace. To ease Hermione's concern, Electra claims that the screams are Orestes', begging Helen's defense from the Argive laws. Hermione pities her cousins and agrees to plead their case to Menelaus. She enters the palaces and cries out as Orestes and Pylades take her captive.

A eunuch arrives with news from within the palace and recounts how Orestes and Pylades manipulated Helen. Orestes asked her to take a seat at Pelops's ceremonial altar so that he could make a request of her. Meanwhile, Pylades locked the guards in other rooms. Orestes and Pylades assailed Helen with their swords and were ready to slay her just as Hermione entered. When Orestes and Pylades turned their eyes toward Hermione, Helen vanished.

When Menelaus hears the news of his wife's death, Orestes and Pylades appear on the roof of the palace with Hermione as a hostage. They threaten to kill the captive and set fire to the palace. When Menelaus refuses to back down, Electra obeys Orestes and torches the building. As the flames scale the walls of the palace and Menelaus cries out desperately for help, the god Apollo appears above with Helen. Helen, Apollo says, is ready to be deified, so Menelaus must find another wife. Apollo sends Orestes to Ephesus for a year, and then on to Athens, where he will be tried for his crimes. Furthermore, Apollo decrees that Pylades must marry Electra and that Orestes must marry Hermione. Apollo assumes the blame for the crimes and makes Orestes king of Argos.

THE BACCHAE

SUMMARY

The Bacchae presents the story of Dionysus, the god of wine, prophecy, religious ecstasy, and fertility. The play focuses on Dionysus's return to his birthplace, Thebes, and his quest to clear his mother's name and punish the insolent city-state for refusing to allow people to worship him.

The prologue provides the background to Dionysus's return by telling the story of his mother, Semele, who once was a princess in the royal Theban house of Cadmus. Semele had an affair with Zeus, the king of the gods, and became pregnant. As revenge, Zeus's jealous wife, Hera, tricked Semele into asking Zeus to appear in his divine form. Zeus, too powerful for a mortal to behold, emerged from the sky as a bolt of lightning and burned Semele to a cinder. He managed, however, to rescue his unborn son, Dionysus, and stitched the baby into his thigh. Semele's family maligned her name and rejected the young god Dionysus by claiming that Semele was struck by lightning for lying about Zeus and that her child, the product of an illicit human affair, died with her.

The action of the play begins with Dionysus's return to Thebes years later. He arrives in town disguised as a Lydian stranger, accompanied by a band of bacchants (revelers), to punish the Theban royal family for their treatment of his mother and their refusal to offer him sacrifices. During Dionysus's absence, Semele's father, Cadmus, handed the kingdom over to his proud grandson Pentheus. It was Pentheus's decision not to allow people to worship Dionysus in Thebes. Dionysus tells the audience that, when he arrived in Thebes, he drove Semele's sisters mad, prompting them to flee to Mt. Cithaeron to worship him and perform his rites on the mountainside.

Pentheus, doubtful that the women's insanity stems from divine causes, sees their drunken cavorting as an illicit attempt to escape the mores and legal codes that regulate Theban society. Despite the opinions of Tiresias, the prophet, and Cadmus, the founder of Thebes, Pentheus sees Dionysian rituals as a danger. He orders his soldiers to arrest the Lydian stranger and his maenads (reveling women), whom he sees as the root of the troubles. Deviously, Dionysus submits to the arrest and goes to Pentheus with the others.

In the first of three encounters, Dionysus begins the long process of trapping Pentheus and leading him to his death. Although Pentheus orders his androgynous prisoner to be chained, bound, and tortured, no one is able to do so. When Pentheus tries to tie Dionysus, he ties only a bull; when Pentheus plunges a knife into Dionysus, the blade passes through shadow. Suddenly, an earthquake shakes the palace, a fire starts, and Pentheus is left weak and puzzled.

After destroying the palace, Dionysus tries to persuade Pentheus to abandon his destructive path, but Pentheus refuses to relent. A cowherd arrives and describes his sighting of the maddened women of Cadmus. The cowherd says that he saw the women resting blissfully in the forest and feasting on milk, honey, and wine that sprang from the ground. They played music, suckled wild animals, and sang and danced with joy. When they saw the cowherd, however, they flew into a murderous rage and chased after him. The cowherd escaped, but the maenads—including Pentheus's mother, Agaue—captured the cattle and tore them apart with their bare hands.

The messenger's marvelous, frightening tale excites and intrigues Pentheus. Dionysus takes note of Pentheus's interest and offers him a chance to see the maenads for himself, undetected. Pentheus, on the verge of launching a military expedition to arrest the women, suddenly cannot resist the opportunity to see the forbidden. He agrees to do all Dionysus suggests, including dressing himself in a wig and long skirts.

Once in the woods, Pentheus cannot see the bacchants from the ground, so he says he wants to mount a tree for a better vantage. Dionysus miraculously bends a tall fir tree, puts Pentheus on top, and gently straightens the tree again. The maenads see Pentheus at once, and Dionysus orders them to attack. With rolling eyes and frenzied cries, the women bring Pentheus down and drag him to the ground. As Pentheus falls, he reaches out for his mother's face and pleads with her to recognize him. But Agaue, driven mad by Dionysus, proceeds to rip her son to death.

At the palace, the chorus is exultant and sings the praise of Dionysus. Agaue returns home with Pentheus's head in her hands. She is still deluded and boasts to all about the young lions she hunted and beheaded. Old Cadmus, who knows what has happened, sadly approaches his daughter and draws her mind back to the palace, her family, and finally, what she is holding in her hands. Agaue begins to weep. Cadmus remarks that Dionysus has punished the family rightly but excessively. In the end, Dionysus finally appears in his true form to the city. He banishes Agaue from Thebes and ordains that Cadmus and his wife will turn into snakes, destined to invade Greek lands with a horde of barbarians.

ANALYSIS

The Bacchae was not performed during Euripides' lifetime but rather reached the amphitheater only after his death. The play won

DRAMA

first prize at the annual contest in which it was performed—ironically, this prize had eluded Euripides all his life. Scholars consider *The Bacchae* one of the finest of Euripides' works, in the same class as Aeschylus's *Agamemnon* and Sophocles' *Oedipus Rex*.

Euripides is interested not only in the nature of Dionysus but in the nature of religious belief itself, so he provides a number of arguments both for and against worshipping the god. In Scene I, the two old men articulate the wrong reasons for taking up new forms of religion: self-preservation and fear. Pentheus, while he rejects the worship of Dionysus, also displays the most extreme and violent form of the same tendency—self-preservation, upholding the family name and rigid rationality, which in itself is a form of madness. Pentheus's understanding of the Dionysian religion is superficial, no deeper than the crude, schoolboy-fantasy level.

In the end, it is Pentheus's own greed and inability to resist the lure of the forbidden that traps him. These details suggest that he is not merely a Dionysian scapegoat but actually responsible for his own fate. When Dionysus arches the tall fir tree and releases it slowly, he displays both his supernatural powers and also his self-control and patience. Once Pentheus falls to the ground, he reaches out to stroke his mother's cheek and begs her not to kill him, and it is only at this last moment that Pentheus understands the full extent of Dionysus's powers. The god's control over human minds proves stronger than even the most fundamental bond between a mother and a son. Pentheus's death feels tragic only at the very end, when he seems repentant and acknowledges his errors. However, Pentheus's mother, Agaue, is the play's most sympathetic character.

IPHIGENIA AT AULIS

Iphigenia at Aulis (c. 410 B.C.) dramatizes the plight of Agamemnon's daughter, Iphigenia, when her father decides to sacrifice her in order to please the gods. Set on the sea coast of Aulis, the play opens as Agamemnon, looking troubled, walks in front of his tent, accompanied by an old attendant. The worried Agamemnon complains about the gravity of his high position in life. He explains to his attendant that his wife, Clytemnestra, is a sister of the beautiful Helen, who had so many lustful suitors that they threatened to kill each other for her hand. To solve the problem, Helen's father, Tyndareus, forced the suitors to pledge an oath: if Helen were ever kidnapped after her marriage, all the suitors would form an alliance and wage war upon the kidnapper.

After Menelaus won Helen's hand in marriage, Agamemnon says, Helen was kidnapped by Paris, prince of Troy. Her former suitors honored their oath, formed a fleet in the bay of Aulis, and got ready to depart for Troy. As the gods would have it, however, the wind remained completely calm, and the ships were unable to sail to Troy. The perplexed Greeks consulted the prophet Calchas, who declared that the sails would be filled and the Greeks would be victorious—but only if Agamemnon sacrificed his daughter, Iphigenia.

Agamemnon sent for Iphigenia and lied to his wife, Clytemnestra, saying that Iphigenia was being summoned to marry Achilles. Now, however, Agamemnon says that he has recanted and that he plans to send orders for Iphigenia to remain at Argos, although he does not explain why. Having finished his story, Agamemnon orders his attendant to intercept Iphigenia on the road to Aulis and return her to her home.

Soon after, Menelaus chases the old attendant from the stage, having seized Agamemnon's letter to Iphigenia. Upon reading it, he discovers Agamemnon's plot to save his daughter. Menelaus reminds Agamemnon, his brother, of his former desire to lead the Greek army and make his name legendary. When Calchas first handed down his prophecy, Agamemnon readily agreed to sacrifice Iphigenia for the Greek army, but now, according to Menelaus, he has turned cowardly.

A messenger enters and announces the arrival of Clytemnestra, Iphigenia, and the infant Orestes. Sadness overwhelms Agamemnon as he sends the messenger away. Menelaus, too, confesses his pain over the situation, telling his brother to spare Iphigenia: to kill her in order to regain Helen, he says, would be an exchange of excellence for evil. Agamemnon confesses his fear that news of the prophecy will spread and that the armies will call for Iphigenia's death. Furthermore, Agamemnon believes that Odysseus will certainly kill him if he does not comply.

Clytemnestra and Iphigenia enter, and Iphigenia immediately notices her father's sadness. Agamemnon tells his daughter that soon they will be separated for a long time. She asks if she may go with him on his ship to Troy, and he responds that soon she will be making a trip alone. After answering his wife's questions about the marriage to Achilles and the wedding plans, Agamemnon insists that Clytemnestra return immediately to Argos. She refuses, however, for she wants to help with the arrangements for the wedding.

Later, Achilles arrives in Agamemnon's tent to say that the troops should be sent home if they will not be moving soon. Clytemnestra approaches Achilles, offering congratulations and words of assurance regarding what she thinks is his imminent wedding to Iphigenia. Achilles, who has never met Clytemnestra before and does not know who she is, insists that he has no knowledge of a wedding or a bride.

As Clytemnestra takes her humiliated leave of Achilles, an old servant stops her and reveals the plan to sacrifice Iphigenia. He also divulges that Agamemnon tried to keep Iphigenia away from Aulis by sending a letter but that Menelaus had intercepted it.

Clytemnestra begs Achilles to protect Iphigenia from her father, but Achilles directs her to beg for Iphigenia's life before he can take action. Clytemnestra agrees and sets off in search of Agamemnon. When Agamemnon enters, he asks Clytemnestra to call Iphigenia, who enters holding young Orestes in her arms. Clytemnestra seizes the moment to challenge her husband directly, demanding to know if he intends to kill their daughter. Agamemnon, realizing he has been betrayed, is consumed with rage.

A fierce argument ensues, during which Clytemnestra declares she married Agamemnon against her will after he killed her first husband and stole her baby. She loves him now, but if he leaves her, kills their daughter, and goes to war for Helen, everything would change very quickly. She says that if anyone must die, it should be the daughter of Menelaus and Helen.

Iphigenia begs her father not to kill her. Agamemnon defends himself, saying that all of Greece needs her to die and that the Greek army will turn against Argos if she does not give herself up. When Agamemnon takes his leave, Achilles arrives and reports that the soldiers are shouting for Iphigenia. She announces her resolve to die for the common good. Achilles, moved by her courage, envies Greece for possessing her and wishes he could call her his wife. He vows to save her from the sacrifice if she desires to live.

In her final moments with her mother, Iphigenia urges Clytemnestra not to hate Agamemnon—everything happened against his will, she says. Iphigenia then encourages her mother to raise Orestes well and remind him often of his dead sister. Iphigenia then bids her mother farewell and heads for the altar.

After Iphigenia departs, a messenger from Agamemnon arrives with news for Clytemnestra: at the very instant the blade was to pierce Iphigenia's throat, she disappeared, and a deer appeared in her place. Clytemnestra, always suspicious, does not believe the messenger, but Agamemnon insists that the story is true—the gods have rescued Iphigenia.

THE CYCLOPS

Written around 408 B.C., *The Cyclops* depicts Odysseus's famous struggle against one of the giant one-eyed Cyclopes. The play opens on the island of the Cyclopes, at the foot of Mt. Aetna. Silenus, a captive of the Cyclopes, recounts how his ships wrecked on the lonely island several years ago, and one of the giant inhabitants captured him and his sons. Now, Silenus and his sons tend the Cyclops's goats, clean his cave, and prepare his meals.

As Silenus's sons and a chorus dressed like satyrs make their entrance, they spy Odysseus and his men, who have just landed on the island. Odysseus asks if he may buy food, for he says that a storm drove him and his men to land and destroyed their provisions. Silenus is quick to alert Odysseus that Cyclopes inhabit the island. Odysseus offers wine in exchange for food, which delights Silenus, who loves wine. As Silenus prepares the food, the chorus questions Odysseus and his men about the war and, in particular, about their relationships with Helen. Just as Silenus returns with the food, the Cyclops appears, and Silenus orders everyone to hide in the cave. Odysseus refuses, declaring that he and his men would rather die honorably than run from the Cyclops.

When the Cyclops discovers Odysseus and his men, he demands an explanation from Silenus, who accuses the visitors of trying to steal the Cyclops's food. The Cyclops craves human flesh and anxiously anticipates devouring the Greeks, who try in vain to defend themselves. Eventually, the chorus corroborates Odysseus's defense by asserting that Silenus offered to sell food to the Greeks.

The Cyclops, after questioning Odysseus about his origins and the Trojan War, invites him into his cave. Odysseus prays to Athena for help and then reluctantly follows the giant inside. Moments later, Odysseus rushes out the cave and says that the Cyclops gorged himself on two of Odysseus's largest men. Odysseus quickly plots his revenge: he will give the Cyclops wine until he is drunk and then stab out his one eye with a spear.

Odysseus hurriedly fashions a large spear out of the trunk of a nearby olive tree and returns to the cave to invite the Cyclops to some wine. The Cyclops drinks greedily and quickly becomes drunk as Odysseus encourages him to take cup after cup. In his stupor, the Cyclops asks Odysseus's name, to which the latter responds, "No-man." The Cyclops promises to eat "No-man" last. The Cyclops, aroused by the wine, drags Silenus into the cave to have sex, for he says that he prefers men to women. Meanwhile, Odysseus readies himself to destroy the monster and heats the sharpened olive trunk in a fire. Not long after, a shriek comes from the cave, and the Cyclops staggers out, groping blindly and screaming that "No-man" has wounded him. As Odysseus escapes, he finally reveals his true name to the blinded Cyclops, who realizes the fulfillment of a prophecy: Odysseus would blind him after the end of the Trojan War but before being forced to wander the seas for many years.

ARISTOPHANES

CONTEXT AND BACKGROUND

Aristophanes was born c. 450 B.C., during the height of Athens under the ruler Pericles. Scholars know little about Aristophanes or his parents, aside from the fact that they were wealthy enough to provide their son with an excellent education that included a firm foundation in literature and philosophy. However, in 431 B.C., when Aristophanes was in his late teens, Athens entered into the Peloponnesian War against Sparta. The war dragged on for decades until a conclusive peace finally was reached in 404 B.C. Thus, much of Aristophanes' adulthood passed amid the turmoil of war, and much of his work, such as *The Acharnians* and *Lysistrata*, suggests how the war taxed the minds, bodies, and souls of the Athenian people.

The only dramatist of Greek "Old Comedy" whose works still exist today, Aristophanes was a contemporary of Socrates and Thucydides, a generation behind Sophocles and Euripides, and a generation before Plato. Although Aristophanes composed anywhere from thirty-six to fifty comedies during his lifetime, only eleven have survived. Evidence of his other, lost plays exists only in papyrus fragments and in brief references in the writings of Aristophanes' contemporaries.

Aristophanes' comedies feature unsparing satire, extravagant wordplay, grand physical comedy, and an insistent moral core. *The Babylonians*, one of his earliest works, earned him persecution from the politician Cleon for slandering the image of Athens and Athenian politics. Aristophanes did not produce—or direct, in the modern sense of the word—his own plays until *The Horsemen* (424 B.C.). He participated actively in the production of his works until his final two plays, which he entrusted to his son Araros to direct. Aristophanes continued to write until close to his death in the 380s B.C.

LYSISTRATA

Lysistrata takes place during the Peloponnesian War. Fought between Athens and the Peloponnesian confederacy, the war was driven by intense hunger—on both sides—for supremacy in Greece and among the Dorian and Ionian races. The war raged for ten years. While massive destruction befell both sides, Athens suffered most, as the war signaled the beginning of the fall of the Athenian empire.

As the play opens, Lysistrata, an Athenian woman, prepares for a meeting she has called among all the women of Greece to discuss the plan to end the Peloponnesian War. As Lysistrata waits for the women of Sparta, Thebes, and other areas to meet her, she curses the weakness of women. She plans to ask the women to refuse to give in to their husbands' sexual demands until a peace treaty has been signed. Lysistrata has also made plans with the older women of Athens to seize the Acropolis later that day.

As Lysistrata relates her plan to her neighbor, Cleonice, a group of women enters. Lysistrata tells Cleonice that these women are from the outskirts of town. Myrrhine, a young matron, leads the group. Another group of women, led by Lampito, a burly Spartan woman, joins them shortly thereafter. Lampito is accompanied by two women: a pretty Boeotian woman and a massive Corinthian woman. At long last, the women from all the various regions assemble, and Lysistrata convinces them to swear an oath to withhold sex from their husbands until both sides sign a treaty of peace. As the women sacrifice a bottle of wine to the gods in celebration of their oath, they hear the sounds of the older women taking the Acropolis, the fortress that houses the treasury of Athens.

A chorus of old men appears, carrying wood and fire to the gates of the Acropolis. An old and bedraggled bunch, the men have great difficulty with the wood and the large earthen pots of fire they bear. The men plan to smoke the women out of the Acropolis but end up only choking on the smoke themselves. Then, a chorus of old women approaches the Acropolis, carrying jugs of water to put out the men's fires. The old women taunt and belittle the old men as they triumphantly pour the jugs of water over the men's heads.

Not long after, the commissioner, an appointed magistrate, comes to the Acropolis seeking funds for naval ships, only to discover that the women have seized the building. In a feeble effort, officers try to regain control of the building, but the women easily beat them back. The commissioner cries out to the men of Athens that they have been too generous and allowed the women of the city too much freedom. As the officers run off, the commissioner and Lysistrata are left to argue about the Peloponnesian War. Lysistrata protests that the war is not just a men's concern but also a women's concern, as women have sacrificed greatly for war by giving their husbands and sons to the effort. Lysistrata adds that, with so many men gone, it is now difficult for a woman to find a husband. As a final insult, the women mockingly dress the commissioner in women's clothing.

Soon enough, the women's sex strike begins to affect the men. Lysistrata spots Cinesias, Myrrhine's husband, approaching the Acropolis. Cinesias, sporting a full erection, cries out for his wife. Myrrhine is steadfast, however, in her refusal to have intercourse with Cinesias until peace exists between Athens and Sparta. Cinesias tells Myrrhine that her child needs her and that he himself needs her and loves her. Myrrhine pretends to listen to her husband's frustrated pleas and hints that she might make love to him, but delays by going into the Acropolis repeatedly to fetch things. As Cinesias promises to think only about a treaty of peace between Athens and Sparta, Myrrhine disappears into the Acropolis and leaves her husband in great pain.

Moments later, a Spartan herald approaches the Acropolis, suffering, like Cinesias, an enormous erection. The Spartan describes the desperate situation of his countrymen and pleads for a treaty. Delegations from both states then meet at the Acropolis to discuss peace. At this point, all of the men have full erections. Lysistrata comes out of the Acropolis with her naked handmaid, Peace. While the men are fully distracted by Peace, Lysistrata lectures them on the need for reconciliation between the states of Greece. She reasons that because Athens and Sparta share a common heritage, have previously helped each other, and owe a debt to each other, the two sides should not be fighting.

Using the naked Peace as a map of Greece, the Spartan and Athenian leaders decide land rights that will end the war. After both sides agree, Lysistrata gives the women back to the men, and a great celebration ensues. The play ends as the chorus of old men and the chorus of old women sing a song in unison while everyone dances.

DRAMA

THE BIRDS

Aristophanes composed *The Birds* in 414 B.C. in the midst of the Peloponnesian War, and the play satirizes the political and military ambition that nearly caused Athens to fall during the war. The play opens in a desolate wasteland, where Euelpides and Pisthetairos, two old men from Athens who are sick of the small-minded local politicians in their town, stand. The men have followed their pet birds, hoping that the birds would lead them to a peaceful place. Having arrived in this wasteland, however, they wish they had not trusted the birds to guide them.

Euelpides and Pisthetairos discover that a nearby house belongs to a bird named Epops. When they meet Epops, the men are relieved to hear that he leads a live of contentment: he, too, was once hounded by problems, but then the gods transformed him into a bird. He now lives a life free of the common struggles of mortal men. Their hopes piqued after Epops's tale, the two old men ask him if he knows of any city where the residents enjoy true friendship and are free to enjoy sex. Epops suggests a town near the Red Sea where money does not exist. Pisthetairos, however, devises his own plan: he wishes to start a city in the sky, called Cloudcuckooland, where birds will rule over humans.

Epops says that he must deliberate with his fellow birds before he can agree to take part in Pisthetairos's venture. But when Epops presents the plan to the birds, they ridicule him for associating with humans and threaten the Athenians with castration. Epops, however, finally gets the birds to listen to the proposal.

The two men get up in front of the birds to give the proposal, and Pisthetairos, to mollify the assembly, emphasizes the superior position of birds in his proposed town. He suggests that the birds could build a wall separating earth from the heavens, severing contact between humans and the gods, thereby increasing the birds' new power even more. He reminds the birds that they used to rule over people, but now their role is entirely diminished.

Although the birds concede that such a plan might enable them to control communications with the gods, they doubt that they would have any influence over the most important thing for humans—money. Pisthetairos, however, argues that the birds easily could control humans by revealing the locations of hidden treasures and offering other information of which only birds are aware. These arguments finally convince the birds, and Epops steps forward with a plan for action. When Pisthetairos and Euelpides return to the stage, they are wearing wings, feathers, and beaks so that they can quickly set the plan in action. They soon complete the wall between heaven and earth.

Just as the birds begin to celebrate, a messenger arrives and announces that a god already has penetrated the wall. Pisthetairos quickly rallies his troops and vows to take up arms against heaven. However, the goddess Iris suddenly appears and reminds the birds that they owe allegiance to heaven just as humans do. Pisthetairos argues that the birds are merely claiming their rightful place in heaven and threatens both Zeus and Iris with violence.

Soon, another messenger enters to announce that the humans are championing Pisthetairos's cause and flocking toward Cloudcuckooland with hopes of gaining citizenship. As the first visitors start to arrive, Pisthetairos either gives them wings or turns them away, depending on their character. One of the first visitors is Prometheus—the Titan who gave humans fire—who warns that Zeus has readied his forces for a retaliatory attack.

A team of negotiators—Poseidon, Heracles, and Triballus—arrives from heaven to mediate. Pisthetairos insists to the negotiators that the birds be granted supreme power, and they finally acquiesce. The play ends as Pisthetairos marries and begins his reign as king of Cloudcuckooland.

THE CLOUDS

SUMMARY
Strepsiades, the father of the spendthrift Pheidippides, cannot sleep, for he is worried about the debts he has incurred due to Pheidippides' expensive passion for racehorses. Strepsiades calls in a slave to bring him his accounts so that he may tabulate his debts. Looking over his debts, he becomes enraged, and his voice wakes Pheidippides. Strepsiades begs Pheidippides to refrain from his expensive ways and to enroll in the Thinkery, a modern school of thought that has opened next door. At the Thinkery, scholars of mystical, natural, and rhetorical wisdom study under the supervision of Socrates. Pheidippides stubbornly refuses Strepsiades' request, leaving Strepsiades to enroll himself.

Strepsiades arrives at the school and meets a student who tells him about Socrates' new experiments involving insects and astronomy. The student shows Strepsiades the other pupils at the school, who are bent over their reading so that they may study geology with their faces and astronomy with their behinds. While the student is showing Strepsiades their maps, Socrates appears in a balloon-basket hanging in midair. Socrates explains that the contraption helps him "suspend" his judgment and open his mind to new ideas. Strepsiades explains his plight and asks for guidance. Socrates enlightens Strepsiades, proving to him that the gods do not exist and that the weather patterns are produced by a chorus of clouds. Socrates fleeces Strepsiades of his coat and hustles him inside.

The chorus of clouds sings a song in defense of the play, berating the audience for not rewarding it when it was first produced. Socrates and Strepsiades reemerge and discuss the gender of nouns, and Socrates puts Strepsiades in a louse-ridden bed to contemplate. After much agony, Strepsiades shares his ludicrous theories about how to win his court case against his creditors. Socrates despairs and calls Strepsiades a worthless pupil. The chorus of clouds convinces Strepsiades to enroll his son, Pheidippides, instead.

Strepsiades runs home and quizzes Pheidippides with his newly acquired Sophistry (deceptive reasoning). He drags Pheidippides to the school, where the two Arguments, Right and Wrong, argue over the proper model for the education of boys. Right suggests a model of education based on traditional poetry and physical fitness, but his descriptions falter when his libido overwhelms him. Wrong unravels Right's argument with examples from myth, and other trivia. Right becomes thoroughly flustered, and Wrong gains Pheidippides as a pupil. The chorus of clouds implies that Strepsiades' forcible education of Pheidippides will be his own undoing. Then, the chorus of clouds turns to the audience and wheedles, bribes, and even threatens them for their approval of the play.

As his day in court draws near, Strepsiades goes to pick up Pheidippides at the school. Socrates promises that Pheidippides is now well-versed in their special brand of specious learning. While Strepsiades gloats that his son is a splendid example of Wrong Argument, two creditors visit him. As they make their demands for money, Strepsiades trounces them with quizzes about the genders of nouns and Sophistic accusations about their religious beliefs. Strepsiades flogs the second creditor until he runs off. The chorus sings a song warning that Strepsiades' "evil" will soon come back to him.

As the song winds down, Strepsiades bursts from the house, Pheidippides beating and striking him, for the two have been quarreling over the recitation of traditional poetry. Pheidippides uses Sophistry to defend his practice of beating his father. Meanwhile, his father mourns that he has exchanged Pheidippides' obsession with expensive horses for his obsession with Sophistry and rhetoric, which is proving to have its own price. In his anger against Socrates, Strepsiades summons his slave Xanthias, and the two set fire to the roof of the Thinkery. As the students flee, Strepsiades crows his "Revenge" and chases off the last of the students by throwing rocks. The chorus appraises the scene and takes its leave.

ANALYSIS

Aristophanes first produced *The Clouds* for a theatrical competition, the City Dionysia at Athens, in 423 B.C. This earliest version of the play no longer exists, but a later edition of disputed date has survived. Although this later version is incomplete and probably was never performed, it provides evidence that the first edition was far from successful. Indeed, in the contest, the first version of *The Clouds* placed third out of the three plays performed.

The "new education" pioneered by the Sophists at the Thinkery represents the first stirrings of scientific theories that were circulating in Athens at the time of the play's production in the fifth century B.C. Aristophanes mocks this new science by making it appear ridiculous and trivial—obsessively concerned with the measurement of insect feet, the digestion of a gnat, and so on. He combines this new scientific experimentation with the new emphasis on rhetoric to present the Sophists as laughably literal: Socrates literally and physically realizes the notion of "suspending one's judgment" when he enters dangling in midair.

Aristophanes' Socrates is undoubtedly a composite figure, a ridiculous mixture of the famous far-flung Sophists, astrologers, mathematicians, and philosophers of Athens at the time. To make his point more clearly and succinctly, Aristophanes consolidates all of these theories and practices into one figure—Socrates, who was the most familiar, accessible figure from philosophy at the time, and a local Athenian to boot. Plato, in his *Apology*, goes to great lengths to refute Aristophanes' portrait of Socrates from *The Clouds*, stating that the image of Socrates as "a clever man . . . who was a thinker about the things up above, investigated everything that was underground, and made the worse argument the better" was purely an invention of a "comic poet"—Aristophanes. Plato denies Aristophanes' suggestion that Socrates charged fees for his school.

Instead, Plato prefers to cast Socrates' interactions with the youth of Athens as informal discussions rather than lectures or lessons.

THE FROGS

First produced in 405 B.C., *The Frogs* opens as the god Dionysus, wearing a lion-skin cloak, arrives at Heracles' house with his servant, Xanthias. When Heracles appears, Dionysus explains that he saw Euripides' play *Andromeda* and now is journeying to the underworld to meet the playwright. Dionysus needs information about the underworld before he sets out on his quest and knows that Heracles can help. Heracles advises Dionysus against the journey but tells him the fastest route nonetheless.

After Dionysus sets out, he meets Charon, the ferryman who conveys visitors to the underworld across a lake. The condescending Charon refuses to row Xanthias across because he is a slave, so he commands Dionysus to row the boat instead. Once they have reached the opposite shore, Xanthias urges his master to give up his quest. Dionysus refuses, however, and instead asks Koryphaios, the leader of a chorus of initiates, for directions to Hades' palace.

Dionysus arrives at the palace gate and uses his lion-skin cloak to disguise himself as Heracles. The doorman at the palace, however, frightens Dionysus, who insists on trading disguises with Xanthias. Inside the palace, the maid of the goddess Persephone welcomes the travelers and tempts them with beautiful young nymphs, at which point Dionysus demands the lion skin from Xanthias so that he can once again play Heracles. Soon after, however, a waitress accuses Dionysus of gluttony, so he again insists on switching disguises with Xanthias.

The doorman, however, ushers three officers onstage and tells them to arrest Heracles for stealing Cerberus, the three-headed dog who guarded the underworld (Heracles had to capture Cerberus to complete the last of his twelve famous labors). Xanthias, however, still disguised as Heracles, suggests that the officers instead torture his slave—motioning to the disguised Dionysus. But Dionysus says that he cannot feel pain because he is divine. The doorman, therefore, forces both the travelers to strip naked and allow the officers to whip them until one cries out in pain, signaling his mortality. As both are whipped, they cry out verses from the works of famous Greek playwrights in order to conceal their pain. Finally, the doorman relents and leaves it to Hades and Persephone to decide which of the travelers is a god and which a man.

Later, an argument erupts between Euripides and Aeschylus over which is the greater playwright. They agree to compete in a poetry contest in order to settle the dispute, and Hades selects Dionysus to act as judge. As the contest proceeds, Euripides argues that he, like Aristophanes, writes plays that are realistic, in contrast to Aeschylus's implausible and unrealistic works. They argue at length, and Dionysus changes his mind repeatedly. In frustration, he tells Hades that it is impossible to choose between the two. Hades, however, declares that Dionysus must make a choice and must go with the winner back to the world of the living. Finally, Dionysus picks Aeschylus, who is allowed to ascend to Earth while Euripides must continue to live in the underworld. As Aeschylus departs, he bequeaths to Sophocles his seat of honor next to Hades' throne.

THE WASPS

The Wasps (422 B.C.) opens at dawn in front of the house of Philocleon, an Athenian man. An enormous net surrounds the house. Two slaves are onstage: Sosias, who is guarding the house, and Xanthias, who is asleep. Philocleon's son Bdelycleon is asleep on the roof of the house. After Xanthias wakes up, he says that he had a strange dream, and Sosias says that he had one also. Xanthias tries to interpret the dreams and decides that they can be seen as a commentary on the state of Athens.

In an extended prologue, Xanthias tells the audience that Bdelycleon is guarding Philocleon's house to keep him from attending the courts, for he has become addicted to participating in trials. Bdelycleon cuts in and warns Xanthias that Philocleon may be about to attempt another escape. Philocleon emerges from the house, admonishes the other men for keeping him from attending the courts, and begs for permission to go to the market to sell a donkey. Bdelycleon, however, tells Xanthias that a troupe of other jurors is due to arrive soon to take Philocleon to the courthouse. Bdelycleon compares the jurors to a swarm of wasps, with stingers able to inflict terrible wounds.

Soon, a chorus of old men dressed in wasp costumes appears at the house and starts to sing outside Philocleon's window. Philocleon appears at the window and begs his fellow jurors to help him escape from his captivity. As they cheer him on, he chews through the net around the house and uses a rope to escape from his room. Bdely-cleon and Xanthias, however, catch him mid-escape and push him back into the house. Bdelycleon tries to reason with his father and convince him of the ridiculousness of his addiction to court cases. Rather than continue a futile argument, the two agree to conduct a formal debate to decide the issue.

Philocleon defends the nobility of the jury and brags about his alleged civic prestige. When Bdelycleon mocks his father's pride, Philocleon accuses Bdelycleon of fearing his power. Bdelycleon insists that the nobility of the jury is all an illusion and that its members earn practically no money. Philocleon gradually starts to see the merit of his son's arguments. Bdelycleon's concern for his father impresses the leader of the chorus, who advises Philocleon to accept his son's help. Philocleon, however, still longs to return to the jury, so Bdelycleon proposes a compromise: Philocleon can practice his hobby from the safety of his home, using his slaves as subjects.

The first defendant is Labes, the family dog, who broke into the kitchen and gorged himself on cheese. The first witness, another dog, makes his case against Labes, declaring that he not only broke into the kitchen but also refused to share the cheese with anyone. Bdelycleon comes to Labes' defense, saying that the dog is entirely ignorant. Philocleon sympathizes and eventually decides to acquit the dog. Entirely pleased with the mock trial, Philocleon agrees to stay at home.

Bdelycleon, however, remains unsatisfied and insists that his father also mingle with refined society. The father and son go off to have dinner with a noble Athenian. Xanthias returns from the dinner first, limping and covered with bruises inflicted by a drunken Philocleon, who enters the stage still drinking and groping a naked woman. The other dinner guests are outraged and threaten to sue Philocleon for his indiscretions.

PEACE

Many critics and scholars consider *Peace* (421 B.C.) Aristophanes' most successful comedy. As the play opens, several slaves are preparing dung to feed to a dung beetle, their master's new pet. The slaves discuss whether or not their master, Trygaeus, is sane. They relate how Trygaeus, in his latest frenzy, attempted to build a ladder to heaven. When this plan failed, he resolved to fly to Zeus on the back of his beetle.

Trygaeus appears overhead, mounted on his giant beetle. When his slaves express concern for their master's safety, Trygaeus assures them that he must undertake his flight in order to save the Greeks from the Medes. When Trygaeus's small daughters beg him to stay, he quotes Aesop's fables in an attempt to calm their fears. With this, Trygaeus takes off upon the back of his beetle.

Trygaeus lands at Zeus's door, where Hermes, the messenger of the gods, immediately launches into a series of confrontational questions. The gods, Hermes says, are disgusted with the Greeks' preference for War over Peace. The gods have decided to abandon the Greeks and move far away, leaving War to destroy the defenseless Greeks.

War makes his entrance, carrying a huge mortar bowl that he uses to grind down the world's cities. He orders his servant, Tumult, to find him a pestle so that he may do some more grinding, but Tumult admits he cannot find the pestle at present. To Trygaeus's relief, War goes off to make his own pestle, temporarily sparing the cities around Greece.

Hastily, Trygaeus rallies all the Greeks to help dig Peace out of the pit in which War has trapped her and piled stones on top of her. A chorus of farmers and workers rushes to help. When Hermes appears and berates them for trying to rescue Peace, Trygaeus pardons himself by lying that the sun and moon are plotting to deliver Greece to the barbarians. Alarmed by this news, Hermes quickly joins the party of diggers.

In due time, the diggers free Peace, along with Opora, goddess of the harvest, and Theoria, goddess of festivals. Trygaeus asks Peace to speak to the assembled crowd, but she refuses out of anger toward the Greeks. She agrees, however, to whisper her message in Hermes' ear. Hermes conveys Peace's words: she said that she brought baskets of truce for the Greeks but that the Greeks ignored her gifts. Hermes then makes Opora Trygaeus's wife and sends Theoria to the Senate. Once back on Earth, Trygaeus prepares sacrifices for Peace. The seer Hierocles insults Trygaeus with absurd prophecies as he is preparing the sacrifice. Eventually, the annoyed Trygaeus drives Hierocles offstage with insults and blows.

At Trygaeus's wedding, various laborers thank him for bettering their business by restoring Peace to her rightful place. Then, the son of a prominent Greek general shows up at the wedding to entertain the guests. He opens with a song celebrating young warriors, but Trygaeus interrupts and requests that the boy sing something more pertinent to Peace. When the boy can think of nothing, another singer steps forward and sings lines from a famous poem about desertion. At this, the wedding banquet commences.

MENANDER

CONTEXT AND BACKGROUND

Menander lived from about 341–291 B.C., during the reign of Alexander the Great. A number of prominent Greeks of the time influenced Menander: he received his training in drama from Theophrastus, who in turn was a student of Aristotle. Moreover, Menander was a student of the comedian Alexis of Thurii, who may also have been Menander's uncle. Amid these influences, Menander garnered a reputation for being a high-living, stylish man. Although he led a relatively quiet life, his affairs with the courtesan Glycera were notorious in Greek society at the time.

Menander wrote more than one hundred plays over the course of his career. These works display a strong, consistent faith in innate human good and feature a tasteful, intelligent comedy directed at everyday subjects. This form of comedy, often referred to as Greek "New Comedy," represented a significant departure from the bawdy, sharply satirical "Old Comedy" of earlier playwrights like Aristophanes. Although the bulk of Menander's works have been lost, several plays exist in close to their entirety, including *Dyskolos*, or *The Grouch*, which scholars discovered in several pieces during the nineteenth and twentieth centuries. Large sections of *The Girl from Samos*, *The Arbitration*, *The Shorn Girl*, and other works provide further evidence of Menander's comedic innovations.

Generally, Menander's plays depict characters from the middle and lower classes caught in circumstances of mistaken identity, coincidence, unrequited love, and other now-staple comedic situations. Despite his use of these stock plots and characters, Menander draws his heroes and heroines with sufficient depth and detail to make them fully rounded individuals rather than mere stereotypes or caricatures.

THE SHORN GIRL

Although large sections of *The Shorn Girl* remain missing, the missing scenes are easily filled with conjecture, and the extant parts offer enough to make the play worth studying. The missing opening of the first act likely introduces the heroine, Glycera, who is an orphan.

When Glycera's boastful lover, Polemon, unexpectedly returns from Corinth, he catches Glycera apparently having an affair with Moschion, her neighbor (and, unbeknownst to either of them, also her twin brother). Outraged at her seeming infidelity, Polemon cuts off Glycera's hair in an effort to shame her publicly.

A character representing Misapprehension explains to the audience the story of two infants, a twin brother and sister, who were abandoned. A peasant woman found the babies, taking the girl, Glycera, into her own care and giving the boy, Moschion, to Myrrhine, a wealthy woman. Just before she died, the poor woman told Glycera of her mysterious origins and of the existence of her twin brother. The poor woman wanted Glycera to know that she was connected to a rich family and to make sure she did not start an incestuous affair with Moschion, who had grown up to become a heavy-drinking ladies' man in town. After the old woman's death, Polemon bought the house next door to Moschion, who remained unaware of his relation to Glycera. Moschion lusted after Glycera upon meeting her and made an amorous advance just as Polemon returned from Corinth. Misapprehension claims responsibility for the ensuing fiasco and promises to make amends.

As the action of the play continues, the newly shorn Glycera seeks the help of her neighbor, Myrrhine. Meanwhile, Polemon sends one of his subordinates, Sosia, to spy on Glycera. Sosia catches sight of Doris, Glycera's slave, as she is leaving the house with a message for Myrrhine. Soon, Glycera exits Myrrhine's house, where she has left both her slave and her clothing. Davus, Moschion's slave, goes to find his master and alert him that Glycera has moved in with Myrrhine. Moschion remains skeptical until he returns to Myrrhine's house and discovers Glycera there. Moschion believes that Glycera is there because she lusts after him, but he soon realizes that he is wrong, for Myrrhine refuses to let him attend her lunch with Glycera.

Polemon, meanwhile, still does not know that Glycera has moved out of the house. When Polemon again sends Sosia to spy on his wife, Sosia finds the house empty, blames the servants for Glycera's disappearance, and assumes that Glycera has moved in with Moschion. Sosia confronts Doris on her way out of Myrrhine's house and accuses her of helping her mistress disappear. Doris insists that Glycera sought refuge with Myrrhine, not Moschion. (At this point, there is a large gap in the text.)

Sosia arrives at Myrrhine's house with a troop of hired soldiers and tries to steal Glycera back. An old man named Pataecus tries to mediate but quickly takes sides and requests that Sosia and the soldiers retreat. Pataecus questions Polemon about his relationship with Glycera, and the two men enter the house to go through her wardrobe. Soon, Moschion arrives, ready to fight. (Here again a large section of the text is missing, during which Glycera arrives.) Glycera makes arguments defending her actions, and when Pataecus urges her to return to Polemon, she refuses. As Glycera tells Pataecus of her mysterious origins, he begins to suspect that she is his own daughter. Pataecus examines a basket of Glycera's baby clothes and recognizes the embroidery. Glycera, however, is repulsed when he reveals his identity, shocked that he could be so insensitive. Pataecus defends himself and recounts the pain of his wife's death during childbirth and his collapse into poverty. Soon, Moschion joins the reunion.

Polemon laments that Glycera will never forgive him and suggests that he may kill himself. Doris, however, comforts Polemon, who apologizes for his overreaction to Moschion and Glycera's embrace. Pataecus blesses his daughter's engagement to Polemon but requests that his future son-in-law leave the army, control his anger, and improve his treatment of Glycera. (At this point, the text of the play ends.)

The Girl from Samos

Menander's farcical play *The Girl from Samos* opens in front of the house of Demeas, who explains that he is hurrying to make arrangements for the marriage of his son, Moschion, and a local girl, Plangon. Demeas relates that, just before he left his house, Moschion's old nurse was whispering to an infant about Moschion's maturation from boyhood to manhood. The nurse handed off the baby to a slave girl, Chrysis, who admonished the old woman for being too loud and disturbing the master of the house. After noting that the slave girl Chrysis hails from the island of Samos, Demeas implies that the baby Chrysis is nursing may well be his own son.

When Parmeno, Demeas's servant, enters, Demeas angrily confronts him and commands him to share all he knows about the infant boy's parents. Parmeno maintains that the boy is the son of Demeas and Chrysis, but Demeas insists that Moschion is the father. Parmeno then changes his mind and agrees that Moschion indeed must be the father. After Parmeno makes his exit, Demeas, reluctant to lay blame on his own son, decides to banish Chrysis from his house. Demeas and Chrysis get into a heated argument, which ends when Demeas slams the door in Chrysis's face.

Niceratus, the father of Moschion's fiancée, Plangon, enters, leading a sheep that he intends to sacrifice for the wedding. Niceratus learns that Demeas is upset because Chrysis refused to abandon the baby when he cast her out of the house. (The text is missing a large piece at this point, but we can conjecture that Niceratus takes Chrysis and the baby into his home. Moschion probably explains the true parentage to Demeas—that Moschion and Plangon are the baby's parents. Niceratus, however, becomes angry when he realizes that he has been housing his daughter's illegitimate child the whole time.)

Demeas hears Niceratus calling for fire and wood so that he can build a bonfire and throw the bastard child into it. Niceratus also briefly considers killing Chrysis for hiding the baby's identity from him. Demeas and Niceratus begin to argue about the infant boy, who Demeas claims is his own son. When Niceratus expresses his skepticism, Demeas suggests that perhaps Zeus slipped into the house and fathered the child without anyone's knowledge. Eventually, Niceratus calms down and agrees to focus on the wedding instead. Moschion, angry with his father for thinking he had an illegitimate child, considers joining the army but decides that he cannot leave Plangon. Parmeno urges Moschion to stay and marry Plangon, but Moschion decides to pretend he is leaving. (At this point, the text of the play ends.)

THE ARBITRATION

The first act of *The Arbitration* exists only in small fragments. Scholars conjecture that the play opens by introducing Pamphilia, the daughter of Smicrines, a greedy Athenian merchant, and telling the story of her recent marriage to a man named Charisius. Pamphilia was raped several months before her marriage and became pregnant. When her husband was away from home, she gave birth to a son and left him out in a field to be exposed to the elements.

Charisius's servant, Onesimus, tells his master about Pamphilia's illegitimate child. The revelation sparks a drastic change in Charisius's behavior, as he starts to spend money lavishly and party wildly, diverging sharply from his typical prudishness and stinginess. Soon, the reason for his change becomes apparent: Charisius intends for his loose behavior to give his wife the opportunity to reject him, thus salvaging her honor and reputation.

Smicrines, however, does not know that his daughter has an illegitimate child, so his son-in-law's sudden sea change infuriates him. On his way into town to seek advice, Smicrines runs into a goatherd named Davus and a slave named Syriscus, who belongs to Charisius's friend Chaerestratus. The two men, who are arguing, ask Smicrines to settle their dispute. They tell him that, one month earlier, they found an infant boy wearing some jewelry. Davus gave the baby to Syriscus to raise because Syriscus's own child died recently. Syriscus says that he claimed the infant's jewelry in the hopes of one day identifying the child's parentage and making sure the child has access to his inheritance, if one exists. Davus wanted to sell the jewelry, but Smicrines insisted that the jewelry belonged to the child and therefore to him as well.

Onesimus arrives, examines the jewelry, and discovers that one piece is a ring identical to one that his master, Charisius, lost during a bout of drinking. Onesimus snatches the ring from Syriscus. Onesimus does not show the ring to Charisius, however, because his latest news— about Pamphilia's illegitimate child—practically destroyed his master. After some consideration, Onesimus surmises that Charisius probably fathered the child during the bout of drinking at which he lost the ring. Further, Onesimus guesses that the foundling is most likely Charisius's own son.

A girl named Habrotonon overhears Onesimus's troubles and says she was at the festival when Charisius was drunk. She says that Charisius raped a rich, beautiful girl, and that she could identify the girl. Habrotonon then devises a plan to pretend to be the rape victim, hoping to force Charisius to admit guilt and confess that he is the baby's father. Indeed, Habrotonon's ploy is successful, as Charisius confesses to fathering the boy and promises to buy Habrotonon's freedom and to help raise the baby boy. This arrangement, however, would invalidate Charisius's marriage to Pamphilia. Smicrines, meanwhile, is thoroughly convinced that Charisius is destroying Pamphilia's reputation. He attempts to tear his daughter away from Charisius, but Pamphilia insists on remaining with him.

Later, Habrotonon walks by with the baby in her arms, and Pamphilia recognizes the jewelry on the little boy. Habrotonon quickly pleads that she only is pretending to be the infant's mother and that Charisius is the father. Onesimus, in the meantime, decides his master is insane after watching him beat his chest and mutter angrily to himself—which Charisius does out of true guilt for the suffering he has caused his wife. Habrotonon confesses her scheme to Charisius, who quickly turns the blame on the meddling Onesimus. Habrotonon also alerts Charisius that Pamphilia is the true mother.

(At this point, there is a gap in the text. Charisius and Pamphilia probably reconcile and reunite, while Habrotonon probably is exonerated and thanked for her assistance.) Smicrines learns of his grandson's existence. (The end of the play also is missing.)

THE GROUCH

This play, discovered in pieces between the 1890s and the 1950s, is one of the foremost examples of Greek New Comedy. The entire play takes place in a cave near Athens. *The Grouch* opens as the god Pan delivers a prologue in which he points out two houses onstage. One belongs to Knemon, a grouchy old man who once was married but whose constantly unpleasant demeanor led his wife to leave him. She now lives in the other house, which is a farm owned by Gorgias, her son from her first marriage. Myrrhine, the daughter of Knemon and his wife, still lives with her father. She spends much of her time worshipping Pan, who, in return, caused a wealthy young man named Sostratos to fall in love with Myrrhine the moment he first saw her.

As the action of the play begins, Sostratos—his toadying companion, Chaireas, and his servant, Pyrrhias, in tow—arrives to see Myrrhine. Pyrrhias, who walks ahead of the other two men, warns Sostratos that an old, very unfriendly man is up ahead and that the old man berated Pyrrhias and threw mud and stones at him. As Sostratos tries to decide what to do, Knemon appears, enraged that there are trespassers on his property. Myrrhine, however, enters, upset that the household nurse dropped her water bucket down a well. Sostratos, head over heels for Myrrhine, is quick to offer to fetch water for Myrrhine himself.

As Sostratos returns with a jug of water, Daos, Gorgias's slave, sees him and suspects that he has less than honorable intentions toward Myrrhine. Daos rushes to tell his master, who lambastes him for not stopping the offender. Sostratos, meanwhile, goes in search of Geta, his father's slave, to ask advice about how to win Myrrhine. He is unable to find Geta, however, and runs into Gorgias instead. Gorgias warns Sostratos about interfering with Myrrhine. Sostratos, however, counters with an oath of love for Myrrhine and wins Gorgias over. Gorgias admits that he is Myrrhine's half-brother and tells Sostratos that he will help him pursue her. Gorgias proposes that Sostratos change his clothes so that Knemon will think he is just a poor farmer. Sostratos, acting the part, sets to work in the fields. Gorgias exits, and Sikon, a cook, calls to Geta, who trails behind. Geta recounts a dream he had wherein Pan captured Sostratos, dressed him up as a farmer, and made him do hard labor in the fields.

Knemon spots Sostratos's sister, Plangon, and Sostratos's mother heading for Pan's shrine, where they plan to make a sacrifice on account of Geta's dream. When Geta appears, he accuses Knemon of spying, which prompts a string of insults from the bitter old man. While preparing for the sacrifice, Geta realizes he has forgotten a pot, and, lacking any other option, reluctantly knocks at Knemon's door to ask for a replacement. Knemon is even grouchier than expected, so Geta forgets his request practically before he can form the words. Soon, Sostratos arrives, exhausted from his day of hard work in the fields, and sees Geta. When Sostratos learns that his mother has arrived for the sacrifice, he decides to invite Gorgias and Daos also.

After an interlude from the chorus, Simiche, Knemon's nurse, bemoans her terrible misfortune: over the course of the day, she has dropped a bucket and a pick down the well. Now, to make matters worse, Knemon himself has fallen down the well. Gorgias and Sostratos follow Simiche to the well. Later, Sostratos narrates the events of the rescue, recounting how Gorgias jumped down the well to rescue his stepfather while Sostratos remained at the top to console Myrrhine. However, Sostratos, still under the spell of Myrrhine's beauty, got distracted and dropped the rope three times before the group completed the rescue successfully.

When Knemon, exhausted by his misadventure, enters with the assistance of Gorgias and Myrrhine, he shows his tender side by fawning over his daughter. He praises Gorgias's manners and bravery and vows to adopt him as a son. Knemon relinquishes Myrrhine to the care of her stepbrother and asks him to find her a suitable husband. At this point, Gorgias suggests Sostratos as a possible husband. (At this point, a portion is missing, but it seems that Knemon agrees to allow Sostratos to marry Myrrhine.) However, Sostratos and his father, Kallipides, disagree over the impending wedding. Kallipides decides to let his son marry Myrrhine even though she is poor, but he is reluctant to allow his daughter to wed Gorgias, who also is poor. Kallipides finally relents, but Gorgias wavers about whether he should marry a noble girl. Ultimately, Gorgias does decide to marry Plangon.

That night, as the families celebrate the upcoming weddings, Geta and Sikon, another servant, plot revenge against Knemon, who remains in the house. Sikon enters the house and asks to borrow a number of pots, tripods, and tables—a request that the grouchy old Knemon naturally refuses. After Sikon departs, Geta enters and asks the old man for mats and an enormous rug. Finally returning to his old ways, Knemon erupts and unleashes a string of insults on Geta. Knemon calls for his nurse, Simiche, as Sikon accuses him of misanthropy and misogyny. Geta and Sikon demand that Knemon join the wedding celebration, so they wreathe him with garlands and push him out to the crowd.

PHILOSOPHY

PRE-SOCRATIC PHILOSOPHERS

THALES OF MILETUS

Thales was born in the city of Miletus in Ionia around 685 B.C. A well-known public figure in his day, he appeared on most lists naming the Seven Sages of Greece. It seems that Thales' fame was due not only to his theoretical achievements but also to more practical triumphs. Among his accomplishments he could count military engineering (he redirected the flow of a raging river so that King Croessus's army could cross), geometry (he devised a means of measuring the height of the pyramids and the distance of ships at sea using triangulation), astronomy (in 585 B.C., using his astronomical knowledge along with the Babylonian tables of lunar and solar orbits, he was the first man to correctly predict a solar eclipse), and authorship of a guide for mariners. Thales also managed to amass a fortune by using his astronomical theories to predict the appearance of a large olive crop and then buying up all the olive presses in the surrounding area. The sole aim of this latter exploit, supposedly, was to prove that philosophers too can make money if they want to.

Among these various activities, Thales also found the time to develop the first known philosophical system. Unfortunately, not even fragments of his original writings have survived to the present day, so all that we know about his theories boils down to five statements found in Aristotle's work. From these five statements we can identify four basic tenets of Thales' worldview: (1) The world derives from water; (2) The world rests on water; (3) The world is full of gods; (4) Soul produces motion. Aristotle offers up even these snippets hesitantly, suggesting that even by Aristotle's time, Thales was known only by report and not through any firsthand evidence.

PYTHAGORAS

Pythagoras (c. 582–507 B.C.) is regarded as both a philosopher and one of the first pure mathematicians. Although he played a central role in the development of geometry, relatively little is known about his actual accomplishments. None of his writings remain, so scholars are forced to rely upon what his contemporaries and followers wrote about him. Plato refers to Pythagoras in several dialogues, most notably in the *Phaedo* and the *Gorgias*. In the *Physics* and the *Metaphysics,* Aristotle makes frequent allusions to Pythagoras and his followers, albeit to disprove their views. Pythagoras moved from place to place throughout his young adulthood until he established a school in Croton in southern Italy. His followers, known as the *mathematikoi,* lived as vegetarians and kept no material possessions. For them, math was not merely about numbers but was also the key to life, religion, and the universe. The Pythagoreans believed mathematics to be capable of spiritual purification; reality to be essentially mathematical in nature; certain figures, such as the dodecahedron, to have mystical significance; and each number to have its own personality—masculine or feminine, beautiful or ugly. The Pythagoreans are most famous for their contributions to geometry, particularly for the Pythagorean theorem, which predicts the lengths of sides in right triangles and is still used today.

HERACLITUS

Heraclitus was born in about 540 B.C. to one of the aristocratic families of Ephesus, near Colophon. His noble birth brought with it an important hereditary role in the life of the city, a position that involved responsibilities as both a political and religious leader (for instance, he would have been in charge of supervising the city's official sacrifices). Heraclitus, however, had no interest in the political life, nor in traditional religion, so he handed over his hereditary ruling position to his younger brother.

Throughout his life and well after his death, Heraclitus had a reputation as a misanthrope and a deliberately obscure thinker. His reputation as a misanthrope was probably based on the unkind words he had for other philosophers and historians. Indeed, Heraclitus called everyone from Homer to Xenophanes an ignoramus—which, according to Heraclitus's theory of knowledge, they technically were. Heraclitus's reputation as an obscure thinker, on the other hand, is probably unjustified.

The basic tenet of Heraclitus's system is his claim that there is a rational structure to the cosmos and that this rational structure orders and controls the universe. Heraclitus calls this single divine law the logos. To Heraclitus, the logos is a physis—something that unifies within nature (or, alternatively, the material from which all other things arose). Indeed, a fundamental part of understanding the logos involves seeing that all things are unified in it. The logos, however, is presumably not the material out of which everything else arose, although it is the origin of all things insofar as it is the arrangement of all matter.

Heraclitus often refers to the logos as the mind of God, although the implications of this assertion for his theory are unclear. Probably, Heraclitus simply identified the logos with the mind of God because it is the controlling, rational force within nature. He views the logos not in anthropomorphic terms but rather as an entirely natural, rather than supernatural, force: the logos exists squarely within the physical world. Oddly, Heraclitus seems to view the logos as part of the world in the same sense that water or air is a part of it—as if he is treating the recipe as one of the ingredients.

A fundamental part of the insight that allows us to make sense of experience is seeing how all that is known constitutes a unity. There are several ways to make sense of this claim that all things form a unity. It is tempting to read this claim as a statement of material monism—the idea that all objects in the world are variations on a single substance. If Heraclitus is a material monist, then the original material out of which everything else derives on his picture is, doubtless, fire. Heraclitus speaks about fire a great deal, referring to it as the principle of wisdom and the material manifestation of the logos. Because the logos is the physis only in the sense of being the unifier in nature, perhaps fire, its material manifestation, is the physis in the sense of the material from which everything arose.

Like all of the pre-Socratic philosophers, Heraclitus is sure that there is an equilibrium in nature, a constant state that is maintained. Unlike the others, however, he believes that the equilibrium state is a state of constant flux. The cosmos is a place of constant change, with a hidden underlying stability in the form of the divine law according to which all change takes place. Returning now to the idea of fire, the reason Heraclitus identifies that substance as the most fitting metaphor for the logos is apparent: fire is a substance of constant change. For this same reason, Heraclitus likens the cosmos to a river: a river both constantly changes (as new water continually flows through) and remains the same (we continue to call the Rhine River the "Rhine," for instance, from moment to moment).

PARMENIDES

Parmenides (born c. 510 B.C.) was the leader of the Eleatic school, a prominent pre-Socratic school of thought that was named for Parmenides' hometown of Elea in southern Italy. In addition to being a philosopher, he also was a renowned legislator, and the Eleans gave him significant credit for the prosperity and quality of life in their town. Parmenides is known primarily for one major work, On Nature, which survives only in fragments. In this work, which is unusual for a philosophical treatise in that it is written in verse, Parmenides rebuts the teachings of Heraclitus and holds that our surroundings do not truly exist. Rather, our world is composed of illusions, and change and variety are hallucinations of our senses. There is only one single reality: Being. All other things in the world are merely different appearances of this single reality—as Parmenides expresses it, "all is one." In this highly illusory world, reason is our only possible guide. Parmenides also sets forth a belief in a supreme being, unseen and unseeing, that dwells in a state of thoughtful absolute rest. Although many Athenians mocked Parmenides' beliefs during his time, his notion of the supreme being influenced Zeno—Parmenides' most famous and outspoken disciple—and, later, Aristotle.

ZENO

A philosopher of the Eleatic school and a student of Parmenides. Zeno (c. 490–430 B.C.) spent his philosophical career defending the views of his teacher. Zeno's major efforts were not to expand Parmenides' philosophy but rather to refute the philosophies of Parmenides' opponents, namely the Pythagoreans. Parmenides believed that True Being is absolutely singular and motionless and that the world consists entirely of multiplicity and motion—therefore, in short, the world is an illusion. The Pythagoreans, on the other hand, argued that common sense indicates the reality of multiplicity and motion.

Although only small fragments of Zeno's work exist, Aristotle preserves Zeno's most famous achievement in the *Physics*. Zeno created a paradox, now known as Zeno's Paradox, to refute the Pythagoreans by disproving the existence of motion. In the paradox, Zeno invites his interlocutors to imagine a race between Achilles and a tortoise. Achilles is ten times faster than the tortoise, so the tortoise receives a head start of ten feet. According to Zeno, it will take Achilles an infinite amount of time to overtake the tortoise. By the time Achilles runs the ten feet to the tortoise's starting point, the tortoise will have crawled one foot—so Achilles still will be one foot behind. By the time Achilles travels that one foot, the tortoise will have crawled another tenth of a foot and still will be ahead. This cycle continues infinitely: each time Achilles reaches the place where the tortoise just was, the tortoise has had time to travel just a little bit farther. Although common sense alerts us to the absurdity of Zeno's argument, his paradox nonetheless has occupied the most brilliant minds for over two millennia because it raises key questions about the divisibility of space. Is space infinitely divisible, or is there a smallest particle that cannot be divided? Great philosophers such as Kant, Hume, and Hegel all have grappled with Zeno's Paradox.

ANAXAGORAS

A philosopher and scientist thought to be the teacher of Socrates, Anaxagoras (c. 500–428 B.C.) founded a school in Athens and taught there for thirty years. However, when he hypothesized that the moon was composed of the same material as the earth and that the sun was a glowing mass at least as big as Greece, the authorities sentenced him to death for impiety. The statesman Pericles intervened on Anaxagoras's behalf, enabling him to flee to his homeland in Asia Minor, where he died. Most of Anaxagoras's works have been lost, aside from fragments of his book *On Nature,* in which he was the first to hypothesize that all material is composed of atoms. He was also the first to introduce the notion of *nous* (mind or reason), a force that stabilized chaos and arranged the atoms in order. This idea inspired Aristotle's metaphysical belief in the prime mover—the idea that thought set the universe in motion.

EMPEDOCLES

Empedocles was born in Acragas, Sicily, around 492 B.C. He was a philosopher, a medical man, an active politician, and a truly flamboyant figure. He supposedly dressed in flowing purple robes and a gold diadem and even went so far as to claim immortality and call himself a god. As a politician, he supported democracy, although his position as an aristocrat would have made him a likelier proponent of the oligarchy. Empedocles' exploits in other fields defied expectation even more dramatically. Legend has it that he managed to keep a woman alive for a month despite the fact that she had lost her pulse and had stopped breathing. When a plague hit the city of Selinus, he managed to divert two streams and thereby rout out the illness.

For unknown reasons, Empedocles eventually was exiled from his home city. He probably died around 433 B.C. in the Peloponnese, although, given his larger-than-life persona, it is not surprising that more exciting stories of his death abound. The most intriguing of these, found in the works of Diogenes Laertius, claims that Empedocles' last act was to leap into a crater of Mt. Aetna in order to prove once and for all that he was a god.

Despite his hijinks and possible madness, Empedocles was a serious and profound philosopher. He wrote in verse, and the poem that survives is dedicated to his lover, Pausanias. In this work, Empedocles tells Pausanias about the nature of the cosmos, describing an original pure state from which humans have fallen and to which they may return through a process of purification involving vegetarianism. Empedocles' poem also delineates the six basic entities of the world: the four elements (earth, air, fire, and water) and the two motive forces (love and strife). According to Empedocles' picture, the actions of love and strife result in cosmic cycles in which love mixes the elements together and strife pulls them apart. These mixings and separations result in the world as we perceive it.

In describing the state and operations of the cosmos, Empedocles floats a theory of the origin of species that hits startlingly close to the idea of natural selection that Darwin proposed more than two thousand years later. Many species, Empedocles explains, arose early on by sheer chance, through the mixing of the elements by love. Only some of these, however, were adapted to survival. Those that were best adapted survived and passed on their characteristics to later generations. Those that were not well-adapted simply died before propagating. Empedocles' examples of maladaptive species are particularly fun to thumb through, for they read like descriptions of characters from a science fiction parody: neckless faces, arms without shoulders, eyes in need of foreheads, men with faces on both sides, ox-men, and androgynous beings.

SOCRATES AND PLATO

CONTEXT AND BACKGROUND

The life and teachings of Socrates (c. 469–399 B.C.) stand at the foundation of Western philosophy. Socrates lived in Athens during a time of transition—the defeat of Athens at the hands of Sparta in the Peloponnesian War (431–404 B.C.) ended the Golden Age of Athenian civilization—and had a tremendous influence on the Athenian youth of his day. Socrates himself never recorded his thoughts, so our only record of his life and thought comes from his contemporaries. These accounts are mixed and often biased by the author's own interpretations of Socrates.

It seems that Socrates led a simple life, renouncing wealth and remaining aloof from political ambitions, preferring instead to mingle with the crowds in Athens's public places, engaging whomever he could in conversation. Nonetheless, he did serve as a hoplite (heavy infantry soldier) in several battles during the Peloponnesian War and was distinguished for his bravery. In 399 B.C., Socrates was brought before a jury of about 500 Athenians on charges of not recognizing the gods recognized by the state, of inventing new deities, and of corrupting the youth of Athens.

The most likely reason for this trial is Socrates' close association with a number of men who had fallen out of political favor in Athens. However, because the government already had declared amnesty for political offenders, officials had to bring other charges against him. The jury found Socrates guilty by a narrow margin and then sentenced him to death. Plato recorded Socrates' response to the charges in the *Apology*.

Plato (c. 427–347 B.C.) was one of Socrates' greatest admirers, and our knowledge of Socrates stems mostly from Plato's dialogues (for other accounts, see Aristophanes' satirical presentation in *The Clouds* and the writings of Xenophon). Plato was born into a prominent Athenian family who would have expected him to pursue a career in politics. However, the short-lived Spartan-imposed oligarchy of the Thirty Tyrants (404–403 B.C.) and the trial and execution of his mentor, Socrates, led Plato to spurn Athenian political life. Instead, he devoted himself to teaching and philosophical inquiry.

To that end, he founded the Academy around 385 B.C., which counted Aristotle among its students. The Academy lasted in some form until 527 A.D.—912 years in total—and has served as the prototype for the Western university system.

Plato's thought is recorded primarily in the form of dialogues that feature Socrates as the protagonist. Apparently, the Socratic dialogue was a small literary genre at the time: not just Plato but many of Socrates' other students recorded philosophical debates in this form. Though the specific dates of composition are uncertain, scholars generally separate Plato's dialogues into early, middle, and late periods. The early dialogues, which Plato wrote soon after Socrates' death, offer the clearest picture of Socrates and Socratic philosophy. As Plato matured, however, he developed an increasingly distinct voice and philosophical outlook. The figure of Socrates in these middle and late dialogues (*The Republic* and the *Phaedo* are two exemplary works of the more mature Plato) becomes more of a mouthpiece for Plato's own views. The *Euthyphro*, one of Plato's earlier dialogues, does not set forth his more characteristic doctrines so much as attempt to present Socrates the teacher. Rather than use positive doctrines or ideas, the dialogue employs Socratic irony in an attempt to teach others to recognize their own ignorance.

EUTHYPHRO

The *Euthyphro, Apology, Crito,* and *Phaedo* comprise the story of the trial and death of Socrates. In the first part, *Euthyphro,* Socrates encounters Euthyphro outside the court of Athens. Meletus has called Socrates to court on charges of impiety, and Euthyphro has come to prosecute his own father for having unintentionally killed a murderous hired hand. Euthyphro sympathizes with Socrates and remarks that Socrates' accusation is probably connected to the divine sign that Socrates claims visits him on occasion. People often disbelieve Euthyphro too when he speaks about divine matters or predicts the future. He reassures Socrates that one must simply endure these prejudices.

Socrates, in turn, flatters Euthyphro by suggesting that Euthyphro must be a great expert in religious matters if he is willing to prosecute his own father on so questionable a charge. Euthyphro concurs that he does indeed know all there is to know about what is holy. Socrates urges Euthyphro to instruct him and to teach him what holiness is, for Euthyphro's teaching might help Socrates in his trial against Meletus.

First, Euthyphro suggests that holiness consists of persecuting religious offenders. Socrates finds this definition unsatisfying because there are many holy deeds aside from that of persecuting offenders. He asks Euthyphro instead to give him a general definition that identifies the one feature that all holy deeds have in common. Euthyphro suggests that what is holy is what is agreeable to the gods. In response, Socrates points out that the gods often quarrel, so what is agreeable to one god might not be agreeable to all.

Euthyphro's most important attempt to define holiness comes with his suggestion that what is holy is that which all of the gods sanction. Socrates sets up an elaborate argument to show that the two cannot be equivalent. What is holy has the gods' approval *because* it is holy, so what is holy determines what has the gods' approval. Because holiness determines divine approval, holiness must be something other than such approval.

Socrates then leads Euthyphro to suggest that holiness is a kind of justice—specifically, that kind of justice concerned with looking after the gods. Socrates wonders what Euthyphro means by "looking after the gods," for surely the gods are omnipotent and do not need humans to look after them or help them in any way. Euthyphro's final suggestion is that holiness is a kind of trading with the gods, in which humans give them sacrifices and they grant humans' prayers. Humans' sacrifices do not help the gods in any way but simply gratify them. However, as Socrates points out, to say that holiness is gratifying the gods is similar to saying that holiness is that which has the gods' approval—which leads back to the previous conundrum. Rather than try to find a better definition, Euthyphro leaves in a huff, frustrated by Socrates' questioning.

APOLOGY

Plato's *Apology* is an account of the speech Socrates makes at the trial in which he is charged with failing to recognize the gods recognized by the state, inventing new deities, and corrupting the youth of Athens. Socrates' speech, however, is by no means an apology in our modern understanding of the word. The name of the dialogue derives from the Greek *apologia*, which means a defense or a speech made in defense. Thus, in the *Apology*, Socrates attempts to defend himself and his conduct, not to apologize for it.

For the most part, Socrates speaks in a plain, conversational manner. He explains that he has no experience with courts of law and that instead he will speak in the manner to which he is accustomed: with honesty and directness. His accusers, many of whom remain anonymous to Socrates, levy two principal accusations against him: first, that he does not believe in the gods, but rather teaches purely physical explanations for heavenly and earthly phenomena; and second, that he teaches how to make a weaker argument overcome a stronger argument by means of clever rhetoric. Socrates complains that he is not certain even who his accusers are, though he makes a passing allusion to Aristophanes (the comic playwright who parodied Socrates in *The Clouds*). As a result, Socrates cannot cross-examine these accusers and must acknowledge that the prejudices they have lodged against him go very deep. All he can do is answer their accusations as best as he can.

Socrates first addresses the accusation that he "inquires into things below the earth and in the sky"—that is, that he tries to provide physical explanations for matters that his society overwhelmingly attributes to the workings of the gods. He refers here to Aristophanes' play, which portrays Socrates as floating about in the air and uttering nonsense about divine matters. Socrates responds that he does not pretend to have any knowledge of these things, nor is he interested in them. He has no complaints against people who do claim to be experts in these affairs, but he is not one of them.

Socrates then distances himself from Sophists (thinkers who garner widespread disdain for teaching their students how to make weaker arguments overcome stronger arguments). These men generally charge a fee for their services, and Socrates denies ever having charged anyone for engaging in conversation with him. He ridicules such behavior, saying that a Sophist will persuade young men "to leave the company of their fellow citizens, with any of whom they can associate for nothing, attach themselves to him, pay money for the privilege, and be grateful into the bargain." These Sophists claim to teach their students about virtue and how to become better citizens. Socrates concedes that such teaching may well be worth a great fee, but that he himself lacks any skill in teaching these matters.

Socrates explains that his inquiring nature stems from a prophecy by the Oracle at Delphi that claimed that he was the wisest of all men. Recognizing his ignorance in most worldly affairs, Socrates concluded that he must be wiser than other men only in that he is aware that he knows nothing. In order to spread this peculiar wisdom, Socrates explains that he considered it his duty to question supposed "wise" men and to expose their false wisdom as ignorance. These activities earned him much admiration among the youth of Athens but much hatred and anger from the people he embarrassed. He cites their contempt as the real impetus behind his trial.

Socrates then proceeds to interrogate Meletus, the man primarily responsible for bringing Socrates before the jury. This is the only instance in the Apology of the elenchus, or cross-examination, that is central to most Platonic dialogues. Socrates' conversation with Meletus, however, is a poor example of this method, as it seems more directed toward embarrassing Meletus than toward arriving at the truth. Under Socrates' questioning, Meletus asserts that Socrates believes in no gods whatsoever. But the affidavit that Meletus himself drew up against Socrates claims that Socrates believes—and teaches others to believe—in supernatural matters. That must imply, then, that Socrates believes in supernatural beings. Since the only kinds of supernatural beings, according to Socrates, are gods and children of the gods, it must follow that Socrates believes in gods, contrary to Meletus's initial assertion.

As a final argument against execution, Socrates contends that putting an innocent man to death is far worse—and thus far more to be feared—than dying oneself. Therefore, it really is the jury, not Socrates himself, that is in grave danger. Socrates claims that, in doing what he does, he is doing Athens a great favor and will not be easy to replace. In a famous passage, he likens himself to a gadfly and the state to a large, lazy thoroughbred horse. He is constantly buzzing about, waking his fellow citizens out of their sleep. Though his presence may be irritating, the state will be more awake and productive thanks to his services.

The jury finds Socrates guilty by a narrow margin and then requires him to propose a penalty. Socrates jokingly suggests that if he were to get what he deserves, he should be honored with free maintenance at the expense of the state for the services he has provided. On a more serious note, he rejects prison and exile and offers to pay a fine instead. When the jury rejects his suggestion and sentences him to death, Socrates accepts the verdict stoically, with the observation that no one but the gods knows what happens after death and that therefore it would be foolish to fear what one does not know. He also warns the jurymen who voted against him that in silencing their critic rather than listening to him, they harm themselves much more than they harm him.

CRITO

This dialogue takes place in Socrates' prison cell, where he awaits execution. Before dawn, Socrates' old friend Crito visits him and tells him that he has made arrangements to smuggle Socrates out of prison to the safety of exile. Socrates seems willing to await his imminent execution, however, so Crito presents as many arguments as he can to persuade Socrates to escape. On a practical level, Socrates' death will reflect badly on his friends—people will think that his friends did nothing to try to save him. Also, Socrates should not worry about the risk or the financial cost to his friends; these they are willing to pay, and they have also arranged to find Socrates a pleasant life in exile. On a more ethical level, Crito presents two more pressing arguments: first, if Socrates stayed, he would be aiding his enemies in wronging him unjustly, and thus would be acting unjustly himself; second, he would be abandoning his sons and leaving them without a father.

Socrates first answers that one should not worry about public opinion but rather listen only to wise and expert advice. Crito should not worry about how his own, Socrates', or others' reputations may fare in the general esteem—they should only concern themselves with behaving well. Socrates refers to the part of us that is harmed by unjust actions and benefited by just actions (Plato leaves this "part of us" ambiguous here but refers to it as the soul in his later works). Socrates suggests that this part of us is far more valuable than the body and that life would hardly be worth living if it were damaged. In this case, it is of even greater importance not to take anyone and everyone's advice but rather to listen only to experts who know best how to handle such matters.

Crito, then, is wrong to worry about public opinion regarding matters of justice. Instead, he should ignore public opinion altogether and pay heed only to those who are wise about justice. Crito objects that, though the public may be ignorant, it has the power to put a man to death. Socrates replies that this issue has no bearing on the argument whatsoever. After all, Socrates is not concerned with what he must do in order to live but rather what he must do in order to live well—that is, to live honorably and justly. Therefore, Socrates and Crito should not worry about the public or about

Socrates' sons or anything else. Rather, they should ask themselves only whether or not arranging an escape would be just and honorable. The only question at hand is whether or not it would be just for Socrates to attempt an escape. If such an action is just, Socrates will go with Crito; if it is unjust, he must remain in prison and face death.

At this point, Socrates introduces the voice of the Laws of Athens, which speaks to him and explains why it would be unjust for him to leave his cell. Since the Laws exist as one entity, to break one would be to break them all, and in doing so, Socrates would cause them great harm. The citizen is bound to the Laws like a child is bound to a parent, so to go against the Laws would be like striking a parent. The Laws go even further to suggest that one's ties to one's country are even stronger than one's ties to one's family. Therefore, it is even more important to respect the judgments of the Laws. Just as one should be willing to suffer and die for one's country in battle rather than flee to save oneself, one should also be willing to suffer and die according to the Laws rather than to destroy them by trying to save oneself. If Socrates wants to avoid execution, he must persuade the Laws that they punish him unjustly rather than simply fleeing, which would disrespect and destroy the Laws.

The Laws of Athens present the citizen's duty to the law in the form of a kind of social contract. By choosing to live in Athens, a citizen implicitly endorses the Laws and is willing to abide by them. Furthermore, the Laws point out, Socrates would be more guilty than most because he has, until now, endorsed Athenian law and the Athenian way of life. Socrates has left Athens on only a handful of occasions—once to attend a festival and the other times to do military service in wars on behalf of the state. Unlike most Athenians, Socrates has never traveled or acquainted himself with the customs or laws of other people—he has been perfectly happy in Athens.

If Socrates were to break from prison now, having so consistently validated the social contract, he would be making himself an outlaw who would not be welcome in any other civilized state for the rest of his life. If he were to do so, when he died, he would be judged harshly in the underworld for behaving unjustly toward his city's laws. Thus, Socrates convinces Crito that it would be better not to attempt an escape.

PHAEDO

The *Phaedo* stands alongside *The Republic* as the most philosophically dense dialogue of Plato's middle period. It contains the first extended discussion of the theory of Forms—four arguments for the immortality of the soul—as well as strong arguments in favor of the philosophical life. The *Phaedo* also contains Plato's moving account of Socrates' final hours and his compelling myth about the fate of the soul after death. More than most of Plato's other writings, the *Phaedo* is in constant dialogue with the pre-Socratic theories of the world and the soul, in particular those of Pythagoras, Anaxagoras, and Heraclitus.

In the remote Peloponnesian township of Phlius, Echecrates meets Phaedo of Elis, one of the men present during Socrates' final hours. Eager to hear the story from a firsthand source, Echecrates presses Phaedo to tell him what happened.

According to Phaedo, a number of Socrates' friends were gathered in his cell, including his old friend Crito and two Pythagorean philosophers, Simmias and Cebes. The account begins as Socrates proposes that, although suicide is wrong, a true philosopher should look forward to death. Death, Socrates explains, is the separation of the soul from the body. Socrates argues that good philosophers distance themselves as much as possible from bodily pleasures—food, drink, sex, fancy clothes, and so on. Rather, they are concerned only with the well-being of their souls and want to free the soul as much as possible from associations with the body. The soul, Socrates asserts, is immortal, and the philosopher spends his life training the soul to detach itself from the needs of the body. He provides four arguments for this claim.

The first is the Argument from Opposites. Everything, Socrates says, comes into existence from its opposite: for instance, a tall man becomes tall only because he was short before. Similarly, death is the opposite of life, so living things come to be out of dead things and vice versa. This Argument from Opposites implies that there is a perpetual cycle of life and death, so that when we die, we do not stay dead but rather come back to life after a period of time. If this were not the case, Socrates notes, soon all the world would be dead: if all living things died, but new living things did not spring from those that had died, the number of dead would soon very quickly supercede and overwhelm the number of the living. If the living could only be made out of other living beings, there would only be a limited stock of living beings before they all ran out.

Socrates' second argument is the Theory of Recollection. This theory suggests that all learning is a matter of recollecting what we already know. For example, we become aware that different sticks and stones are equal to one another through our senses, and similarly, we sense their deficiency with respect to true Equality. There are no instances of perfect equality in the sensible world, and yet we have had this notion of Equality for as long as we have been alive. Socrates infers that we cannot have come to learn of Equality through our senses but rather that we obtained our knowledge of it before our birth. If such holds true for the Form of Equality, it should hold true of all the other Forms as well. Therefore, it would seem that we lose knowledge of these Forms at birth, and that it is through a process of learning that we come to recollect them and know them again. This is why Socrates claims that all learning is recollection. We forget much of our knowledge at birth but can be made to recollect it through proper questioning. The fact that we had such knowledge at birth and could forget it suggests that our soul existed before we were born.

The third argument is the Argument from Affinity. Socrates draws a distinction between those things that are immaterial, invisible, and immortal and those things that are material, visible, and perishable. The body is of the second kind, whereas the soul is of the first kind. This distinction suggests that the soul ought to be immortal and survive death.

At this point, both Simmias and Cebes raise objections to Socrates' arguments. Simmias suggests that perhaps the soul is like the attunement of a musical instrument. The attunement can exist only as long as the instrument exists and no longer. Although Cebes admits that perhaps the soul is long-lived and can outlive many bodies, he argues that this point does not demonstrate that the soul is immortal.

Socrates replies to Simmias by noting that his theory of attunement is in conflict with the Theory of Recollection, which proposes that the soul existed before the body. As for Cebes, Socrates embarks on a complex discussion of causation that ultimately leads him to lay out his fourth argument, which posits the unchanging and invisible Forms as the causes of all things in this world. All things possess what qualities they have only through participation in these Forms. The Form of Life is an essential property of the soul,

Socrates suggests, so it is inconceivable to think of the soul as ever being anything but alive.

Socrates concludes with a myth about what happens to souls after death. He maintains that all the hollow regions of the earth are connected by great subterranean rivers of water, fire, and mud, which flow between the several regions. One of the cavities in the earth is so large and so deep that it pierces right through to the other side of the earth. This cavity, often referred to as Tartarus, is where all the rivers flow together and the place from where they flow forth again. The greatest of these rivers is Oceanus, the ocean that surrounds the world. The great underworld rivers of Acheron, Pyriphlegethon, and Cocytus also flow to and from Tartarus.

When people die, those who lived a neutral life set out for Acheron and spend a certain period of time in the underworld, where they are punished for their sins, rewarded for their good deeds, and then returned to the earth once more. Those who have been irredeemably wicked are hurled into Tartarus, never to return. Those who have been good, however, ascend to the true surface of the earth, and those who have completely purified themselves through philosophy live without a body altogether and reach places indescribably more beautiful even than the true surface of the earth.

After concluding his arguments, Socrates has a bath, says some last goodbyes, drinks the poisonous hemlock, and drifts imperceptibly from this world to the next.

MENO

The *Meno*, which takes the form of a dialogue between Socrates and Meno, a young nobleman, is one of Plato's earliest surviving dialogues, set around 402 B.C. As the dialogue sits nearly at the beginning of Western philosophy, Socrates and Plato are working not so much amid a context of preexisting Western philosophies as amid a complete lack of them. Furthermore, the teachings that Socrates sets forth in the *Meno* seem to represent a relatively early stage in his own thought.

Socrates' discussion with Meno begins as Meno asks whether virtue is taught, learned through practice, or a trait inherent to certain individuals. Socrates answers by reminding Meno that Meno's own countrymen, the Thessalians, have recently gained a reputation for wisdom, due chiefly to the rising fame of Gorgias, a Sophist teacher. Gorgias, Socrates says, has taught people "to give a bold and grand answer to any question [they] may be asked, as experts are likely to do."

Meno moves quickly, at Socrates' behest, to give a definition of virtue. Meno says that there are different virtues for men (managing public affairs, helping friends, harming enemies, and protecting oneself), for women (managing the home, protecting possessions, and being submissive to one's husband), for children, slaves, the elderly, and so on. Meno's effort, however, is not a definition but a list of different kinds of virtue. Socrates points out this error with a metaphor about Meno's "swarm" of virtues being like a swarm of bees. The bees differ in size and shape but "do not differ from one another in being bees." In other words, Socrates is after the definitive characteristics of virtue in general—the Form (eidos) of virtue.

Meno offers several more definitions, each of which Socrates easily shows to be flawed. Then, Meno defines virtue as "the power of securing good things." Even this definition is not enough for Socrates, however, who points out that the acquisition of good things is good only if it is done "justly and piously"—otherwise, such acquisition is "wickedness."

Socrates and Meno renew their efforts, for they have made little progress in their attempt to define virtue. First, however, Meno brings up a difficult question: "How will you look for [virtue]," he asks, "when you do not know at all what it is?" This question presents a serious paradox—if we seek the nature of something that we do not know, how do we know when we have found it? How do we even know where to look?

Socrates' long, complex answer introduces his theory of recollection and the immortality of the soul. Because the soul is immortal and has therefore seen the Forms and the world many times before, one does not have to learn to identify virtue—one simply has to recollect it. When Meno seeks evidence of recollection, Socrates calls over a slave boy. Through a series of questions, Socrates elicits the answer to a geometric problem from the simple boy, proving that the boy needed merely to recollect the answer rather than learn it from scratch.

Now that Socrates and Meno have resolved the question of whether it is possible to seek the definition of virtue, they decide to try a new approach. Meno suggests that they return to the original question of whether virtue is taught, learned through practice, or inherent in some people's nature. Despite Meno's certainty that virtue is a type of knowledge, Socrates is suspicious about virtue being taught. After all, if something as important as virtue can be taught, where are the teachers? Socrates claims, as he does at the beginning of the dialogue, that he has yet to find any such teachers of virtue. If Socrates' claim is true, it would indicate that virtue cannot in fact be taught and that virtue therefore is not a form of knowledge.

Socrates, Meno, and Anytus—an Athenian statesman who enters the conversation late and feels that Socrates has insulted him—conclude that virtue is, at least in part, a kind of wisdom. However, they also believe that even the most beneficent men cannot be virtuous simply due to knowledge, for none of these men seems capable of teaching virtue. This last point, Socrates suggests, is one reason why he and Meno may have failed to find a definition of virtue itself in considering such virtuous men. This suggestion puzzles Meno. Socrates explains that, though they have been looking for virtue as a kind of teachable knowledge, the good deeds of virtuous men could be the result not of knowledge but of "true opinion."

In the end, Socrates and his interlocutors decide that virtue is neither teachable nor innate, for virtuous men are not always virtuous. This conclusion leaves virtue as "a gift from the gods which is not accompanied by understanding." Although this puzzling uncertainty may seem like an unsatisfying end to the dialogue, it emphasizes the fact that awareness of a lack of knowledge is a form of knowledge in and of itself. In the *Meno*, Socrates succeeds in convincing two prominent citizens and men of politics not only that they have no understanding of virtue but also that no one does. This idea of *aporia*, the state of knowing that one does not know, is a major theme in Platonic philosophy and one that clears the ground for the pursuit of more exacting and rigorous truth than previous philosophers had sought.

ION

In this dialogue, Socrates engages Ion of Ephesus, a professional reciter of odes who has just returned from a recitation victory at a competition in Epidaurus. Ion brags to Socrates that he has a closer relationship with the verses of Homer than any other living man. Socrates, full of admiration for Ion, asks him to demonstrate his poetic skill.

Socrates asks Ion if he is skillful at reciting the works of poets other than Homer, and Ion admits that he has mastered only Homer.

Through a series of questions, Socrates elicits from Ion the statement that anyone has the ability to distinguish between the excellent and the merely good or adequate—in this case, the distinction between the master Homer and the lesser poets. Although Ion grows visibly excited at the mere mention of Homer, he finds the lesser poets boring.

Socrates and Ion then discuss how experts throughout the arts—sculptors, painters, singers, and so on—can distinguish between good and bad artists in their respective fields. Ion repeats his assertion that he is the best living reciter of Homer. Socrates then suggests that perhaps Ion gains his skill by divine inspiration, that the muse makes Ion's recitations beautiful through a godlike possession. Socrates declares that Ion is like a magnet attracting stones, for great poetry is drawn to him. Because of this association with the muse, Socrates continues, Ion is the greatest reciter of Homeric verse.

Naturally, the boastful Ion is quick to accept Socrates' assertions. However, Socrates adds that Ion, though an expert in Homeric verse, cannot have complete familiarity with every episode that Homer mentions in his epics. Accordingly, Ion cannot fully understand verses about prophecy or medicine, but only those about recitation, since that is his area of expertise. Ion counters Socrates by stating that all of Homer is concerned with recitation. Socrates, however, refuses to accept this assertion and cites example after example of Homeric verses concerning arts other than recitation.

Socrates culminates his rebuttal of Ion by asking one question: since Ion claims to be an expert of Homeric verse, and so much Homeric verse concerns military matters, is Ion then the greatest general in all of Greece? Overwhelmed by the majesty of this proposal, Ion eagerly agrees that he is in fact the greatest Greek general. Socrates then asks why Ion, if he is the greatest general in the land, wastes his time reciting poetry? Ion insists that Athens needs no more generals, especially foreign ones such as himself. Socrates, now exasperated, accuses Ion of misleading him. He compares Ion to Proteus, a deceptive god who assumes any shape he pleases. Socrates offers Ion a choice: he is either a deceiver like Proteus or divinely inspired. Ion is quick to claim divine inspiration, and Socrates closes the dialogue by stating that Ion is not an artist himself but rather a mouthpiece for the gods.

Symposium

As the dialogue opens, Apollodorus relates to an unnamed companion a story he heard about a symposium, or dinner party, given in honor of the tragedian Agathon. The guests at this elite dinner party include the highest-ranking statesmen, poets, and philosophers of Athens: Socrates, the philosopher; Phaedrus, a friend of Plato; Eryximachus, a doctor; Pausanias, a disciple of the Sophist Prodicus; Aristophanes, the legendary Greek dramatist; and Alcibiades, a statesman, general, and admirer of Socrates.

Socrates arrives at the party late, as he was lost in thought on the porch of a neighboring house. After the group has finished eating, Eryximachus picks up on Phaedrus's suggestion that each person present should make a speech in praise of the god of love. Phaedrus begins by saying that love is one of the oldest of the gods and the one that does the most to promote virtue in people. Pausanias follows Phaedrus, drawing a distinction between common love, which involves simple and mindless desire, and heavenly love, which always takes place between a man and a boy. In the case of heavenly love, the boy, or loved one, sexually gratifies the man, or lover, in exchange for education in wisdom and virtue. After Pausanias, Eryximachus speaks and suggests that good love promotes moderation and orderliness. Love does not restrict itself to human interaction but also can be found in music, medicine, and many other fields.

Next to speak is the comic poet Aristophanes, who suggests that humans used to be twice their current size until their threat to the gods prompted Zeus to cut them in half. Ever since, each human individual has wandered the earth looking for his other half in order to rejoin with it and become whole. When an individual finds his other half, he is overwhelmed with affection, concern, and love for that person. Although this great amount of care cannot result simply from a desire for sex, humans have difficulty articulating precisely what it is that makes them care so much. If Hephaestus, the blacksmith god, were to offer to weld a couple together so that they could become one and never be parted, even in death, the couple clearly would leap at this opportunity. Love is the name that humans give to their desire for wholeness, to be restored to their original nature.

Agathon follows with a rhetorically elaborate speech that identifies love as young, beautiful, sensitive, and wise. He goes on to speak about the virtues of love: love is just because he is never forced and never uses force, for everyone consents to his authority. Love practices moderation, for he can master pleasures and desires. Love is braver even than Ares, the god of war, for Ares fell in love with Aphrodite and was thus mastered by love. Love is wise, for he is the inspiration for all other acts of wisdom. No poet could be wise without love, nor could the gods or muses master their respective arts without love for those arts. The gods became organized only when love came into being and motivated them with a love of beauty. Agathon also sees love as responsible for implanting all the virtues in humans.

Socrates questions this speech and suggests that Agathon has spoken about the object of love rather than love itself. In order to correct Agathon, Socrates relates some information that a wise woman named Diotima once told him. According to Diotima, love is not a god at all but rather a spirit that mediates between people and the objects of their desire. Love is neither wise nor beautiful but rather is the desire for wisdom and beauty. Love expresses itself through pregnancy and reproduction, either through bodily, sexual love or through the sharing and reproduction of ideas. The greatest knowledge of all, Diotima confides, is knowledge of the Form of Beauty, which we must strive to attain.

By surrounding oneself with images of beauty, Diotima contends, one can ascend from loving particular kinds of beauty to loving Beauty itself, from which all beautiful things derive their nature. Diotima suggests that a life gazing upon and pursuing this Beauty is the best life that one can lead. Many individuals can give up all luxuries in order to gaze upon and be with someone whom they love. Imagine, then, Diotima urges, what it would be like to gaze upon Beauty itself, which is so much greater than the beauty of boys, men, clothes, money, and all other lesser things. Such a person would be able also to produce true Virtue rather than images of virtue. Those who are obsessed with images of beauty can produce only images of virtue; on the other hand, those who can see Beauty itself can produce Virtue itself, making themselves immortal and loved by the gods.

CHARMIDES

Another of Plato's earlier dialogues, the *Charmides* is, along with the *Lysis*, studied less frequently than many of Plato's other works.

Perhaps the primary reason for this neglect is the fact that the *Charmides* includes a fair amount of inconsistent or even muddled argumentation.

The *Charmides* begins as Socrates arrives back in Athens after years of service in the army and a recent escape from a brutal battle. He heads for a *palaestra* (a sports school or gymnasium) to find his old friends, who ask him about the battle. Socrates asks them, in turn, about the state of philosophy in Athens. He also inquires whether there are any particularly wise or beautiful youths currently in the city. Socrates learns of one such youth, Charmides, who allegedly possesses unsurpassed beauty and solid temperance.

By coincidence, Charmides enters the temple just moments later. Socrates, awestruck and aroused by Charmides' beauty, persuades Critias—Socrates' friend and Charmides' older cousin—to convince Charmides to come over by telling him that Socrates has a cure for Charmides' headaches. Socrates tells Charmides that the mystical "cure" treats not just the body but the soul as well, for it makes the soul temperate.

Charmides agrees to receive the cure, but Socrates first wants to find out whether Charmides truly is temperate of soul already, as everyone says he is. Socrates proceeds by asking Charmides to define temperance. Charmides claims that temperance is always good. He then tries to define it as "quietness" and "modesty," but Socrates shows that both fail to match the definition of temperance: quietness is not good in some pursuits, and modesty is sometimes bad (when one is needy, for example). Charmides then uses a borrowed definition: temperance is "doing our own business." Socrates refutes this definition as well, on the grounds that craftsmen, for example, can be temperate even though they do, or make, things for other people.

At this point, it becomes clear that this latest definition came from Critias, who is brought in to defend it. (Critias is the interlocutor from here until just before the end of the dialogue.) Critias begins with a defense of his definition based on a nitpicky distinction between doing, making, and working. Socrates puts Critias's words in simpler terms: temperance, Critias argues, lies in doing good. Socrates expands this proposition to involve doing good both for others and for oneself. However, he quickly shows that people often do not know which of their actions will be beneficial in these ways. Therefore, it seems possible to be temperate without self-knowledge.

Critias objects to this suggestion that one might be temperate without knowing of temperance, so revises his argument and decides to define temperance as "self-knowledge." The two debaters decide that if temperance is a kind of knowledge, then it must be a kind of science. Critias suggests that temperance is "the science of a man's self"—but it remains unclear, as Socrates points out, what product or effect such a science would have. At this point, there is a brief but significant interruption in the argument, as Critias accuses Socrates of trying only to refute whatever he says rather than trying to develop the argument. Socrates replies by noting that refutation has nothing to do with positive arguments attached to individuals; rather, refutation is precisely the way an argument does proceed.

Socrates develops the assertion that temperance is a kind of self-knowing science into the hypothesis that temperance must be a science of itself and of all the other sciences—a "science of science." Further, Socrates adds, in order to be truly self-knowing, such knowledge must include a knowledge of what it *does not* know. This "science" of temperance, then, proves to be a difficult notion to pin down and perhaps even a paradox. Socrates is unsure whether such a knowledge can exist at all. Further, he is unsure whether it would do any good at all. Socrates and Critias decide to drop the question of whether such a "knowledge of knowledge" can exist at all. Rather, they decide to focus on whether, if it did exist, such knowledge would be of any use.

As the debaters try to find a use for this reflexive knowledge, they quickly encounter difficulty in their attempts to link knowledge whose "subject matter" is purely knowledge with knowledge that has concrete subject matter, such as medicine or architecture. Socrates suggests that perhaps he and Critias aimed too high when they defined temperance strictly in terms of pure, idealized self-knowledge: after all, how can pure self-knowledge rule over all knowledge of concrete people and things? Socrates proposes a different, less ambitious version of the same idea: knowledge of knowledge helps to frame or guide more concrete learning.

The debaters promptly drop this revised hypothesis, however, as Socrates recounts a "dream" of the perfect state ruled by wisdom (knowledge of knowledge). Try as he might, Socrates cannot convince himself that, even in such a perfect state, everyone really would be happy. Again, the problem is the link between pure, ideal temperance or wisdom and specific happiness: what exactly is it about knowledge of knowledge that makes us happy? Critias briefly suggests a compromise solution in a kind of "science of the good" or "science of advantage," which would apply to all other sciences but which would itself be a specific, concrete science. Socrates rejects the suggestion on the grounds that even this science of advantage does not seem to have any intelligible links to temperance as the "science of sciences."

At this point, the participants declare the discussion dead. Even after accepting as "givens" a number of things that did not seem very likely at first, the two men still are unable to come up with even a definition or a use value for temperance. The failed discussion does not dissuade Charmides, however, and the men decide that Charmides will see Socrates frequently to continue to learn from him and to pursue the true meaning of temperance.

GORGIAS

Much of the content of the *Gorgias* stems directly from events in the Athenian political world at the end of the Peloponnesian War in 404 B.C., just before Plato wrote this dialogue. Although images of classical Greece often suggest the epitome of a proper and successful democracy, by the time Plato completed the *Gorgias*, this balanced Athenian government had disintegrated considerably. When the war ended, a new political authority came into power in Athens—a group of wealthy, corrupt, and opportunistic citizens interested more in their own prosperity than in their society's well-being. Not only was the new government tainted by corruption, but to make matters worse, the transition of power was anything but smooth.

The *Gorgias* presents a detailed study of virtue that, in turn, is based on inquiries into the nature of rhetoric, art, power, temperance, justice, good, and evil. The dialogue is significant in itself but also relates closely to Plato's other works, especially to his overarching philosophical project of defining noble and proper human existence.

The dialogue takes the form of a mostly friendly, but occasionally scathing, conversation among Socrates and four fellow citizens. Chaerephon, an apparent contemporary of Socrates, speaks with the philosopher at the beginning of the dialogue but says little else afterward. Callicles, another of Socrates' peers, and his harshest critic in the *Gorgias*, plays host to the famous orator Gorgias and, at the end of the dialogue, opponent to Socrates. Gorgias, for whom the text is named, serves as the catalyst of the dialogue's debates through his answers to various questions that Socrates asks him.

Polus, the fourth citizen, is Gorgias's inexperienced, overeager student. Although the dialogue depicts a fictitious conversation, we must remember that Socrates was indeed Plato's teacher. As a result, Socrates' words, for the most part, mirror the actual Socratic framework and presentation and also serve as an expression of Plato's own positions.

Although Plato does not divide the *Gorgias* into explicit sections, the text does divide smoothly into general topics. In the first section, Socrates and Chaerephon discuss Gorgias's status as a famous rhetorician. Socrates desires to question Gorgias about the scope and nature of rhetoric, so he and Chaerephon go to the home of Callicles, where Gorgias is staying. An intense discussion ensues, leading to a more general consideration of true vs. false arts (flattery vs. routine), a distinction based on the idea of the good existing as different from the pleasant. This conversation provides the first hint at the dissimilarity between the good and the pleasant, but the point is not developed until much later in the dialogue.

The second part of *Gorgias* investigates the true essence of power. Eventually, the participants conclude that power exists both in an overall lack of need and in one's ability to perform only those actions that he wills independently. By this reasoning, a tyrannical leader does not have actual power, for he must perform certain actions—executions, for example—simply because they benefit the state, not because the tyrant independently wills them. This inquiry into the essence of power leads to an attempt to identify the worst wrong a person can commit. Socrates and his companions ultimately conclude that no evil surpasses that of inflicting wrong and escaping punishment. This conclusion provides the dialogue's first suggestion of an overarching question of right and wrong—the issue that eventually results in a mapping of virtue.

The next general portion of the dialogue diverges from the investigative tone characteristic of the rest of the *Gorgias*. Callicles spends a fair amount of time chastising Socrates, especially the fact that a grown man would remain immersed in the pursuit of philosophy. Callicles sees this continued practice as a disgrace in adults. Here, more than anywhere else in the work, the prevalent beliefs of Socrates' contemporaries directly threaten his pursuit of truth.

In the fourth section, the participants inquire into the nature and value of temperance and justice. During this discussion, Socrates supplies a somewhat abstract logical proof of the distinction between the good and the pleasant, thereby resolving an issue begun in the first section of the *Gorgias*. For Plato and his teacher, the chaos of contemporary Greek society—especially Athenian society—stemmed from the inability of most people to recognize this fundamental difference. This widespread oversight, in turn, leads to a confusion of flattery for art, persuasion for truth, and other such illusions. The conversation moves on to conclude the topic with a grounding of proper existence in temperance and justice.

As the dialogue closes, Socrates attempts to show how virtue arises from an appropriate balance of the arts defined earlier in the dialogue. He also attempts to show how virtue manifests itself in a righteous life. Socrates describes virtue of the body (through gymnastics and medicine) as well as of the soul (through temperance and justice). Interestingly, Socrates' response here smacks of rhetoric and oration more than of dialogue, and his tone takes on a passion and urgency unusual even for him. This intense passion suggests the vital significance for Socrates—and thus for Plato—of the topics being examined. At the conclusion of the *Gorgias,* Socrates relates a mythology of death that illustrates the importance of virtue in both this world and the world beyond.

On one hand, the *Gorgias* epitomizes Plato's exploration of the general nature of good living, for its insights arise from a specific, conversational consideration of what makes a good leader, a good act, a good body, and a good soul. The general definition of good evolves from more specific topics, just as the general themes of Platonic philosophy evolve from Plato's individual texts. On the other hand, the *Gorgias* is somewhat atypical among Plato's body of work, for Socrates' standard professions of ignorance are virtually absent, and Socrates displays uncharacteristic confidence in his conclusions. However, given the tight relation between the political events that preceded the *Gorgias* and the text's investigations of power, justice, and virtue, Plato may have felt this certainty necessary to preserve morality in Athens. In other words, we can see the dialogue's unusual confidence and urgency as a product of its time. Nonetheless, its subject—the investigation of virtue—is in keeping with Plato's other early dialogues and with his overall philosophical pursuit.

LACHES

According to legend, Socrates originally began his quest for knowledge because the Oracle at Delphi told him that he was the wisest

PHILOSOPHY

man in Greece. This advice puzzled Socrates, however, because he felt that he knew absolutely nothing. To discover what the Oracle possibly could have meant, Socrates traveled around Athens speaking to wise men so that he could see how wise he was in comparison. Upon speaking to these men, Socrates realized that the Oracle must have meant that whereas Socrates knew that he knew nothing, these other men often were mistaken and did not know that they knew nothing. The fact that they were convinced, mistakenly, that they had knowledge made them less wise than Socrates. From that point onward, Socrates dedicated himself to making others wiser by revealing to them that in fact they had no knowledge.

The *Laches* portrays Socrates' quest to point out to others their lack of knowledge. Plato portrays Socrates asking questions of his friends to show them that they in fact cannot answer his questions— thereby deepening their wisdom. In large part, the dialogue addresses the virtue of courage. Throughout, two distinguished generals, Nicias and Laches, take turns attempting to define the nature of courage while Socrates mediates and responds. Ultimately, Socrates defeats each of the generals' arguments and proves to them that they do not know the nature of courage. Although Socrates, Nicias, and Laches are all, in a sense, examples of courageous men, none has any real knowledge of courage because none is able to define it. In the end, Socrates instructs the whole company to go back to school again and says that he also will do so himself.

As the dialogue begins, Lysimachus makes a speech to two of his friends, Nicias and Laches. Lysimachus says that he and his friend Melesias want their sons to become honorable men. Therefore, they want the advice of two generals about how they should educate their sons; specifically, they want to know what the generals think of the art of fighting in armor. Nicias says that the art of fighting in armor would be good for the boys to learn, for it would make them want to learn other things about war. Laches, for his part, believes the art of fighting to be a kind of knowledge without value. He argues that most of the men he knows who are teachers of this art make fools of themselves on the battlefield. Laches relates a long anecdote concerning a teacher named Stesilaus whose companions in battle all laughed at him. Laches believes that although fighting may be a form of knowledge, this knowledge is not worth knowing because it does not make a person a better fighter.

Lysimachus asks Socrates to decide between the two generals' differing opinions. Socrates, however, insists instead that they determine who among them is the expert and then ask his advice. If they find no expert among them, then they must seek the advice of another teacher. Then, Socrates clarifies that his goal is to find the one man among them who is an expert not in the art of fighting with armor, but rather an expert in the soul of youth—for that is the end product of what they are discussing.

Socrates proposes that he, Nicias, and Laches each give proof of their expert status by showing the others who their teachers have been and who their students are. Socrates sarcastically states that he, of course, is unqualified, for he never has been able to afford the teaching of the Sophists. Therefore, he recommends Nicias or Laches instead.

Nicias accuses Socrates of carrying the conversation in circles, with no aim but to frustrate the other participants. Laches claims that he dislikes conversation that is "out of tune"—his term for a disparity between a person's words and deeds. However, Laches states that he will listen to anything Socrates has to say on the subject of virtue, for he knows that Socrates' deeds in battle are themselves so virtuous.

Socrates shifts the conversation to focus on the nature of what they are attempting to discuss. In general terms, Socrates calls this thing virtue, but specifically, they are discussing only a part of virtue—courage. Laches defines a man of courage as one who does not run away from an enemy. Socrates explains that this definition does not cover all instances of courage, so Laches must come up with a more general definition. Laches then defines courage as "an endurance of the soul." Socrates presses Laches to narrow his definition to a "wise endurance of the soul" and then proves to him that courage actually is more akin to a foolish endurance of the soul.

Then, Nicias defines courage as a kind of wisdom, a "knowledge of the grounds for fear and hope." Laches criticizes this definition because it includes non-courageous men such as physicians or soothsayers. Socrates tells Nicias that his definition fails to consider courageous animals, such as the boar or the lion, who have no knowledge. Nicias defends his definition by drawing a distinction between courage, which is a form of wisdom, and fearlessness, which is what animals possess. Socrates attacks this assertion, claiming that Nicias's definition of courage as "knowledge of the grounds of fear and hope" deals with only the future of courage and neglects the present and past.

Nicias extends his definition to include not only the knowledge of hope and fear—that is, knowledge of future good and evil things—but also knowledge of *all* good and evil things, past, present and future. However, Socrates notes that a man who has knowledge of all good and evil things at any time would embody *all* virtue, not merely a part of it. This refutation prompts Nicias to abandon his definition.

Ultimately, none of the men is able to get any closer to a definition of the nature of courage. Nonetheless, the men choose Socrates as the teacher for the children of Lysimachus and Melesias. Jokingly, Socrates suggests that all men—not only children—should go to school in order to learn the nature of courage.

LYSIS

On his way from the Academy to the Lyceum, Socrates runs into two men, Hippothales and Ctessipus, who suggest that he join them for some conversation in the newly constructed palaestra. The men talk, and the conversation soon turns to Hippothales' overpowering crush on the boy Lysis. Ctessipus recounts how Hippothales constantly sings the boy's praises to the point of being obnoxious. Socrates asks Hippothales about his method of wooing Lysis and criticizes him for inflating the boy with too much praise, thus making him harder to catch. Socrates offers to come inside and meet the boy himself, in order to show Hippothales how to woo him.

Inside, Socrates, Lysis, and Lysis's friend Menexenus sit down to talk. Socrates convinces Lysis that he currently is a "slave" to his parents and that the only way to escape this situation is through greater knowledge and understanding. Socrates initiates a lengthy dialogue about the nature of friendship, during which Socrates proposes ideas and Lysis and Menexenus alternate in brief expressions of agreement.

During the dialogue, the participants consider and reject a number of causes of friendship and definitions of "friend." First, Socrates considers whether the lover or the beloved is the friend. Ultimately, he rejects both, for it always is possible that the beloved hates the lover. Next, Socrates considers whether like is the friend of like and whether unlike is the friend of unlike. He rejects the former on the grounds that like can desire or need nothing from like, and the latter because it seems a "monstrous" idea that the good would be the friend of the bad.

Socrates' third hypothesis suggests that the good is the friend of that which is neither good nor bad, and that this neutral element is motivated to befriend the good because of the presence of surrounding evil. This answer seems good, but Socrates rejects it, saying that the ultimate cause of friendship never can be found in friendship "for the sake of" something else. Therefore, evil cannot be the motivating cause of friendship.

Finally, Socrates concludes simply that desire—which is in itself neither good nor evil—causes friendship. Furthermore, he concludes that desire occurs between two things when they are "congenial." However, congeniality does not avoid the earlier problem that like has no reason to befriend like, so Socrates rejects this final thesis as well. As the boys' tutors arrive to take them away, the conversation ends.

PROTAGORAS

Among Plato's dialogues, the *Protagoras* is something of an anomaly in that it takes place before Plato's own birth, at a time when Socrates is still young. Plato sets the *Protagoras* before the beginning of the Peloponnesian War, around 433 B.C. At the end of the thirty-year war, political power in Athens changed hands from a democracy to an oligarchy of "Thirty Tyrants"—and this upheaval in turn led to Socrates' condemnation, trial, and execution in 399 B.C. We must take this historical context into account when reading Socrates' and Protagoras's discussion of political virtue in the *Protagoras*.

The dialogue begins with a conversation between Socrates and an anonymous friend, and the rest of the dialogue consists of Socrates speaking to this friend. The friend does not reappear at the end of the dialogue, however, so the text feels oddly unfinished as a narrative.

Socrates' story concerns the famous Sophist Protagoras, at the time the most famous thinker in Greece. Socrates relates how his friend Hippocrates awakens him one day, excited by Protagoras's arrival in Athens. Hippocrates intends to become Protagoras's disciple. When Socrates questions Hippocrates as to what he hopes to learn from Protagoras, however, Hippocrates is unable to answer. The two men therefore set out to ask Protagoras himself exactly what he teaches.

PHILOSOPHY

When the men find Protagoras, Socrates questions him about what he teaches his pupils. Protagoras says that he educates his students in politics and in the management of their personal affairs. Socrates questions whether the latter really is a subject that can be taught. Protagoras responds by giving a long speech about the creation of the world. Virtue is indeed teachable, argues Protagoras, because political systems are founded on the basis that all citizens can possess virtue. Similarly, systems of criminal justice are based on the notion that people can reform—that is, learn how to be virtuous.

Socrates shifts the subject of discussion to focus more precisely on what virtue is: is it one thing or many things? Before this line of argument can progress very far, the dialogue breaks down, as Socrates and Protagoras begin to bicker about how long their answers to each other's questions should be. Socrates favors short answers and rapid questioning, while Protagoras prefers to answer at length. Other speakers intervene and persuade the two men to return to the subject at hand. They decide to let Protagoras question Socrates first and then have Socrates take his turn.

Protagoras takes this opportunity to change topics and discuss a poem by Simonides. He points out a contradiction in the poem and challenges Socrates to explain it. Socrates responds with his own interpretation of the poem, saying that the poem is a reaction to a famous sage's assertion that it is difficult to be good. In Socrates' interpretation, the poem contends that it is hard to become good and that it is impossible to be good all the time, for inevitable misfortunes force humans to behave badly. Socrates elaborates, saying that misfortune here does not mean poverty or scarcity but rather ignorance. The only evil, Socrates argues, is a lack of knowledge, for it is impossible for one to behave badly when one knows what is good.

Socrates continues to pursue this line of reasoning when it is his turn to ask Protagoras questions. The only good, Socrates reasons, is pleasure, so to commit an evil action is to opt unwittingly for pain over pleasure. Socrates believes that he and Protagoras must devise a technique that can identify without fail the more pleasurable course of action in any situation. Protagoras assents. Then, Socrates argues that cowardice is failing to fear the right things and fearing things that should not be feared. Courage, too, is therefore a form of knowledge.

Because Protagoras earlier accepted that wisdom, temperance, justice and holiness all name the same thing—virtue—Socrates has proven (at least to the satisfaction of Protagoras) that courage is also synonymous with these other terms. Therefore, virtue itself is simply another name for knowledge. If virtue is knowledge, then people can learn it. Thus, both Protagoras and Socrates end up arguing the opposite of the positions they held at the beginning of the text. The dialogue ends as Socrates complains about a missed appointment.

THE REPUBLIC

MAJOR CHARACTERS

Socrates   Probably the most important element of Socratic philosophy is the Socratic *elenchus.* Sometimes called the dialectic, the *elenchus* is a cross-examination meant to amend or improve the beliefs of Socrates' conversational partner. Most of Plato's dialogues progress as follows: Socrates runs into someone, and the topic of some specific virtue—piety, for example, in the *Euthyphro*—somehow comes up. In that work, Socrates asks for a definition of piety, and Euthyphro confidently gives one. Socrates points out the ways in which this general definition conflicts with Euthyphro's other beliefs about piety. Euthyphro alters or edits his statement. Socrates shows how this new definition conflicts with old ones. Often, a dialogue concludes with both participants—Socrates and his interlocutor—admitting that they simply are unable to define the virtue they are discussing. The important thing is that the interlocutor *thought* he knew, and by subjecting him to the *elenchus*, Socrates has morally and intellectually improved him.

Glaucon and Adeimantus Plato's brothers in real life, and Socrates' primary interlocutors in *The Republic.* We can infer from the text that Plato likes and respects his brothers; indeed, the mere fact that he recreates them as characters provides some proof. Glaucon's and Adeimantus's personalities are not prominent or well-defined. Plato does, however, convey that Glaucon is competitive and loves young boys—a socially acceptable taste in ancient Greece—and that Adeimantus, who sometimes disagrees vehemently with Socrates, is perhaps the bolder of the two. Both brothers are very intelligent.

Thrasymachus One of the key interlocutors of *The Republic,* even though he is active only in Book I. Thrasymachus claims that the unjust get more benefits from life and thus are happier, which forces Socrates to address the question of whether it is better to live justly or unjustly. Although Socrates is able to refute Thrasymachus's argument somewhat, Thrasymachus complicates matters by insisting that someone offer positive assumptions about justice to counter his own, and thus in a way sets the tone of the rest of the work.

SUMMARY: BOOK I
As Socrates and his friend Glaucon return from watching a religious festival, they run into another friend, Polemarchus, and Adeimantus, Glaucon's brother. All four men go together to spend the afternoon at Polemarchus's house. There, they join Polemarchus's aging father, Cephalus.

Socrates questions Cephalus's definition of just behavior, but before they can discuss the matter, Cephalus departs, leaving his argument to Polemarchus. Polemarchus defends his father's definition of justice, saying that justice is giving each what is owed to him—treating friends well and enemies badly. Socrates finds numerous problems with this definition. First, because people are sometimes mistaken about who their true friends are, such a definition appears to endorse treating bad people well and good people poorly. Second, because injustice breeds injustice, Polemarchus's definition implies that it is the just person's job to create injustice.

Just as Polemarchus agrees that his initial definition is incorrect, Thrasymachus, another guest at the house, roars into the conversation. Thrasymachus announces, with some pomp, that justice is "nothing other than the advantage of the stronger." In all cities, the rulers enact laws that are in their own best interests, and these laws are declared just; therefore, justice serves only the powerful. Socrates responds by saying that all crafts are in the service of that over which they are set—medicine over a patient's health, shipbuilding over a ship and crew, and so on. It ought to then follow that the craft of rulership sets the ruler out for his subjects' benefit.

Thrasymachus notes that the just man gets less, and therefore is less happy, than the unjust man. He declares that injustice is a virtue, for dishonesty and thievery can get a person far in life. Socrates notes that, if justice is a craft, then Thrasymachus's assertion makes no sense. All musicians tune their instruments to the same key, and all doctors give similar diagnoses when correct. In both cases, a desire to rise above and outdo one's colleagues is a sign of ignorance and vice—not virtue—since it generally means being incorrect. The craft of justice ought to follow the same principles.

Thrasymachus concedes that the unjust all want to outdo their "colleagues" in justice and, therefore, unjust behavior is a sign of ignorance and vice, not wisdom. Socrates then proves that justice brings unity to any group of people, for it allows them to trust and rely on each other. He points out that the gods are just, so an unjust person is the gods' enemy. Lastly, he asserts that justice is the virtue of a person's soul. Because the virtue, or arete, of something, is what permits it to function well, a just person will function well—that is, live happily—and an unjust person will not. By the end of Socrates' argument, Thrasymachus has conceded defeat. Socrates ends Book I by noting that he is still dissatisfied, for these discussions of justice are useless without a definition of the thing itself.

ANALYSIS: DEFINITION OF JUSTICE

In this beginning portion of *The Republic*, Plato introduces the fundamental question of the rest of the text—whether it is more beneficial to live justly or unjustly. Although Plato devotes the entire middle section to the creation of the just city, the question of justice remains central. Plato does not argue whether it is more moral to live justly. Rather, he argues whether it is more beneficial to live justly, whether the just life will make a person happier. This argument develops clearly in Book II.

SUMMARY: BOOK II

Glaucon now enters the conversation. He divides all things into three categories: those things that are pleasurable for themselves and their results; those that bring good results, but with difficulty; and those things that bring no results but are pleasurable. Glaucon asks Socrates which category justice falls under, and Socrates places it in the first category. Glaucon notes that the general view is that justice falls in the second category. Glaucon then speaks at length in praise of the unjust life, not because he believes it best, but rather to divine the specific nature of justice.

As an example, Glaucon discusses a fable about the ring of Gyges, a magical ring that renders its wearer invisible. Glaucon argues that both an unjust person and a "just" person would use the ring to commit a variety of crimes, for the only reason people behave justly is because they are aware of their powerlessness in the face of society. People publicly praise justice but privately do not care for it. In this view, the best thing is for a person to be thought to be just while in fact reaping the benefits of injustice. The worst thing is for a person to be reviled as unjust for whatever reason when in fact he leads a good and virtuous life. This dilemma brings the difficulty of justice with no rewards.

Although Socrates is impressed with the thoroughness of Glaucon's arguments, he refutes them as promised. Socrates' goal is to define and praise justice by itself, and, centrally, to discover whether it is truly more beneficial to lead a just or an unjust life. Using the argument that the Form of justice will be the same on any scale—the beauty of a rose and the beauty of a great building, though different in size and type, are both beauty—Socrates notes that it would probably be easiest to look for justice on a large scale and then compress his argument down to the level of the individual. He suggests a city as the example model, and everyone agrees.

Socrates then proceeds to construct a hypothetical just city from scratch. He starts with what he calls the "healthy city"—a city in which labor is divided so that everyone's basic needs are met. The division of labor is efficient and practical, and the people live well but wholly without luxury. They have no fine foods, no arts, no culture, no comforts or amenities. Socrates expands this healthy city to the "luxurious city," which has comforts and amenities. The luxurious city is much larger, so Socrates adds an army to defend this city's extensive land and properties, making particular note that the soldiers must be a specialized class. The luxurious city, then, has two groups—farmers or craftsmen, and guardians who lead and protect. The character of the city guardians is important. They must be spirited enough to defend the city, but their aggressiveness must be tempered by philosophy to make them gentle and moderate, preventing them from turning on the populace.

Education is the key to developing this balanced character in the guardians. This education must encompass physical education for the body and music and poetry education for the soul. Teachers must choose carefully which stories to tell the young guardians-in-training: the students must never hear stories of the gods behaving in cowardly or immoral ways, for these stories would teach the young guardians to behave in cowardly or immoral ways. Furthermore, such stories are untrue, for the gods are good, and no untrue story may be told in the city. Socrates says that the guardians must be educated to be as god-fearing and godlike as possible. To this end, teachers must give the students only examples of godly excellence upon which to model themselves.

SUMMARY: BOOK III

Socrates continues his discussion of stories that cannot be told in the just city. Stories that depict Hades as terrible or depressing must be forbidden, for they will make the guardians fearful of death. Socrates notes that, if anyone must have access to any falsehoods (like the stories of the gods behaving immorally), it must be the guardians, because they can then control this information.

Socrates then enumerates other types of stories that must be forbidden in the just city: stories about lamenting, for lamenting is unmanly and weak; stories about sex and revelry, because they encourage immoderation; and stories about greed, because love of money is base. Now that he has discussed stories about heroes and gods, Socrates says that he must pause, for it is impossible to decide what stories about people are appropriate until he has established what it is that makes people just or unjust.

Then, Socrates discusses the styles of stories and songs that will be allowed. He lays out what he considers appropriate modes and meters for music and wonders whether these stories ought to be in dramatic or in lyric form. He sets out restrictions on musical instruments and on the types of rhythms that are permitted in songs. After concluding his discussion of music, Socrates moves on to the other arts, such as painting and architecture. In all of these arts, as in poetry, he forbids the artists to represent characters that are vicious, unrestrained, slavish, or graceless. Any characteristics besides those that the guardians should emulate must be excluded.

Now that Socrates is satisfied with the basic education of the guardians, he considers the question of their physical training. This area requires much less care, because if the guardians follow the prescriptions Socrates has laid out regarding the education of their minds, it will be almost unavoidable for them not to follow suit by working their bodies into shape. Socrates' only recommendation is that the guardians maintain simplicity, as in Homer's epics, in which the military men live very simple lives without luxury.

Socrates then discusses doctors and judges in the just city. Ideally, doctors, from an early age, should have experience with the widest range of people and illness possible, for such experience prepares them to provide the best quality treatment. Judges, on the other hand, should have their early experience limited to virtuous people, for then injustice will be unfamiliar, repugnant, and easily recognizable to them later in their careers.

Returning to the subject of the guardians, Socrates stresses that their education must be balanced between philosophy and physical training so that they become neither too "soft" and cerebral nor too harsh and warlike. Socrates then divides the guardian population into complete guardians and auxiliaries. The complete guardians are the true leaders, while the auxiliaries are the deputies and soldiers. According to Socrates, the city obviously should pick the best guardians to lead, which probably means choosing the eldest among the physically fit men of the founding population of the city, since the eldest are bound to be the wisest. Socrates believes, however, that this method is not really sufficient for selection of leaders, so he proposes a series of tests and trials that show which children born in the city are up to the heavy challenges of leadership. He opens these tests to *all* children born in the city, including those born of the lower class—farmers, craftsmen, and so on. The tests must be designed to discover who has the correct mix of intellectual tenacity, spiritedness and aggressiveness, and philosophical moderation to lead the city—a rare mix of traits, in Socrates' opinion. Socrates also considers it important that there be tests that challenge the potential guardians' beliefs in the city, for such tests would reveal who has absorbed the most from their education. These select few would exemplify all the qualities of a good leader.

Socrates then devises a scheme to convince the populace of this arrangement. He relates the Phoenician "myth of metals" as a possible means to do so: tell the people that all their education and upbringing was a sort of dream, and in fact they all came from the earth and are related. When the gods made them, they mixed certain metals in each of them, and the mix of metals from which a person was made defines that person. Those people with gold mixed in them become complete guardians, those with silver become auxiliaries, and those with iron and bronze become farmers and craftsmen.

It is possible, however, for a child of gold to be born to parents of iron and bronze; such children must always move into the guardian class. Likewise, anyone born of guardians who does not have silver or gold metal at their core must be demoted to tradesman, for a prophecy has stated that the city will fall if ever one of these inferior people attains a position of leadership. Thus, a system of trial and test will ensure that the best and most worthy of the population will always be in a position of leadership.

ANALYSIS: THE GOLDEN LIE

From the start, the myth of metals comes across as a dishonest method of implementing a policy of eugenic racism on the part of the city's leadership—and further examination seems to confirm, rather than deny, this view. Therefore, the myth of metals raises new issues in any consideration of Plato. He clearly believes that there are people of superior and inferior natures and that those of superior natures have a genetic right to rule over those of inferior natures. Plato's assertions come across as less extreme if we replace his terminology—"superior natures"—with the word smart, however, for most people would concede that there are smart people and less smart people. Speaking in simple terms, many would agree that the smarter people in a population should be in positions of leadership. We might even agree that, in general, we would guess that smarter parents would generally have smarter children, although less smart parents might also have smart children. These assertions are the essence of what Plato says in Book III, and they are fairly acceptable even by modern standards. Where Plato does run awry of modern values is in his rigidity in social structuring: he more or less establishes a caste system under which individuals have no mobility whatsoever.

Perhaps the most important thing the myth of metals teaches is Plato's view of human talent, which is, it seems, wholly informed by his belief in objective human good. Modern society is cautious about claims to define human intelligence alone, let alone human worth in its entirety. Plato, on the other hand, feels comfortable defining, or at least categorizing, human worth. Admittedly, this tendency stems in part from the lack of any egalitarian sentiment in classical Greece as compared to modern America. But it is also partially due to Plato's particular brand of philosophy. Plato was not a cautious philosopher: he employed a moral perspective almost all of the time, and *The Republic* as a whole is an emphatic testament to that.

PHILOSOPHY

SUMMARY: BOOK IV

Adeimantus asks how the guardians of the just city could possibly be happy with the situation Socrates describes—living without owning land, without family, in barracks their entire lives. He claims that the guardians would watch as the populace gains wealth and luxury, while they themselves labor in protection of that wealth but are unable to share it. Surely, Adeimantus claims, such an arrangement goes against the spirit of the ideal city, for it ensures the unhappiness of one class.

Socrates responds that the guardians would not be unhappy, for their education would improve their understanding of things. Moreover, this arrangement is, in fact, exactly in keeping with the spirit of the city, for it guarantees the whole city's greatest common happiness, which is the goal in the first place—not the guarantee of excessive happiness on some part. Each sector of the population would fulfill its function, and this would contribute to the greatest common good. To this end, Socrates notes that both wealth and poverty pose threats, for each makes the bearer less productive: wealth makes a tradesman or farmer slothful, but poverty prevents him from having enough food, tools, and time to do his work well.

The conversation then turns to the making of laws in the just city. While Socrates concedes the needs for the basic laws that they have discussed as a constitution for this city, he feels that, beyond those basic laws, things might well be left to the guardians because of their education. Once the guardians' education is in line, the laws they create are guaranteed to be just and sensible, and the society as a whole is guaranteed to be healthy and well-run.

At this point, Socrates deems it time to take stock of whether this city is just. He says that the city is completely good, and therefore wise, courageous, moderate, and just. He ascribes each virtue to a different part of the population. The city is wise because its guardians, who have passed all the trials, are wise; it is courageous because the auxiliaries are courageous; and it is moderate because "the desires of the inferior many are controlled by the wisdom and desires of the superior few." Speaking broadly, the city is in control of its baser appetites.

Socrates now expresses amusement at his own foolishness, for the definition of justice appears to have been underneath his nose this entire time. He defines justice, at this point, as "doing one's own work." The assumption made from the outset—that the wise should lead, the less wise should be tradesmen and craftsmen, and each should focus on performing their duties and avoid meddling in the affairs of the other—is what makes this city just. The city becomes unjust when its different classes start to meddle in one another's affairs, as when a moneylender, arrogant because of his wealth, feels he should lead.

Now that Socrates has defined justice on the level of the city as a whole, he must collapse his arguments into a definition of justice for the individual. First, he divides the human soul into three parts—the appetitive, the spirited, and the rational. These categories are drawn from the city—the rational part of the soul corresponds to the wise rulers of the city; the spirited part to the aggressive auxiliaries; and the appetitive part, although less explicitly detailed, to the desires for various satisfactions that lie within both society and the individual. When an individual displays moderation then, the rational part of his or soul rules the appetitive and spirited parts of the soul.

Socrates then presents his definition of justice in the individual: "one who is just does not allow any part of himself to do the work of another part or allow the various classes within himself to meddle with each other." Again, Socrates simply compresses the virtues of the city into the individual. To act justly, then, is to act in accordance with this inner harmony of the different parts of the soul.

The dialogue then returns to the original question—although Socrates has defined justice, the question remains whether it is beneficial and profitable to behave justly and perhaps suffer the consequences, or to live unjustly with the corresponding benefits. Glaucon feels that the question has been answered already, for Socrates has described unjust behavior as a condition of a soul in disorder and turmoil. How could anyone whose soul is so unbalanced be happy?

Socrates, on the other hand, is not satisfied that they have resolved the question, so he suggests a further examination of virtue and vice. He says that there is one form of virtue and infinite forms of vice, four of which are worth mentioning. Socrates matches these five forms (one virtuous, four not virtuous) to types of souls and civil constitutions and says that he has been discussing the first form this whole time. The first form has two names: if ruled by a single leader, it is called a kingship; if ruled by a group of leaders, it is called an aristocracy. Together, these form one kind of constitution, as there is no real difference if there is a king or a group of leaders.

PHILOSOPHY

SUMMARY: BOOK V

Socrates affirms that the kingship / aristocracy described at the end of Book IV is the one good form. Just as he is about to discuss the four bad ones, Polemarchus and Adeimantus interrupt him and demand that he explain something (the discussion of the four bad forms is put off until Book VIII). In his description of the guardians' education, Socrates hinted that the guardians would possess all wives and children in common. Polemarchus and Adeimantus ask him to explain this notion, as it seems controversial. Socrates responds that he indeed meant that the guardians would all share their wives and children. This affirmation leads to a discussion of the place of women in the city.

In the first of several radical claims that he makes in this section, Socrates declares that females should be reared and trained alongside males, receiving the same education and taking on the same political roles. Though he acknowledges that in many respects men and women have different natures, he believes that in the relevant respect—the division among appetitive, spirited, and rational people—women fall along the same natural lines as men. Thus, there is no reason not to train women to join the men in all the activities of ruling.

Socrates then discusses his plans for breeding guardians in the city. The best women would be chosen to be guardians, just as the best men would be. Then, comparing the rulers to any animal population in which one breeds from the best animals to produce the best offspring, Socrates lays down a strict set of rules surrounding sex and procreation in order to guarantee the finest genetic stock possible in the city. Socrates' laws to reach this goal are as follows:

1. People may have sex only within their own group, and the city rulers must sanction all sex.
2. The rulers must take all babies when they are born. They must expose the babies of inferior people to the elements, leaving them to die, whereas they must give the superior infants to nurses for care.
3. People may have sex only during the prime years of their life. Any baby born to people having sex beyond those years must be exposed.
4. To avoid accidental incest, people must not have sex with anyone who, by age, could be their children or parents.

5. All people in the city must refer to their peers as "brother" or "sister," their elders as "father" or "mother," and their juniors as "son" or "daughter."

Socrates notes that the guardians must hide some of these practices from the people in general, so he proposes a rigged lottery to guarantee that the best men will have sex with the best women. Also, people must not know what becomes of their babies after the rulers have taken them—whether they lived or were exposed. These measures would provide the benefit of the entire population being one family, thus providing an unprecedented sense of camaraderie.

Next, Socrates outlines his views on war in the just city. When the rulers go to war together, they should bring their children in order to train the younger generation in the military arts. Socrates proposes allowing the children to have swift horses on the battlefield so that they can escape if the need arises. Warriors who distinguish themselves on the battlefield should get better access to women and other rewards. Fallen auxiliaries should receive a decent burial befitting their great lives and virtuous deaths.

Finally, Socrates explains the practical means by which this ideal just city could come about. He starts by qualifying his statements, noting that some concessions to reality are inevitable. Socrates claims, however, there is great merit to these ideas even if they cannot be implemented. In any case, there is a way to make the just city come to pass as he has described and work well: to make sure that the king of the city is a philosopher, making the city a lover of all wisdom. As a philosopher, the city would be enamored with the Forms of Beauty and Justice.

ANALYSIS: THE FORMS

For the first time in *The Republic*, the theory of Forms plays a part in Plato's account of justice. Plato presents philosophy as the ideal calling, the only true calling that leads a person to an understanding of truth—through the theory of Forms—that is necessary for leadership.

A rigorous examination of Plato's theory of Forms shows that:

1. Forms are free of the contradictions that plague other things—a "tall" tree is taller than some trees but shorter than others. The Form of Tall is just tall. It does not represent this duality.

2. Forms are wholly unchanging and stable. All other things are in a constant state of flux.
3. Our senses cannot tell us about the Forms. Anything that we sense both constantly changes (as in no. 2) and represents opposites (as in no. 1) and therefore is not a Form.
4. Forms are removed from sensible things: the Form of Tall does not change as a tall tree decays and dies. The Form of Tall would exist even if there were nothing tall in the world.

Each of the defining characteristics of the Forms (except perhaps the fourth) is key to an understanding of the remaining portion of *The Republic*, which is a discussion of the joys of philosophy—joys that, in turn, are based on the Forms.

SUMMARY: BOOK VI

Socrates continues his argument about why philosophers must lead the just city. Philosophers love the Forms and all learning and, therefore, love truth. A philosopher's focus on learning also perfectly prepares his temperament for leadership. Philosophy is moderate by definition, as it is a love of wisdom that drives it. At this point, Adeimantus interjects with another challenge: how can Socrates expect people to accept a philosopher-king, when all the contemporary philosophers are either vicious or useless? Surprisingly, Socrates agrees but also says that he can explain the causes of both these types of philosophers, neither of which are accurate representations of true philosophy.

First, Socrates uses a metaphor to explain why people think philosophers are useless. He describes a ship in which there is no leadership—every soldier fights to navigate the ship and be captain all the time. Regardless of any individual soldier's skill as a navigator, his getting the job is based not on navigational ability but rather on the ability to trick or convince his fellow sailors into allowing him to navigate. Furthermore, the other soldiers might say that he is a good navigator, despite the fact that he has no skill, for he has other skills that get him the position. The most unfortunate aspect of this situation, according to Socrates, is that there are a few soldiers who do know navigation well but are stuck on the sidelines, "useless," because they lack the other skills necessary to take control of the situation. Those men are the philosophers whom others presume useless—the men who should be ruling but are not, simply because they lack the political skills to assume leadership.

The vicious philosophers are another matter entirely. Socrates explains that this viciousness is the result of bad education: someone with the unique and strong nature of a philosopher is in fact more likely to be wicked and vicious if brought up incorrectly, because those strong personality traits that become virtues when well cultivated become too extreme when poorly cultivated. Socrates lists the Sophists as an example of bad teaching, for they teach not wisdom but simply a set of values that is slavishly based on the conventional wisdom of the people. Potential philosophers so taught do not learn wisdom, so they cannot learn of the Forms.

Socrates then reminds his listeners that they still are discussing virtue and vice. At this point, he is reluctant to continue that discussion without examining the principle at the root of it—the Form of the Good. Some people think the good is pleasure, while the more sophisticated feel it is knowledge. But no one, when asked what kind of knowledge, can really come up with an answer. Socrates says that he himself cannot come up with an adequate explanation of the good at the moment, but that they can discuss what he considers to be an "offspring" of the good in order to understand it better.

Socrates sets off to explain this idea of the "offspring" of the good. He starts by discussing the eyes. The virtue, or arete, of the eyes is vision, for their function is to see. In order to perform that function, however, the eyes need light from the sun. This light illuminates the world and thus makes seeing possible, and yet it itself also is seen. Socrates links this idea to the good: "What the good itself is in the intelligible realm, in relation to understanding and intelligible things, the sun is in the visible realm, in relation to sight and visible things." He goes on to explain that when we turn our understanding to something "lit" by the truth of the good, we come to understand that thing. When something lacks that illumination, all that we can do is speculate. Likewise, just as we can see sunlight, so can we turn our understanding to the good itself—the good is the thing that makes understanding possible, and can itself be the subject of inquiry. Furthermore, just as the sun nourishes the plants and animals we see with its light, so does the good nourish those things that we try to understand by it: "their being is also due to it although the good is not being, but superior to it in rank."

With Glaucon and Adeimantus urging him on, Socrates continues to try to explain his idea using the metaphor of a line. He imagines a line divided into two unequal sections. The smaller section represents opinion, the larger knowledge. Then, he imagines dividing those sections again in the same ratio as the original division of the line. The divisions of opinion are imagination (the smaller) and belief (the larger). The divisions of knowledge are thought (the smaller) and understanding (the larger). This line now represents the modes of human understanding. The only way to reach the top, understanding, is through an understanding of the Forms. Sensory perceptions alone can take a person only as far as belief. Thought also is possible without the Forms (intelligent hypotheses fall into the category of thoughts—this is as far scientific inquiry goes). The Forms are required, however, for understanding. Finally, the length of each section along the line indicates what portion of true understanding it comprises.

SUMMARY: BOOK VII

Book VII begins with Socrates' famous allegory of the cave, in which the philosopher tries to explain his theory of the good and its place in human understanding. He describes a situation in which people are born and raised in a very dark cave and chained so that they can face only the back of the cave. Behind them is a fire, and behind that a ledge on which sit several statues that can be manipulated like puppets. Throughout their lives, all that the people in the cave see is the shadows of the puppets moving on the back wall of the cave. To these people, a shadow of a puppet on the wall is a person. If you were to free one of these people and force him out of the cave, he would be blinded by the sun at first and able to look only at shadows. Eventually, he could look at actual things—up at a tree, for instance, rather than at its shadow. Finally, his eyes would become accustomed enough to the light that he could look up at the sun itself and see the light that it brings to the world. If this person were to return to the cave, he would be ridiculed by his former companions because he would no longer be able to see in the dark and so would seem blind and stupid to them.

Socrates draws several important lessons from this allegory. Just as the sun is the last thing that the cave man is able to look at, "in the knowable realm, the form of the good is the last thing to be seen, and it is reached only with difficulty." Furthermore, it is crucial to note that the cave man is blind both when he emerges from the cave into the light and when he returns to the cave from the light. The implication of this idea is that when someone appears to have trouble understanding something, it could mean either that they have come from a better place (from outside into the cave) or from a worse place (from the cave to the outside).

The cave allegory also proves that the role of education is not to teach—in the sense of feeding people information they lack—but rather to shed light on things that people already know. Education "isn't the craft of putting sight into the soul. Education takes for granted that sight is there but that it isn't turned the right way or looking where it ought to look, and it tries to redirect it properly."

Socrates goes on to elaborate on the specifics of the guardian's education in light of this allegory of the cave. The guardians must receive a basic education in poetry, music, and mathematics. Afterward, they must accomplish two or three years of compulsory physical training. At this point, when the youth are about twenty, the best of them must be selected to go on to another ten years of education in mathematical sciences. After this ten years there must another selection process, after which those who are chosen to continue as potential guardians would receive five years of training in dialectic (see comments for Book VII). Finally, there must be one final selection process, after which those who make the cut must go on to fifteen years of practical political training, before being ready, at the age of fifty, to become rulers of the city. Socrates then reiterates his point that, for all of this education to take place, the only thing that must happen is for a philosopher or group of philosophers to come to power in a city, send out all the citizens over the age of ten, and start that society over again.

ANALYSIS: THE ALLEGORY OF THE CAVE

The allegory of the cave is one of the clearest explanations in all of Plato's work of his view of how human beings learn. This view is linked to his idea of the immortality of the soul (discussed in Book X) and works as follows. Because the soul is immortal, we are born "knowing" everything we will ever know. All we have to do is remember it or be guided into remembering it. In the dialogue Meno, Socrates proves this assertion by leading a slave boy into "remembering" a geometric proof rather than teaching it to the boy. Plato feels that all learning works in this way—a teacher's job is to guide students into remembrance of things known rather than to fill them with new knowledge.

Moreover, the allegory of the cave connects with Plato's metaphors of the sun and the line. The light of the sun, or the good, shines down upon things and helps the student to remember them. The student does not have to be told what things are once the light is on them; rather, he recognizes what they are now that he can see them. Likewise, the four stages of the cave man's journey are equivalent to the four segments of Plato's line. Imagination corresponds to the time when the cave man is still in the cave, watching only the shadows of things against the wall. Belief corresponds to the time when the cave man has left the cave and is starting to look around, although his eyes are not yet accustomed to the sun. Thought corresponds to the time when the cave man is able to look at things in the light of the sun and tries to come to an understanding of their true nature. Finally, understanding corresponds to the time when the cave man is finally able to look up at the Sun itself and see the light that shines. To a degree, this interpretation of the line metaphor modifies the earlier idea of the line, for it makes understanding a cohesive whole—it seems to be difficult, in Plato's mind, to master only some of the forms. Once a person is ready to look up at the sun and bask in the splendorous light of the good, he understands the unity that brings the Forms of all things together.

SUMMARY: BOOK VIII

At this point, Socrates returns to the discussion that was interrupted at the beginning of Book V—the four bad kinds of people and the constitutions that correspond to them. He hopes to use this examination to compare, at last, the benefits of justice and injustice and find out whether it is better to behave justly or unjustly. Socrates asserts that there are four kinds of bad city constitutions and individual traits that correspond to them. These are, from best to worst, the timocracy, the oligarchy, the democracy, and the tyranny. The just city, in decay, passes through these stages in the above order.

The first type of government is the timocracy. The timocracy occurs when, inevitably, the guardians of the just city make mistakes in the eugenics system, and mistaken births force them to put people with iron and bronze natures into positions of leadership. These mistakes do not change the structure of the city enormously—the guardians are still separate from the tradesmen, and so on—but a few important and sinister changes take place. The mixing within the ruling class leads to a large group of leaders who are not philosophers but rather are ruled by their spirited parts—and therefore are overly warlike and proud. When leaders are overly proud, the state tends to be always at war. Moreover, proud leaders often tend to keep private treasuries of money.

The transition from timocracy to oligarchy occurs as these leaders with their own treasuries start to bend the laws that govern their ability to spend the money on themselves. As the leaders bend the laws, the constitution of the just city ultimately is wholly destroyed, and wealth becomes more important than virtue in measuring a person's worth. Indeed, the oligarchic personality is defined by a disinterest in anything but money. The transition to oligarchy leads to a total dissolution of the just constitution for several reasons:

1. Justice disappears, for those making lots of money—traders, merchants, and so on—and the leaders are one and the same. The separation of roles that defines justice is now gone.
2. Whereas the population of the city previously was unified, it becomes divided between rich and poor—two groups that have different interests.
3. The greatest of all evils is realized when truly poor people are not part of the society, as they are not part of any of its parts (soldiers, craftsmen, and so on). In short, the poor have no stake or involvement in the city.
4. The state becomes powerless because of war. Either the weak oligarchs are forced to fight and are always defeated because they are unfit and few, or they are forced to arm the poor, who may well rebel.

When the poor people finally do rebel, kick out the wealthy, and redistribute the land and goods, democracy arises. Democracy is characterized by a total freedom of anyone to do anything. Although this state of affairs may seem ideal at first, it ultimately lapses into anarchy, chaos, hedonism, and lack of personal or societal discipline. Socrates says that democracy eventually lapses back into a semi- oligarchy in which a few members take advantage of their freedom and amass great wealth and power, and the people—justly or not—seek to depose them.

To depose these purported oligarchs, the people choose a champion. The many, being more powerful than the few, are able to put their champion in control. At first, this champion is promising, but soon he starts to amass power and destroys anyone who threatens his own power—which ultimately means killing anyone wise, brave, or strong. The champion thereby cripples the state and amasses power for himself until the state becomes a full-blown tyranny.

SUMMARY: BOOK IX

After describing the tyrannical state, Socrates embarks on a description of the soul of the tyrannical man. He starts by enumerating the base desires that everyone has—appetitive instincts that, unchecked, can lead people to do horrible and unnatural things. Most people—and philosophers most of all—are able to rule their appetitive part with their rational part. A man becomes tyrannical when he loses control of these appetites. The tyrannical man is vicious because his uncontrolled desires drive him to do terrible things in order to fulfill them. He is also the most wretched and unhappy of men because he is never satisfied, as his appetites always sting him into worse and worse actions. Happiness eludes him because his rational, good part is wholly subjugated.

The only thing worse than the private tyrannical man is the tyrannical man whom fate offers the chance to take power in public life. As a slave to his own base desires, the tyrant uses his power to fulfill them, alienating everyone and making enemies. Thus, the metaphorical prison of the private tyrant—the prison of his own desires—becomes a literal prison as the political tyrant surrounds himself with people who want him dead and ousted. He can never leave his city or even the protection of his guards.

With this information, Glaucon declares it clear, and Socrates agrees, that the just man is happier than the tyrannical man, in the same way that the just city is a better place than the tyrannical city. Glaucon bases his decision on the description of the just man's soul—which is contented and ruled by its rational part—in comparison to the tyrant's soul. Socrates has two additional proofs of their conclusion, however.

The first proof is based on the superiority of the rational part of the soul. Socrates says that, clearly, the money-loving person (appetite), the honor-loving person (spirit), and the philosopher (rational) all think that their joys are the best joys and that their way of life is best. However, of the three, only the philosopher has any understanding of the joys of the other two. The philosopher's study of truth and the theory of Forms—combined with the fact that it is the rational part that judges things and compares them—makes it clear that the philosophical man has the best vantage point from which to judge which is the best way of life. Therefore, the philosophical man's conclusion that his way is best has more credibility than the money-lover's or the honor-lover's.

Socrates considers his second argument to be the most important, the "greatest and most decisive of overthrows." This argument asserts that the pleasures of philosophy—filling oneself up with a knowledge of Forms, truth, and virtue—are greater pleasures than all others because they involve great, unchanging things, whereas the other pleasures (food, sex, power, and so on) are limited because they are based in short-lived, worldly things. Socrates then calculates that the just man is 729 times happier than the tyrant.

Socrates ends by painting a mental picture of the tripartite soul. The spirited part can be represented by a lion, the appetitive part by a many-headed monster, and the rational part by a human being. In the just person, these three parts live in harmony, with the human controlling the other two. In the unjust person, the other two parts overpower the human and dragging it about, powerless.

SUMMARY: BOOK X

Socrates now returns his attention to subject of poetry about human beings, which he left off in Book III. He states that imitative poetry is bad and must not be allowed into the just city. To explain why imitative poetry is so bad, Socrates uses an analogy involving carpenters. When a carpenter makes a bed, he is making something that contains the Form of Bed but that is not itself that very form. Rather, the bed is a copy of that form. Then, if a painter happens to paint a picture of the bed, he makes an imitation of a copy. There are three kinds of things, then: the original form, produced by the god; the copy, produced by the carpenter; and the imitation of the copy, produced by the painter. Imitation, then, is three degrees removed from truth (the Greeks always included the first item in a series). The painting is simply an imitation of the appearance of the bed, and the painter has no understanding of the craft of bed making or of the true Form of "bed."

A poem written about the bed is just like a painting—it is an imitation three degrees removed from the truth. Therefore, as Socrates sarcastically puts it, "a poetic imitator is an accomplished fellow when it comes to wisdom about the subjects of his poetry!" His implication is that poets—whom many people consider wise because they are able to represent so many things and therefore seem to understand so many things—in fact have an understanding of nothing that they represent. Therefore, Socrates states, there is nothing to be learned from imitative poetry, for it feeds the irrational part of the soul. Imitative poetry cannot exist in the just city—

only hymns to gods and eulogies to great citizens. Socrates does say, however, that he would be willing to hear arguments proving that poetry was beneficial in an attempt to mend the "ancient quarrel between [poetry] and philosophy."

Socrates' final subject in *The Republic* is the immortality of the soul. To prove that the soul is immortal, he notes that anything, when it is destroyed, is destroyed by its own natural badness. However, there does not appear to be any natural badness that destroys the soul. It is a mistake to say that the body's evil destroys it, for nothing can be destroyed by something else's natural badness. Injustice of the soul, though terrible, does not destroy the soul, as evidenced by the fact that unjust people do not die of their own accord—rather, they are killed by others. If something has no natural badness, there is nothing that can destroy it, and it therefore must be eternal.

Socrates concludes his argument with the myth of Er, a tale of a man who was brought back from the dead to tell people how things work after life. One is sent to either heaven or Hades, depending on the justice of one's life, and spends a thousand years there—ten times longer than a life span. Then, when it is time for a soul to return, all the souls draw lots to choose what sort of life they will lead when they return—a rich tyrant, a poor farmer, and so on. The souls are no wiser than people: some make wise choices, some foolish. Then, the souls go, forget everything of their previous life, and are sent back to earth to live again. This cycle continues without end. By living justly, Socrates concludes, one can assure one's happiness while on earth and on the thousand-year journey that lies beyond.

ANALYSIS: THE MYTH OF ER

Plato's opinion about the soul implies that, because souls are eternal, they know everything and therefore have only to be reminded of it in order to recollect it. Plato brings together the work of *The Republic* with the myth of Er in his conclusion not only that it is more beneficial to live justly while on Earth, but also that it guarantees another thousand years of beneficial living after our earthly lives are done. He intends this argument to be the deciding factor for anyone who might have been unconvinced of the fact that, even if justice is better, it is better to live justly all things considered. For Plato, then, the immortal soul is not a sentimental belief but rather an idea linked to the core of his philosophy, an idea that supports his teachings about learning, understanding, and the theory of the Forms.

From the point of view of argumentation, Plato's placement of the myth of Er at the end of his work is clever. The myth of Er, as Socrates tells it, is beautiful, ethereal, and fantastic. It seems wonderful—to live well, experience a thousand years of pleasure, and then get to choose what sort of life we get to live again. This entire section of *The Republic*, from the visual description of the part of the afterlife Er saw, to the description of the souls, to the inclusion of famous Greek literary figures among those souls, is enchanting and magical. Plato ends his work with a stirring passage that links to his philosophy, certainly, but is told with greater flourish, splendor, and detail than his philosophy dictates. This ending is a skilled rhetorical move on Plato's part and an evocative way to end his lofty discussion of human good and justice.

PHILOSOPHY

ARISTOTLE

CONTEXT AND BACKGROUND

Aristotle was born in 384 B.C. in ancient Stagira, part of Macedonia—a region in northern Greece that the residents of the more southerly cities of Athens, Sparta, and Thebes did not consider a true part of Greece. Nonetheless, the Macedonians were a Hellenistic society, and Aristotle received a characteristic Greek upper-class upbringing. His father, Nicomachus, was the personal physician of Amyntas, king of Macedonia and grandfather of Alexander the Great. Nicomachus profited well by the association and became a wealthy man with many estates.

Around the age of seventeen, Aristotle left Macedonia to attend Plato's Academy in Athens. He quickly became a leading student, and then a leading teacher, at the Academy. After some time, however, Aristotle's thought began to conflict with portions of Plato's doctrines, and the close relationship between the two deteriorated. After being passed over for the position of head of the Academy in 347 B.C., Aristotle left Athens in disgust to teach prominent men throughout Greece. Perhaps most famous, in 343 B.C., Aristotle was enlisted as the tutor of Alexander (soon to be the Alexander the Great), the young son of Philip of Macedonia. Although Aristotle tutored Alexander for three years, we know little of the association between the two. Their relationship ended badly, as Alexander grew extremely suspicious of Aristotle, who barely avoided execution on charges of treason. At the end of the three years, Aristotle returned to his homeland to teach once again.

In 335 B.C., after once again having been passed over as head of the Academy, Aristotle founded his own school in Athens, called the Lyceum. The Lyceum, founded on Aristotelian rather than Platonic philosophy, enjoyed great success. Aristotle gave his lectures while walking, so his followers came to be known as Peripatetics ("those who walk up and down"). After years of teaching, Aristotle was forced to flee Athens in 323 B.C., when Alexander's death resulted in political retaliation against Macedonians such as Aristotle. He retired to a property in Chalkas, where he lived for a year in peaceful solitude before his death.

Aristotle's philosophy is rooted in the work and methodology of his first and greatest teacher, Plato. However, there are also great differences between the two, which center on their conflicting metaphysical (Plato) and scientific (Aristotle) approaches to knowledge. One of the fundamentals of Plato's philosophical system was his theory of Forms. Plato believed that, after a point, scientific observation of the world was bound to be flawed. Thus, truth could only be sought by resorting to metaphysical ideas about the Forms or essences of things (see Plato's *Phaedo* or *Republic* for a more extended discussion of Forms). Plato's philosophy requires a belief in these Forms, which, by definition, never are observable.

Aristotle, in contrast, believed that scientific inquiry and the rigorous organization of knowledge could explain the world. He was devoted to a systematization of learning that consisted of set rules and methods that could be defined and repeated. It was this urge towards systematization that led Aristotle to develop the fundamental concepts of logic. Although Plato did appreciate the importance of rational thought, Aristotle took this approach far further than Plato ever did. Indeed, Western logic can trace its origins to Aristotle's work.

Unfortunately, none of Aristotle's own words have survived. All the texts we have by Aristotle are, in fact, compilations of lecture notes from his time at the Lyceum. The fact that the *Ethics* is such a compilation of notes explains both its repetitiveness and its style. Moreover, the *Ethics* is not the definitive version of Aristotle's thought but rather a work in progress that likely changed from year to year. Because of these factors, it is hard to place the *Ethics* chronologically with respect to Aristotle's other works.

This uncertainty about the chronology of Aristotle's ideas does not, however, prevent us from discussing the place of the *Ethics* within Aristotle's larger philosophical system. Aristotle divided learning into three types: theoretical, productive, and practical. Theoretical science encompassed "physics" (what we would call metaphysics), mathematics, theology, and natural science. Most of Aristotle's surviving work is theoretical in nature. The *Ethics*, however, is squarely practical. It seeks to make us good people; that is, it does not merely discuss virtue in the abstract but also provides us with a blueprint for virtuous behavior and happy living.

PHILOSOPHY

ETHICS

SUMMARY: BOOK I

The "good" can be defined as the end, or goal, of any activity. The good can either be an activity or a product. When the good is a product of an action, the product is superior to the action. There are, therefore, many "goods," for every activity has its own good.

There is also a hierarchy of goods. Any activity that can be considered part of another activity, or subordinate to it, has a good that is correspondingly subordinate. For instance, all the skills involved in making a meal (cutting, frying, measuring, and so on) and their corresponding goods (cut meat, fried meat, measured flour) are subordinate to that activity and to the ultimate good—the complete meal. The good of the meal is therefore more important than any of the individual components that compose it.

The most central good therefore comes from the most central activity. That activity, according to Aristotle, is political science. Political science is the science to which all others are subordinate because it dictates how and when all of these other sciences are taught and implemented. All activities exist in order to service the goal of politics—the betterment of the society.

The end of political science is happiness. Happiness is not something superficially manifested, such as wealth or fame, although that is what many people think. Happiness itself is worthwhile: it defines all other goods, since all other goods strive towards it as an end.

People lead their lives according to their understanding of happiness, and there are three major styles of life—that of gratification, that of political activity, and that of study. The life of gratification is the basest because it consists of pursuing happiness in the form of superficial pleasures, which are never really ends in themselves. The political life is less base, for it strives for honor. However, this too is somewhat superficial, because honor is dependent on the judgments of other people. The ultimate good is, presumably, independent of such judgments. The life of study, which is discussed in more depth later in the text, is the least base.

There is no universal concept of good by which we can judge things. If there were a single Idea of the Good, then there would have to be a single corresponding activity that works to that end. In truth, there are many ways of accomplishing any good. Furthermore, were there a single Idea of the Good, then the Idea of the Good would, by definition, be identical to any individual good, making the entire discussion pointless. Lastly, the fact that the Idea of the Good is eternal does not make it any more of an example of good.

How does one achieve happiness? Perhaps the solution is to fulfill one's function as a human being. For example, the good of a flutist insofar as being a flutist is the goal of fine flute playing. What, then, is the good of a human being insofar as being a human being? To reach an answer, we must discern what is unique about being a human being, for the good of a human being must be unique to human beings. Rationality alone is what makes humans unique. Therefore, it must be some action of the individual on behalf of rationality that is the activity of human good.

The human function, then, is to act in pursuit of reason itself, or to act in such a way that obeys the reason of another person. Because the fulfillment of a good is a virtue, and given that the human purpose is to pursue a life of reason, the pursuit of a life of reason to its fullest extent must fulfill some kind of virtue. Therefore, living rationally in pursuit of the human good is the soul's most virtuous activity. These conclusions agree with common beliefs that most people and other philosophers hold. By common sense, goods can be divided into three types: external (outside the individual), goods of the body, and goods of the soul. Goods of the soul are said to be the best of the three, so it is sensible to focus on them.

We can use several common beliefs about happiness to form a fuller definition: first, that happiness in its true form is best, finest, and most pleasant; second, that by doing that which we ought to do, we come to the greatest personal pleasure; and third, that since happiness can be aided by external goods—such as wealth or physical gifts—it would seem that virtue needs some prosperity added to it truly to bloom into happiness. Happiness, then, is behaving virtuously at all times, with an adequate (but not resplendent) supply of external goods—all of which provides a guarantee that one's end will be suitable. We should praise happiness as a perfect good unto itself rather than as a means to anything. This conclusion must be true because happiness is itself the ultimate means to which all other things aim—and it cannot be said that something can be a means to itself.

The soul can be divided into rational and irrational parts, and then the irrational part can be divided into two further parts. One part may be called the vegetative part, the cause of nutrition and growth, which is not unique to humans but is possessed by all crea-

PHILOSOPHY

tures. The vegetative part has no interaction with the rational part. The other part of the irrational soul may be called the appetitive or desirous part, and this part does interact with reason. In fact, reason must master and moderate this desirous part.

SUMMARY: BOOK II

We can divide virtue into two categories: intellectual and moral. Intellectual virtues are developed by teaching and instruction, whereas moral virtues are developed by force of habit. People do not possess moral virtues intrinsically. Although the soul is designed to receive moral virtues, these virtues must grow through the exercise of good habits if they are to develop into guiding forces. The soul acquires moral virtue by exercising it, just as the pianist learns to play the piano by playing it and not by thinking about it. In short, virtuous activity breeds virtuous character.

The first thing we can say about virtuous conduct is that it is inconsistent with excess or deficiency. Any moral quality (courage, for instance) can be present in excess (rashness) or deficiency (cowardice). In all things, virtue represents a middle ground between too much and too little. A virtuous person will react moderately to both pleasure and pain.

If a person commits a virtuous act accidentally, the act is still worthwhile, but we cannot consider it part of our examination of human virtue. In order to be fully virtuous, an act must be performed by someone who is aware of what he is doing and why he is doing it. This is particularly true if we consider that virtue, if it is to be taught, must be strengthened by habit. If a person commits virtuous acts without awareness of their worth, those acts cannot strengthen the person's habits.

We may speak of the feelings, faculties, or dispositions of the soul. Feelings are emotions, faculties are the capability of having emotions, and dispositions are our inclinations to have emotions. Virtues must be dispositions, for no one is praised or condemned for their emotions alone or their ability to feel them, but rather on their reactions (and therefore inclinations). Furthermore, human excellence must be the disposition that makes a person most inclined to be a good person and fulfill the human function—to live a virtuous, rational life.

The doctrine of the mean can help uncover the nature of the virtuous dispositions. Virtue consists of seeking the mean in one's responses to other people and the world. This path of moderation is difficult and leaves an infinite amount of space for error—people can be bad in countless ways, but there is only one way to be virtuous. Certain evil acts—murder, adultery, and so on—cannot be practiced at the virtuous mean. There is no right way or right time to commit murder: it represents an absolute evil, and one must avoid it always if one is to maintain virtue.

We can apply the doctrine of the mean to any personality trait we choose. In so doing, we can find the virtues that we should seek to make habitual. We generally refer to the virtuous mean as being the opposite of one of the extremes, not a middle ground between them (i.e., we say that courage is the opposite of cowardice and that temperance is the opposite of licentiousness). We do so for two reasons: first, the virtuous mean may sometimes be closer to one extreme than the other; second, we are inclined to say that the virtue is the opposite of that extreme to which we are more naturally drawn. For instance, people generally are drawn more to cowardice than to rashness, so we see courage as the opposite of cowardice rather than rashness. Despite this idea of opposites, virtue in all things is that which seeks the mean.

Summary: Book III

Actions can be voluntary or involuntary. Involuntary actions are those that people perform in ignorance or under compulsion. An act is compulsory only when its sole cause is an external force or person. When someone acts out of irrational emotion—anger, for instance—the act is not involuntary, as the emotion comes from that person's own disposition. An act is performed through ignorance when the performer is ignorant of the particular situation—acting through ignorance must be dissociated from acting in ignorance (out of drunkenness or moral depravity, for instance), which is far worse.

Moral conduct is rooted in voluntary action, which implies that moral conduct involves choice. Choice is distinct from desire or temper: all animals have desires and anger, but only human beings are capable of choice. True choice involves rational consideration, an ability unique to human beings. True choice also implies that the person choosing can determine that one action is preferable to another. This rational consideration requires deliberation: the person must consider a situation in which the proper action or outcome may not be clear. People deliberate not about ends but about how to *achieve* the best ends. Clearly, we can only deliberate among options that are within our power. Therefore, choice is a considered review of things that lie within our power.

In choosing, people of good character will always aim for the good. However, people lacking good character may understand things incorrectly and may wish only for the apparent good. Both good and vice, therefore, lie within human power, and it is possible for people to voluntarily choose vice. This explanation is supported by common laws of reward and punishment: people are punished for their bad behavior except in cases of ignorance or involuntary action.

Just as people are responsible for their own bad actions, they are also responsible for their moral states. If someone falls into a bad moral condition, it is his own fault for leading a bad life. Once established, a bad moral state is hard to remedy because it is based on habit. Just as developing virtue depends on developing habits of good behavior, bad behavior strengthens the individual's tendency toward bad behavior.

In returning to a discussion of the virtues, it is best to discuss them individually. Courage is the mean between rashness and cowardice. The courageous man, therefore, *is* afraid of certain things. We can define courage as fearless behavior in the face of honorable death or harm. This virtue appears most clearly in war. It is not always pleasurable to show courage; in fact, it may be painful. The truly courageous person is courageous on the part of a good and noble end. Many dispositions resemble courage in some way—civic courage, experience of risk, desperation, optimism, and ignorance are five examples. One must never mistake these things, which resemble courage only superficially, for true courage.

Temperance is the mean with regard to pleasures. The pleasures it concerns are physical, not psychological. The specific pleasures it concerns are those of touch and taste—sexual and gourmet desires. It is concerned not with pain or an avoidance of pain but only with pleasure itself. A desire for the wrong sort of things, or an overly strong desire for these pleasures, is licentiousness. There is no word for someone who has abnormally minimal desires for pleasure. Licentiousness differs from cowardice in that it is more voluntary—it involves choosing to indulge in pleasures—and is therefore even more reprehensible. Licentious people are like spoiled children.

Summary: Book IV

Liberality is the virtue of having the right attitude toward money. It is the mean between prodigality (excessive giving) and illiberality (excessive greed). Liberality concerns both giving and receiving money but is more concerned with giving, for virtue is better measured by the actions that people choose to do than by those things that others do for or to them.

Prodigality, or excessive generosity, is far better than illiberality, for it is a mark of foolishness rather than moral failing and because it benefits others. The prodigal person has good in him and can be taught moderation. Illiberality stems from greed or avarice. It consists of either excessive stinginess or in taking too much money from others. People are inclined more toward greed than toward excessive generosity.

Magnificence is a special kind of liberality concerned with the giving of public gifts. Excessive magnificence is defined not by giving too much but rather by giving in tasteless or ostentatious ways—one could call it garishness. A deficiency in magnificence is defined as giving less than one's means allow. A very wealthy person is expected to give public gifts of a certain scope, whereas a poor person cannot be held to the same standard. Regardless, small acts also can be magnificent.

Magnanimity is a gracious and accurate sense of self-worth. Excessive sense of self-worth is vanity; a deficient sense of self-worth is pusillanimity. A person must be of great worth to be magnanimous; a person who is of little worth and knows it is temperate but not magnanimous. The magnanimous person is great and knows it. He therefore accepts honors that are given to him, for he knows he deserves them; he does not, however, take excessive pleasure in these honors. Aware of his greatness and status, he is uncomfortable with anything that puts him in an inferior position to anyone and always seeks his rightful superior place. Pusillanimity is the opposite of magnanimity, because it is more common and a worse fault than vanity.

There is a satisfactory mean for a love of honor, but it has no name. This virtue seems particularly sensitive to context—sometimes we praise honor-loving behavior as noble, but other times we scorn it as evidence of greed for glory. The mean consists of seeking the correct amount of honor from the correct people at the correct time. Since this happy medium has no name, it seems that the two extremes are the opposites in this case (rather than the mean and one of the extremes).

The correct disposition toward anger also is difficult to name but might be called patience. An excessive tendency toward anger could be called irascibility. Patient people are not easily perturbed but get angry only when it is appropriate. Just as it is possible to be overly quick-tempered, it is possible to be overly patient and too slow to anger, which is lowly and servile. It is difficult to determine the correct degree of anger in any situation. Because irascibility is more common than excessive patience, irascibility is considered the opposite of the mean in this case.

In social interactions, amiability is the virtuous mean between obsequiousness and quarrelsomeness. Regarding honesty and self-presentation, sincerity is the virtuous mean between boasting and understatement or irony—boasting being the worse failing. In light conversation, tactful wit is the mean between buffoonery (always joking about everything) and boorishness (the inability to take or make a joke).

Lastly, modesty is not a virtue except in young people. Older people should not require modesty—since a wise person has no desire to do bad things, modesty is wholly unnecessary.

SUMMARY: BOOK V

Justice is a state of character. Since it is often easiest to understand a particular state by examining its opposite, this is the path we will pursue with regard to justice. Unjust means either lawless or unfair; therefore, justice means either lawful or fair. The just person must behave to the best advantage of any social or political association. Behaving lawfully, he will follow all social laws to the benefit of those around him, and being fair, he will in all his societal interactions bring benefit to the same. Justice, then, is a universal virtue with sovereignty over all others. It is the only virtue that encompasses not only one's own good but also the good of those with whom one associates.

Now we must turn from universal justice to look at a different justice—the justice that is a part of virtue. People tend to consider a bad action unjust only if the person performing it gains some benefit from it—if the offender does not profit, it is simply attributed to some other vice (cowardice, licentiousness, and so on). Such cases are called particular justice; that is, justice as it relates to individual actions. One kind of particular justice is concerned with the distribution of benefits (money, honor, and so on) or the rectification of an unjust allocation of these benefits.

Distributive justice concerns geometric proportion—the ratio of the worth of the people concerned in the transaction and of their shares in the goods distributed. Justice is that which keeps each person's proportion of the proceeds equal to their merit in the transaction. An unjust transaction is one in which this proportion is violated.

Rectificatory justice remedies situations in which injustice leads the proportion to be violated. This type of justice is like an arithmetical progression—a certain portion of the good must be subtracted from one party and added to another. The purpose of this type of justice is to restore equality. A judge displays rectificatory justice in deciding damages in court cases: to the best of his ability, the judge restores equality (even in cases, like murder, in which the arithmetic analogy fails).

How do we define the proportion that marks an interaction as just? Inasmuch as such a thing can be labeled, proportional reciprocity appears to be the clearest governing principle for fair exchange. This principle is called "proportional" because it is affected by the other factors in the situation (whether the action was voluntary or involuntary, the rank of those concerned, and so on). Therefore, all exchanges must be made so that the two things exchanged are of equal value.

Political justice satisfies the needs of those who live together as citizens of equal status. This justice is attainable only when set laws govern the mutual relations of individuals. These laws may be of two types—natural or civil. Natural law has the same validity everywhere, amongst all peoples; civil laws, on the other hand, must be established by each society.

When someone does something to harm someone else, we can classify the harm as one of three things. The harm is a mistake if the person perpetrated it in ignorance—that is, either by accident or not voluntarily. When the harm is not done in ignorance, but the outcome is not what one would have expected, we can call it a misadventure. When the agent deliberately but without premeditation acts to harm, the harm is an injury. This last category of action may be attributed to temper.

It may seem easy to act justly, for all that just action requires is a choice to commit just action or, inversely, not to commit unjust ones. However, just action is not easy. Truly, to act justly, one must act from a just moral state, which is a difficult and challenging thing to develop.

One cannot be unjust to oneself, but one can be unjust to a part of oneself. Sometimes, we permit the appetitive, irrational parts of the mind to rule over the good, rational parts, thereby betraying the good parts.

SUMMARY: BOOK VI

Just as the soul has two parts, rational and irrational, so does the intellect—the contemplative intellect and the calculative intellect. We divide the intellect in this manner because there are two ways to divide things—those that are variable and those that are invariable. The contemplative or scientific part of the intellect is concerned with invariable things, whereas the calculative or deliberative part is concerned with changing and variable things (because no one deliberates over that which is invariable).

Both parts of the intellect seek truth, but the deliberative part aims at achieving truth through the exercise of correct choice. By this truth we mean practical truth—not universal truths relating to invariable ideas. Because choice is required, a good moral state is required if we are to reach this truth. Choice is a matter of choosing the truth that corresponds to the correct balance of appetite and rationality.

Five modes of thought can elicit the truth: Science, Intuition, Art, Prudence, and Wisdom. Scientific knowledge is concerned with things that are eternal and unchanging. Knowledge may proceed either through induction or deduction: induction starts from first principles and builds universals, whereas deduction starts from universals and works down to specific cases. Scientific knowledge must include first principles, because a scientist wants to be able to explain why things are. Yet, though scientific knowledge requires knowledge of first principles, it cannot itself generate them.

Intelligence, or intuition, is the state of mind that grasps first principles. Art is concerned with production, as opposed to action, and must be reasoned correctly (that is, with truth) to really be art (rather than "non-art"). Prudence, perhaps better translated as "practical commonsense," is concerned with deliberating practical matters—that is, developing solutions that maximize the human good.

Wisdom is a combination of intuition and scientific knowledge: it apprehends all things fully, knowing their first principles and the universals that stem from them. It has little to do, however, with prudence and other practical things, for it is unconcerned with particulars. Political science, though well served by wisdom, has much more to do with prudence. In political science, the matter of most immediate concern is always the particulars of the situation. The most important thing is the ability to understand these particulars and find a solution in them.

Let us look closer at good deliberation or resourcefulness. Good deliberation is that which succeeds in its end. Understanding is like prudence—it is a state that is concerned not with any particular sphere or science but rather with correctly judging other peoples' accounts of various matters. Understanding well, therefore, is much like learning well. Judgment is similar in that it is the general faculty of correctly judging what is equitable.

We tend to consider all of these things—intelligence, judgment, understanding, and prudence—together when describing a person. This practice is correct, for these attributes are interrelated: a person who displays one often displays another.

One might ask what the intellectual virtues are good for. Wisdom is not concerned with human affairs, and prudence simply guides one to a knowledge of what is good, not an ability to do good things. In response to this question, it should be said that, these things being virtues, they are desirable and good in and of themselves even if they have no external benefits. Second, these things do result in happiness—not directly, but because they are part of virtuousness as a whole, which brings happiness. One needs both prudence and moral virtue to fulfill the human function—moral virtue to ensure the correctness of one's wants and aims, and prudence to ensure that these good ends are achieved. Prudence is aided in this effort by a faculty we have not yet discussed: cleverness. Cleverness is absolute—it can be put to any end, good or bad. Prudence is not absolute because no one can be prudent without being good.

PHILOSOPHY

SUMMARY: BOOK VII

There are three bad states of character: vice, incontinence (hedonism), and brutishness. There are many mistakes and inconsistencies in the common beliefs about incontinence. These inconsistencies center on the question of whether a person can knowingly act incontinently or whether they must be unaware of goodness to act incontinently. The answer is that a person cannot knowingly act incontinently, for anytime a person acts incontinently, he does so either out of total ignorance or because his mind is clouded by desire, drink, or illness. The issue of incontinence (and continence) relates to the sphere of pleasure and pain. Things that give pleasure can be divided into two types: biological necessities and pleasures that are desirable but not necessary. Physical pleasures—those relating to food and sex—fall into the first category; things like wealth and honor fall into the second. Generally, we do not refer to those who indulge in the second class of pleasures as "incontinent." However, those who seek excessive physical pleasure and shun discomfort are incontinent or soft. Thus, this idea groups the incontinent and the licentious person together, as well as the continent and the temperate person.

Thus far, we have discussed things that are naturally pleasant to all people, at least in varying degrees. There are other pleasures that people come to enjoy through mental imbalance, habit, or depravity. These include cannibalism, necrophilia, and other atrocities. A person who is drawn to these sick pleasures may be called morbid; someone excessively drawn to ordinary vice (such as licentiousness regarding natural pleasures, or cowardice, or irritability) is called brutish. Incontinence, on the other hand, is only concerned with natural (non-morbid) desires.

We can speak of incontinence as it relates to non-physical pleasures or unnatural desires as long as we qualify it—for instance, by saying "incontinence of temper." Incontinence of temper is much less shameful than incontinence of desire, for the person who is incontinent of temper is more governed by reason than the person who is incontinent of desire. Additionally, temper may arise from a sense of being mistreated, which may be exaggerated but is based in truth. Desire, in contrast, never arises from a grievance.

Regarding pleasures, someone may be continent or incontinent. Regarding pain, we may call someone enduring (tough) or soft. These are states, not virtues or vices. The vice of licentiousness is worse than incontinence because the incontinent person is in some ways helpless to control his desires; the licentious person, on the other hand, has more control and acts on his choices. The incontinent person is never convinced that he is right, whereas the licentious person may believe that he is. The incontinent person behaves wickedly but is not himself wicked; the licentious person is wicked. The incontinent person may understand virtue but does not have the strength to adhere to his (possibly good) choices.

The continent, or temperate, person, has the strength to stand by his convictions. Continence is different from stubbornness, however, because the continent person can be moved by arguments, whereas a stubborn person cannot. Stubborn people can be divided into the opinionated, the ignorant, and the boorish. The opinionated are motivated by the pleasure of feeling superior in their beliefs.

We must also discuss pleasure, for we are discussing moral virtue, and virtue and vice are tied up with pleasure and pain. Some say that no pleasure is good, others that only some pleasures are good, and still others that all pleasures are good—but all agree that pleasure itself cannot be the supreme good. These views are incorrect, for they stem from flawed understandings of pleasure, human nature, and the nature of true pleasure. The fact that all animals and human beings pursue pleasure is evidence that pleasure is the supreme good.

Summary: Book VIII

Friendship is a kind of virtue, one that is necessary for living. Friends define and preserve our characters and well being. Without them, we are robbed of human contact and security. It is hard to say what makes people friends—some say it is similarity, others that it is opposition. Whatever its cause, friendship is the state of wishing another good for his own sake in a way that he knows about and reciprocates.

There are three types of friendship: utility, pleasure, and goodness. Friendships based on utility generally are found among the elderly and those in middle or early life seeking their own advantage. Such friendships are limited because these friends take pleasure in each other only inasmuch as they are able to gain advantage from each other. Friendship based on pleasure, including erotic friendship, is found among the young, who are most inclined to live for pleasure. Erotic friendship also is obviously limited, in this case by its dependence on the friends' ability to give each other pleasure. Perfect friendship is the kind that is based on goodness. These friendships arise between people who are good; they are friends not for their own sake—for advantage or pleasure—but rather because they love the other person for what they are. These friendships— true friendships—develop slowly but are strong and last until one party or another changes from his or her state of goodness.

Friendship is a state between two people. It has an active component, such as whenever the friends join for activity or conversation, but can exist without this active aspect. For this reason, friends who are parted are still friends, even though they may not be able to act on that friendship for long periods of time. Friendship spawns a feeling of affection but is greater than this mere feeling. Friendship also presumes that the affection is reciprocal.

One may have many superficial friendships of the lesser types, but it is not possible to have a great many true friendships. True friendship may exist between unequals so long as proportion is maintained—that is, so long as the greater party in the friendship is loved more than he loves the other. Giving, rather than receiving, affection is the most important thing in a friendship; loving is the distinctive virtue of friends. Friendship—both the true type and the lesser, secondary types—is an important force in keeping a community together. Indeed, every community is expected to have its own kind of justice and its own mutual friendly feelings.

There are three kinds of political constitutions—monarchy, aristocracy, and timocracy (rule by those who hold property). Of the three, monarchy is the best and timocracy the worst. Each type of government also has a bad form and can be transformed into that form: monarchy turns to tyranny, aristocracy to timocracy, and timocracy to democracy. Each of these governments has a type of friendship associated with it—the paternal friendship between a monarch and his subjects, the friendship between betters and inferiors of an aristocracy, and the friendship between brothers of a democracy. There are various types of relations in society with corresponding levels of affection. Friendship between relations ultimately derives from paternal or maternal affection, as parents love their children more than their children love them. Fraternal or sororal affection exists because brothers and sisters spring from the same origins.

ANALYSIS: FRIENDSHIP

In this section, Aristotle demonstrates a strong interest in friendship as a social institution. His devotion of so much space to the subject, and some individual aspects of his discussion of it, can be explained by the fact that the ancient Greek conception of friendship was broader than our own. Friendship could encompass the feelings that countrymen were supposed to feel for each other or even the feelings between two parties in a successful business interaction. Friendship, in the sense that Aristotle uses it, seems to encompass all positive social interactions. At the same time, Aristotle is careful to distinguish what he regards as the best and truest form of friendship, which is close to our idea of the same.

The notion of proportionality returns with Aristotle's discussion of friendships between unequals. The idea of inequality between two friends belies the almost contractual view of friendship that was prevalent in ancient Greek society. Aristotle also notes that in true friendship, the friends' feelings for one another are born not of their emotions but of their good moral states. Aristotle implies that the love between friends is less an emotional response than a philosophical one. This conclusion demonstrates that good moral character is central to Aristotle's analysis. For him, even the quality of an interpersonal relationship is based on the moral characters of the people within it.

Summary: Book IX

Great problems can result when two friends have different understandings of the motives for their friendship. Problems arise particularly in regard to the giving and repayment of services. The best way to decide how a service should be evaluated is to measure its worth to the recipient: if the price has not been set beforehand, the recipient should determine it. To avoid discord, it is best (particularly among friends) to set the price before the act. When someone does a service for another from pure benevolence, as in the case of parents rearing their children, it is impossible to fully repay the deed. In such cases, the beneficiary simply should do his or her best.

A utilitarian or pleasure-based friendship may be broken off easily whenever its primary aim—utility or pleasure—is no longer being served. What becomes of a friendship based on goodness, however, when one of the friends changes for the worse? If the changed person is curable, it is probably best to remain friends and try to help him return to a state of goodness. However, if his vice becomes incurable, the friendship may be broken off in good conscience, because one should not associate with base persons. In the reverse case, when one party becomes greatly superior to the other, it is similarly difficult for the old friendship to persist. One should always treat an old friend in the light of the fact that he once was a friend, except when the friendship was broken off because of his or her wickedness or vice.

Our feelings toward our friends are a reflection of our feelings toward ourselves. If we do not have a correct understanding of the good for ourselves, then we cannot have a correct understanding of the good for our friends. We extend to friends the relation we have with ourselves—if that relation is good, then our relations with others will be good; if that relation is bad, then our relations with others will be bad. We can reverse this argument to realize that the person who behaves badly toward others must feel bad about himself as well.

Goodwill is different from friendship in that it need not be mutual, and the recipient of another's goodwill need not know of its existence. Goodwill generally is aroused by some merit or goodness on the part of the recipient. Concord is like friendship but is not the same; it is a kind of political amity in which the citizens of a political unit agree on what should be done in a situation. When concord is lacking, factions arise and the state can grind to a standstill.

Although people often criticize self-love, if defined correctly, it is, in fact, the trait of an admirable person. People generally describe self-loving people as those who take the most money, physical pleasure, or public honors for themselves. Yet if the person who behaves with virtue is assigning himself the most in honor (true honor), dignity, and happiness (from behaving well), we must realize that this person is also self-loving. It is a good thing to be self-loving in such a way.

To be truly happy, a good person must have virtuous friends. Friends are necessary both in good fortune (so that one can be kind to them) and in bad fortune (so that one can enjoy their kindness). In fact, friendship between good people is not only enjoyable but also increases the goodness of the participants, for a person will adopt the traits he admires in his friends.

SUMMARY: BOOK X

We now must view pleasure in more detail, particularly since it is a topic of some controversy. Some hold that pleasure is the Good itself, others that it is bad. However, pleasure cannot be the Good, because a pleasurable life can be made better by adding intelligence and learning to it. Something that can be improved cannot be the ultimate Good, for the Good, by definition, cannot be improved upon. Likewise, those who say that all pleasure is bad are mistaken: all people seek pleasure, including those who are wise and good, and the good would not seek something that is not itself a good thing. In fact, the argument that all pleasures are bad is a weak one, because those pleasures that bring harm, or that are achieved through amoral means, are not true pleasures, for good and just people would not seek them.

An activity will be most pleasurable when executed in the best way. Each sense has a corresponding pleasure, which is obvious because we describe certain sounds, sights, and tastes as pleasurable. Pleasure, then, perfects all activity if it is performed correctly, and thus can perfect life if it is lived properly. Different activities— intellectual, physical, and so on—have different pleasures associated with them. When an activity is performed correctly and is therefore pleasurable, a positive feedback cycle is established: the activity becomes easier, which makes it more pleasurable, which in turn makes it even easier. Likewise, activities that have no pleasure, either because they are bad actions or because they are performed badly, become more arduous and unpleasant when they are repeated.

As has been established before, the good person is most trustworthy in regards to which pleasures and desires are best. Therefore, it is not unreasonable to say that only the good man's pleasures are true pleasures and can be called human in the sense that they are above all other pleasures.

What, then, is a true description of happiness? It is not a state, for it is dependent on activity—specifically, on the kind of activity that leads to a good moral state of the soul. Happiness is a good to be chosen for itself; it is self-sufficient and is not to be chosen in the service of anything else. Happiness is not amusement or relaxation, because these things are a means to happiness, or a means of recuperation before more activity.

If happiness is the ultimate end, then it is in accordance with the highest virtue, which must itself stem from the highest part of ourselves. The intellect is the highest thing in us, so contemplative activity must be the highest activity. Moreover, contemplative activity seeks the highest, most virtuous things and is not dependent on anything else. The pursuit of philosophy, then, leads to the purest and most permanent pleasures. The philosopher is the most self-sufficient type of person, needing nothing but himself to fulfill his pleasures.

Thus, happiness necessitates leisure, for it stems from intellectual rather than practical activity. Politics and warfare, though best among practical activities, do not allow for leisure. The life of intellectual leisure is the only life that allows time for contemplation and the only one that puts a person in touch with the divine part of him-

PHILOSOPHY

self—his mind. Other lives, when moral, do bring happiness, but this happiness is not as great as a philosopher's happiness.

Other arguments confirm this view of the philosophical life. The gods themselves are limited to contemplation—their divinity makes anything else beneath them, so they must devote themselves to philosophy. Tradition holds that the gods are supremely happy. Furthermore, the lower animals have no happiness themselves and are incapable of reasoning.

As has been noted earlier, even the philosopher needs some external goods to be happy, or else he will be starving, cold, and wretched. With philosophic happiness, however, only minimal external goods are necessary—enough to survive comfortably, and nothing more.

Although this discussion of happiness and pleasure is useful in itself, how can we put it into effect? Goodness must be taught; it is not a character trait, although a person must have a character that is receptive to virtue if he or she is to understand goodness. Education in goodness is a task best left to the state, because law is the best way to make sure that this learning is trained into people's minds at a young age. If the state fails in this duty, a parent may take it up. However, it is important that anyone seeking to teach theoretical knowledge of goodness and virtue have some knowledge of legislation and laws, for it is by these means that people are best taught.

Who can teach knowledge of legislation to the teachers? Certainly not the Sophists, for none of them have any practical experience. Someone who wants to understand how, practically speaking, to live happily—rather than just understand the philosophical basis of such a life—must therefore apply himself to a study of politics to acquire this necessary experience.

ANALYSIS: HAPPINESS

The last section of the *Ethics* provides Aristotle's answer to the problem of happiness: the philosopher's life is the way to true happiness. To understand this conclusion, it is useful to compare the *Ethics* with *The Republic* by Plato. In *The Republic*, Plato also concludes that philosophers should lead society, for the pleasures related to philosophy are great and its grasp of the world unsurpassed. Plato's and Aristotle's conclusions may seem strange to modern ears, but philosophy had a very different place in the ancient world than it does in the modern world. First, philosophy, mathematics, and science were more tightly linked in Greece than they are now: philosophy and science did not become truly distinct until the Renaissance and the Scientific Revolution. Thus, we can see Aristotle's advocacy of philosophy as an advocacy of learning and study in general. Second, philosophy—especially the form practiced by Aristotle—had important practical and moral implications.

It is worth noting that Aristotle singles out the Sophists as incapable of providing any learning of worth in this area. The Sophists were, by various accounts, either traveling wise men or traveling con men. In practice, they were tutors who traveled from place to place and charged young men fees for their teaching. It was a great sore spot with Plato that Socrates was accused and tried as a Sophist, especially since Plato considered his and his master's philosophy to be in absolute opposition to what he considered the Sophists' word games. At any rate, both Plato and Aristotle regard the Sophists with scorn.

POETICS

Aristotle wrote prolifically on myriad subjects from ethics to biology, but he left perhaps his greatest mark on literary criticism. In the *Poetics*, Aristotle analyzes the structures of tragedy and comedy. Unfortunately, his section on comedy has been lost.

As Aristotle begins his study, he states that all forms of poetry, from epics to tragedies, are a type of imitation. Although they differ in medium, structure, object, and rhythm, all forms of poetry work toward the same end. When depicting people, poets have the choice to display people as better than, the same as, or worse than common people in reality. Comedy typically shows people as worse than in reality, whereas tragedy depends on depicting characters better than most people. A writer must not only choose his characters but also decide upon a form of narration: characters may act out their own stories themselves, or the poet can narrate the action instead.

Next, Aristotle analyzes the roots of poetry. Human beings differ from animals because they have a sense of imitation, rhythm, and poetry. The poetic art thus arose from a natural ability in humans and, as it developed, branched off in two directions: comedy and tragedy. Aristotle recounts how far tragedy has come since its inception as a one-character drama: Aeschylus introduced a second actor, Sophocles a third.

Tragedy and epic poetry are similar in that they both concern noble characters. The greatest differences between them lie in their length, meter, and form. Aristotle asserts that the action of a tragedy should be contained to one day, whereas epics should not be so constrained. Because of tragedy's time constraints, the plot must be tight and must work quickly to establish its goal—eliciting pity and fear from the audience and thereby purifying them of these emotions. To achieve this goal, tragedies must include six crucial elements, which Aristotle lists in order of importance: plot, character, fiction, thought, song, and spectacle.

Plot is the most important element because no action can occur without it; spectacle is the least important because it is the least related to the art of poetry. Plot, says Aristotle, must be like a living organism and possess a beginning, middle, and end. Furthermore, in the case of tragedy, the plot must be long enough to allow a movement from good fortune to calamity. Because suspense is crucial to the plot of tragedies, and because everything must happen in a short period of time, Aristotle advises that every action of the play must work toward the conclusion. If a scene or speech can be removed without disturbing the plot as a whole, it is not necessary to the play.

Aristotle asserts that poetry is a higher form of art than history. Whereas history deals with what happened, poetry deals with what might happen. Because of this tendency, poetry expresses more philosophic and universal sentiments than history. However, not all poetry is good, especially not episodic poetry, which usually is written simply to entertain audiences or win competitions. Tragedy, the highest form of poetry, uses surprise, through reversals or recognitions (such as Oedipus realizing that his wife is his mother), to arouse fear and pity. Nonetheless, it is crucial that plausible cause-and-effect relationships link all that transpires during the play.

The greatest tragic heroes must be noble individuals who accidentally or unavoidably bring about their own downfalls. The characters' natures must remain constant, and their motives for their actions must be clear. The plot itself must be probable and not dependent on the interference of divine forces and supernatural occurrences. If the author constructs the tragedy properly, it will end with complications and unraveling of mysteries. All quality poetry should convey a sense of a rise and fall.

Aristotle concludes his study by pondering the individual merits of tragedy and epic poetry. He decides that tragedy is a higher form of art than epic poetry because it emphasizes unified actions and because people can both read it and perform it.

HISTORY

METHODS AND THEMES OF THE GREEK HISTORIANS

In keeping with the rational, scientific nature of ancient Greek culture, the Greeks developed a unique kind of history that had a profound effect on the still-developing Western world. Unlike their ancient neighbors, the Egyptians, who recorded the conquests of ancient dynasties in a mixture of fact and fiction, or the Hebrews, whose history was largely rooted in theology, ancient Greek historians focused on strings of cause and effect. Their approach to their subject is apparent in the very definition of their word for history—*historia*, which Herodotus coined to mean research or study.

This study of history as an investigation of cause and effect first arose in the Greek state of Ionia, where the mathematician Thales sparked a period of great philosophical and scientific inquiry that started in the early sixth century B.C. As this interest in rational study grew in Ionia, scholars began to question and seek alternatives to the mythology that, until that time, had dominated all accounts of Greece's history. Furthermore, because the Ionians were sea traders and frequently came in contact with foreign merchants and emissaries, they grew increasingly aware of cultures with religious and historical traditions sharply different from their own. This foreign contact, along with the Ionians' own love of travel, only fostered the people's already skeptical views of myth.

One of the earliest Ionian historians was Hecataeus of Miletus, who wrote a geography tome called the *Travels*, which recounted historical, ethnographical, and biographical information about peoples and places that Hecataeus or his compatriots had visited. Although much of the *Travels* has been lost, scholars are certain that the work had considerable influence on Hecataeus's follower, Herodotus, the first great Greek historian.

As a citizen of a country constantly skirmishing or warring against it neighbors, Herodotus (c. 484–428 B.C.) recognized the importance of wars in any historical record. Countless chroniclers of history since Herodotus—from his immediate successor, Thucydides, to historians of the present day—have taken to heart this lesson that war is of the highest importance to historical accounts. For, as Herodotus alerts readers of his *Histories of the Persian Wars*, war is a powerful force in testing and establishing cultural identities.

Herodotus paid close attention to his representations of Greek politics and often recreates in his chronicle long speeches given by political leaders. Thucydides and other Greek and Roman historians copied this technique, which allows students of the *Histories* to scrutinize the motives of the ruling political institutions.

Herodotus, however, differed from his successors in his methods of obtaining historical information for his chronicle. Whereas Thucydides and most Roman historians limit themselves to contemporary events—preferably those they had witnessed themselves—Herodotus chronicles events long before his time, forcing him to rely on rumors and second-hand accounts for information.

Throughout his dramatizations of important speeches and seemingly accurate accounts of battles, Herodotus is careful to keep his *Histories* from becoming dry. He expected others to read the *Histories* aloud to an audience, which meant that the text had to be stylistically pleasing. To be certain of entertaining his audience, Herodotus styles his history to read like a story, with a beginning, middle, end, and a consistent "plot" running through it all—a practice that his successors imitate. Even though the *Histories* covers a long period of time, Herodotus achieves a coherent plot by searching for and elucidating recurrent themes, motifs, and morals in history. Perhaps the foremost theme that Herodotus articulates is the unending struggle for power that defined the ancient world—both in myth and in true history—that led countries and individual leaders to destroy one another and themselves. Indeed, many of Herodotus's leading characters discover the disastrous effects of excessive complacency and pride or realize the power of wisdom over riches.

Whereas Herodotus often attributes the forces of history to individuals, Thucydides credits the masses with the movements and great events of history. He displays a great reluctance to grant individuals sole responsibility or agency behind the actions of an entire country. Not surprisingly, whereas Herodotus searches for recurring traits and actions among the great individual figures of history, Thucydides seeks to chronicle the repeating motifs of nations and peoples as a whole.

HERODOTUS

CONTEXT AND BACKGROUND

Herodotus was born under Persian rule in Halicarnassus around 484 B.C. As a relative of Panyassis, a reputable epic poet, he had the advantage of a good education and an aristocratic upbringing. During his youth, his family was exiled after falling into political disfavor with the ruler of Halicarnassus. Eventually, Herodotus made his way to Athens, where he wrote his most famous work, the *Histories of the Persian Wars*, which chronicles the war between the powerful Persian empire and the scattered Greek states. As he began to give public readings from his work, he gradually entered the higher social circles in Athens and befriended the great Greek tragedian Sophocles. In his mid-forties, he left Athens for Thurii, where he lived until his death in 428 B.C., just after the outbreak of the Peloponnesian War.

As a young man, Herodotus traveled extensively in order to collect the raw material for the *Histories*. His wanderings covered much of the ancient world, including Libya, Egypt, Syria, Phoenicia, Macedonia, Thrace, and other lands. Although he attempted to collect a great deal of information through interviews, the fact that he knew only Greek limited his endeavor significantly. Because Greece had kept few records of the Persian War, and because records outside of Greece were largely inaccessible, Herodotus depended almost entirely on observations from his own travels and on gossip, rumor, and legend. Accordingly, the *Histories* are a mixture of military fact, political science, religious tradition, local legend, and ethnic traditions.

Herodotus does, however, seek to differentiate fact from fiction as much as possible; to ensure clarity, he frequently indicates the source of his evidence. He states whether he witnessed an event firsthand, whether he learned of an event from a firsthand witness or by more circuitous sources, whether multiple sources confirmed a particular account. Although some of the tales in the *Histories*—such as an account of a dolphin rescuing a princess after she is hurled from a ship—clearly are implausible, Herodotus includes such oddities nonetheless because of their interest as folklore.

Although scholars have discovered information that supports a number of Herodotus's stories, his style as a historian differs greatly from that of most modern historians. For one, Herodotus does not concern himself with researching other historical documents. Whereas most modern historians value historical evidence over rumor, Herodotus seems to take such delight in local legends that he cannot bring himself to withhold them from his text. Of course, the fact that Herodotus, as a member of the Greek civilization, subscribed to many of the Greek beliefs about omens, oracles, and divine intervention, lends his histories an element of magic. Moreover, in his effort to present his histories as narrative stories, he often gives his historical characters fictional characteristics as he leads them to seemingly fated tragic or heroic destinies similar to those depicted in Greek myth and drama.

In spite of all these caveats, Herodotus, through his close attention to ethnographies and characters of the Greek states and their neighbors, does paint an instructive and revealing picture of the philosophy, politics, and histories of the ancient world and its inhabitants. This picture, as he states in the opening paragraph of the *Histories*, is part of his purpose. He declares that his threefold aim is to prevent the deeds of men from being forgotten over time, to preserve the marvelous works that both Greeks and some non-Greeks have produced, and to identify and remember the factors that caused war to break out between Greece and Persia.

The structure of the *Histories* likewise has three major parts. First, Herodotus tells of the Persian empire's string of conquests that lead its territories to border Greece. Second, he recounts the Greeks' resistance to the Persian onslaught, including the famous battle at Marathon in which the Athenians defeated the Persian king Darius. Finally, Herodotus tells of the unsuccessful efforts of Darius's son, Xerxes, to invade Greece ten years later.

HISTORIES OF THE PERSIAN WARS

The nine books of Herodotus's *Histories* tell the story of the various wars that Persia, under the leadership of Darius and Xerxes, made against the disjointed Greek city-states and their neighbors. Throughout these books, Herodotus sets forth themes and fates that manifest themselves in the lives of his historical characters.

BOOK ONE

In Book One of the *Histories*, Herodotus illustrates the transience of power and the corruptive effects it has on those who wield it. He recounts how Croesus, the wealthy king of Lydia, and Cyrus, the king of Persia, wage war against each other to appease their appetites for increased power and dominion. As is often the case throughout the *Histories*, divine forces interfere with human affairs, as Croesus consults the Oracle at Delphi before waging war. The Oracle prophesies that Croesus will topple an empire if he wars with the Persians.

Following the Oracle's advice, Croesus sets his forces upon Persia, only to find his armies overwhelmed in strength and number. Croesus and his forces briefly find safety at Sardis, but before long, the Persian forces make Croesus their captive. Croesus understands the words of the Oracle too late to save himself—the empire he has destroyed is his own. Only divine intervention is able to save Croesus's life: as he lies upon his funeral pyre, waiting for Cyrus to burn him alive, a sudden, unexpected downpour extinguishes the flames.

Cyrus, meanwhile, continues his military campaign and conquers Babylon and much of Asia Minor. From Babylon, he marches against the Massagetae and the forces of Queen Tomyris. Cyrus slays the queen's son in battle before he finally falls himself. The queen, devastated and enraged by the loss of her son, savagely desecrates Cyrus's body after his death.

BOOK TWO

Book Two tells the story of Cyrus's son, Cambyses, who invades Egypt. Herodotus, who himself traveled to Egypt while researching the *Histories*, explains at length the nature of Egyptian culture. The Egyptian deities, he explains, are the predecessors of the Greek gods. Herodotus seems to admire the philosophy and ritual of the Egyptians. He notes the Egyptians' acute awareness of mortality and provides a detailed account of the different methods of mummification. Herodotus also notes the Egyptians' careful preservation of their own history, both through the building of pyramids and other monuments and through the keeping of careful records. The Egyptians are able to trace their history of their kings back eleven thousand years. When Cambyses invades, the Egyptians are under the rule of King Amasis.

BOOK THREE

At the beginning of Book Three, Herodotus relates how the Persian king demanded Amasis's daughter as a prize from the Egyptians. Notably, Herodotus acknowledges two different versions of the story: in one, the Persian king is Cambyses; in the other, he is Cyrus. The first version claims that Cambyses is overwhelmed by egomania and greed after defeating the Egyptian army. He destroys the Egyptian nobility and then plans to continue his conquests by attacking Ethiopia and Carthage. When these plans fail, Cambyses loses control and goes on a spree of madness, desecrating Egyptian temples and monuments, killing his brother and sister, and turning on his advisors. However, Cambyses dies of an infected wound while making his return to Persia.

BOOK FOUR

Book Four relates the rise of Cambyses' successor, Darius. Eager to duplicate the victories of his father and grandfather, Darius sends his forces to Scythia, where he challenges a barbaric enemy infamous for their cruelty and cannibalism. The Scythians draw Darius and his forces far into their own country and then launch a powerful, delayed attack. As supplies run low, Darius orders a hasty retreat and barely escapes with his life.

BOOK FIVE

Book Five describes the effect of the Scythian experience on Darius. His defeat at the hands of the Scythians quells his blind ambition and turns his mind to the governance of the state. The Persian empire meets with happy times as Darius begins to take into serious account his colleagues' advice. He removes himself from military affairs and no longer accompanies his troops into battle. He does, however, instigate a new campaign against Ionia.

BOOK SIX

In Book Six, Herodotus recounts the famous battle of Marathon (490 B.C.). In the months before the battle, Darius's armies make strong advances against Ionia and turn their attention to Sparta and Athens. As the Persian forces push into Greece, however, a storm wrecks their navy, and the Thracians launch a surprise attack on their army. After the Persian forces regroup, Darius reroutes them across the safer Aegean Sea, and they conquer Eretria, due largely to the help of Eretrian traitors.

HISTORY

Led by an exiled and vengeful Athenian leader, Hippias, the Persian forces reach Marathon, a plain near Athens that Hippias believes will provide a strategic advantage to the Persian cavalry. When the Athenian forces learn of the Persian advance, they send a runner, Pheidippides, to Sparta to enlist help. The Spartans offer to help but, because of religious reasons, cannot send aid before the next full moon. Only Plataea, a small independent Greek state, sends troops to succor Athens. Against all odds, the Greeks defeat the Persians at Marathon. Immediately after the Persians retreat, however, they set sail for Athens in the hopes of launching a surprise attack on the city. Nonetheless, the remnants of the Athenian army manage to repel the attackers and force them to retreat to Persia.

Book Seven
In Book Seven, Darius organizes another invasion of Athens but dies in the midst of his preparations. His son, Xerxes, assumes the leadership of the Persian state and quickly institutes an iron-fisted rule. After brutally quashing an Egyptian rebellion, he announces his own overblown dreams of conquest—a war to conquer all of Europe. Over the next five years, Xerxes raises an enormous force of 2,500,000 men and 1,200 ships. Despite a series of bad omens that occur just before his armies are due to depart, Xerxes pushes on, unwilling to heed the warnings of the gods.

On the way to Greece, the Persian fleet is caught in a storm, and nearly one-third of the ships sink. Nonetheless, Xerxes' enormous army still far outnumbers the Greek forces when the two armies finally meet at Thermopylae, a narrow mountain pass near Delphi. The narrowness of the pass, however, prevents Xerxes from deploying all of his forces against the entrenched Greeks. Over the course of three days, the Greeks dismantle and delay the Persian armies. Soon, however, a Greek traitor reveals an alternate route through the mountains, which leads the Persian forces farther into Greece. Leonidas, the commander of the Theban army, makes a brave stand but eventually falls as his army is devastated. The tenacity of the Greek forces enrages Xerxes, who alleviates his frustration by desecrating Leonidas's corpse.

Book Eight
Book Eight of the *Histories* recounts the Persian forces' continued assault on the Greeks and their razing of numerous Greek towns. Then, at the port of Salamis, the Greek and Persian forces clash again, the Greeks angered by recent news that Xerxes has burned

the Acropolis in Athens. Through a combination of good fortune and smart tactics, the outnumbered Greeks defeat the Persian navy, which, in the confusion of battle, inadvertently destroys a number of its own ships. The Greek victory forces Xerxes' armies to retreat to Persia.

BOOK NINE

In Book Nine, Herodotus details the exploits of Mardonius, a Persian commander who stayed in Greece with his forces and renewed fighting against the Greeks the following spring. In 479 B.C., Mardonius marches on Athens and burns the city. The Greek army, though outnumbered yet again, challenges Mardonius at Plataea. The Greeks sustain grievous losses but still manage to kill Mardonius and drive out the Persian forces once and for all.

HISTORY

THUCYDIDES

CONTEXT AND BACKGROUND

Born around 460 B.C., a generation after Herodotus, Thucydides was the son of Thracian and Athenian aristocrats. Unlike Herodotus, who drew his material from a relatively distant past, Thucydides wrote primarily about events that took place during his lifetime, some of which he witnessed firsthand. Scholars believe that Thucydides enlisted in the Athenian army at the outbreak of the Peloponnesian War, around 430 B.C. Despite his relative obscurity as a soldier, he became a general several years later. He was, however, stripped of his rank when he and his fleet arrived too late to save the city of Amphipolis when it was under attack from Sparta. Disgraced by his failure, he lived in self-imposed exile from Athens and stayed in Thrace, where he wrote his masterpiece, the *History of the Peloponnesian War*.

The *History* remained unfinished upon Thucydides' death in 399 B.C. Although he had written outlines of his final chapters, he had not had time to fill them out with the detail and color found in the completed chapters. Some scholars believe that Thucydides' daughter took up where her father left off, finished the final chapter, and took responsibility for preserving the text.

Sincerely motivated by a quest for truth behind the fog of war, Thucydides placed special emphasis on events he was able to witness firsthand. His exile in Thrace not only enabled him to gain perspective on the events taking place in Athens but also gave him access to interviewees from both sides of the conflict. Therefore, he was able to achieve objectivity and balance in his accounts of the war's causes and the motives and strategies of the opposing armies.

In contrast to his predecessor, Herodotus, Thucydides concentrates on one particular aspect of human nature—wartime behavior. Rather than place responsibility for victory or defeat in the hands of fate or the gods, as Herodotus does, Thucydides identifies consistent qualities and characteristics that he believes make leaders great. To Thucydides, stupidity and lack of foresight are an army's greatest enemies. Conversely, decisiveness, pragmatism, and intelligence are the foremost qualities of an ideal military leader.

Although Thucydides' political philosophy may at times seem cold and rational, his prose reveals poetic gifts and an acute sensitivity to the plight of the human individual. His accounts of the plague in Athens and the treatment of the Athenians after their defeat at Syracuse, for example, epitomize his ability to capture historical moments in a short turn of phrase. The combination of rhetorical prowess and rigorous factual accuracy makes Thucydides foremost among reliable sources for life in the ancient world.

HISTORY OF THE PELOPONNESIAN WAR

BOOK ONE

At the opening of Book One of the *History*, Thucydides explains his aim in writing the work. He says that he wishes simply to record the events of the Peloponnesian War (431–404 B.C.)—the biggest war, both militaristically and geographically, in Greek history.

Before Thucydides begins his account, he sets down a brief history of Greece in an attempt to understand the beginnings and fundamental causes of the war. After the defeat of the Persian armies (the subject of Herodotus's *Histories*), two major powers emerge within Greece—the Athenians and the Spartans. As the rivalry between these two groups heats up, they begin a cycle of skirmishing, peacemaking, and political warring for control of smaller satellite states. Naturally, Thucydides states, such a relationship eventually must lead to a major, prolonged conflict.

Indeed, the debate about all-out war comes to the forefront when the revered Athenian statesman Pericles argues in favor of making a stand against the growing threat from Sparta. He declares that war will come whether Athens looks for it or not. Therefore, he concludes that if the financial costs of a war are not too severe and if the army is ready, Athens should strike first.

BOOK TWO

In Book Two, Thucydides recounts how the debate about war comes to an abrupt end when Thebes suddenly attacks Plataea, ending a prolonged period of peace in the region. When Athens rushes to help Plataea, war breaks out in full. The Spartans march on Athenian territories, and Athens sends a fleet to the Peloponnesus to retaliate. The Athenians pause during the first winter of fighting to pay tribute to their fallen soldiers. Pericles delivers an eloquent funeral oration in which he argues that Athens is a place of greatness where individuals have an unmatched capacity for great works and self-reliance.

Athens suffers a significant setback the next summer, when a terrible plague passes through the region and baffles both doctors and priests. The symptoms, which include fever, chest pain, and excruciating stomach pain, kill victims within days. Some people dive into wells out of thirst, only to contaminate water supplies of entire villages. Poor men become rich after looting but spend their money more quickly than they received it because they know their deaths are imminent.

BOOK THREE
Book Three tells of the spread of the war to the far reaches of the Athenian and Spartan territories. The island of Lesbos breaks away from Athenian rule to join Sparta but soon returns to Athens voluntarily to avoid starvation. The Athenians kill all the leaders of the revolt and enslave the women and children of Lesbos. Later, more Athenian-controlled territories revolt, including Ionia, Messina, and Megara. Meanwhile, Sparta continues its conquest by capturing Plataea and razing the city.

BOOK FOUR
In Book Four, Thucydides documents the Athenians' reversal of fortune as they rally against the tiring Spartans. However, Brasidas, a Spartan commander, successfully engineers major uprisings in Amphipolis and other areas throughout the Aegean region. After several more military and diplomatic setbacks, Athens accepts a year-long truce from the Spartans.

BOOK FIVE
Book Five holds the story of the death of Pericles, which leaves Athens without a strong political voice to dictate wise military action. In his absence, self-promoting, hawkish politicians seize power in the senate. A second truce breaks down when Athens enlists Argos as an ally. These Athenian moves toward war anger the Spartans, who attack the Argives and force them to break their alliance with Athens.

In a famous episode of the *History* called the Melian Dialogue, Thucydides recounts the mercilessness of Athens in its dealings with the Spartan territory of Melos, which wishes to remain neutral in the war. Athens absolutely refuses Melian neutrality and eventually loses patience with negotiations. Athenian forces storm the city, slaughter the men, and take the women and children captive.

Book Six

Book Six recounts the escalation of violence that occurs when both the Athenian and Spartan leaders set their military goals too high and stretch their armies too thin. The Athenian forces do find some solace in the leadership of their two great generals, Nicias and Demosthenes, just as Sparta continues to follow the leadership of Brasidas. However, the Athenian general Alcibiades defects to the Spartan side when other Athenian leaders accuse him of treason.

Book Seven

In Book Seven, Thucydides tells of the war's shift in location to Sicily, which Athens hopes to secure in order to resupply its poorly equipped forces. Athens commences its plan by invading parts of Sicily and constructing a fort at Syracuse. In an epic sea battle, Spartan soldiers rush to the Sicilians' aid and destroy the Athenian navy, forcing it to retreat by land. On shore, the Sicilians clash with the retreating Athenian forces, capturing part of the army and trapping another part in a mountain pass. The Spartans put the Athenian generals to death and enslave the Athenian soldiers.

Book Eight

Book Eight, the final section of the *History*, recounts the Athenians' last attempt to vanquish the Spartans. However, low morale and desertion undermine any chance of Athenian victory. The democratic system in Athens collapses as the Spartan navy nears the city. In the last complete section of the *History*, which recounts the events of 411 B.C., Athens's empire begins to fall apart at the seams, and the city's period of greatness gives way to the beginnings of the period of darkness to come.

XENOPHON

CONTEXT AND BACKGROUND

Xenophon (428–354 B.C.) is remembered primarily as a historian, especially for the *Hellenica*, his attempt to complete Thucydides' account of the Peloponnesian War. Xenophon's studies and expertise, however, were by no means limited to the field of history. In addition to serving in the Athenian cavalry during the war with Sparta, he was also a student of Socratic philosophy, a mercenary soldier, and a farmer. Xenophon was raised in a small town outside of Athens but complemented his country upbringing with travel and militaristic ambition. According to legend, he literally fell into the Socratic school when he was unhorsed during the battle of Delium. Socrates, himself a noted soldier, rescued the toppled Xenophon and became his friend and mentor.

Although Xenophon was a capable student, the philosophical life never grabbed him as it did Socrates. Accordingly, despite his lessons with Socrates, he remained devoted to the army and the study of history. When Athens made peace with Persia after the Peloponnesian War, Xenophon sold his soldierly services to the Persian commander Cyrus the Younger, who was raising an army against his brother, Artaxerxes, the king of Persia. After Cyrus died and Artaxerxes' forces routed the enemy, Xenophon lead a troop of thousands of surviving Greek soldiers across 4,000 miles of rugged terrain in just over a year. Despite Xenophon's heroics, Athens disapproved of his alliance with Persia and banished him from the state. After his banishment from Athens, Xenophon went to Sparta, where he joined the army and fought against Persian tyrants in Asia Minor. His valor and leadership in these battles earned him a consulship under the king of Sparta, Agesilaus II.

With his consulship and a large estate near Olympia, Xenophon entered the quiet years of his life. He spent the next twenty years sporting and writing until his estate was captured in a local skirmish in 371 B.C. By that point, Athens and Sparta were allies against Thebes, so Athens forgave Xenophon's past transgressions. Xenophon moved to Corinth and sent his sons to join the Athenian cavalry.

Fourteen of Xenophon's works still exist today, among them *Anabasis*, a description of Cyrus's failed war against his brother; and the *Hellenica*, a history of Greece in the first half of the fourth century B.C. While these two works deal exclusively with history, a number of Xenophon's other texts explore different subjects, including Spartan politics, philosophy, economics, agriculture, and animal breeding and training.

Despite Xenophon's greater military experience, his historical accounts of war cannot compare to those in the work of Thucydides. Critics praise Xenophon's descriptions of battle and his understanding of the common soldier—no doubt because he was one himself—but assert that he lacks the insight into the broader picture of history that makes Thucydides' works so notable.

ANABASIS

The *Anabasis* is Xenophon's account of his experiences as a hired soldier of Cyrus the Younger during Cyrus's aborted military expedition against the armies of Artaxerxes. The account, probably based upon daily notes that Xenophon made, illuminates the powers and shortcomings of Cyrus's mercenary army.

When Cyrus's army is forced to retreat, Xenophon finds himself thrust into a position of leadership. He recounts how he navigated the retreat of a throng of weary and battered soldiers over rugged terrain without provisions or money. While some critics cast doubt upon Xenophon's account of the events—which portrays the author as a genius and hero—his detailed story of the retreat is remarkable in its own right and is complemented by interesting discussions of military strategy.

Xenophon opens the *Anabasis* with a discussion of the history of Cyrus and Artaxerxes' relationship, noting that the two men fell into hostilities after their father, Darius, died. Not surprisingly, Xenophon sides with his commander, Cyrus, and praises him for his charm and strength as a leader. Xenophon recounts how Cyrus raises a host of mercenaries and leads them in search of Artaxerxes. Cyrus is killed, however, by a javelin during a battle along the banks of the Euphrates River. After the battle, Cyrus's lieutenant deliberates over the best course of action. He concludes that, with Cyrus fallen, the army has no grudge against Artaxerxes and no interest in his kingdom. The attack, therefore, is called off, and Xenophon sets out on his long journey home.

HELLENICA

In the *Hellenica*, Xenophon continues retelling Greek history where Thucydides leaves off, covering political and military developments within Greece over the period from 411–362 B.C. When Xenophon begins his account, Athens is in the midst of internal turmoil, as democracy and oligarchy struggle for control. The *Hellenica* recounts the war between Sparta and Persia (399–387 B.C.); the Corinthian War (395–386 B.C.) between Sparta and the allied forces of Corinth, Athens, Thebes, and Argos; and the subsequent infighting among Greek states as they sought to form effective alliances with one another against the Persian empire.

In the second part of the *Hellenica*, Xenophon describes the formal peace that the Greeks and King Artaxerxes of Persia eventually achieve. After this assurance of peace with Persia, the Greek leaders turn their attention to the state of Thebes, which poses the largest danger of disrupting the fragile balance of power within Greece. Xenophon ends his history with the battle of Mantinea (362 B.C.), during which the Thebans emerged victorious despite losing their great commander Epaminondas.

CYROPAEDIA

The *Cyropaedia* is Xenophon's biographical account of the life of the Persian ruler Cyrus the Great. Despite the inaccuracy of certain facts—Xenophon confuses the political institutions of Athens and Persia, for example—the *Cryopaedia* does provide a rich portrait of Cyrus's life. Xenophon, who clearly admires Cyrus's ability to rule people and nations, discusses the great leader's education, lifestyle, administrative talents, military expertise, and conquests.

MEMORABILIA

In the *Memorabilia*, Xenophon attempts the task at which only Plato succeeded—an accurate, philosophically moving account of the trial and death of Socrates. Xenophon, unfortunately, did not attend the trial himself and therefore could not report it with great accuracy. In addition, the defense that Xenophon presents against Socrates' accusers is based not on the actual events of the trial but on Xenophon's reading of a secondhand account by Polycrates.

In the first part of the work, Xenophon presents the charges against Socrates—that his teachings are impious and dangerous in that they corrupt the youth of Athens. Xenophon goes to great lengths to defend his teacher, reminding us of Socrates' virtues, frequent sacrifices to the gods, self-discipline, and respect for Athenian law. Later, Xenophon records a number of aphorisms and short dialogues on the subject of citizenship, some of which recall Socrates' service and valor as a soldier. As Xenophon draws his argument to a close, he pays tribute to Socrates' strength as a teacher. Socrates, Xenophon testifies, encourages his students to recognize and depend upon their own intrinsic intelligence—the only true source of happiness.

HISTORY

ORATION AND PROSE WRITING

LYSIAS

The speechwriter and orator Lysias (c. 459–380 B.C.) grew up among the upper classes of Athens, although he was not Athenian by birth. In Lysias's early teens, his father, Cephalus, sent him and his brother, Polemarchus, to Italy to study rhetoric and philosophy. After their sojourn to Italy, Lysias and his brother worked for their father, a manufacturer of shields, until Polemarchus fell out of political favor and was sentenced to death. Fearing for his life, Lysias fled to Corinth.

Several years later, more sympathetic political forces regained power in Athens, so Lysias returned and started his own school of oratory. He soon changed his focus to speechwriting, establishing a career penning speeches for clients who were in the lower classes or who did not have adequate experience to defend themselves in court cases. More than thirty of Lysias's speeches survive today.

Unlike his contemporaries, the Sophists, who relied upon ornate, overcomplicated, and usually specious arguments, Lysias distinguished himself with the directness and clarity of his prose. One of Lysias's most famous speeches, *Olympicus*, calls for Greek unity against foreign tyrants—perhaps because Lysias himself always was considered a foreigner in Athens. Lysias maintains his political bent in several other speeches by attacking Alcibiades, a shameless Athenian rhetorician and general who shifted his allegiances back and forth between Athens to Sparta. Other speeches focus directly on court cases and on specific calls for punishment or exoneration. In the only speech he delivered himself, *Against Eratosthenes*, Lysias calls for the punishment of his brother's murderer. *On the Murder of Eratosthenes*, in contrast, defends Euphiletus, who killed Lysias's wife's lover.

DEMOSTHENES

Deemed too fragile for military service, Demosthenes (384–322 B.C.) gave his energies to the art of oration and went on to become the most skillful speaker in fourth-century-B.C. Athens. Orphaned at a young age, he studied rhetoric and law—skills that came in handy several years later, when he leveled charges of embezzlement against his guardians, who had squandered his inheritance. These lawsuits earned Demosthenes a reputation as an orator, and by the age of thirty he was earning his living, like Lysias, as a speechwriter and professor of rhetoric. Sixty of Demosthenes' speeches still exist today. One of the earliest of these, *On the Symmories* (354 B.C.), argues in favor of what would become recurring subjects in Demosthenes' speeches: the need to support the Athenian military and the importance of the survival of Athenian independence. Demosthenes frequently, but often futilely, argued against the complacent, isolationist mentality of the Athenian state.

In the later part of his career, Demosthenes began a heated and dangerous rivalry with Aeschines, a supporter of King Philip II of Macedonia, a foreign tyrant who threatened the independence of the Athenian state. When Demosthenes accused Aeschines of mishandling an embassy to King Philip, Aeschines barely escaped conviction. Aeschines, in turn, frequently leveled his speeches against Demosthenes, and the two traded rhetorical blows until Demosthenes finally emerged victorious, and Aeschines was forced to abandon Athens.

Demosthenes' victory, however, was short-lived: he lost his political advantage when Alexander the Great succeeded King Philip, and then, in 323 B.C., he became embroiled in a bribery scandal and was publicly humiliated. After paying a large fine, Demosthenes fled Athens in embarrassment. Although he returned to Athens in 322 B.C., after Alexander's death, Demosthenes was unable to restart his career. When the Macedonian forces finally destroyed Athens' military, Demosthenes fled to an island, where he committed suicide by poisoning rather than face capture or arrest.

AESOP

Although Aesop's name will forever be associated with his collection of fables, concrete facts from his life are few. Aesop (c. 620–564 B.C.) was a slave from Lydia but eventually was freed from his master on the island of Samos. He went on to write or compile more than three hundred fables—brief tales that teach moral lessons.

As legend has it, Aesop's career also proved his downfall: a mob, envious of his fame, stuffed a golden chalice in his bags, accused him of theft, and threw him off of a cliff near Delphi. Legend also holds that Delphi went on to suffer a terrible plague and was forced to make monetary gifts in compensation to the descendants of Aesop's former master.

Aesop's wise, simple, yet perplexing and ironic tales existed primarily in oral form until the late fourth century B.C., when they were recorded for the first time. Then, in the first century A.D., a Roman slave named Phaedrus assembled the "definitive" compilation of the fables as they appear today. The stories, which often feature talking animals who display human qualities, each end with an overtly stated moral, such as "One good turn deserves another," "Slow and steady wins the race," or "The gods help those who help themselves." For their brevity and simple moral teachings, many of Aesop's fables are popular even today and stand as staples of children's literature.

ENCYCLOPEDIA

PEOPLE, PLACES, & IDEAS IN GREEK ANTIQUITY

ACHILLES

The strongest of the Achaean (Greek) warriors in the Trojan War and the son of the goddess Thetis. When Achilles is a child, Thetis dips him into the magical waters of the river Styx, making his body invulnerable. As she dips him, she holds him by the heel—the only part of his body not to be submerged in the water. Accordingly, Achilles' heel remains mortal and thus his one point of vulnerability. Achilles grows up to be a proud, obstinate warrior who quickly takes offense when he perceives that someone has insulted his honor. During the Trojan War, the Trojan archer Paris shoots Achilles in his heel, causing a wound that eventually leads to Achilles' death. In 1693 A.D., the Dutch anatomist Verheyden coined the phrase Achilles' heel upon dissecting his own amputated leg and discovering the large tendon behind the heel. While this phrase remains a reference to the human anatomy, literary tradition has given the phrase another meaning—a dooming, unmistakable weakness. Some critics read the weakness in Achilles' heel as a metaphor for his pride, the flaw that leads to his eventual downfall. See AGAMEMNON, TROJAN WAR.

AENEAS

A Trojan warrior and mortal son of the goddess Aphrodite. Although Aeneas makes several appearances in the *Iliad,* he is more important in Roman mythology than in Greek. At the end of the Trojan War, Aeneas is one of the few Trojan captains to escape. He sets sail along with his ailing father, young son, and a host of bedraggled and war-torn Trojan families. After losing his father, Aeneas finally finds his way to Sicily, where he visits the Sibyl, a prophetess. The Sibyl leads Aeneas into the underworld and reveals to him his fate, showing him the past, present, and future. In the future, Aeneas sees the great Roman leaders Caesar, Antony, and Brutus, and learns that they will lead a country inhabited by his descendants. In short,

Aeneas learns that he will be the father of Rome. For more information on Aeneas, see SparkNote on Virgil's *Aeneid*.

AGAMEMNON

A great warrior, king of Mycenae, and leader of the Achaean (Greek) forces during the Trojan War. Agamemnon, also called Atrides, is arrogant, self-centered, and rash but often an outstanding leader nonetheless. Agamemnon steals Achilles' war spoils—the maiden Briseis—for himself, which offends Achilles and leads him to withdraw temporarily from combat. Much of Homer's *Iliad* concerns Achilles' anger at this slight on Agamemnon's part. Agamemnon is perhaps most famous for his sacrifice of his daughter, Iphigenia, in order to gain favorable winds to propel his ships to Troy. This sacrifice enrages Agamemnon's wife, Clytemnestra, who, with the help of her lover, Aegisthus, later murders Agamemnon in revenge. This cycle of bloodshed in the house of Atreus is a staple topic in Greek drama, most notably in Aeschylus's *Oresteia*. See ACHILLES, TROJAN WAR, ELECTRA, ORESTES.

AGES OF MAN

The periods of human history that the poet Hesiod defines in *Works and Days*. According to Hesiod, humankind descended in distinct races and ages named for the materials that the gods used to mold each generation. During the time of the Titans, the gods created a race of men out of gold, heralding the start of the Golden Age. While not immortal, this first race of men lived alongside the gods in bliss. When Zeus came to power, he destroyed this race and replaced them with a race of men made from silver. This race proved rebellious, so Zeus destroyed them as well and created a new race from bronze, ushering in the Bronze Age. The members of this race proved violent and killed themselves off without a trace. Zeus then created a race of men who resembled the gods, and from this race came the heroes of Homer's epics. Finally, when these men died, Zeus created a race of iron, the race that still inhabits the world today. According to Hesiod, because this race is greedy, warlike, impious, and deceitful, Zeus ultimately will destroy it as well.

ALCIBIADES

A disciple of Socrates who appears in Plato's *Symposium* and in Thucydides' *History of the Peloponnesian War*. Alcibiades (450–404 B.C.) studied under Socrates and then rose through the ranks of the Athenian army, earning a reputation for flair and wildness that subjected him to animosity and jealousy from his fellow statesmen. During the Peloponnesian War, Alcibiades was unjustly accused of defiling the statues of Hermes that stood in Athens. Alcibiades defected to the Spartan side and gave them intelligence on Athenian battle plans. When the Spartans grew weary of Alcibiades, he fled to Persia. Although he later returned to Athens, he aroused suspicion by failing on an important military mission and fled to Persia again. Ultimately, a gang of Spartan mercenaries assassinated him.

ALEXANDER THE GREAT
King of Macedonia and one of the most famous conquerors in the history of the world. Alexander (356–323 B.C.) built his reputation as a great tactician and leader and a cruel and fiery soldier. The son of King Philip II of Macedonia, he was educated by Aristotle, who instructed him in politics, ethics, and war. At age twenty, Alexander inherited the throne after his father's assassination. Some suspected Alexander of the crime, for his ambitions were well known and his relationship with his father shaky at best. Alexander quickly set his sights on Persia and destroyed the 40,000-man Persian army while losing only about 100 of his own soldiers. Alexander then conquered Egypt, where he was hailed as a liberator. In 331 B.C., he founded the city of Alexandria, captured Carthage, and continued to Babylon. With all of Persia subdued, Alexander then turned to India. Although his forces overwhelmed the Indian army, their weariness gradually showed, and at the banks of the Hyphasis River, they refused to go forward. Alexander had no choice but to go home. After a short break, he planned an assault on Arabia but fell ill with a fever and soon died. According to legend, when his generals pressed him to name a successor on his deathbed, Alexander replied, "The worthiest," and died without giving a name.

ALLEGORY OF THE CAVE
A parable that Socrates, as portrayed in Plato's *Republic,* uses to illustrate the effects of education on the human soul. Socrates asks his student to imagine a group of people born and raised in a dark cave, tied up, facing a wall, and unable to turn around. Behind them is a fire, and between them and the fire are a number of statues that can be manipulated like puppets. The fire casts moving shadows of the statues on the wall, which the prisoners, knowing no other reality, believe to be people. One of the prisoners frees himself and emerges from the cave to the outside world, where the sun blinds him. The experience is unpleasant, but gradually his eyes adjust to

the light, he sees objects clearly, and eventually is able to look at the sun itself. He can see a new world, truer than the one he knew previously. If he were to return to the cave, the other prisoners would ridicule him because he would no longer be able to see in the dark and would appear blind and stupid to them. This situation, according to Socrates, mirrors that of the philosopher who enters the daily life of the ordinary man. The philosopher has no skill in the everyday business, politics, or leisure activities of the city—his skill lies in perceiving the true nature of the universe and the soul. Where most men find pleasure, the philosopher finds only boredom and pain. Socrates sees the philosopher as the ideal ruler of a city, for the greatest rulers, he asserts, have no desire to rule.

AMAZONS

A savage, man-hating race of warrior women who seek the company of men only for the purpose of procreation. The Amazons play a part in several stories involving the great Greek heroes. At the outbreak of the Trojan War, the Amazons come to support the Trojans against the Achaeans (Greeks). Achilles slays Penthesilea, the Amazon queen, only to fall desperately in love with her as she dies in his arms. In another story, the Amazons, led by Hippolyta, interrupt the wedding banquet of the hero Theseus and Phaedra. The jealous Hippolyta wants to claim Theseus, who already is her husband and has given her a son. However, Theseus kills her when the doors of the banquet hall close and separate her from the other Amazons. Finally, Heracles, as part of his Twelve Labors, is sent to retrieve Hippolyta's girdle, which was a gift from the god Ares. Although Hippolyta willingly gives Heracles the girdle, the Amazons attack him as he leaves, forcing him to slay Hippolyta. See THESEUS.

APHRODITE

The goddess of love. According to Hesiod, Aphrodite emerges from the foam that forms around the genitals of Uranus after Cronos tosses them into the sea. Aphrodite takes her place among the Olympians and marries Hephaestus, the limping metalsmith of the gods, although her true love is for Ares, the god of war. Aphrodite is perhaps best known for her role in inciting the Trojan War. When Hera, Athena, and Aphrodite argue over which of them is the most beautiful, Zeus chooses Paris, a Trojan prince, to be the judge of their beauty contest. Aphrodite bribes Paris by offering him the most beautiful woman in the world if he choose Aphrodite above Hera and Athena. Paris chooses Aphrodite, and Aphrodite awards Helen, a Greek queen, to Paris. Aphrodite is the mother of the Trojan hero Aeneas.

APOLLO

The god of prophecy, artistic inspiration, archery, and medicine. Apollo features prominently in the Greek classics, especially in Aeschylus's *Oresteia*. In *Agamemnon,* his rage causes disbelief in Cassandra's prophecies; in *The Libation Bearers,* he advises Orestes to slay his mother; and in *The Eumenides,* he protects Orestes from the Furies.

Apollo arrives in the world after his mother, Leto, struggles for nine days to give birth to him and his twin sister, Artemis. When Leto is in labor, she tries to hide from Hera, who seeks to revenge Leto's love affair with Zeus. According to some legends, the newborn Artemis and Apollo send a plague upon all the homes that turned their laboring mother away for fear of Hera's punishment. Later, Apollo takes over the oracular duties at Delphi. Apollo becomes the god of medicine when he has a son, Asclepius, to whom he gives the power not only to prevent men from dying but also to resurrect the dead. Appalled that Apollo would give such powers to a mortal, Zeus smites Asclepius. Apollo, in turn, slays the Cyclopes. Zeus threatens to hurl Apollo into Tartarus, but Leto intervenes, and Zeus agrees instead to exile Apollo from Olympus and condemn him to serve a mortal for one year. Apollo serves his year as a herdsman for King Admetus—a story retold in Euripides' *Alcestis.*

ARCHERON

The river of woe across which the ferryman Charon transports the souls of the dead in Hades. The bottomless Archeron flows in and out of Tartarus and into the Archerusian Lake, where the souls of the dead wade until the time of their rebirth. See CHARON, HADES, TARTARUS.

AREOPAGUS

See ATHENS.

ARES

The god of war and protector of Olympus. The vain and moody Ares loves Aphrodite despite the fact that she is married to Hephaestus. Upon learning of Aphrodite's infidelity, Hephaestus traps her and Ares in bed with a net and suspends the entangled lovers to the merriment of the other Olympians. During the Trojan War, Ares fights for the Trojans, breaking his promise to fight alongside Athena and Hera on the Achaean (Greek) side. In revenge for the broken promise, Athena dons the helmet of Hades, makes herself invisible, and wounds Ares.

ARGONAUTS
See GOLDEN FLEECE.

ARIADNE
The daughter of King Minos of Crete. Ariadne falls in love with the young hero Theseus, helps him find his way out of the Labyrinth in Crete, and escapes with him. See THESEUS.

ARISTOCRACY
Government by the best. In more modern times, such as revolutionary France, aristocracy came to mean government by the wealthy nobility. In ancient Greece, however, aristocracy literally meant government by the best. In Plato's *Republic,* Socrates declares that aristocracy is the best form of government and that, in his imagined ideal city, the "best" would be the philosophers. Socrates would, therefore, put philosophers in charge of the city.

ARISTOTELIAN MEAN
Aristotle's idea that a person achieves happiness by living in moderation. This idea, one of the most famous in Greek philosophy, advises moderation in every aspect of life. In the *Ethics*, Aristotle examines various vices and determines that their corresponding virtues lie somewhere along the spectrum between pairs of extremes: bravery lies between rashness and cowardice, gentleness between malevolence and apathy, and so on. These virtues do not necessarily lie at the midpoint between extremes, however: bravery, for instance, lies closer to rashness than to cowardice. The key to happy living is identifying and following these appropriate moderate paths between extremes.

ARISTOTELIAN PHYSICS
Natural science, as opposed to the study of the physical world. The English word physics comes from the Greek word *phusis*, which means "the nature of things" or "the order of nature." Although the Greeks were far from accurate in many of their scientific inquiries, Aristotle's *Physics* remains a science classic. Aristotle built his study of physics on one key deduction—that everything in nature happens for a reason, for all of nature is in constant search of perfection.

ENCYCLOPEDIA

When a tree grows, for example, it grows a certain way because its growth is governed by necessity.

ARTEMIS

The goddess of the moon and the hunt. Although Artemis forever remains chaste and modest, she quickly and ruthlessly punishes those who attempt to intrude upon her womanhood. In one legend, Actaeon, a hunter, inadvertently sees Artemis unclothed when he stumbles upon her bathing. He quickly covers his eyes and seeks her forgiveness, but she transforms him into a stag and sets his own hunting hounds upon him. In another story, Agamemnon, just before the Trojan War, incurs the wrath of Artemis when he shoots a stag and brags that Artemis herself could not do better. To repay the insult, Artemis strands Agamemnon and his fleet and refuses to send wind until Agamemnon sacrifices his daughter, Iphigenia. Euripides retells this story in *Iphigenia at Aulis*.

ASTRONOMY

The study of the stars and planets, which the ancient Greeks pursued intensely. Farmers, who composed the majority of the Greek population, wanted to understand the heavens because their livelihood depended on understanding the changes of the seasons. The earliest Greek guesses about the nature of the heavens appear in the works of Homer, who describes the universe as an inverted bowl of a definite size and with stars hanging from its walls. Even as Greek society advanced and scientists began to tackle the nature of the universe in earnest, the picture that Homer presents remained remarkably unchanged. However, whereas Homer and his followers attributed the motion of the heavens to the will of the gods, later scientists began to think that there might be laws governing the motions of the heavens. These laws came to fruition around 585 B.C., when Thales of Miletus—widely regarded as the father of philosophy and science—accurately predicted an eclipse by studying past astronomical cycles. Despite Thales' discoveries, the Greeks continued to struggle in their attempts to explain the universe. Gradually, philosopher-scientists tried to reconcile their philosophies with the movements of the heavens. Heraclitus argued that the universe, like the Earth, constantly struggled to maintain equilibrium between love and strife. Parmenides argued that the universe never changed and that the movements of the heavens were governed by necessity. Empedocles tried to combine the ideas of Heraclitus and Parmenides by envisioning an unchanging universe perfectly balanced between harmony and discord. Later, Aristotle argued in favor of a geocentric universe in which the sun, the moon, the planets, and other heavenly bodies orbit the earth in concentric circles, with the stars hanging on the outmost sphere. As the spheres rotate, they resonate with a harmonious music. Centuries passed before anyone realized that this theory, though elegant, was insupportable in light of scientific evidence.

ATHENA

The goddess of wisdom, often called Pallas Athena. Athena, who inspires courage and skill in the just, is the daughter of Zeus and the nymph Metis. According to legend, Zeus impregnates Metis and then remembers a prophecy that Metis would give birth to a wise god who would take over heaven. Zeus, fearing he will be overthrown, swallows Metis whole. When the time comes for Athena's birth, the Titan Prometheus hits Zeus in the head with an axe, and Athena bursts out of Zeus's forehead in full armor. Athena is renowned for her loyalty to Odysseus, whom she helps repeatedly throughout the *Iliad* and *Odyssey*. She leads the Trojan warrior Hector to his doom when she takes the shape of a fellow Trojan as Achilles chases Hector around the walls of Troy. Believing that he has backup, Hector turns to face Achilles, only to see his seeming ally disappear when Athena takes flight.

ATHENS

The greatest city-state in ancient Greece and the birthplace of Western culture, philosophy, mathematics, and government. Athens, named for the goddess Athena, was built upon rich farmland with ready access to the sea, allowing for prosperous trade. Originally, a king ruled the city, but the monarchy gradually gave way to the Areopagus, a council of nobles named for the hill where they held their meetings. By the eighth century B.C., the Areopagus was in full control. The Areopagus elected nine *archons,* or rulers, who ran the state but submitted their decisions to the approval of the Areopagus. Gradually, the divide between the wealthy Areopagus and poor commoners increased, and many commoners were forced to sell their wives or children into slavery to make money. Tensions brewed until 594 B.C., when the Areopagus transferred all their power to one man, Solon.

Effectively a tyrant, Solon annulled all debts, retrieved as many people as possible from slavery, and reinvented the Athenian government into a system with more balanced power. Although common Athenians welcomed Solon's reforms, the economy continued to worsen until it nearly collapsed into anarchy. Backed by a mercenary army, the militaristic Pisistratus seized power and set about changing Athenian culture and religion. He actively pursued artists and poets to bolster Athenian culture and transferred more power to the lower classes.

After Pisistratus's death, his son Hippias took power and quickly earned many enemies. In 510 B.C., the Spartans defeated Hippias and replaced him with Athenians of their choosing. After a period of political unrest, Cleisthenes seized power. Cleisthenes implemented several reforms that led to the success of the Athenian democracy: he made citizens of all free men living in or around Athens and established a council that would be the chief arm of the government. Any citizen over the age of thirty was eligible to sit on the council, and every year, council positions were chosen by lot. This council could veto any motion by other branches of the government, and only this council could declare war. Athenian democracy took hold, and with it, art and philosophy prospered.

ATLANTIS

A mythical island lost beneath the sea. According to Plato's *Critias*, the Greeks learned of the myth of Atlantis from the Egyptians. According to the legend, Zeus and his brothers divide the world into three realms. Poseidon receives dominion over the seas, including a group of islands stretching from the Mediterranean Sea to modern-day Spain. The largest of these islands, Atlantis, is the most beautiful piece of land Poseidon has ever seen. On the island, he meets the beautiful Cleito, who soon bears him ten sons. The first of these sons is Atlas, after whom the island and the surrounding Atlantic Ocean are named. Atlantis blossoms into a powerful and cultured land, but its kings grow greedy and fail to share with the world. They raise a large army and conquer several countries on the mainland before setting their sights on Greece. They attack Athens and believe they have won, but as they sail home, the Atlantians see the sky fill with clouds and turn blood red. Zeus, believing that the inhabitants of Atlantis have lost their way, strikes them down and engulfs their island forever in the depths of the ocean.

ATLAS

A Titan who is assigned the task of holding up the sky to keep it from collapsing onto the earth. When Zeus overthrows the Titans, he gives this job to Atlas as punishment. Later, Heracles famously tricks Atlas during his completion of the Twelve Labors, one of which requires Heracles to steal the golden apples of the Hesperides (four nymphs who live near Atlas in the far west). The apples are too high to reach, so Heracles asks Atlas to get the apples and promises to support the sky while Atlas is away. Atlas returns with the apples, believing he is free of his punishment. However, Heracles asks Atlas to hold the sky momentarily while he positions a cushion on his shoulders. When Atlas takes the sky again, Heracles grabs the apples and leaves. According to some stories, Atlas meets his end soon after receiving a prophecy that an offspring of Zeus will destroy his home. When Peleus, a son of Zeus, arrives at Atlas's house, Atlas asks Peleus to leave and threatens to hurt him if he does not. Peleus shows Atlas the severed head of Medusa, the Gorgon, which turns Atlas to stone. He still exists as part of the Atlas mountain range in northern Africa. See TITANS.

ATREUS, HOUSE OF
The family that includes Atreus, Menelaus, Agamemnon, and others. The curse on the house of Atreus figures prominently in Greek drama. Atreus, the patriarch of the family, and his brother, Thyestes, are not fond of each other. After Thyestes steals the Golden Fleece from his brother, Atreus kills Thyestes' children and invites Thyestes to a feast in which the children are the main course. Thyestes flees from the feast and curses his brother. His lone surviving son, Aegisthus, harbors hatred for the house of Atreus throughout his life. Eventually, Aegisthus avenges his siblings by taking Agamemnon's wife, Clytemnestra, as his lover and plotting with her to murder Agamemnon after the Trojan War.

BACCHIC REVELRY
Festivals and merrymaking in honor of the god Dionysus (from his Roman name, Bacchus). Although the Greeks believed overwhelmingly in moderation in all aspects of life, they also made room for revelry in honor of Dionysus. Accordingly, Athens rang in the changing of the seasons through weeklong Bacchic festivals that honored the god of wine and the harvest with hearty drinking, merriment, and artistic displays. Greek playwrights used these festivals as opportunities to showcase their latest tragedies and comedies. See DIONYSUS.

BRONZE AGE
See AGES OF MAN.

CADMUS, HOUSE OF
See THEBES.

CALCHAS
A seer who famously predicts that Troy will fall within ten years of the arrival of the Achaean (Greek) army. After unfavorable winds detain the Achaean army on its way to Troy, Calchas prophesies that the winds will not return until Agamemnon sacrifices his most beautiful daughter to the goddess Artemis. Euripides retells this story and the results of this prophecy in *Iphigenia at Aulis*. The winds do return, but only after Agamemnon sacrifices Iphigenia and incurs the wrath of his wife, Clytemnestra, who later murders him (see Aeschylus's *Agamemnon*). Calchas also foresees the fall of Troy by means of the Trojan horse.

CALLIOPE
The muse of epic poetry. Calliope, the oldest of the muses, also delights in philosophy. Her marriage to Oeagrus produces the inspired musician Orpheus, who is able to soften rocks and bend trees with his sweet music. See MUSES.

CASSANDRA
A prophetess famous for making predictions that no one believes. The daughter of Priam and Hecuba, Cassandra plays a romantic and tragic role in Greek history. She gains prophetic powers as a child after spending the night in Apollo's temple. Years later, she again spends the night in Apollo's temple but shuns Apollo when he makes advances on her. Enraged, Apollo curses Cassandra to make prophecies that are always correct but never believed. Upon returning from Apollo's temple, Cassandra repeatedly foretells the fall of Troy, but Priam judges her insane and locks her away. After the fall of Troy, Agamemnon claims Cassandra as a spoil of war. Once again, she repeatedly warns Agamemnon of trouble waiting for him at home in Argos, but he ignores her warnings and walks into the murderous hands of his wife, Clytemnestra, who kills Cassandra as well. A number of works of Western literature document Cassandra's plight, notably Aeschylus's *Agamemnon*, Virgil's *Aeneid*, and Ovid's *Metamorphoses*.

CATHARSIS
The experience of emotional purgation or cleansing that, according to Aristotle, an audience experiences upon seeing a tragedy. The word catharsis comes from a Greek word meaning "to purge." In

his *Poetics*, Aristotle sets forth his view that people are drawn to tragic plays because of a desire to experience tragedy without suffering the consequences themselves. The audience members' spirits are purged when they watch a tragedy unfold onstage and suffer along with the characters. At the end of the play, the audience, having experienced these emotions vicariously, feels renewed. To Aristotle, catharsis is one of the most important elements of a tragedy.

CERBERUS

A three-headed dog that menaces the spirits of the dead as they enter the underworld. The guardian of the gates of Hades, Cerberus prevents the unwanted from entering and the unexcused from escaping. Cerberus plays a central role in the myth of the Twelve Labors of Heracles. The last of Heracles' tasks—which Hera assigns him as penance for Heracles' killing of his family—demands that he steal Cerberus from the underworld. Hades agrees to let Heracles wrestle with his dog but requires Heracles to use only his bare hands. Cerberus also figures in the myth of Orpheus, the musician and son of the muse Calliope. After the tragic death of his wife, Eurydice, Orpheus travels to the underworld to beg Hades to release his love. At the gates of the underworld, Cerberus menaces Orpheus, who lulls the three-headed beast to sleep with the magic of his music. See HADES.

CHARON

The god who ferries dead souls across the river Styx when they reach the underworld. The son of Erebus (Darkness) and Nyx (Night), Charon often is represented as a bad-tempered old man with a grizzled gray beard, a crooked nose, and fiery, piercing gray eyes. Rowing an old and rotting wooden boat, Charon demands a payment of one gold coin for his troubles. According to myth, if a spirit fails to provide payment, he is left to wander the far shores of the underworld for eternity, never finding rest in Hades. The ancient Greeks, therefore, placed a gold coin in a person's mouth upon his or her burial.

CHARYBDIS

A whirlpool-like sea monster that, along with the monster Scylla, waits in a rocky strait and threatens passing ships. Initially, Charybdis lives happily as a sea nymph, but Zeus transforms her into a monstrous, gaping whirlpool that engulfs even large ships. Odysseus navigates between Scylla and Charybdis in Homer's *Odyssey*. See SCYLLA.

CHIMERA

A three-headed beast that is part lion, part dragon, and part goat. The offspring of Typhon and Echidna, the Chimera belches fire and can level a building with a swat of its tail. The predatory Chimera torments the countryside of Asia Minor until the hero Bellerophon finally slays it.

CLEON

A greatly disliked general and political leader of Athens. Cleon (mid-400s B.C.) was the target of endless, biting satire from the comic playwright Aristophanes. He was notorious for executing the citizens of Mytilene, the capital of Lesbos, after quelling a revolt there. Cleon died during the battle of Amphipolis in the Peloponnesian War, in which the Spartan leader Brasidas defeated Cleon's forces.

CLIO

The muse of history. Clio is the mother of Hyacinthus, a young man whose beauty rivals that of Narcissus.

CONTEMPLATIVE LIFE

The life of philosophy, which the great Greek philosophers claim to be the most worthwhile and fulfilling life possible. In an argument over the merits of philosophy, Socrates asserts that the non-contemplative life—the life without philosophy—is not worth living. Aristotle, too, asserts in the *Ethics* that the greatest man is he who devotes his life to contemplation and the pursuit of philosophic truths.

CRETE

A large island in the Mediterranean. According to legend, Crete rises to power after Europa (see Thebes) returns to the world and marries Asterius, who inherits the kingdom of Crete. Under the reign of Asterius and his son and grandson, Crete flourishes. However, Crete crumbles under the rule of Asterius's corrupt greatgrandson, Minos. Pasiphae, Minos's wife, gives birth to a monstrous son with the head of a bull. Minos imprisons this son—the Minotaur—in a labyrinth under his palace. Later, the hero Theseus slays the Minotaur and steals Minos's daughter, Ariadne. See MINOTAUR, THESEUS.

CRONOS

The youngest of the Titans and the father of a number of the Olympian gods, including Zeus. Cronos follows the orders of his mother, Gaia (the Earth), and castrates his father, Uranus (the Heavens). Cronos becomes the ruler of the universe, which flourishes under him. Known as the Golden Age (the first age of man), this era is peaceful and prosperous. However, Cronos ultimately grows corrupt like his father, and Gaia alerts him that the same fate that destroyed his father will destroy him as well. Fearing a revolt from his children and his wife, Rhea, Cronos ingests each of his children as they are born—Demeter, Poseidon, Hades, Hera, and then Hestia. When Zeus is born, however, Rhea hides him and feeds Cronos a rock in baby clothes instead. Later, Cronos regurgitates his other children, who join Zeus in a battle against their father and the other Titans. Zeus frees the Cyclopes from Tartarus and promises them freedom if they fight on his side. The Olympian gods emerge victorious, and Zeus casts Cronos and the other Titans into Tartarus. See OLYMPIAN GODS, TITANS, URANUS.

CYCLOPES

Strong, stubborn, one-eyed monsters who are the progeny of Uranus. Upon seeing the disfigured Cyclopes, Uranus casts them into Tartarus. When Cronos revolts against Uranus, he frees the Cyclopes from their dark prison to help in the fight, only to banish them once again after his victory. Later, when Zeus revolts against Cronos, Zeus again frees the Cyclopes. In thanks for their freedom, the Cyclopes award Zeus the thunderbolt, Poseidon the trident, and Hades the helmet. With these gifts, Zeus and his brothers defeat the Titans. In Homer's *Odyssey,* Odysseus has a famous encounter with the Cyclops Polyphemus on his journey home to Ithaca. See POLYPHEMUS.

DAEDALUS

A highly respected engineer, architect, and artisan who builds the famed Labyrinth at Crete. After Daedalus builds the Labyrinth for King Minos, he reveals the secret of how to escape from the Labyrinth to Ariadne, Minos's daughter. Ariadne then reveals the secret to the Athenian youth Theseus, who uses it to slay the Minotaur and escape from the Labyrinth. In punishment, Minos imprisons Daedalus and his son, Icarus, in the Labyrinth. However, Daedalus uses feathers and wax to fashion two pairs of wings that enable him and Icarus to escape. Icarus, however, flies too close to the sun, and the wax on his wings melts, causing him to fall to his death. See ICARUS, LABYRINTH, MINOTAUR.

DELPHI

The site of the temple of Apollo, home of the Oracle at Delphi. The temple and the Oracle play crucial roles in Greek myth and literature. The Greeks believed that the temple, which was built over a sacred spring, stood upon the *omphalos,* or navel, of the earth. At a number of key moments in Greek mythology, individuals make pilgrimages to Delphi to ask the Pythia, the priestess of Apollo, to shed light upon the future. The Pythian priestess is an inspired woman responsible for communicating with Apollo and foreseeing the future. When those with questions arrive, the priestess takes her seat on a tripod over a deep chasm in the earth and falls into a trance by inhaling vapors from inside the earth. Generally, the Oracle's answers are vague. When Greek generals consult the Oracle during the Peloponnesian War, for example, she tells them that Athens will be saved by a wooden wall—which ultimately turns out to be the Athenian navy. Sometimes her answers are more specific, as when she tells Laius that his son, Oedipus, will murder his father and sleep with his mother.

DEMETER

The goddess of the harvest and the earth. The daughter of Rhea and Cronos, Demeter loses her own daughter, Persephone, to the god Hades, who abducts her and carries her off to the underworld. The loss of Persephone saddens Demeter, and no crops grow on the earth during her mourning. Ultimately, Persephone and Hades make an arrangement that obligates Persephone to spend only a portion of each year in the underworld. During the time when mother and daughter are separated, the earth falls into the barrenness of autumn and winter. When Persephone returns from Hades, the earth blossoms into spring and summer. Demeter is also the mother of Artemis and Apollo. See OLYMPIAN GODS, HADES, PERSEPHONE.

DEMOCRACY

Government by the people. Although Athens built its reputation as the first successful democracy, Plato maintains that a democracy is far from the best from of government. Throughout Plato's *Republic* and other works, Socrates asserts that all men are *not* created equal. Aristotle supports this notion with his belief in natural slaves. While Athenian citizens enjoyed far fewer privileges than the citizens of most modern-day democracies, Plato still viewed democracy as a dangerous form of government because of the power it gave to the masses—whose appetites he considered uneducated and untrustworthy.

DEUS EX MACHINA

A convention in Greek drama wherein a god appears onstage to bring sudden and unexpected resolution to a conflict or difficulty. Many Greek playwrights, particularly Euripides, used this technique—literally "god from a machine"—frequently. When a play called for an appearance from above by a god or ghost, the stagehands would use ropes and pulleys to raise an actor above the stage and simulate flight. Occasionally, as in the *Medea*, the playwright would employ *deus ex machina* to achieve a surprise or miraculous ending—Medea flies away in a chariot drawn by dragons.

DIONYSUS

The god of wine and revelry. Dionysus is the child of Zeus and Semele, a mortal. Hera, jealous of Zeus's passion for Semele, advises Semele to make a special erotic request of Zeus: that he make love to her as he makes love to Hera. When Zeus complies, he overwhelms Semele, inadvertently killing her and causing her to give premature birth to Dionysus. Zeus sews the embryonic Dionysus in his thigh until the infant is ready to enter the world, whereupon Zeus bestows him to the care of the nymphs. All the while, Hera harbors a deep hatred for Dionysus and persecutes him forever. Dionysus is perhaps best known for his tendency to inspire an animal madness in his followers. In Euripides' *Bacchae,* Dionysus enters the city of Thebes and incites madness in the Theban women, who take to the hills, where they bare their breasts and hunt like wild beasts. The ancient Athenians heartily celebrated Dionysus with festivals and considered him the patron god of drama and playwrights.

ECHO

A young, beautiful nymph who incurs the wrath of the goddess Hera by distracting her deliberately while Zeus runs off and has trysts with other goddesses and mortal women. In revenge, Hera destroys Echo's capacity for speech, allowing her only to repeat words spoken by others. According to one story, the god Pan falls in love with the muted Echo, who spurns him. Enraged, Pan drives a group of shepherds mad so that they turn on Echo and tear her limb from limb. Gaia, however, loves the nymph's music and preserves her voice in the mountains. In yet another version of the story, Echo falls madly in love with the vain young man Narcissus, who rejects her. Overwhelmed by self-loathing and heartbreak, Echo retreats to the mountains, where she gradually fades away until her bones turn to stone and only her voice remains in the air. See NARCISSUS.

ELECTRA

The daughter of Agamemnon and Clytemnestra and sister of Orestes. When Clytemnestra murders her husband—Electra and Orestes' father—Electra plots with her brother to kill their mother in revenge. Both Sophocles and Euripides retell this story in plays entitled *Electra*. The nineteenth-century psychoanalyst and theorist Sigmund Freud loosely based his theory of the "Electra complex" on this story, claiming that every young girl has a latent envy of her father and blames her mother, shifting her affections to her father. This theory's far more famous counterpart is the Oedipus complex, based on the legend of Oedipus. See OEDIPUS.

ELYSIAN FIELDS (ELYSIUM)

The fields in Hades were the spirits of the chosen dead rest in eternal bliss. As the dead make their way into the depths of the underworld, the road forks. One road leads to Elysium, and the other leads to Tartarus, the dwelling place of the cursed. At the fork, the shades of the dead encounter three judges—Aeacus, Rhadamanthys, and Minos—who used to be mortal kings. Those great souls who pass the judgment of the three dead kings make their way toward Elysium. Ruled by Cronos, Elysium has a sun and moon of its own. The dead frolic in grassy fields, sleep peacefully on the banks of a river, and never again experience the pain and suffering of life. The great souls that rest there include the musician Orpheus, the prophet Musaeus, and the Trojan hero Hector. According to some accounts, Elysium is also inhabited by the souls of those mortals not yet born.

EPIMETHEUS

A Titan and the brother of Prometheus. Epimetheus marries Pandora, the first mortal woman, against his brother's warnings. See PANDORA, PROMETHEUS.

ERATO

The muse of love poetry. The poets who earn Erato's favor become highly desirable lovers. See MUSES.

ERINYES
See FURIES.

EROS
The god of love and sexual desire. The source of the modern word erotic, Eros exists in one or both of two different manifestations. In the most common story, Eros is the child of Aphrodite and is armed with a bow and arrows of love—the image of Cupid (Eros's name in Roman mythology) popularized by Valentine's Day. Both Hesiod and Aristophanes, however, contend that Eros is one of the oldest gods and that he played an important role in the formation of universe. According to Hesiod, Eros impregnates Gaia with Uranus, Oceanus, and the hills. According to Aristophanes, Nyx (Night) lays an egg in Erebus (Darkness) from which Eros hatches. Eros then impregnates Chaos, who gives birth to Gaia, Uranus, and Oceanus.

The myths of Eros's participation in the formation of the universe undoubtedly influenced Greek philosophy through Plato and Aristotle. In Plato's philosophy, Eros plays a crucial role in the philosopher's quest for truth, as the philosopher longs for truth with an erotic love. Likewise, Aristotle considers Eros central, as a force who fosters desire in a universe governed by the Prime Mover—a bodiless, shapeless, benevolent entity that sets the universe in motion.

EUCLID
A disciple of Plato's school, often considered the father of modern geometry. Euclid (late 300s B.C.) taught geometry at Alexandria, where he founded a school of mathematics and wrote his seminal work, the *Elements*. In this twelve-volume work, Euclid sets out definitions for the most basic concepts in geometry—points, lines, planes, parallelism, and so on—and from there shows how to construct everything from triangles to dodecahedrons. The *Elements*, which Euclid wrote in verse, makes poetry of geometry, as he constructs definitions from statements such as "A line is breadthless length" and "A point is that which has no part." Euclid's fifth postulate, which states that parallel lines never meet, remains a central point of mathematical philosophy—even today, no one has proved or disproved the veracity of this statement. In addition to his work in geometry, Euclid wrote about optics, the heavens, and music.

ENCYCLOPEDIA

EUTERPE

The muse of lyric poetry and music. Euterpe delights those who hear her sing. See MUSES.

FATE

The all-powerful force that the ancient Greeks believed determined an individual's destiny in life. Fate was of great concern to the Greeks, and its workings resonate throughout many of their myths. Countless characters go to great lengths in attempts to alter or avoid fate—and sometimes display hubris, or excessive pride, in the process—but such endeavors always prove futile. The three Fates, or Moerae, decide the fate of each individual—mortal or immortal—when he or she is born. No individual can do anything to alter his fate or prolong his life. Even the mighty Zeus is subject to the will of the Fates, as we see in his hounding of Prometheus to divulge the name of the woman who will bear the offspring that one day will kill him.

The Greek belief in the primacy of fate is both optimistic and pessimistic: individuals can take comfort in knowing that what happens to them is meant to happen, but at the same time, the prospect of free will is remote. Perhaps the most famous example of fate is the story of Oedipus, whose father, Laius, goes to great lengths to prevent Oedipus from fulfilling his destiny to kill his father and marry his mother. Despite Laius's efforts, the prophecy comes true, as Oedipus kills Laius and marries Jocasta. Ironically, it is Laius's exercise of free will—his attempt to alter Oedipus's fate—that causes that fate to come true. See FATES, OEDIPUS, HUBRIS.

FATES (MOERAE)

Three sister goddesses who spin the web of life that decides human fate. The Fates—Clotho, Lachesis, and Atropus—are alleged to be the daughters of Nyx (Night) and often are depicted as old women. Together, the three decide the fates of all mortal beings and exercise influence over even the mightiest of the gods. Each mortal's life is represented by a thread: Clotho spins the strand, starting the individual's life; Lachesis determines its length, and thus the length of the individual's life; and Atropus cuts the string, indicating it is time for the individual to die. The omnipotence and wisdom of the Fates make them the most powerful and revered of all gods.

FURIES (ERINYES)

Three goddesses who avenge crimes that mortals commit, especially patricide. The Furies—Alecto, Megaera, and Tisiphone—form when Cronos rebels against his father, Uranus, and castrates him. The blood from the castration falls to the ground and causes Gaia, the Earth, to give birth to the Furies. The Furies' primary task is to hunt down and torment mortals who are guilty of heinous crimes. The Furies also dwell in Hades, where they menace the souls of the dead as they make their entrance into the underworld. Tisiphone stands guard in Tartarus, where the most wicked face their punishments.

The Furies figure prominently in the story of Orestes, who kills his mother, Clytemnestra, in revenge for her murder of Orestes' father, Agamemnon. According to Aeschylus's *Eumenides,* the Furies chase Orestes to Athens, where he seeks Athena's protection. Athena rules that Orestes murdered his mother justly. As a peace offering to the Furies, Athena unburdens them of their role as tormenters and makes them patron goddesses of Athens.

GAIA

The goddess of the Earth, often termed Mother Earth. Gaia appears out of Chaos, a dark, inscrutable entity with unexplained origins. From Gaia comes Uranus, the Heavens. Together, Gaia and Uranus produce the first race of gods, the Titans. Uranus, however, begins to eat his children out of fear they will rebel against him, so Gaia commands her youngest son, Cronos, to castrate his father. Later, Cronos grows similarly paranoid about his own children, so his wife, Rhea, gives one of their sons, Zeus, to Gaia so that she can watch over Zeus until he grows strong enough to challenge his father. Zeus eventually topples Cronos, and Gaia, who mourns the loss of her first children, breeds a second race of enormous gods, the Giants, who soon besiege Olympus. See CRONOS, ZEUS, OLYMPIAN GODS.

GOLDEN AGE
See AGES OF MAN.

GOLDEN FLEECE

The wool of a flying golden ram that the hero Jason and his crew, the Argonauts, are sent to retrieve. According to legend, a man named Pelias usurps the throne of Jason's father, a Greek king. The scheming Pelias tells Jason that the gods have decreed that someone must retrieve the Golden Fleece for the kingdom. In reality, Pelias believes that sending Jason on the dangerous quest will mean his certain death. The Golden Fleece belongs to Aeëtes, the king of Colchis, so Jason assembles a group of heroes—including Heracles, Theseus, Peleus, and Orpheus—to help him. Their ship is called the *Argo,* so the group is called the Argonauts. The Argonauts face many dangers on the way to Colchis, but when they arrive, Hera and Aphrodite assist the quest. Aphrodite causes Aeëtes' daughter, the witch Medea, to fall in love with Jason. Medea helps Jason through the tasks that Aeëtes sets before him and even kills her own brother to help Jason's quest. Ultimately, Medea leaves Colchis with Jason, helps him overthrow his father, and marries him, although their marriage ends with tragedy and bloodshed. See MEDEA.

GORGIAS
A leader of the Sophists. Gorgias (485–380 B.C.) played an important role in the development of Attic prose, excelling as he did in rhetoric. He is the title character of Plato's dialogue *Gorgias,* in which he and Socrates engage in an argument over the nature of happiness. Gorgias, a nihilist, believed that nothing exists; that if something does exist, it cannot be known; and that if something happens to exist and can be known, it cannot be communicated. See SOPHISTS.

GORGONS
Three female monsters whose hair is made of living snakes and whose horrible appearance turns mortals to stone. The three Gorgons are named Euryale, Medusa, and Sthenno. See MEDUSA.

HADES (PERSON)
The brother of Zeus and Poseidon and the god of the underworld, which bears his name. Hades gains control of the underworld when he and his two brothers divide the dominions of the world. After the Olympian gods defeat the Titans, the Cyclopes award Hades a helmet that renders its wearer invisible. Later, Hades, lonely in the underworld, abducts Persephone, the daughter of Demeter, as his bride. The saddened Demeter searches night and day for her daughter, and the earth bears no fruit during her mourning. When Zeus commands Hades to return Persephone, he tricks her into eating pomegranate seeds, and she is forced to stay in Hades one month of each year for each seed she eats in the underworld. During the

remainder of the year, Hades permits Persephone to return to her mother. See DEMETER, PERSEPHONE, OLYMPIAN GODS.

HADES (PLACE)

The underworld, named for its ruler, the god Hades. According to Greek mythology, the souls of the dead inhabit this realm, which lies under the surface of the earth. There is no annihilation after death—only the flavorless, sometimes painful, sometimes blissful existence of souls in Hades. When mortals die, the god Hermes leads their souls to the edge of Hades, where they must wait for Charon, the immortal riverman, to ferry them across the river Styx. However, the unburied and those without money to pay for their ride are left forever on the far shores of the river. At the gates of Hades stand many dark gods and goddesses, including Thanatos (Death), Hypnos (Sleep), Geras (Old Age), Eris (Discord), and the Erinyes (the Furies). In the midst of these are monsters—centaurs, gorgons, harpies, and others—and a tall elm tree with false dreams clinging under its leaves. Guarding the entrance to the underworld is Cerberus, a fierce three-headed dog.

As the dead make their way past Cerberus, they come to Limbo, the home of the souls of children, suicides, and the falsely condemned. Next are the Asphodel Fields, reserved for the majority of the dead, where shades are confounded by confusion, darkness, and boredom. Nearby is the Vale of Mourning, home to those who died unhappily in love. In the farthest fields dwell the souls of soldiers. Those deemed worthy of a happier afterlife are sent to the Elysian Fields, where they dwell in eternal bliss. Those who passed their lives in wickedness are condemned to Tartarus—an utterly black pit where the Furies torture the souls of the dead.

Although the underworld is meant to hold souls captive until they receive permission to leave, a number of well-known characters from Greek mythology heroically journey to Hades and return to the world above. Among those who succeed are Heracles, who goes to capture Cerberus as part of his Twelve Labors; Orpheus, who goes in search of his deceased wife, Eurydice; Theseus, who dies but is rescued by Heracles; Odysseus, who goes in search of the prophet Tiresias; and Aeneas, who wishes to consult the spirit of his dead father. The accounts of these individuals who enter Hades vary. While all describe the underworld as a dark and confusing place, some report more pain and suffering than others. According to Odysseus's account, everyone in Hades wishes desperately to return to life and longs for contact with the living. At the same time, the *Odyssey* depicts a conversation between Agamemnon and Achilles that leaves the impression that the deceased old war heroes stand around all day reminiscing about their heroics. See CHARON, CERBERUS, ELYSIAN FIELDS, TARTARUS.

HAPPINESS

The state of contentment or fulfillment that many Greek philosophers attempted to define. In the *Ethics*, Aristotle asserts that the endeavor of every individual's life is the pursuit and attainment of happiness. The nature or definition of this happiness, however, was a point of constant dispute among Greek philosophers. Whereas Sophists like Gorgias argued that anyone can be happy, Plato and Aristotle maintained that the wicked never can know true happiness. Rather, happiness exists only for those who spend their lives in pursuit of wisdom, for with wisdom comes happiness. Other Greek thinkers believed that wisdom was not the only source of happiness. In Homer's *Odyssey,* for instance, Odysseus reports that the warrior Achilles broods unhappily in Hades because of the nature of his death. In another scene from the *Odyssey,* Agamemnon and Achilles discuss the unhappiness of their deaths, placing the origin of happiness on the nature of death rather than the nature of life. In another ancient story, the legendary Greek ruler Solon, famous for his wisdom, advises the rich Croesus on the nature of happiness. When Croesus asks Solon to name the happiest man, Solon responds with stories of triumphant deaths and counsels Croesus to count no man happy until his death.

HECTOR

A modest, dutiful, and just Trojan warrior and the eldest son of King Priam. Hector, who dies at Achilles' hands outside the walls of Troy, plays a key role in two prophecies during the Trojan War: one prophecy states that Troy never will fall to the Achaeans (Greeks) as long as Hector remains alive, while the other states that Achilles will die soon after killing Hector. Despite the efforts of Priam and Hecuba to save their son from his own sense of duty, Hector refuses to shy away from battle with Achilles. Hector senses, as he confesses to his wife, Andromache, that Troy soon will fall. After Hector's death, Achilles desecrates his body by dragging it through the dirt, stabbing it repeatedly, and refusing to bury it. After the war, Hector's family meets similarly horrible fates. Priam dies at the hands of Achilles' son, Neoptolemus; Hector's young son, Astyanax, is hurled from a tower; and Andromache is awarded to Menelaus as a spoil of war.

HELEN OF TROY
Reputedly the most beautiful woman in the world and the "face that launched a thousand ships" in the Trojan War. The goddess Aphrodite gives Helen, the wife of King Menelaus of Sparta, to the Trojan prince Paris as a prize when Paris judges Aphrodite to be the fairest goddess. Paris kidnaps Helen, which prompts Menelaus and the Achaeans (Greeks) to attack Troy. As the war drags on, at great cost to both sides, some begin to blame Helen for inadvertently causing so much death and destruction. See TROJAN WAR.

HEPHAESTUS
The metalsmith of the gods and the son of Zeus and Hera. Hephaestus is born weak and physically lame. According to one story, when Hephaestus is young, his mother sends a storm upon Heracles, the son of Zeus by another woman. In retaliation, Zeus chains Hera to a rock, but Hephaestus pities his mother and releases her, enraging Zeus, who casts Hephaestus out of heaven. Hephaestus falls through the sky for nine days and nights and breaks his already weak legs when he lands. Despite his physical lameness, he weds the beautiful Aphrodite, even though her affections remain with Ares. Hephaestus occasionally bestows his pieces of metalwork upon mortals. For Heracles, he fashions an impenetrable breastplate; for Achilles, he makes a suit of armor and a shield, which Homer describes in detail in the *Iliad*.

HERA
The wife of Zeus and queen of the gods. The frequently jealous and vain Hera resents any comparisons of her beauty to other goddesses or mortal women. Many Greek myths show how Hera retaliates against Zeus and his amorous partners in revenge for Zeus's infidelities. See ZEUS.

HERACLES
A legendarily strong hero most famous for the Twelve Labors he is assigned to complete. Heracles is the son of Zeus and Alcmena, a mortal woman. Hera, jealous of Zeus's infidelity, sends two serpents to kill the baby Heracles, but the infant strangles them. When he comes of age, the gods award him with weapons: a sword from Hermes, a bow and arrows from Apollo, a breastplate from Hephaestus, and a robe from Athena. Heracles continues to grow stronger as

he ages, and Hera continues to persecute him. In her cruelest moment, she inflicts him with a fit of madness that causes him to kill his wife and children.

When Heracles snaps out of his spell of insanity, he rushes to the Oracle at Delphi to ask what he must do to atone for his crimes. The Oracle tells him to go to Eurystheus, who, along with Hera, invents twelve seemingly impossible tasks for Heracles to perform. In a single day, he must kill the monstrous Demean lion, conquer the nine-headed Hydra, capture the golden-horned stag of Artemis, subdue the terrifying boar of Mt. Erymanthus, and clean the Augean stables—home to thousands of cattle. He completes all of these successfully and, for the stable-cleaning task, goes so far as to divert two rivers to reroute them through the stables. With these five labors complete, Heracles then is commanded to destroy the man-eating Stymphalian birds, capture the Cretan bull, harness the man-eating mares of Thrace, obtain the girdle of the Amazon queen Hippolyta, capture the cattle of the monster Geryon, and steal the golden apples of the Hesperides. Heracles' final task is to capture Cerberus, the three-headed dog that guards the gates of the underworld. Hades permits Heracles to wrestle the monster as long as he uses no weapons. While in the underworld, Heracles spots his good friend Theseus—trapped in Hades before his time—and returns him, along with Cerberus, to the land of the living. The playwright Euripides details Heracles' labors in his play *Heracles*. See ATLAS, HADES (PLACE).

HERMES
The herald and messenger of the gods. The fleet-footed Hermes brings dreams to mortals, acts as an ambassador for peace, is the patron of travelers, and leads the souls of the dead to the gates of the underworld. Hermes fights valiantly in the war between the Olympians and the Giants. When Typhon the Giant binds Zeus, tears the sinews from his arms, and hides them away, Hermes recovers them and secretly returns them to Zeus.

HIPPOLYTA
See AMAZONS.

HUBRIS
Excessive pride or arrogance, especially the pride that leads humans to challenge fate or hold themselves up as equals to the gods. Hubris is one of the worst traits that an individual can exhibit in the world

of ancient Greece, as mortals foolish enough to display hubris inevitably are punished. Tales warning of the dangers of hubris pervade Greek mythology and tragedy. Perhaps the most commonly cited story of hubris in Greek myth is that of Icarus, the son of Daedalus, the architect who designed the Labyrinth on Crete. When King Minos imprisons Daedalus and Icarus in the Labyrinth, Daedalus engineers their escape by fashioning wings out of wax and feathers for himself and his son. Daedalus warns Icarus not to fly too high because the heat from the sun will melt the wax holding the wings together. But Icarus, overwhelmed by the freedom of flight and his proximity to the gods, grows overconfident and soars higher and higher as he and his father escape over the sea. As Icarus climbs, the wax on his wings begins to melt until the wings suddenly give out altogether, sending Icarus plummeting to his death in the ocean. Other examples of hubris in Greek myth include that of Phaëthon, who pridefully believes he can drive the chariot of his father, the Sun; Bellerophon, who bridles the winged Pegasus and tries to ride to the summit of Mt. Olympus to join the gods' revelry; and Arachne, who dares to challenge Athena to a weaving contest.

HYDRA

A monster that makes its home in the caves of Lerna and torments nearby villages. The Hydra's physical description varies according to different accounts of the monster: they variously claim that it has nine heads, one of which is immortal; or a hundred heads; or countless heads; or only one head. Heracles is sent to slay the Hydra as one of his Twelve Labors. To provoke the Hydra, Heracles shoots arrows into its cave. When the monster rears its ugly heads, Heracles chops them off with his sword, but for every head he cuts off, two more heads take its place. Heracles realizes the fruitlessness of his tactic and orders his companion, Iolus, to sear each severed neck with a branding iron in order to prevent the growth of more heads. When only the immortal head remains, Heracles cuts it off, sears the neck closed, and buries the head on the road to Lerna. See HERACLES.

HYPERION

A god identified with the sun. Hyperion, who is the first to understand the movements of the heavens, has offspring who include Helios (the Sun), Selene (the Moon), and Eos (the Dawn).

ICARUS

The son of the great inventor Daedalus. Icarus and his father escape the Labyrinth of Crete when Daedalus fashions wings out of feathers and wax, which enable the father and son to fly. However, Icarus fails to heed his father's warnings and flies too high, and the heat from the sun's rays melts the wax on his wings and sends him tumbling to his death in the sea. See DAEDALUS, HUBRIS.

IRON AGE

See AGES OF MAN.

ISOCRATES

A student of both Socrates and Plato who founded a famous school of rhetoric in Greece. Isocrates (436–338 B.C.) wrote speeches for lawyers, taught the art of essay writing, and challenged the Sophists. He argued vehemently for the union of the Greek city-states against the Persian and Macedonian empires. Disappointed by the rule of Dionysus of Syracuse, Isocrates invited Philip II of Macedonia to join the union of Greek city-states, but the plan fell apart when Philip sacked Athens and robbed the Athenians of their independence. Heartbroken and perhaps shamed, Isocrates starved himself to death at the age of ninety-eight.

JASON

The husband of Medea and the hero who, along with the Argonauts, retrieves the Golden Fleece. See GOLDEN FLEECE, MEDEA.

LAESTRYGONIANS

Cannibalistic people who live in the hills near Mt. Aetna. In Homer's *Odyssey,* Odysseus and his men encounter the Laestrygonians after the men open a mysterious bag that Odysseus received from Aeolus, ruler of the winds. The men presume that the bag holds gold, but when they open it, it releases the winds that Aeolus gave to Odysseus, and the gusts send the ships swirling away from Ithaca. The ships land on a rocky island, and when Odysseus sends three men to investigate the island, the Laestrygonian chieftain, Antiphates, devours two of them. The survivor makes a hasty retreat to the ships, but the Laestrygonians have already stormed the cliffs, hurling rocks and spears down on Odysseus's men. Odysseus sees that all is lost, boards his own ship with his men, and sails away. The Laestrygonians eat the rest of the men in the fleet. See ODYSSEUS.

LAOCOÖN

A prophet who, like Cassandra, makes predictions that fall upon deaf ears. During the Trojan War, when the Trojans awake to find the Achaean (Greek) armies sailing away and an enormous wooden horse waiting at their gates, they initially are suspicious. Laocoön vehemently opposes accepting the horse and declares that a Greek army lies waiting inside. In an effort to prove his point, Laocoön hurls his spear into the horse, expecting to wound the Greeks that he is certain are hiding inside. When the tip of his spear comes back free of blood, the tide turns against him. Laocoön refuses to give in and continues to rant against the horse. Finally, the goddess Athena sends two serpents to attack his sons. She blinds Laocoön as he tries to save his family, and the serpents kill his boys. The Trojans decide to accept the horse to avoid further offending Athena—which proves to be their fatal mistake, as Odysseus and his men leap from the horse and seize the city later that night. See CASSANDRA, TROJAN HORSE.

LETHE

The river of forgetfulness in Hades. The river Lethe flows across the plain of Lethe in the underworld, where it murmurs through the caves of Hypnos and induces drowsiness. Before souls of the dead can be reincarnated in the afterlife, they must drink from the waters of the Lethe in order to forget about their previous lives on earth.

LOTUS EATERS

A group of island people whom Odysseus and his men encounter on the way home to Ithaca. The Lotus Eaters habitually eat the sweet, delectable lotus flower, which is a narcotic that leaves them in a constant blissful stupor. When Odysseus's ships land on the island in search of provisions, the men find the lotus, and some of them begin to satisfy their ravenous appetites. They discover that, with their first bite, all their thoughts of home vanish. They lose their desire to leave and want only to eat more of the lotus. Ultimately, Odysseus is forced to abandon a portion of his men on the island because they have no desire to leave.

MARATHON

A famous battle in the Persian War and the source of our modern term for a lengthy race or endeavor. Darius, the king of Persia, invaded Greece in 490 B.C. and met the Athenian forces on the plains of Marathon, outside Athens. The Athenians, though outnumbered four to one, stood strong against the Persian advance for eight days. On the ninth day, the Athenians mounted a bold offensive, took the Persians by surprise, and succeeded in routing the invading army. As the Persians regrouped, they turned their ships toward Athens. Miltiades, the Athenian commander, quickly realized the imminent threat to Athens and sent a runner, Pheidippides, to warn the city of danger. Pheidippides ran the twenty-six miles to Athens—the first marathon—in just over three hours and delivered his message with his final breath. The Athenians successfully countered the Persian attack, and the tide of the war turned.

MEDEA

A sorceress and princess who marries the hero Jason and becomes one of the most prominent female figures in Greek mythology. Under the influence of Aphrodite, Medea falls in love with Jason when he comes to retrieve the mythical Golden Fleece from her father, Aeëtes. She uses her powers to help Jason succeed in his quest, several times at her own expense and at the expense of her family. Then, Medea marries Jason and helps him overthrow Pelias, the man who has usurped his throne. Despite Medea's devotion and assistance, Jason cruelly abandons her for another woman after several years of marriage. Medea takes revenge—again at terrible cost to herself—by killing Jason's new bride, his new father-in-law, and her own two small children, whom she and Jason had together. Medea then rides off in a chariot drawn by dragons. Euripides retells this story in his play *Medea*. See GOLDEN FLEECE.

MEDUSA

One of the Gorgons, female monsters whose hair is made of living snakes and whose appearance turns mortals to stone. Medusa dies at the hands of Perseus, who uses a mirrored shield to avoid gazing upon Medusa directly. Perseus cuts off Medusa's head and brings it to the goddess Athena, who places it in the center of her shield. See GORGONS.

MELPOMENE

The muse of tragedy. According to some sources, Melpomene is the mother of the Sirens, the women with bewitching voices who cause sailors to crash upon the shores of their island. See MUSES, SIRENS.

MIDAS

An ancient king of Phrygia whose story is the source of the expression "Midas touch." One day, Silenus, the leader of the group of satyrs that follows the god Dionysus, gets drunk and passes out in King Midas's garden. Midas recognizes the satyr and entertains him magnificently for several days. In return, Silenus offers to grant Midas any wish he desires, so Midas requests that everything he touch turn to gold. Delighted, he touches the objects around him, and each of them instantly turns to gold. When he tries to eat, however, his food also turns to gold. Later, Midas touches his daughter, and she turns to gold. The curse lifts only when Midas consults Dionysus, who instructs him to bathe in the waters of the Pactolus River. Midas's gold settles in the silt of the riverbed and washes downstream to the kingdom of Lydia, which is renowned for its wealth. To this day, "Midas touch" denotes a remarkable knack for making money in business or other financial ventures.

Minotaur

A monster, with the head of a bull and the body of a man, that haunts the great Labyrinth of Crete. Minos, the king of Crete, prays to Poseidon to send him a fine white bull as a sign of the god's approval. Minos promises to sacrifice the bull as a token of appreciation and obedience. Poseidon causes a white bull to emerge from the sea, but the bull is so beautiful that Minos yearns to keep it himself and opts to sacrifice a different bull instead. Enraged at Minos's substitution, Poseidon strikes back by inducing Pasiphae, Minos's wife, to fall in love with the bull. Pasiphae, overcome with lust for the bull, consults the engineer and architect Daedalus to construct a hollow wooden cow wrapped in the skin of a real cow. The cow is placed in a field near Minos's bull, and Pasiphae climbs inside and waits until the bull approaches and mates with the wooden cow. The impregnated Pasiphae later gives birth to the Minotaur. Minos casts Daedalus into prison for his part in the affair and puts the Minotaur into the Labyrinth, a giant maze that Daedalus constructed. Every year, Minos forces the Athenians, whom he earlier conquered, to send seven of their young men and seven of their young women into the Labyrinth as fodder for the Minotaur. One year, one of the young Athenian men, Theseus, falls in love with Ariadne, Minos's daughter. Ariadne, hoping to save Theseus's life, tells him a way to escape the Labyrinth. As Theseus makes his way through the maze, he takes the Minotaur by surprise, kills it, and escapes from Crete with Ariadne. See THESEUS.

ENCYCLOPEDIA

MNEMOSYNE
The goddess of memory and the mother of the nine Muses. The English word mnemonic, which refers to memory, derives from Mnemosyne's name. See MUSES.

MOERAE
See FATES.

MT. OLYMPUS
See OLYMPIAN GODS.

MUSES
Nine goddesses who inspire all human art, music, and knowledge. Soon after the fall of the Titans, Zeus takes the form of a shepherd and seduces Mnemosyne, the goddess of memory. He lies with her for nine nights, and she soon gives birth to nine daughters—Calliope, Clio, Erato, Euterpe, Melpomene, Polyhymnia, Terpsichore, Thalia, and Urania—who become the Muses. Together with Apollo, the Muses inspire humans to the artistic callings: each muse is associated with a specific art, such as comedy or lyric poetry or history. Many works of Greek literature begin with invocations of the Muses—appeals for guidance in the forthcoming artistic endeavor. The poet Hesiod even claims in his work that he met the muses in person on Mt. Helicon, where they bestowed upon him a gift for poetry. Mortals also turn to the Muses for truth, as the Muses, the daughters of Memory, are the only beings with the ability to tell absolutely true tales. The Muses inspire immortal beings as well as mortals: they provide the Sphinx her riddle, give birth to the Sirens and to Orpheus, and teach Echo to play music.

MYTH OF ER
A story that Socrates tells in Plato's *Republic* in order to assert that living justly is the key to happiness. According to Socrates' story, the warrior Er dies in battle, and his body is taken to a funeral pyre. Just as the fire is lit, however, Er sits up, amazed, and returns to the land of the living. Er says that the gods of the underworld permitted him to leave so that he could act as a messenger to humankind. After death, he says, the souls of the dead gather in a large meadow where they wait to be judged for their actions. For every bad deed, souls suffer for one hundred years; for every good deed, they receive one hundred years of bliss. After this period, the souls of the dead meet with Lachesis, one of the Fates, who has them draw lots for their reincarnated existences. The souls choose, according to their lot,

what kind of life they will have when they are reborn. They are offered lives as rich men, kings and queens, paupers, martyrs, and animals. Many souls lack foresight and choose lives as kings, not seeing that their wished-for power often spells doom. Some, however, choose wisely according to their experiences in life. Er claims that he saw Orpheus, the singer, choose a life as a swan. Odysseus, Er says, chose the life of a modest man without ambitions. Agamemnon picked an eagle, Ajax a lion. After all choose their lots, the Fates send the souls to the river Lethe, the river of forgetfulness where they all drink measures of water that cause them to forget about their previous lives.

NARCISSUS
A mortal youth renowned for his incredible good looks, which lead him to excessive self-love—or, as we say today, narcissism. When Narcissus is young, his parents ask the seer Tiresias if their son will lead a long life. Tiresias says that Narcissus will grow old "only if he never knows himself." As a young man, Narcissus spurns all those who fall in love with him, including the nymph Echo. One day, however, Narcissus sees his own reflection in the still water of a pond and is immediately transfixed. He continues to sit by the pond, gazing down at himself, until he finally dies and turns into a flower—the showy-blossomed, aptly named narcissus. See ECHO.

NYMPHS
Female nature spirits who protect forests, seas, mountains, and other natural spirits. Greek myth depicts the nymphs as minor goddesses who take the form of attractive, benevolent young women. There are a number of different types of nymphs, including the Naiads, or river nymphs; Dryads, or forest nymphs; Oceanids, or sea nymphs; Nereids, or nymphs of the Mediterranean Sea specifically; and Oreads, or mountain nymphs. The satyrs are the male equivalent of the nymphs. See SATYRS.

OCEANUS
The eldest of the Titans and the god who personifies the ocean. According to myth, Oceanus takes the form of a backward-flowing river that binds the earth and gives water to all rivers and oceans. According to Homer's *Odyssey*, it is necessary to cross the river Oceanus to reach the underworld. When the Titans revolt against Uranus, only Oceanus refuses to attack his father. He also is alone in

ENCYCLOPEDIA

his compassion for Prometheus, his brother, who stole fire and gave it to humans. See PROMETHEUS, TITANS.

OEDIPUS

The son of Laius and Jocasta, famous for inadvertently fulfilling a prophecy that he will kill his father and marry his mother. The story of Oedipus, which Sophocles tells in *Oedipus Rex* and *Oedipus at Colonus*, has long fascinated scholars because of its cutting insights into human nature, especially into human psychology. The nineteenth-century psychoanalyst and theorist Sigmund Freud famously based his theory of the "Oedipal complex" on this story, claiming that every young boy has a latent desire to kill his father and sleep with his mother. See section on Sophocles' *Oedipus Rex*.

OLIGARCHY

The rule of the few, sometimes called plutocracy. In Plato's *Republic*, Socrates calls into question the merits of the oligarchical state. He especially worries that an oligarchy's emphasis on the wealthy minority turns people to avarice. The virtuous, unwilling to entertain the ambition and greed necessary to succeed in an oligarchy, cannot exist in such a state. See section on Plato's *Republic*.

OLYMPIAN GODS

The pantheon of twelve gods—Zeus, Hera, Poseidon, Athena, Apollo, Artemis, Ares, Aphrodite, Demeter, Hermes, Hephaestus, and Hestia—who rule the heavens from Mt. Olympus. Various accounts include Hades or Dionysus in the pantheon at the expense of Hestia. According to myth, after Zeus and his siblings overthrow the Titans, they move their court to the peak of Mt. Olympus. Although Mt. Olympus exists as a real mountain in Greece, the Mt. Olympus of Greek mythology possesses fantastic qualities. A mortal, for example, cannot reach the summit where the Olympian gods hold court. The weather at the summit never changes: there is no rain, wind, snow, or cloud cover, and every day brings unlimited visibility through crystalline skies. When the gods of Olympus are not meddling with human affairs or attending sacrifices in their honor, they feast upon heavenly ambrosia and nectar as Apollo strums his lyre and the Muses sing.

The earliest existing works of Greek literature—Homer's *Iliad* and *Odyssey* and Hesiod's *Theogony*—depict the Olympian gods actively interfering with the lives of mortals. The gods pick their favorites among mortals and ceaselessly protect them: Athena stands by Odysseus, Apollo by Paris, Zeus by Sarpedon, and Aphrodite by Aeneas. The gods appear to mortals frequently, sometimes in their true forms, sometimes transformed. In later works of Greek literature, however, this close relationship between humans and gods falls away. The Olympian gods appear only rarely in the plays of Sophocles, Euripides, and Aeschylus. Characters sometimes speak of encounters with the gods, but the playwrights keep the gods offstage.

Later works by Greek philosophers go even further by calling the nature of the gods into question. In Plato's works, Socrates refers to various gods as if they exist, but his words are laced with irony. For Plato, the Olympian gods came to represent manifestations of his Forms—Aphrodite represented perfect love, Athena perfect wisdom, and so on. While Aristotle could not renounce the Olympian gods directly, his metaphysics completely ignores them. According to Aristotle, the only important force in the universe is the Prime Mover, the original, formless, benevolent entity that set the universe in motion. Despite these assertions, even the most revered Athenian philosophers could not proclaim open disbelief in the Olympian gods. City authorities levied charges of blasphemy and atheism against Socrates, and Alcibiades, a student of Socrates and a famous statesman and general, was accused of defacing the statues of Hermes—a crime repulsive to the Athenian public.

ORACLE AT DELPHI
See DELPHI.

PALLAS ATHENA
See ATHENA.

PANDORA
The first mortal woman. After Prometheus angers Zeus by giving mankind fire and other gifts, Zeus orders Hephaestus to create Pandora as a punishment for mankind. The gods give Pandora a box containing all forms of evil and suffering, previously unknown to men, and tell her never to open it. The Titan Epimetheus marries Pandora against his brother Prometheus's warnings. Overcome by insatiable curiosity, Pandora opens the box and releases the catalog of plagues on humankind. After all of these have escaped into the world, hope floats up from the box to ease humankind's suffering. See EPIMETHEUS, PROMETHEUS.

PANTHEON
The group of twelve Olympian gods. See OLYMPIAN GODS.

PERICLES
The most famous and revered of all Athenian statesmen. Pericles (c. 495–429 B.C.) grew up in an aristocratic family but earned the affection of the common people of Athens through his natural patriotism, eloquence, and sense of justice. He was a great proponent of democracy, and historians have labeled his rule as the golden age of Athens. Pericles received his education from Damon, a Sophist. Afterward, he showed favoritism to art, and his friends included the most prominent poets and philosophers of his time, including Sophocles, Socrates, Protagoras, and Herodotus. Pericles was renowned for his natural eloquence and remarkable public speaking ability, which he displayed on the floor of the Athenian senate. He fought to restore important buildings and symbols of Athenian culture, like the Parthenon, and in the process created jobs for the poorest citizens. Under Pericles' rule, Athens became the strongest Greek city-state both in culture and government, a center of poetry and philosophy where democracy thrived and the military increased its already formidable strength. However, this rise in power incited jealousy and fear in other countries and eventually led to the Peloponnesian War between Athens and Sparta. Pericles took full responsibility for the outbreak of war and offered Athens as a refuge to the citizens of surrounding cities. He never lived to see the end of the war and the beginning of Athens's fall, however, as he and his two sons died, along with countless others, during a plague that swept through Athens.

PERIPATETIC
A follower of the philosophy of Aristotle. Today, the word is used to indicate a pedestrian or a person who walks back and forth. Originally, Aristotle's school became known as the Peripatetic school because of Aristotle's tendency to pace back and forth during his lectures.

PERSEPHONE
The daughter of Demeter, the goddess of the harvest. One day, Hades, the lord of the underworld, abducts Persephone by force as she gathers flowers in a meadow. He then takes her as a bride and forces her to live with him in Hades. Persephone is given to gathering flowers even in the underworld, where she plucks a fruit of the

pomegranate tree and eats some of its seeds. Because she eats the food of the underworld, however, she is unable to escape fully from Hades' grasp. Rather, she is allowed to visit her mother in the world above for only a portion of each year. When she is in the underworld, Persephone adds a touch of beauty and sympathy to its otherwise bleak landscape. When the musician Orpheus visits the underworld in search of his deceased love, Eurydice, he enchants Persephone with his music and convinces her to permit him an audience with Hades. Also, when the seer Tiresias arrives in Hades, Persephone allows him to maintain his mental acuity and clear-headedness amid the fields of numb and empty-minded dead souls. See DEMETER, HADES (PERSON), HADES (PLACE).

PHILOCTETES

A famously skilled archer who plays an important role in the outcome of the Trojan War despite the fact that he is not featured in Homer's *Iliad*. Philoctetes comes into the possession of Heracles' bow and arrow—originally gifts from Apollo—when he helps Heracles die peacefully after the hero is poisoned. Later in his life, Philoctetes is a suitor of Helen of Troy and, like all of her other suitors, goes to fight the Trojans after Paris abducts her. During the voyage to Troy, however, a water snake bites Philoctetes on the ankle, and the wound does not heal, leaving Philoctetes in agony. Moreover, the wound emits such a stench that the other Achaean (Greek) leaders, unable to bear his presence on the ships, decide to abandon him on the shores of Lemnos, where he stays until after the death of Achilles. Despite the Achaeans' efforts, Troy remains impregnable, and the seer Calchas declares that the city will not fall until the weapons of Heracles fight on the side of the Achaeans. Therefore, Odysseus goes with Neoptolemus, the son of Achilles, to fetch Philoctetes, whom they compel to leave Lemnos either by trick or by force—an episode that Sophocles recounts in his play *Philoctetes*. When Philoctetes enters the war, he slays Paris, and Troy quickly collapses.

PHOENICIA

An ancient land on the eastern shores of the Mediterranean, approximately the same as modern-day Lebanon. Phoenicia earned its name from Phoenix, the son of Agenor who founded the country after a long and fruitless search for his sister, Europa. Until around the eighth century B.C., the Greeks lacked a written language. According the Greek historian Herodotus, this changed when Cadmus, the brother of Phoenix, arrived in Greece and founded the city of Thebes. He brought with him the written alphabet the Phoenicians had developed and taught this writing system to the Greeks. Over time, Greece adopted the alphabet and gradually made small changes. Because the English alphabet descends directly from the Greek alphabet, we also are indebted to the Phoenicians for our written language system. See THEBES.

PHOENIX

An enormous bird with the head of an eagle and bright red and gold feathers, famous for its ability to reincarnate itself. The Phoenix makes its home in an unknown area, and only the people of Heliopolis, the city of the sun, claim to have seen it. According to Herodotus, every 500 years, the Phoenix reaches the end of its life, perches itself in its nest, bursts into flames, and disintegrates into ashes. However, it rises from its own ashes in its original dazzling form. Each time the Phoenix is reborn, it bears the ashes of its previous self to Heliopolis, where it deposits them at the temple of the sun.

PIETY

Reverence for the gods, a virtue that many Greek philosophers attempted to analyze and define. Piety is perhaps the most important virtue in a world ruled by petty, unforgiving gods who play favorites. In some cases, however, excessive piety for one god can be construed as disrespect for other gods. Hippolytus, the son of Theseus, incurs the wrath of Aphrodite because of his zealous worship for Artemis, the goddess of chastity. Ajax, through no fault of his own, earns the hatred of Athena because he dislikes Odysseus, whom she favors. Moreover, the gods' retribution for a mortal's disrespect or impiety often outweighs the mortal's original insult. According to one story, Agamemnon shoots a stag and brags that Artemis could not have done better—an offense for which Artemis demands the sacrifice of Agamemnon's daughter, Iphigenia. In another story, Actaeon, a worshipper of Artemis, accidentally sees her bathing naked when he is hunting in the forest. Despite his pleas for forgiveness, Artemis transforms Actaeon into a deer and sets his own hounds on him to devour him. In real life, the Athenian authorities accused Socrates of impiety and sentenced him to death for it—a charge that Plato details in his *Death of Socrates* dialogues.

PLATONIC LOVE

The highest form of love, which centers on an individual's search for truth. According to Plato, this form of love ascends from passion for an individual to contemplation of an ideal. In the Socratic dialogues, the greatest lovers are those whose love depends on the search for truth while suppressing sexual urges. In modern usage, a Platonic relationship signifies a close relationship, such as between a man and a woman, in which sexual urges do not exist or are not acted upon.

PLUTOCRACY

See OLIGARCHY.

POLYHYMNIA

The muse of sacred poetry. Polyhymnia—or "many hymns"—often is depicted wearing a veil. See MUSES.

POLYPHEMUS

One of the Cyclopes, or one-eyed giants, who dwells on an unkempt island and herds goats. The proud Polyphemus and his brethren pay no heed to the gods, to each other, or to the development of their island. Despite his isolation, Polyphemus is unable to avoid the arrows of love and develops a frenzied passion for the sea nymph Galatea. The nymph, however, does not return Polyphemus's love, and his heartsick pleas fall upon deaf ears. When Polyphemus one day sees Galatea in the arms of the young shepherd Acis, he hurls a boulder from a cliff and crushes him. Polyphemus is most notable for his encounter with Odysseus in Homer's *Odyssey*. Long before encountering Odysseus, a prophet declares to Polyphemus that Odysseus one day will blind him. When Odysseus and his men land on the island of the Cyclopes on their return to Ithaca, Polyphemus captures them and traps them in his cave. Polyphemus devours the men one by one but promises to save Odysseus for last. Odysseus, who introduces himself to Polyphemus as "Nobody," gets Polyphemus drunk on wine until he passes out. Odysseus fashions an enormous spear and stabs the giant in his eye. Polyphemus awakens with a roar, gropes helplessly for his assailants, and cries out in pain. When other Cyclopes come to the mouth of the cave, Polyphemus declares that Nobody is attacking him, so the other Cyclopes disperse. The next morning, Polyphemus lets his sheep out to pasture, and Odysseus and his men cling to the bellies of the sheep and escape undetected. As they sail away, Odysseus yells back to Polyphemus

ENCYCLOPEDIA

and reveals his true name. Polyphemus, realizing that the prophecy has come true, calls upon his father, Poseidon, and begs him to torment Odysseus as he makes his way home. The god of the sea raises storms, Odysseus and his men are shipwrecked, and only Odysseus survives. See CYCLOPES.

POSEIDON

The god of the sea and the brother of Zeus and Hades. Poseidon, who has the power to control the ocean and earthquakes, often is moody and vindictive. He holds a special disdain for Odysseus because Odysseus blinds Poseidon's son, the Cyclops Polyphemus. In Homer's *Odyssey*, Poseidon torments Odysseus as he struggles to find his way home from the Trojan War, repeatedly destroying Odysseus's ships, tossing him about on the waves, and punishing those who seek to help him. In Euripides' *Hippolytus*, Poseidon answers the prayers of Theseus by sending a herd of bulls from the sea and causing Hippolytus to crash his chariot on the rocks.

PROMETHEUS

A Titan who steals the secret of fire from the gods and gives it to mankind. According to the myth, after the gods create mortal creatures, the brothers Epimetheus and Prometheus are charged with the distribution of skills and faculties to the different creatures. Epimetheus persuades Prometheus to let him handle the work and simply come inspect the work when Epimetheus is done. With this freedom, Epimetheus gives wings to some creatures, speed to others, the ability to swim or live underground to others, and so on. When Prometheus arrives to check Epimetheus's allocations, he notices that Epimetheus has given nothing to man, so Prometheus takes art, wisdom, and fire from the gods and gives them to mankind. When Zeus learns of Prometheus's theft, he orders Hephaestus, the metalsmith god, to bind Prometheus to a rock in the Caucasus Mountains. Zeus subjects Prometheus to years of torture in which an eagle swoops down from the sky every day to feast upon Prometheus's liver. Every night, his liver regenerates so that the process can be repeated indefinitely. Finally, the hero Heracles stops this endless punishment by killing the eagle. Prometheus's indiscretion also spurs Zeus to punish mankind by creating the first mortal woman, Pandora. See PANDORA.

PROTAGORAS

A philosopher regarded as one of the foremost Sophists. Protagoras (c. 485–410 B.C.), a great friend of Pericles, taught grammar, rhetoric, and the interpretation of poetry to his students in Athens. Protagoras did not believe in absolutes, but instead maintained that good and bad, true and false, and other such oppositions were subject to human opinion. He famously stated that man is the measure of all things—by which he meant that, because opinions differ so greatly, one man's truth is another man's falsehood, and thus an absolute truth does not exist. According to Plato, Protagoras also believed that individuals are punished for their crimes to ensure that the same crime never happens again. However, Protagoras himself eventually was punished for what others believed were his crimes—atheism and impiety—and he drowned while attempting to flee to Sicily. See SOPHISTS.

PROTEUS

A shape-shifting sea god who is the son of either Poseidon or Oceanus. Proteus has unequaled abilities as a seer or prophet but dislikes making predictions and will do so only if he is captured and forced to. Capturing him is difficult, however, as Proteus changes shapes rapidly and repeatedly when pursued. If caught, he takes the form of an elderly man and tells his prophecy. Proteus appears in the *Odyssey* when Menelaus tells Telemachus of his encounter with the shape-shifting god. Menelaus recounts how the gods waylaid him and his men on their way home from Troy as punishment for their failure to make sufficient sacrifices to the gods. Stranded at the mouth of the Nile, Menelaus encountered Eidothea, Proteus's daughter, who took pity on the lost warrior. She alerted Menelaus to Proteus's presence and said that Proteus would tell Menelaus everything he needed to know about his journey home—if Menelaus could capture him. Eidothea told Menelaus to wait for Proteus to fall asleep and then leap on him and cling to him no matter what shape he took. Eventually, he would return to his normal form as an old man. According to Menelaus, Proteus turned first into a lion, then a snake, a panther, a boar, a tree, and finally running water, until his repertoire was exhausted. Once subdued, Proteus revealed to Menelaus the fates of all his compatriots.

PYTHIAN PRIESTESS

See DELPHI.

ENCYCLOPEDIA

REVENGE

Perhaps the most common theme in Greek literature. Revenge or retribution, often through violent means, perpetuates many of the central stories of Greek mythology. The various stories involving the cursed house of Atreus, for instance, all involve a self-perpetuating chain of revenge: first, Agamemnon shoots a stag and boasts that Artemis herself could not have done better; then, the angered Artemis strands Agamemnon's ships and forces him to sacrifice his daughter Iphigenia to gain wind; when Agamemnon does so, his wife, Clytemnestra, kills him in revenge for his killing of their daughter; then, their son, Orestes, kills Clytemnestra and her lover, Aegisthus, in revenge for their murder of Agamemnon—and so on. In this story and in many others, crimes or offenses between families, between gods, or between mortals and gods never are forgotten or resolved but rather lead to further revenge crimes.

RHEA

The wife of Cronos and mother of the original Olympian gods—Demeter, Hades, Hera, Hephaestus, Poseidon, and Zeus. Rhea protects Zeus from the wrath his father, Cronos, who fears that his own children will grow up to overthrow him. Cronos decides to eat his children, but when Zeus is born, Rhea gives Cronos a rock swaddled in baby clothes to swallow. Rhea hides Zeus until he is old enough to fend for himself. See CRONOS.

SACRIFICE

Ritual offerings to the gods that mortals must perform to keep the gods happy. In Greek myth, regular sacrifices are an important measure mortals must take to protect themselves from the gods' moodiness and animosity. The sacrificial objects, which range from goats and bulls to sons and daughters, frequently depend upon the vague insights of the prophets. Moreover, even those mortals who make regular sacrifices risk incurring the wrath of the gods by performing the sacrifices improperly or sacrificing unacceptable livestock. Any such insult to the gods, whether intentional or accidental, can spell doom for the individual or his or her family.

SALAMIS

A strait west of Athens where the Athenian and Persian forces clashed in a climactic battle in the Persian Wars in 480 B.C. As was often the case during the war, the Persian forces, led by Xerxes, greatly outnumbered the Greeks on both land and sea. The Greek general and statesman Themistocles, however, devised an ingenious battle plan that enabled the nimble Greek ships to encircle the slow Persian vessels in the strait. The Greeks, aware that the Persian ships could not move swiftly and that many of the Persian soldiers—being from the desert—could not swim, rammed the Persian boats while assailing their crews with spears and arrows. The Persians who withstood the collisions fell victim to the Greek assault, while those who fell into the water drowned. At the same time, the Greek forces on land ambushed the retreating Persians. The battle turned the tide of the war, and Xerxes, who watched the battle from afar, returned home defeated. See THEMISTOCLES.

SATYRS

Male nature spirits who take the form of men with the horns and hindquarters of goats. The satyrs, the male equivalent of nymphs, are the followers of the god Dionysus. They spend their time protecting the forests and mountains, drinking wine, and pursuing nymphs. See NYMPHS, DIONYSUS.

SCYLLA

A terrifying six-headed monster who once was a lovely sea nymph. Scylla inhabits a cave on the sea and menaces ships along with Charybdis, a deadly whirlpool that gapes on the other side of the strait. According to legend, when Scylla is still a young nymph, Glaucus, a fisherman who transformed into a sea-god, falls madly in love with her. Scylla retreats to land so that Glaucus cannot follow her. Desperate, Glaucus consults the sorceress Circe for help, but Circe herself falls in love with Glaucus as he tells the story. Glaucus scorns Circe's love, however, and the sorceress directs her rage at Scylla, resolving to poison the water where she bathes. Circe follows through with her threat, and the poison transforms Scylla into a hideous monster with six heads, each with three rows of teeth. Below the waist, her body is suddenly composed of beasts. Overcome with hatred and self-loathing, Scylla situates herself in a strait where she can reach for passing ships and snatch up their crewmen in her jaws. In Homer's *Odyssey*, Odysseus's ship passes through Scylla's strait. As they take care to avoid Charybdis, the whirlpool on the other side, the six-headed Scylla snatches six unsuspecting men from Odysseus's ship. See CHARYBDIS.

SILVER AGE
See AGES OF MAN.

ENCYCLOPEDIA

SIRENS

Creatures with the heads of women and the bodies of birds who live on a rocky island and sing alluring songs that lure sailors in passing ships to their doom. By most accounts, there are either three or four Sirens, and they are the daughters of the river god Achelous and one of the Muses (either Melpomene or Terpsichore). The Sirens have beautiful voices, and their songs are so enchanting that no men can resist their temptation. If the sailors of a passing ship hear the songs, they helplessly steer the ship toward the Sirens' island, where it is dashed to pieces on the treacherous, rocky coast and lost forever. According to some accounts, the Sirens are not born bird-women but originally are the companions of the goddess Persephone. They are present when Hades abducts Persephone but fail to interfere with the abduction, so Demeter punishes them by changing them into bird-women. Odysseus and his men encounter the Sirens in the *Odyssey.* Aware of the danger of the Sirens, Odysseus commands his men to stuff their ears with wax in order to block their hearing. Because he himself longs to hear their song, he orders his men to tie him firmly to the ship's mast and ignore whatever commands he gives them as they sail past the Sirens' island. When Odysseus hears the Sirens' song, he frantically demands that his men untie him, but they only tie him tighter, so he remains the only mortal to hear the Sirens' song and live to tell about it. See PERSEPHONE.

SISYPHUS

A Thessalian prince who angers the gods by betraying their secrets. In one notable story, Zeus steals away with Aegina, the daughter of a river god, but Sisyphus discloses the secret lovers to Aegina's worried father. In punishment for his whistle-blowing, Zeus sentences Sisyphus to an eternal punishment of hard labor in the underworld. In Tartarus, Sisyphus is forced to roll a large boulder up a steep hill, and just when he nears the top, the boulder tumbles back down to the bottom. He must repeat his efforts for all eternity.

SOLON

A famous leader of Athens who instituted major political and economic reforms. When Solon (c. 639–559 B.C.) was fifty-five years old, the leaders of Athens—the Areopagus—approached him and asked him to lead the city. They trusted Solon enough to give him the power to restructure the Athenian government completely. With this authority, Solon went on to create the judicial system, the people's assembly, and the senate. He increased the people's role in

Athenian government significantly until democracy finally came to fruition. Solon also created laws dealing with economic issues, marriage, punishment of crimes, and other areas. In his efforts to bolster the public's interest in government, he even decreed that any man who failed to take sides in political debates would have his belongings confiscated. See ATHENS.

SOPHISTS

A school of teachers in ancient Greece who were the first professional peddlers of wisdom. The Sophist school came into being when demand for higher education in Greece increased dramatically in the fifth century B.C. By most definitions, the Sophists were teachers rather than philosophers, for whereas most philosophers frowned upon taking money for their teachings, the Sophists readily charged large sums for their lessons. Originally teachers of virtue, the Sophists expanded their lessons to cover other areas as demand continued to rise. Ultimately, they offered lessons in everything from mathematics to grammar. As political careers rose in popularity after the reign of Solon, the Sophists made rhetoric their specialty as well. Some Sophists, like Gorgias, prided themselves on teaching their students how to make the weaker of two arguments appear stronger. Gorgias boasted that he could argue any subject, even one of which he had no knowledge. For the Sophists, truth was not a priority—a stance that earned them the derision of philosophers such as Socrates and Aristotle. Indeed, a number of the Sophists embarked on political careers by employing complicated logic, ensnaring their opponents with semantics, or simply shouting down the opposition. The modern word sophistry, meaning the use of fallacious arguments while knowing them to be such, derives from the practices of the ancient Sophists.

SOUL

The aspect of an individual that Greek thinkers from Homer to Aristotle viewed as the one indestructible part of the mortal self. Many writers and philosophers pondered the question of what happens to the soul after death. In Homer's epics and in many Greek tragedies, newly deceased souls travel to the banks of the river Styx, where they take the ghostlike shapes of the deceased and wait for the ferryman Charon to convey them across the river to Hades. According to popular belief, the soul of an unburied body cannot reach the comfort of Hades—a problem that serves as the focal point of many myths, most notably Sophocles' *Antigone*. Once in Hades, souls pay for their mortal crimes and sins in a period of atonement, then drink from the river Lethe to forget their past lives. Finally, they are reborn in another form.

Although Plato and Aristotle do not challenge directly any of these beliefs in the afterlife—Aristotle never even mentions them—they do spend considerable time questioning the nature, origins, and destinations of the soul. Several of Plato's dialogues, including the *Phaedo,* the *Timaeus,* and the *Gorgias,* deal almost exclusively with the nature of the soul. Although Plato does explore the ideas of resurrection and atonement for sin, he excludes the mythical monsters of Hades in his depictions of the afterlife. Plato is concerned about the afterlife more in terms of wisdom than in terms of punishment.

SPARTA

Athens's rival city-state, located in the south of Greece. Whereas cultural and artistic institutions were central to the Athenian city-state, the military was the dominant force in Spartan society. At age seven, every healthy male commenced military training, in which he learned toughness through severe conditioning, pain, and tests of endurance. At age twenty, after thirteen years of training, Spartan males became soldiers. Although they were allowed to marry, they lived in the barracks and rarely saw their wives. Not until the age of thirty were Spartan males allowed to live in their own houses. Each man remained in the military until the age of sixty, when he finally could retire if he still was alive. Spartan women were held to similarly rigorous standards. Infant girls suffered the same screening process as infant boys—if an infant was decidedly too weak, he or she would be exposed and allowed to die. While the men went away to military school, the women were sent to a grueling education of their own, designed to instill belief in and duty to the state. Sparta achieved an incredible stability through this system of severe education, coupled with large and intrusive military government. In nearly every aspect of everyday life, the state refused any luxuries that possibly could be construed as causing human weakness. Today, the word Spartan still is used to refer to people or things that are exceedingly self-disciplined or that avoid luxury or comfort.

SPHINX

A monster—part woman, part lion, and part bird—that terrorizes the city of Thebes in Sophocles' *Oedipus Rex,* although she does not appear in the story herself. After a stranger murders King Laius of Thebes and his herald on the road to Delphi, the Sphinx appears at the gates of the city, apparently enraged by Laius's unsolved murder and the rise of the new ruler, Creon. The Sphinx torments the citizens of Thebes and refuses to relent until someone solves her riddle, which the Muses gave her. Moreover, the Sphinx promises to make the person who solves the riddle the husband of Queen Jocasta and therefore king of Thebes. The riddle asks which creature walks on four legs in the morning, two in the afternoon, and three in the evening. The answer, which Oedipus guesses correctly, is a man. In the early years of his life, before he learns to walk, a man crawls on four legs; in middle age, he walks upright on two legs; in his elderly years, he walks with a cane—hence, four legs, then two, then three. When Oedipus answers the riddle, the Sphinx throws herself to her death, and Oedipus becomes king of Thebes, unwittingly fulfilling the prophecy that he will kill his father, Laius, and sleep with his mother, Jocasta. See OEDIPUS.

STYX

The river of hate in the underworld. The ocean god Oceanus divides in the underworld and produces his daughter, Styx, who is the first to come to Zeus and the Olympians in support of their war against the Titans. Because of Styx's generous support, Zeus requires that gods swear their oaths on the waters of Styx. If a god should swear by Styx and break his oath, he is made to lie spiritless and voiceless, far from the ambrosia of Olympus for a full year, after which he is banished from sacrifices and councils of the gods for nine more years. Examples of oaths to Styx can be found through out the *Iliad* and *Odyssey*. According to many accounts, the ferryman god Charon transports the shades of the dead across the river Styx as they make their way to Hades.

TANTALUS

A king who earns Zeus's wrath when he arrogantly tests the gods' divinity. At first, the gods favor Tantalus and allow him to attend their banquet on Mt. Olympus. However, Tantalus grows prideful and decides to test the gods by killing his own son, Pelops, and serving him as a sacrifice to the gods to see whether they notice. Zeus immediately knows what Tantalus has done and, in anger, condemns him to eternal punishment in the underworld—a punishment that Odysseus reports in the *Odyssey*. According to Odysseus, Tantalus stands in a pool of water that reaches his chin, and just above him, ripe apples, pears, and pomegranates dangle from trees above. Tantalus is forever parched and famished, but whenever he bends down to drink the water, it recedes and dries up, and whenever he stretches to grasp the fruit from the trees above, a wind arises and blows the branches up beyond his reach. Tantalus's constant frustrated desire to reach the impossible gives us our modern word tantalize, meaning to tease or torment by withholding something.

TARTARUS
A deep cavity in the underworld where the wicked are sent for punishment. Tartarus, the origin of all waters, yawns deep below the surface of the earth and is the realm of Erebus, pure darkness. In Tartarus, the condemned are held behind walls of bronze and iron, encircled by Pyriphlegethon, the river of fire. The gates to Tartarus are built of adamant and can withstand even an attack by the gods. At the entrance, Tisiphone, one of the Furies, sits in a bloody robe upon a pillar of iron. Behind the gates of Tartarus, the worst sinners, both mortal and immortal, meet their punishments. Among them are the Titans who rose against Zeus, the Cyclopes, Sisyphus, and Tantalus. Many of the punished are bound by the Furies and prevented from reaching for food placed in front of them. The incarcerated include those who hated their brothers, killed their parents, cheated their clients, raped their daughters, acted as traitors, ruled with injustice, or killed for adultery. Occasionally, the less wicked among those trapped in Tartarus are carried away by the Pyriphlegethon and cast onto the shores of Archeron, where they beg for forgiveness from the people they wronged. Should they prevail upon their victims, their punishments cease; if not, they are cast back into Tartarus, where their sufferings continue. In some myths, Tartarus is also a god, the father of such monsters as Typhon and Erebus. See CYCLOPES, TITANS, SISYPHUS, TANTALUS.

TERPSICHORE
The muse of dance. According to some sources, it is Terpsichore, not Melpomene, who gives birth to the Sirens. See MUSES, SIRENS.

THALIA
The muse of comedy. See MUSES.

THEBES
The richest and largest city in the part of Greece known as Boeotia. Both mythology and history concur that Cadmus of Boeotia founds Thebes after bringing the Phoenicians' written alphabet to Greece (see Phoenicia). According to the myth, Cadmus's father, Agenor, sends his three sons in search of their sister, Europa, after Zeus steals

her away. Each son goes in a different direction, but ultimately, all of their quests are fruitless. At one point, Cadmus loses his way and consults the Oracle at Delphi, who tells him to follow a cow with a white, moon-shaped spot on each flank. Eventually, the Oracle says, the cow will collapse in exhaustion, and Cadmus should build a city at that site. Cadmus follows the cow until it can go no more and then sends his men to a nearby river for water so that they can wash the cow and prepare it for sacrifice. When none of the men return, Cadmus himself goes to the river and finds a dragon bloated on the meal it has made of Cadmus's men. In a rage, Cadmus kills the beast, only to discover it was the son of Ares, the god of war. Bewildered, Cadmus consults Athena, who tells him to plant half of the dragon's teeth in the ground. Cadmus does so, and the planted teeth quickly spring forth from the ground, transformed into a menacing army of soldiers. The hordes of soldiers attack each other, and in the end, only five soldiers survive. From these five, the five royal families of Thebes arise, calling themselves the Sparti. Cadmus becomes the first king of Thebes. The trials and tribulations of Cadmus's descendants, including Oedipus and Antigone, are well documented in Greek drama, particularly in Sophocles' *Oedipus Rex* and *Antigone*. Cadmus himself appears in Euripides' *The Bacchae*. See OEDIPUS, SPHINX.

THEMISTOCLES

A general famous for his participation in the Persian Wars. According to legend, when the Oracle at Delphi predicted that only a wooden wall could save the Athenians from the Persians, Themistocles (527–460 B.C.) rightly interpreted the "wooden wall" to mean the Athenian fleet. While others took refuge behind the wall skirting Athens, Themistocles and his fleet set sail for Salamis, where they won an unlikely and tide-turning victory against Xerxes' Persian forces. Themistocles not only provided valiant leadership for the Athenian navy but also suggested using the money from an Athenian silver mine to construct the triremes (a type of boat common in the ancient world) that defeated Xerxes. However, Themistocles' accomplishments on the battlefield could not mask his shady politics, which led the Athenian authorities to ostracize him 471 B.C. In search of work and a home, Themistocles wandered to Persia, where he presented himself to Xerxes' son, Artaxerxes, who made him a Greek governor of a city in Asia Minor, where he died. See SALAMIS.

ENCYCLOPEDIA

THERMOPYLAE

A narrow mountain pass near Delphi that is the site of a pivotal battle in the Persian Wars in 480 B.C. When the Persian king Xerxes led his enormous army into Greece, a small Greek force led by Leonidas, a Spartan, made a stand against Xerxes in the pass at Thermopylae. Although Leonidas and his men were vastly outnumbered, they withstood the Persian attack for three days and prevented Xerxes from attacking with his full force: only a handful of men could enter the pass at once, which dramatically reduced the Persian advantage. After three days of fighting, however, a Greek traitor told Xerxes about an alternate route through the mountains. Leonidas learned of the treachery and sent the majority of his men to support a small volunteer infantry guarding the alternate route. Only three hundred of Leonidas's men stayed behind—just enough to distract the Persians until the other route could be secured. These remaining three hundred died in their efforts to save Greece, and a memorial to them still stands at Thermopylae.

THESEUS

A great mythical king of Athens who plays a part in a large number of Greek legends. Theseus is perhaps most famous for his defeat of the Minotaur, the half-man, half-bull monster that inhabits the Labyrinth in Crete. When Athens is under Crete's control, King Minos of Crete demands that Athens send him seven young men and seven young women every year so that he may cast them into the Labyrinth as food and sport for the Minotaur. One year, Theseus volunteers to be one of the seven young men in the hopes of killing the Minotaur. When he goes to Crete, he and Minos's daughter, Ariadne, fall in love. Ariadne tells Theseus how to find his way out of the Labyrinth, so he follows her instructions, slays the Minotaur, and escapes from Crete with Ariadne. However, when the couple reaches Naxos, Theseus grows tired of Ariadne's company and abandons her. He returns to Athens, becomes king, and marries Ariadne's sister, Phaedra. However, Phaedra soon falls in love with Hippolytus, Theseus's son by the Amazon queen Hippolyta. Although Hippolytus rebuffs Phaedra's advances, a misunderstanding ensues and Theseus thinks that his boy has fallen in love with Phaedra. Theseus therefore curses Hippolytus and sends him to his death—a story that Euripides tells in his play *Hippolytus*. Theseus also is known for giving sanctuary to Oedipus, kidnapping the beautiful Helen for a short time, punishing wrongdoers, and being a close friend of Heracles. In fact, when Heracles journeys to the underworld during his Twelve Labors, he rescues the deceased Theseus from Hades.

Few characters appear as frequently as Theseus in the great works of Western literature. In addition to his appearances in numerous Greek myths and plays, Theseus plays a role in Chaucer's *The Canterbury Tales,* Shakespeare's *A Midsummer Night's Dream,* Racine's *Phaedre,* and Renault's *The King Must Die.* These different authors have created a number of different versions of Theseus: some draw out his love affairs, his wildness, and his seemingly endless search for trouble. Others focus on his character as a leader, his cool reasoning, and his innate sense of justice. Perhaps because of this chameleonic aspect, Theseus remains one of the most enduring characters from Greek myth. See MINOTAUR, AMAZONS.

THETIS
A nymph and the mother of Achilles. See ACHILLES.

TIMOCRACY
A government based on honor. In *The Republic,* Plato considers timocracy the second best form of government behind aristocracy. He fears that problems arise in timocracies when citizens and the government disagree over the merits of certain actions, or when citizens become overly ambitious in the quest for recognition.

TIRESIAS
A famous blind prophet who makes numerous appearances in ancient Greek literature. According to one account, Tiresias accidentally sees Athena naked and, either by edict of the gods or anger from Athena, is struck blind. However, Athena takes pity on his blindness and makes up for it by giving him unerring prophetic powers. She also gives Tiresias the ability to understand the language of the birds. Tiresias lives an exceedingly long life; by some accounts, he lives for at least seven generations, from the time of Cadmus (when Thebes is founded) to long after the death of Oedipus. Tiresias finally dies when he voluntarily drinks the waters from the spring of Tilphussa, a spot in Boeotia.

Tiresias's prophecies figure prominently in Homer's *Odyssey,* Euripides' *The Bacchae,* Aeschylus's *The Seven Against Thebes,* and Sophocles' *Oedipus Rex,* among many other major classical works. In the *Odyssey,* Odysseus travels to the underworld to consort with the spirit of the deceased Tiresias, who alerts Odysseus that Poseidon is angry at Odysseus's blinding of the Cyclops Polyphemus, that many dangers await Odysseus and his crew on the way home, and that suitors have infiltrated Odysseus's palace in Ithaca. In *Oedipus Rex,* Tiresias tells Oedipus the truth about his murder of his father and marriage to his mother, despite Oedipus's outcries against the seer.

TITANS

A race of giant creatures who are the descendants of Uranus and Gaia. The Titans include Cronos, Atlas, Prometheus, Epimetheus, and Oceanus. After Cronos ascends to power, his children, led by Zeus, rise up against the Titans and overthrow them. When the Olympian gods emerge victorious, Zeus casts the Titans into Tartarus as punishment. The Titans' giant size gives us the modern word titanic, meaning of enormous size or power. See URANUS, CRONOS, RHEA, ATLAS, PROMETHEUS, EPIMETHEUS, OCEANUS, ZEUS.

TRIPARTITE SOUL

Socrates' conception of the soul composed of three distinct parts. In Plato's *The Republic,* Socrates and his interlocutors question the nature of the soul, and Socrates asserts that the soul is composed of the appetitive part, the emotional part, and the rational part. The appetitive part is neither good nor bad—it simply wants or does not want. The emotional part, however, poses some danger to the balance of the soul, for it can be influenced but cannot be reasoned with. The rational part of the soul is the best part, for its decisions are based solely on reasoned conclusions. However, its power is limited by the strength of the emotional part. These three parts join together to form a soul that continually struggles to achieve the best balance between the emotional part and the rational part.

TROJAN HORSE

An enormous wooden horse that Odysseus and his forces use to breach the gates of Troy at the end of the Trojan War. Despite monumental effort on the part of the Achaean (Greek) forces, the walls of Troy still show no signs of collapsing after ten years of war. At Odysseus's suggestion, the Achaean army constructs a gigantic wooden horse with a hollow belly. Odysseus and a handful of soldiers climb inside and seal the hole, and the remaining Achaeans roll the horse to the walls of Troy and present it to the Trojans as a peace offering. Despite the warnings of the prophet Laocoön, the Trojan leaders accept the horse as a gift, and the Achaeans return to their boats and pretend to sail away. When night falls, Odysseus and his men creep out of the horse and open the gates of Troy from the inside, allowing the Achaean forces to storm the city. Although Homer never documents the episode with the Trojan horse directly, Odysseus refers to it in the *Odyssey*. To this day, the phrase Trojan horse is used to indicate someone or something that defeats insidiously or from within. See TROJAN WAR, ODYSSEUS, LAOCOÖN.

TROJAN WAR

The great war between the Trojans and the Achaeans (Greeks) that is central to Greek mythology and forms the backdrop for Homer's *Iliad*. For ten years, the Achaean forces attempt to seize the city of Troy, which is located on the western coast of present-day Turkey. The war has its roots in the wedding of Achilles' parents, Peleus and Thetis, especially their failure to invite Eris, the goddess of discord, to the wedding. Enraged, Eris storms into the wedding reception, throws a golden apple on a table, and declares that it belongs to whoever is the fairest. However, Athena, Hera, and Aphrodite all reach for the apple at the same time. To resolve the dispute, Zeus declares that the Trojan prince Paris—regarded as the most beautiful man alive—must act as a judge in the divine beauty contest. Hera promises Paris power, Athena promises him wisdom, and Aphrodite promises him the most beautiful woman in the world. Paris awards the apple to Aphrodite, who in turn promises that Helen, the wife of King Menelaus of Sparta, will be Paris's wife. Against the warnings of his prophetic sister, Cassandra, Paris sets off for Sparta, where Menelaus receives him as a royal guest. When Menelaus leaves Sparta for a funeral, Paris abducts Helen. Upon learning of the theft, Menelaus raises an enormous army led by Helen's former suitors and wages war against Troy. After ten years of war, Troy burns as Odysseus and the Achaean army seize the city. After Troy falls, Aeneas, a Trojan warrior, escapes with a number of other Trojans and sets sail for Rome—a story that the Roman poet Virgil tells in the *Aeneid*. Aeneas is generally regarded as the father of the Roman Empire. According to Greek mythology, Troy was home to the noble King Priam, his wife Hecuba, and their daughters and sons, including Hector and the infamous Paris. See ACHILLES, AGAMEMNON, ODYSSEUS, TROJAN HORSE, HELEN OF TROY, PHILOCTETES, AENEAS, LAOCOÖN.

ENCYCLOPEDIA

TWELVE LABORS OF HERACLES
See HERACLES.

TYRANNY
Government by an individual with absolute—and often oppressive—power. Although today we tend to remember ancient Athens as a paragon of early democracy, the Athenian political system often teetered on the edge of tyranny. The early tyrants of Athens—the Areopagus, Solon, Pisistratus, and others—set the stage for the development of democracy through remarkable good judgment and a willingness to share power. Even after democracy was long established in Athens, however, its existence remained in danger. During the waning years of the Peloponnesian War, the Thirty Tyrants seized power in Athens, only to return it when Athens regained its feet. In his dialogues, Plato displays great interest in the nature of tyranny and frequently ponders the state of a tyrant's soul.

URANIA
The muse of astronomy. Urania, who foretells the future by reading the position of the stars, is the mother of Hymenaeus, the companion of Eros. See MUSES, EROS.

URANUS
One of the oldest gods and the father of Cronos, who in turn is the father of Zeus. By most accounts, Uranus, who embodies the heavens, is both the son and wife of Gaia, the Earth. Gaia and Uranus have three sets of children: the Titans, the Cyclopes, and the Hecatoncheires. These last two monstrous groups particularly displease Uranus, so he casts them into Tartarus to rid them from his sight. Gaia, however, advises the Titans to revolt against their father. She gives Cronos a jagged sickle with which he castrates his father. According to some accounts, Uranus's genitals fall into the ocean, and the goddess Aphrodite rises from the surrounding foam; the blood from his genitals falls onto the earth and spawns the Furies. See GAIA, CRONOS, TITANS, FURIES.

ZEUS
The king of the Olympian gods and the most powerful among them. When Zeus is born, his mother, Rhea, hides him from his father, Cronos, who is determined to swallow all his children to keep them from revolting against him. Rhea hides Zeus in a cave in Crete and feeds Cronos a rock swaddled in baby clothes to fool him. When Zeus comes of age, Rhea feeds Cronos a drug that causes him to

regurgitate his other children. Zeus frees the Cyclopes from Tartarus, leads his brothers and sisters in a revolt against their father, and ultimately overthrows him. To thank Zeus for their freedom, the Cyclopes award him the power of the thunderbolt, with which he rules the heavens. Zeus's hold on the reigns of power is not secure at first. After he and his siblings subdue the Titans, Gaia, the earth, spawns another race of monsters, the Giants. Led by Typhon, a monster with a body of vipers that spew fire, the Giants nearly topple the Olympian gods. Typhon captures Zeus, binds him to rock, and tears the sinews from his arms. But Zeus, aware of a prophecy saying that only a mortal could save the Olympian gods, calls upon his mighty mortal son, Heracles. The god Hermes recovers Zeus's sinews and, with Heracles' help, chases the Giants into retreat. As a final blow, Zeus crushes Typhon with Mt. Aetna, creating a volcano in Sicily that, to this day, remains active. Once his grip on power is assured, Zeus rules the universe with his queen, the goddess Hera. Zeus is renowned for his philandering with nymphs, mortal women, and other goddesses, and his trysts often drive Hera into a jealous rage. See CRONOS, HERA, HERACLES, TITANS, OLYMPIAN GODS.

ENCYCLOPEDIA

Index

A

SPARKNOTES
TEST PREPARATION
GUIDES

The SparkNotes team figured it was time to cut standardized tests down to size. We've studied the tests for you, so that SparkNotes test prep guides are:

Smarter
Packed with critical-thinking skills and test-
taking strategies that will improve your score.

Better
Fully up to date, covering all new features of the tests,
with study tips on every type of question.

Faster
Our books cover exactly what you need to
know for the test. No more, no less.

SparkNotes™ Literature Guides